ABORIGIN/

Current Crisis and Future Alternatives

ABORIGINAL EDUCATION

Current Crisis and Future Alternatives

Edited by

Jerry P. White, Dan Beavon, Julie Peters, and Nicholas Spence

THOMPSON EDUCATIONAL PUBLISHING, INC.

Toronto, Ontario

Information on how to obtain copies of this book is available at:
Website: http://www.thompsonbooks.com
E-mail: publisher@thompsonbooks.com
Telephone: (416) 766–2763
Fax: (416) 766–0398

Library and Archives Canada Cataloguing in Publication

Aboriginal education : current crisis and future alternatives / edited by Jerry P. White ... [et al.].

Includes bibliographical references.
ISBN 978-1-55077-185-5

1. Native peoples--Education--Canada. I. White, Jerry P. (Jerry Patrick), 1951-

E96.2.A24 2009   371.829'97071   C2009-900341-4

Production Editor: Katy Bartlett
Cover Design: Tibor Choleva
Copy Editor: Rachel Stuckey
Proofreader: Gillian Urbankiewicz
Cover Illustration: Daphne Odjig, Hide and Seek, 1982
                     serigraph, ed. 125, 20" x 18"
                     Reproduced with permission from Daphne Odjig
                     Courtesy of Gallery Phillip

Thompson Educational Publishing, Inc.

20 Ripley Ave

Toronto, Ontario, Canada, M6S 3N9

Statistics Canada information is used with the permission of Statistics Canada. Users are forbidden to copy the data and redisseminate them, in an original or modified form, for commercial purposes, without permission from Statistics Canada. Information on the availability of the wide range of data from Statistics Canada can be obtained from Statistics Canada's Regional Offices, its World Wide Web site at http://www.statcan.ca, and its toll-free access number 1-800-263-1136.

We acknowledge the support of the Government of Canada through the Book Publishing Industry Development Program for our publishing activities.

Printed in Canada. 1 2 3 4 5 6   13 12 11 10 09

Table of Contents

Part One: Understanding the Current Situation

Part Two: Causes, Costs, and Possible Solutions

Part One:
Understanding the Current Situation

1

Aboriginal Education: Current Crisis, Future Alternatives

Jerry P. White and Dan Beavon

Introduction

Every Aboriginal language in Canada has words for learning. In the Cree language *Kiskinohamâw* means being taught, learning, or going to school. There are words for study, words for student, and many words for needing to learn. Aboriginal cultures across this country hold the educational processes very dear, yet the First Nations, Métis and Inuit peoples all face serious problems of underachievement.

We find that Aboriginal educational attainment lags significantly behind the Canadian population. While we can see overall improvement for Registered Indians between 1981 and 2006, improvement in educational attainment has not been continuous. In the 1981 to 1991 period there was a narrowing of the gap with the Canadian population in terms of the proportion with high school or higher, whereas in the 1991 to 2006 period the gap actually increased.

As we have noted before (White, Beavon, et al. 2007) younger cohorts of Aboriginal peoples have greater educational levels then older age groups. However, the gap between non-Aboriginal and Aboriginal education is even greater at the younger age levels. In other words, the gains Aboriginal youth are making vis-à-vis their elders is being eclipsed by the rising education levels of Canadians in general.

Canadians generally agree that the development of human capital is very important in the self-actualization of a person. It allows one to choose when and how to integrate into the economic enterprise of the country, region or community in which one lives, and it also contributes to the production of citizenship.

There is a long scientific tradition in sociology and economics that has established that educational attainment, that is, the acquisition of human capital, is highly correlated with income, wealth, occupational diversity and a host of other positive outcomes (see Becker 1964, Coleman 1988). This relationship has been demonstrated to hold for Aboriginal people as well (Richards 2008, Spence et al. 2007, Spence 2007, White, et al. 2004, White, et al. 2005).

Given that Aboriginal peoples culturally prize education and there are these very positive associations with education concerning self-growth and prosperity, we might hope that Aboriginal attainment would be close to the national average. If we look closely at the situation for education we see a different trend. We can see in **Figure 1.1** that the Registered Indian population on reserve (measured in

Figure 1.1: Comparing the Proportion of Aboriginal Population with High School Completion to all Other Canadians

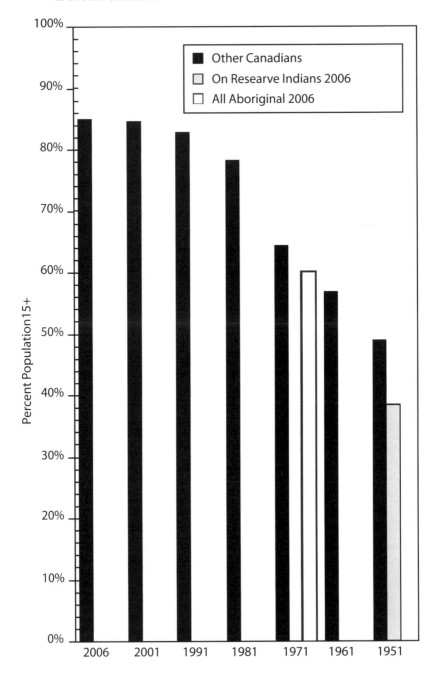

Figure 1.2: Proportion of Registered Indians and Other Canadians with a University Degree, 2006

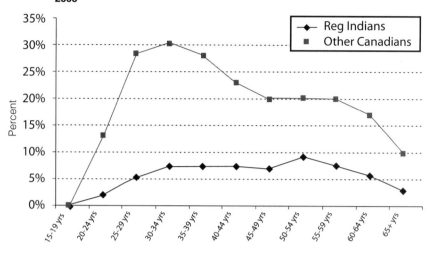

2006) has a high-school completion rate roughly equal to the rate of non-Aboriginals in 1951; thus, the former are more than 50 years behind the latter. If we include the entire population identifying as Aboriginal, the rate is about the same as in 1971 representing, about a 35-year lag.

If we look at **Figure 1.2** we see that in 2006, the Registered Indian population had much lower overall university degree attainment rate (5%) than the "Other Canadian" population (18%). As John Clement notes in this volume (Chapter 5), for certain age groups, the proportion of the "Other Canadian" population with a university degree is almost six times that for the Registered Indian population (20–24 and 25–29 year olds).

There is a large gap in educational attainment and, as we said earlier, it is not narrowing.

The Arguments Made in this Book

Just how bad is the situation? What jumps out to anyone reading the discussions of our research teams is the following:

1. All Aboriginal groups share a problem of low educational attainment and a large gap with the non-Aboriginal population.

2. For all Aboriginal groups, the gap is widening.

3. There are differences between identity groups. Those peoples in the cities, and those who are closer to market centres and economic development have higher educational attainment. Those in the North or in First Nations communities (reserves) fare most poorly. This can be related to several factors not the least of which is the lack of opportunity to use one's education where one

is far from any development. Without the pull of jobs and productive work, youth are not as likely to stay in school.

4. Those who are uprooted or choose to migrate often—those moving from neighbourhood to neighbourhood or community to community—fare much worse than those who are rooted in one place. This may be related to the levels of social capital that families can call on. Networks and supports do not get developed, or once developed they get broken, as families move.

5. Women are outperforming men in all Aboriginal groups. Therefore, we see a reduced gap between Aboriginal females and the rest of the Canadian population. For males, we see a larger gap that is widening more quickly than for women.

6. The families where educational attainment norms are low tend to reproduce the low attainment in their children. This may also be related to social capital. Low norms in strong networks can be a negative thing. This may account in part for the situation in First Nation communities where residential schools had the effect of reducing educational attainment and creating a negative attitude to schooling.

7. The current structure of education, with federal and provincial jurisdictions out of synchronicity, negatively effects educational attainment. If we add the Aboriginal administrations of education into the mix, we face multiplying problems in delivering an appropriate education that captures the needs to train and skill-up people while respecting cultures and ethnic particularities.

8. Movements to transfer control of education to Aboriginal communities may be simply downloading the right to fail. Many communities have no revenue base, or population base to run schools or school systems. So while leaving schooling out of Aboriginal hands is wrong, so too it may be wrong to transfer control given economies of scale and capacity. We know there are wide ranging differences in capacities between communities (see White, Beavon, et al. 2003).

9. The low levels of economic development, whether we look at entrepreneurship or externally driven investments, are clearly related to low educational attainment. This could be because there is no future that young people can see in terms of work, occupation, or career. Therefore there is no draw to higher education. At the same time the low levels of educational attainment discourage investments because there is a perceived lack of skilled labour available in that region. Likely these trends reinforce each other.

10. There is a "brain drain" from the North and from Aboriginal communities generally. This is because there is a very clear benefit to those who seek higher education. They get better salaries through better jobs. Given these opportunities are not located in the North or on the reserves (for the most part) the brightest migrate south or to the cities. It also seems that when the youth leave to seek college or university, they never return.

11. Everyone is losing from low Aboriginal educational attainment. We see lower incomes for the Aboriginal peoples and the resulting poverty for too many. We see a loss of tax revenue for the provinces and Canada. We also see increased expenditures to deal with the social and health consequences associated with lower income and unemployment.

So if that is the current situation, and some of the causes, what can be done? Some of the chapters have proposed solutions. Our teams of researchers have tried to present an evidence-based assessment of the situation and have introduced a range of ideas, even ones we do not necessarily agree with. We do urge everyone to consider them all.

Some arguments support creating less-balkanized, less-inefficient collectivities of communities (and peoples). They argue this will permit real control over education with the resources to be successful. The amalgamation into larger units could allow real self-governing and hence educational reform.

We see arguments for more market driven approaches, where parents get report cards on the success of the school and can move their children out. This, it is argued, leads to schools improving or dying; getting rid of the worst and encouraging the others to improve. Peters and White have labeled this proposal from Richards (2008) the "free market approach," as it best approximates a range of proposals that are geared to allowing market forces and freedom of choice to force change.

Peters and White also introduce the Assembly of First Nations' proposals for more self-governmental-style control by Aboriginal communities and collectivities of communities. This might include regional Aboriginal school boards and other innovative structures.

Funding issues and quality issues are of utmost importance. We see proposals for stabilized funding through appropriate incentive systems based on standardized testing regimes that work to build the schools, improve teacher effectiveness, and put the students first.

Policy is called for that targets economic development. Authors argue that transfer payment systems, and the dependency associated with those systems, do not encourage educational attainment. Quite the opposite, they discourage education and reinforce the low norms created in the residential schools period.

Conclusion: Which Way Forward?

A great scientist once said that true ignorance is doing the same thing over and over again and expecting a different result. It is obvious that despite the enormous resources and thought we have put into improving our educational systems, we have not succeeded in solving the problems linked to Aboriginal educational attainment. It should be obvious that we can not simply push forward on the same path and expect things to get better. We argue that there is a need to confront this current situation, based on the evidence, and not turn away from the difficult decisions. Thinking outside the box will mean raising issues that some people do not want raised, such as the viability of certain communities and certain social, economic, and bureaucratic structures.

We are facing a crisis. Not only because there is such a large gap between Registered Indians and the rest of Canada. It is not only because *all* Aboriginal identity populations are achieving much lower attainment. It is all this and more. The crisis comes from the fact we are not improving the situation despite the enormous resources we throw at the problem. The gap is getting worse! Those who think we might have "got it right" in the 1981–91 period because we saw the gap reduce slightly are wrong. During that time we simply saw several processes working themselves out that changed the population we were measuring. There was an influx of higher educated people who regained their status through Bill C-31 in 1985 (See White et al. 2003, White et al. 2007). They were joined by an ethnic drift of people who chose to declare themselves as having an Aboriginal identity where before they had not (see Guimond 2003). This group also had higher general educational attainment. This resulted in an increase in average educational attainment that appeared to narrow the gap. We see that since 1991 the gap has increased again.

So, we need to think about the problem in a different way: seek new ways of thinking about the causes and develop new potential solutions.

First, we don't think it is the schools and their curriculum that are the key problems. We do agree the schools need secure funding so they can attract and retain good teachers and administrators while marshalling resources for quality programs. We have developed some innovative proposals on ways to do that in this book. White, Peters, and Beavon call for stabilized funding through appropriate incentive systems based on standardized testing regimes that work to build the schools, improve teacher effectiveness, and put the students first. We think that the regularization of funding through a mechanism that empowers the teachers to adjust the delivery of education to help students facing particular issues and roadblocks is crucial. A case study of a pioneering Aboriginal school is included in Chapter 7 and seems to support our contention.

We argue that communities and families are one very important key to rectifying the crisis. The external influences outside the schools are most important in lowering educational attainment. First, communities that have no economic development, either externally driven or through intra-community entrepreneurialism have relatively little chance of improving educational attainment over the medium or long term. There are compelling reasons for this:

1. Youth need to be encouraged to stay in school through the potential of jobs, careers, and improved lifestyle. No development means no jobs and no encouragement.

2. Where communities offer no opportunities for educated youth (other than the

service jobs that come with the transfer payments), those young people leave. They may leave to get an education and never return, or if they do come home, they do not stay. Simply put, there will be a continued "brain drain."

This raises very difficult questions that relate to whether all communities are viable. This may seem like heresy, but we need to confront the question, discuss it, and consider the implications. It may be that some communities with rich histories and culture have no long-term future outside of being propped up by transfer payments. Paquette, et al. argue that true self-government is necessary to rectify the educational attainment crisis but that true self-government can only come about when there is a community (or group of communities) that is of a size to be self-sufficient and sustainable. While their argument is developed on slightly different lines, in a way this is supportive of our general conclusion that we need to confront the issue of sustainability.

Non-sustainable or semi-dysfunctional communities can also create particular problems. They create conditions where some of their members migrate. When people migrate to cities for housing or jobs or health care, they uproot from family and clan networks that provide social supports. When people are in the cities, these urban communities can also create the conditions that forces movement. Unemployment, inadequate housing, lack of family support services and lack of health care can force intra-urban migration. These movements depress educational attainment. So we argue that support services and better housing will improve educational attainment. This applies in the cities and in other communities.

This bridges us to a third issue we wish to raise. Part of the reason that youth, whose families move a lot, have lower educational attainment is because they have less bonding, bridging, and linking social capital to call on. We outline how these processes work in a chapter that looks at several countries, including Canada, but suffice it to say in simple terms, the families don't have the networks to rely on and use for support. Networks can support through in a myriad of ways, whether it is a family member that can look after kids while one works, or clan neighbours that can go to the store for food when you are sick. White and Spence go further and point out that social capital operates in many ways, even those with strong family networks can be divorced from the schools and the educational processes of Aboriginal communities. They point out that getting families and clans involved in the schools and in education is crucial. Recruiting mothers and elders into the school and developing educational officers of Aboriginal origin to promote education in the communities can be very important in overcoming the low educational norms in many families.

Lastly, we want to draw attention to the obvious. Putting resources into education, either directly to the schools or through economic development, is investment. We will get returns. As several of the authors argue, such as Clatworthy, there is a real cost to low educational attainment and inversely there will be a great gain as we solve this crisis.

The complex relationships that exist between the constitutional provincial educational responsibilities and the treaty-based federal educational responsibilities creates real problems. We feel they need to be made seamless and transparent to allow improvements to Aboriginal educational attainment. We know this is another very difficult question, but one that we must grapple with if this crisis is going to come to an end.

We will be successful in dealing with this crisis because we have to; failure will mean that the current difference in the status and standard of living between populations that share Canada will deepen. This relative deprivation experienced by Aboriginal peoples living in cities or living out in home communities, will lead to serious social unrest and will most certainly increasingly undermine the fabric of Canadian society. We either solve the problem or the tremendous wealth and social stability Canada enjoys will be eroded at an ever increasing rate.

References

Becker, G.S. 1992. "The Economic Way of Looking at Life" Nobel Lecture, December 9, 1992. Accessed January 4, 2009 at <**home.uchicago.edu/~gbecker/Nobel/nobellecture.pdf**>.

Coleman, J. 1988. "Social Capital and the Creation of Human Capital." *American Journal of Sociology* 94: S95–S120.

Guimond, É. 2003. "Changing Ethnicity: The Concept of Ethnic Drifters" In *Aboriginal Conditions: The Research Foundations for Public Policy.* J.P. White, D. Beavon, and P. Maxim (eds). Vancouver: University of British Columbia Press. 91–107.

Richards, J. 2008. "Closing the Aboriginal/Non-Aboriginal Gaps." Toronto: C.D. Howe Institute Backgrounder #116 .

Richards, J., J. Hove and K. Afolabi. 2008. *Understanding the Aboriginal/Non-Aboriginal Gap in Student Performance: Lessons From British Columbia.* Toronto: C.D. Howe Institute Commentary # 276.

Spence, N. 2007. *New Vistas on the Income Inequality-Health Debate: The Case of Canada's First Nations Reserve Population.* PhD Dissertation, Department of Sociology, The University of Western Ontario, London, Ontario.

Spence, N., J. White, and P. Maxim. 2007. "Modeling Educational Success of First Nations Students in Canada: Modelling Community Level Perspectives." *Canadian Ethnic Studies.* 39(1/2): 145.

Walker, I. and H. Smith (eds). 2002. *Relative Deprivation: Development, Specification and Integration.* Cambridge: Cambridge University Press.

White, J., S. Wingert, D. Beavon. 2007. *Aboriginal Policy Research: Moving Forward, Making a Difference Volume IV.* Toronto: Thompson Educational Publishing.

White, J.P., E. Anderson, and W. Cornet (eds). 2007. *Aboriginal Policy Research: Moving Forward, Making a Difference Volume V.* Toronto: Thompson Educational Publishing.

White, J., S. Wingert, D. Beavon, and P. Maxim (eds). 2006. *Aboriginal Policy Research: Moving Forward, Making a Difference Volume III.* Toronto: Thompson Educational Publishing.

White, J., N. Spence, and P. Maxim. 2005. "Social capital and educational attainment among Aboriginal peoples: Canada, Australia and New Zealand." In *Policy Research Initiative Social Capital Project Series, Social Capital in Action: Thematic Studies,* edited by Policy Research Initiative. Ottawa: Policy Research Initiative, Government of Canada. 66–81.

White, J., P. Maxim and N. Spence. 2004. "An Examination of Educational Success" In *Aboriginal Policy Research: Volume I: Setting the Agenda for Change.* J. White, P. Maxim and D. Beavon (eds). Toronto: Thompson Educational Press. 129–148

White, J.P., D. Beavon, and P. Maxim. 2003. *Aboriginal Conditions: The Research Foundations for Public Policy.* Vancouver: University of British Columbia Press.

White, J. and P. Maxim. 2003. "Toward an Index of Community Capacity: Predicting Community Potential for Successful Program Transfer." In *Aboriginal Conditions: The Research Foundations for Public Policy.* J.P. White, D. Beavon, and P. Maxim (eds). Vancouver: University of British Columbia Press.

White, J.P., P. Maxim, and N. Spence (eds). 2003. *Permission to Develop: Aboriginal Treaties, Case Law and Regulations.* Toronto: Thompson Educational Publishing.

White, J.P., P. Maxim, and D. Beavon (eds). 2004. *Aboriginal Policy Research: Setting the Agenda for Change. Volume I.* Toronto: Thompson Educational Publishing.

White, J.P., P. Maxim, and D. Beavon (eds). 2006. *Aboriginal Policy Research: Setting the Agenda for Change. Volume III.* Toronto: Thompson Educational Publishing.

2

A Short History of Aborigii Education in Canada

Jerry P. White and Julie Peters

Introduction

In this chapter we trace the development of European-led "education" of Aboriginal peoples in Canada from the establishment of New France where the Récollets, and later the Jesuits, engaged in attempts to assimilate the First Peoples into French culture, through the British shift from partnership to integration and finally through the twentieth century where remarkably similar tactics continued. The sweep of history is only briefly explored, but we can see that the more policy changed the more it reverted to being much the same.

Education in New France

The first known educational institutions for Indigenous youth were established near Quebec by the Récollet missionaries in 1620. The French policy on Indigenous education at the time has been referred to as "[f]rancization," which was based on the Récollets' belief that Indigenous peoples needed to be turned into "Frenchmen" before they could be converted to Christianity (Jaenen 1986). A thoroughly French education was thus required. To this end, the Récollets would single out Indigenous boys for schooling, educating them at the seminary or sending them to France where they could be fully immersed in French culture and language. It was assumed that these students would then return to their communities and form part of an Indigenous elite that could assist in Christianizing the rest of the population (Jaenen 1986). However, the Récollets were largely unsuccessful. They were never able to attract large numbers of students to their seminary or to France, due largely to parents being unwilling to part with their children for extended periods of time. In 1629 the English captured Quebec, and the Récollets along with the Jesuits, who had arrived in New France by this time, were forced to leave the colony. When Quebec was returned to France in 1632, it was the Jesuits who were given a monopoly over missionary activity (Magnuson 1992).

The Jesuits initially adopted quite a different approach to the education of Indigenous peoples than that taken by the Récollets. Rather than instructing only a few students in separate, thoroughly French educational institutions, the Jesuits focused on delivering education within Indigenous villages and in Indigenous languages. The focus of instruction was on Christian doctrine rather than on French language and customs. However, by the mid-1630's the missionaries to feel that the greatest impediment to the Christianization of the Indigenous peoples was their nomadic lifestyle. Thus, the Jesuits concluded that rendering the Indians sedentary was an important step in conversion to Christianity. A plan was devised that involved establishing permanent settlements for the Indians near French settlements, where the missionaries could be in constant contact with the tribes and the Indians[1] could become accustomed with the French language and way of life. The first settlement, the Sillery habitation, was established in 1637 near Quebec (Magnuson 1992). While these early "reserves" did not have formal schools, missionaries would conduct instruction in various places around the settlements. In addition to Christian training, education was largely of a practical nature, focusing on teaching the Indigenous peoples agricultural practices with the goal of transforming them into self-sufficient farmers.

While the attached settlements were somewhat successful in winning Christian converts, they experienced less success in encouraging the Natives to take on a French way of life. The reserves were also plagued by disease and social and economic problems. Thus, despite initial success, most of the reserves experienced sharp population decline leading many, like the Sillery reserve, to fade into non-existence (Magnuson 1992). By this time, the Jesuits had already begun to shift their emphasis, focusing on residential or boarding schools in French towns as the primary means of delivering education to the Native population (Jaenen 1986).

Residential schools were seen by the French as an attractive option for educating Indigenous youth, as the children could be removed from the influence of their parents and fully acculturated into the French way of life. Attracting and retaining students to attend residential institutions, however, proved to be a difficult task. Parents were often apprehensive about allowing their children to live among the French, and children who were sent to attend residential institutions would often run away. The schools were also expensive to run, as the communities and parents who offered their children to the Jesuits for instruction expected gifts and continued material assistance for doing so, and the children attending the institutions needed to be housed and fed (Jaenen 1986). For these reasons, day schools were also in operation, with the day school pupils always outnumbering those in residential institutions.

French teaching and instruction styles, which involved treating the students like adults, using strict discipline, fostering competitiveness, and emphasizing recitations and examinations, were largely incompatible with the traditional education of Native students. Students resisted and refused to cooperate, and the French found that those who were successfully educated and Christianized were ineffective at preaching the word to their people (Miller, 1996). One Ursuline sister, Mother Marie de l'Incarnation commented that "out of a hundred that have passed through our hands scarcely have we civilized one" (as quoted in Jaenen 1986, 58).

Around 1668, after the elevation of New France to a Royal Colony, there was renewed pressure from the French government to use boarding institutions to educate and ultimately assimilate Indian youth. The French administration saw the conversion of Natives into Frenchmen as a means of securing and populating their colony in the New World without depopulating Old France. Seen to be failing in this regard, the Jesuits were accused by the Crown of not working effectively towards teaching the Indians French customs and language. However, what the French administration did not realize was that the Jesuits had attempted to convert the Indian peoples to French ways, but had found this approach wanting. The Ursalines, brought to New France to educate Indigenous girls, supported the Jesuits stating that acculturation had not been successful due to the "tenacity of the Indigenous culture" (Magnuson 1992, 61). In addition to the difficulty of "Frenchifying" the Indigenous peoples, it began to be clear that assimilation made little sense for the fur traders and the military who found the Indigenous peoples to be essential to the fur trade and strong military allies just as they were. Thus in 1685, the governor of New France stated that the policy of Frenchification was not working and called on the Crown to alter their policy. By the end of the century, assimilative residential schools for educating Indian youth had been largely abandoned and few Indian children were attending French schools (Miller 1996).

Pre-Confederation in British North America: Assimilative Segregation for Integration

Prior to the War of 1812, the British were not concerned with assimilating Indigenous peoples, as their knowledge and skills were useful to the British in their roles as military allies and as essential partners in the fur trade. Maintaining these partnerships was of the utmost concern. After the War of 1812, however, with hostilities subsiding and the fur trade on the decline, the Indigenous population began to be seen as an impediment to European settlement. It was at this time that there began to be a shift in focus from maintaining Natives as allies, to, in the words of a former secretary of state for the colonies, "reclaiming the Indians from a state of barbarism and introducing amongst them the industrious and peaceful habits of civilized life" (as quoted in Wilson 1986, 66).

Reflecting this shift in thinking, responsibility for Indigenous peoples was formally transferred from military to civilian authorities in 1830. Civilian authorities quickly adopted a new Indian policy that was based on "civilizing" the Indigenous peoples through education. While there had been educational institutions established in British North America prior to this change in policy, these institutions were run entirely by church organizations without assistance from the Crown (Chalmers 1972). After 1830, however, the colonial government began to take an express interest in the establishment and operation of schools for Native peoples and numerous new schools were opened. The operation of the schools was largely left in the hands of missionary organizations, and the costs for building and running schools was shared between the colonial government, missionary groups, and the Indigenous peoples themselves (Nock 1988).

As part of the new policy of civilizing and assimilating the Native population, efforts were first made to establish reserve lands on which the Indigenous peoples could settle. Similar to earlier attempts by the French, the hope was that the Indigenous peoples would abandon their nomadic lifestyles and become sedentary farmers, adopting a European way of life. Schools were established on the reserves to provide rudimentary education and Christian teachings. The reserves proved to be a failure, however, after a number of the first experiments were unable to retain a sizable Indigenous population (Miller 1996).

By the mid-1840's, realizing that the traditional livelihood of Indigenous peoples had been eroded due to the rapid expansion of British settlement, the government shifted its focus to manual labour schools, as recommended by the Bagot Commission in 1844. In addition to Christian training, these schools were to teach Indigenous peoples practical skills that could help them to survive in the "White man's world" while promoting assimilation. According to Captain Anderson, a superintendent of Indian Affairs, by attending manual labour schools Indigenous children were to "forget their Indian habits, and be instructed in all the necessary arts of civilized life, and become one with [their] White brethren" (as quoted in Wilson 1986, 72). Boys would be taught trades such as carpentry, shoemaking, and blacksmithing, while the girls would learn domestic skills such as sewing and knitting. That the proposed industrial schools were to be large and centrally located was seen to have the added advantage of removing students from the influence of their families.

In 1846 the colonial administration met with various "chiefs" in Orillia, Ontario, to persuade them to accept the government's plans to establish manual labour schools for the education of Indigenous children and to settle larger, permanent areas around the schools. The Indigenous bands were to put one fourth of the annuities they received from the government towards supporting the educational institutions. Despite some objections to their relocation into concentrated settlements and to the Christian nature of the schools, the assembled chiefs ultimately gave their support to the proposed plan. Many of supporters, however, hoped that the schools would eventually be run by their own people (Miller 1996).

While numerous manual labour schools were opened in the decades following the commission, they quickly lost the support of the Indigenous peoples. An 1856 Special Commissioner's report on Indian Affairs found that authorities were having difficulty persuading Ojibwa parents to send their children to manual labour schools on the Sarnia reserve, and less than half of the potential school population was attending school on the Six Nations reserve on the Grand River. The report came to the conclusion that "this benevolent experiment has been to a great extent a failure," and the focus began to shift to day schools (as quoted in Miller 1996).

Confederation to World War II: Assimilation, Segregation, and Separation

Under the *British North American Act* of 1867, all aspects of Indian affairs became the responsibility of the Canadian federal government. This included education, which had been promised in the various treaties signed for the surrender of Indian lands. While the treaties generally promised day schools on-reserve, problems with attendance and the perception that day schools were ineffective in assimilating Indigenous peoples led to a search for alternatives (Miller 1996). After the establishment of the *Indian Act* in 1876, member of parliament Nicholas Flood Davin was assigned the task of investigating the United States' use of residential schools for educating American Indians to see whether this would be a suitable model for Canada. In his 1879 report, Davin recommended that similar institutions be established in Western Canada (Haig-Brown 1988). Although the federal government was responsible for Indian education, the administration of the schools was to be delegated to the various church missions that were already engaged in the venture. Thus, unlike provincial schools at the time, schools for Indigenous children were to be denominational and, wherever possible, existing mission schools were to be used. While Davin also recommended that the schools both employ and teach Métis peoples, who he saw as the "natural mediator between the Government and the red man," the government insisted that it would only provide funds for the education of Status Indians and there are no records of attempts to recruit Métis staff (Miller 1996, 101).

Similar to the earlier experiences with manual labour schools and with boarding institutions in New France, recruitment and retention of Indigenous children at the residential schools became a key issue. In 1893 the government, looking to cut costs, instituted a per capita school funding system that shifted more of the financial burden for schooling onto missionary organizations and students. Maintaining maximum enrolment became of utmost concern for missionary groups, while at the same time, inadequate financial resources led to poorer school conditions, which made the residential institutions less attractive to Indigenous families. In order to counter declining enrolments and ensure steadier funding, missionary groups pressured the government to make school attendance mandatory. Heeding their concerns, the *Indian Act* was amended in 1894 to make school attendance at a day, boarding, or industrial school compulsory for ten months of the year for all Indigenous children over age 6 (Grant 1996).

By the turn of the century serious concerns were being raised about the health and safety of students attending the schools. Diseases such as tuberculosis ran rampant and mortality rates were alarmingly high. A 1907 report from the department's chief medical officer stated that the death rate due to tuberculosis among Indigenous students in the West was 24% and Duncan Campbell Scott, the deputy superintendent general of Indian Affairs, conceded that about half of the children who attended boarding institutions did not live to benefit from the education they received (Miller 1996, 133). For those students who did survive their years in boarding establishments, the education they received was minimal at best. The schooling often focused more on religious indoctrination and manual labour than on academic knowledge. When students left the schools they were ill-equipped to compete for jobs in the "White man's world," and were alienated from their own societies (Chalmers, 1972).

In 1910, concerned with the high costs associated with educating Indigenous youth and the failure of educational institutions to transform students into successful members of the dominant society, the government again shifted its educational policy. Abandoning the prior focus on preparing Indigenous students for life in White society, the new objective was to prepare students for life on the reserve, marking a policy shift from integration to segregation (Miller, 1996). The curriculum, already far less advanced than that of provincial schools, was simplified further and any new facilities built were to be basic day schools which could offer education to Indigenous youth at a far lower cost to the government (Barman, Hébert, and McCaskill 1986). In the 1920s, the industrial school model was completely abandoned and all former industrial and boarding establishments came to be known as residential schools (Miller 1996).

The education received in both residential and day schools in the early- to mid- twentieth century was minimal and basic. The teachers usually did not hold a teaching certificate and the principals were normally clergymen who had little experience with developing instructional programs (Chalmers 1972). With regard to residential schools specifically, a half-day system was typically followed in which students were to receive classroom instruction for half of the day and learn practical skills, usually agricultural, for the remainder of the day. In addition to ensuring that Indigenous pupils received only a very basic scholastic education, this system allowed the administration to extract free labour from students by having them perform chores around the schools as part of their "practical instruction." In fact, officials at the time had expressed hope that residential schools might become financially independent through the manual labour of their students (Miller 1996, 157). Needless to say, few students progressed past the primary grades regardless of how many years were spent in school. In 1930, only 3% of Indigenous students had progressed past grade 6 and three-quarters of all those in school were in grades 1 to 3. In comparison, about one third of students were beyond grade 6 in the provincial school system at the time (Barman, Hébert, and McCaskill 1986).

Aware of the dismal academic results, various Aboriginal individuals, leaders and groups brought their concerns to the government. For example, a parent of a student at Battleford residential school refused to send his child back, telling the Indian agent that his son could not read, speak, or write English after five years of attendance, his time having been spent performing farm labour rather than learning (Miller 1996). In 1911, a delegation from Saskatchewan to the superintendent of Indian Affairs requested that less emphasis be placed on farming, and more on class work (Barman, Hébert, and McCaskill 1986). Two decades later, the League of Indians of Western Canada passed a resolution asking that the Department of Indian Affairs develop local day schools on-reserve since students in residential schools were progressing so slowly (Sluman and Goodwill 1982). The next year the League pushed the department to require that teachers have proper certification and that students in residential schools spend more time in the classroom (Barman, Hébert, and McCaskill, 1986). Little was done to respond to these requests.

As would later become more widely known, not only did little academic learning occur in residential schools, for many First Nations students, residential schools were places of emotional, physical, and sexual abuse. Children were taken, often forcefully, from their homes, their hair was cut, they were clothed in European style of dress, and they were placed in unsanitary living conditions. Students were taught to be ashamed of their culture and to see themselves and their people as inferior and immoral, often facing punishment if they spoke their native language (Miller, 1996). Physical abuse was also common in residential schools, and it is clear from government documents from the time that church and department officials were aware of the abuse and chose not to stop it. For example, in the early 1900s, an inspector of Indian Agencies named W. Graham brought numerous cases of abuse to the attention of the Department of Indian Affairs. One such case involved a principal at Crowstand School who had tied ropes to the arms of a number of boys who had attempted to run away, making them run behind a horse and buggy for eight miles. In another case, a boy from the Anglican Old Sun's School who had run away was shackled to a bed, stripped, and beaten mercilessly. In all of the cases brought forward by Graham, the Department refused to have the offenders removed from the schools, siding instead with the churches, which defended the actions of their employees (Milloy 1999). Despite numerous suggestions that regulations on the acceptable use and limits of punishment should be sent to school principals, no such regulations were ever issued. Principals and school staff thus disciplined children as they saw fit, with records showing that students experienced a litany of abuses including chaining and shackling; being locked in small, dark spaces; having their heads shaved; and being severely beaten with whips and fists (Milloy 1999).

While almost entirely absent from government documents of the time, reflecting the general lack of discussion of sexual matters in that period, it is now widely known that sexual abuse was also pervasive. According to the Aboriginal Healing Foundation, while residential school students had long spoke about their negative experiences, it was a BC social worker working with clients from the Nl'akapxm First Nation in 1987 that acted as a catalyst in bringing to light the full extent of the abuses endured by former students. Examining the personal disclosures of Nl'akapxm clients, she discovered that most of the Nl'akapxm who had attended St. George's Residential School had been sexually abused during their time there. A criminal investigation followed and a former dormitory supervisor was convicted of sexual assault, drawing media attention to the issue and setting the stage for other former students to bring charges forward (Aboriginal Healing Foundation 2005). Former students of St. George's Residential School also brought a lawsuit against the Anglican Church and the Canadian Government, becoming the first such civil case to come to trial in Canada. By 1999, 2500 lawsuits had been launched over abuse at residential schools (Miller 2000). While it is not known exactly how many students experienced sexual abuse, one study estimated that 48% to 70% of residential school students in one First Nations community were sexually abused (Chrisjohn, Belleau et al. 1991).[2]

Winding Down Residential Schools: From Segregation to Integration

It was not until the 1940s and 1950s that the government began to once again rethink its education policy. Funding cutbacks during the First World War, the Great Depression, and the Second World War had left federal schools severely under-resourced. At the same time, the atrocities of the Second World War brought an increased awareness of institutionalized racism and human rights issues to the general public, drawing attention to the treatment of Indigenous peoples. Impetus for change was also provided by the large number of Indigenous men returning from war who were increasingly unwilling to accept inferior treatment after fighting for their country (Miller 2000).

In 1946, a Special Joint Committee of the Senate and House of Commons was formed to examine and formulate suggestions for how to improve the *Indian Act*. With regard to education, the committee noted that residential schools were failing to both educate and assimilate Aboriginal children and should thus be abandoned. It was proposed that where possible, Indigenous students should be integrated into provincial schools (Nicholas 2001). Based on these suggestions, the revised *Indian Act* of 1951 included provisions for the federal government to strike tuition agreements with provincial and territorial authorities for Aboriginal students to be educated in provincial schools. By 1960, about one quarter of Aboriginal students were attending provincial institutions (Barman, Hébert, and McCaskill 1986). Among the first generation of students to attend public schools, however, drop out rates were alarmingly high, with approximately 94% of Aboriginal students leaving school before graduating grade 12, compared to 12% of non-Aboriginal students (Hawthorn, 1967).

Despite the Joint Committee's clear proposal to abandon residential schools in 1946, strong resistance from the churches, and in some cases from Aboriginal communities themselves, lengthened the process of winding down the residential school system. By 1960, over 60 residential schools remained in operation (Aboriginal Healing Foundation, 2007). Over the next decade, however, a number of factors combined to produce more rapid change. For one, the government formally ended its partnership with the churches in 1969, effectively secularizing

Aboriginal education and stifling a key source of opposition (RCAP 1996). In terms of public attitudes, the civil rights movement in the United States and decolonization struggles in Asia and Africa were bringing attention to equal rights for minority groups and made addressing the issue of Aboriginal well-being a moral imperative (Miller 1996). Further, various government reports were commissioned during this time to investigate the needs of the Aboriginal population, with two such reports explicitly condemning residential schools. Both released in 1967, Caldwell's *Indian Residential Schools* and Hawthorn's *A Survey of the Contemporary Indians of Canada*, commonly known as the Hawthorn Report, provided strong criticisms of the residential school system and supported the government's policy of integrating students into provincial schools. Both recommended that the government cease to operate residential schools and Hawthorn suggested that the former residential establishments be converted to hostels where children could board to attend regular schools. Rather than disputing the criticisms of the federal school system, the government endorsed the reports and used them to support their position on integration (Milloy 1999).

Education in the North

The development of European-style education in the North[3] occurred at a different pace and a different time than elsewhere in Canada, but followed largely the same overall pattern. From 1670 to 1870, the Hudson's Bay Company (HBC) controlled large swaths of land in the North and West due to a royal charter granted by King Charles II. Interested solely in trade, HBC initially discouraged missionary activity on its land and had no desire to educate or assimilate the Indigenous population (Carney 1995). After these lands, known as the North-Western Territory and Rupert's Land, were ceded to the newly formed Dominion of Canada in 1870, missionaries began to have a larger presence in the North and expanded on the few mission schools that had been opened in the 1860's (Macpherson 1991). However, like the Hudson's Bay Company, the Canadian government had little interest in educating the Northern Indigenous population, as it was assumed that having a formal education was futile for peoples living in such isolated regions. The Canadian government also hoped that Indigenous peoples in the North would maintain their traditional lifestyles and thus not rely on the government for assistance (Milloy 1999).

With little involvement from the Canadian government, education was left in the hands of the religions groups that operated missions in the North, primarily the Anglican and Catholic Churches. A number of day and residential facilities were slowly established and, after repeated appeals to the federal government for assistance, limited funding began to be provided in the 1890s (Coates 1991, Macpherson 1991). The government was not convinced, however, that education in the North was necessary or desirable and remained generally disinterested in Northern educational activities. Unwilling to establish a territory-wide education system, new schools were opened only when missionaries pressured the government to provide funds, and, even then, funding was provided reluctantly (Coates 1991). Reflecting the government's sentiment, Frank Oliver, minister of the interior, granted the capital and operating costs for a new boarding school in the Yukon in 1909 but stated, "I will not undertake in a general way to educate the Indians of the Yukon. In my judgment they can, if left as Indians, earn a better living" (as quoted in Coates 1991, 138). Due to the lack of government support and the meager funds available, the schools that were established were marked by inadequate facilities, unqualified teachers, a lack of supplies and curriculum, and they operated intermittently, closing and opening based on the availability of teachers and funds and on the migratory patterns of the Native populations (Coates 1986, Macpherson 1991).

It was not until after World War II that the federal government began to become truly involved in the education of Northern Aboriginal peoples. In the post-war period, a renewed interest in issues of social justice and the well-being of disadvantaged Canadians brought a flurry of new programs to the North designed to improve everything from health, to housing, to employment. Education also became a concern, and a number of reports were commissioned to investigate the current state of affairs and what should be done. In 1955 it was arranged that the Department of Northern Affairs and National Resources would take on responsibility for educating children in the Northwest Territories, and in 1956 all mission school teachers were made federal employees. An aggressive school construction program to expand the meager education system was also announced in 1955. Many of the new schools were accompanied by hostels to house students from outlying areas and, in line with the federal government's wider push towards integrated schooling, the schools were to educate both Indigenous and non-Indigenous students (Macpherson 1991). According Gordon Robertson, Deputy Minister of the Department of Northern Affairs in the 1950s, the number of schools in the Northwest Territories grew rapidly from only 18 in the entire territory in 1953 to 30 schools in the Mackenzie Educational District and 25 in the Arctic Educational District in 1962 (Macpherson 1991).

The move towards federal control also brought a dramatic shift in the curriculum being offered in Northern schools. Under federal authority, school programming began to more closely resemble the curriculum in southern schools and English or French were the only languages of instruction (Coates, 1991; Milloy, 1999). While the Department of Northern Affairs, professing to have learned from the mistakes of the southern school system, stated that their educational policy was to "maintain the native way of life" and "preserve the pride of the race," critics asserted that inside the classroom, assimilation remained the primary goal (Milloy, 1999).

By the late 1960s, jurisdiction over Northern education was once again changing hands. The creation of a new government in the Northwest Territories with Yellowknife as its capital led to the devolution of a number of federal powers in 1967. Education was devolved soon after, and by 1970 the Northwest Territories government had full jurisdiction over education (Macpherson 1991). In the Yukon, virtually all of the schools were under the authority of the Yukon territorial government by the late 1960s (Coates 1991). Arctic Quebec followed a similar pattern, with provincial schools being established in most communities in the 1960s. The Quebec government, seeking to assert control over Inuit affairs, offered an alternative education system to the pre-existing federal system but both federal and provincial schools continued to operate (Vick-Westgate 2002).

Indian Control of Indian Education

The real watershed in Aboriginal education across the country occurred in 1969 with the release of the "White Paper" and the subsequent Aboriginal response. Produced by Trudeau's Liberal government, the White Paper argued that in order for the conditions of Aboriginal peoples to be improved they needed to be made full and equal citizens in Canadian society. To achieve "full equality" the *Indian Act* was to be repealed, the Department of Indian Affairs eliminated, and all special legal status for Indians was to be removed. Aboriginal peoples were to become just one more element in a multicultural society.

First Nations reacted swiftly to the proposed policy, condemning the paper as an attempt by the government to shirk its responsibility to First Nations and as promoting cultural genocide. Soon after, various Aboriginal organizations began producing position papers voicing their intense opposition to the terms of the White Paper, with education becoming a key concern. One of the most significant of these position papers was the National Indian Brotherhood's 1972 paper titled *Indian Control of Indian Education*. At this time, the government had already abandoned the White Paper due to the strong and united Aboriginal opposition and had promised to consult with First Nations groups in the formulation of a new policy. The National Indian Brotherhood's paper was a comprehensive statement of the need for local control of Aboriginal education, inspired in part by events such as the 1970 Blue Quills Residential School sit-in, in which the community successfully resisted the school's closure, demanding it remain open under Indian control. The government, already committed to phasing out the failed and costly residential schools and finding that integration was not more academically or socially successful, acquiesced and accepted the Brotherhood's position paper in principle (Longboat 1986).

After accepting *Indian Control of Indian Education* as the national policy statement on Aboriginal education, the government began to devolve some administrative control of schools to First Nations communities. In most cases, the devolution of responsibility to First Nations communities resulted in very little actual control over the content and delivery of education. More comprehensive change came about in Northern Quebec due to the James Bay and Northern Quebec Agreement (1975), which was the first major land claim settlement in Canada. The agreement contained detailed provisions on education, including the creation of a Cree and an Inuit school board. The two school boards were given the power to develop and deliver culturally appropriate curriculum and to use Cree and Inuktitut as the languages of instruction (Vick-Westgate 2002).

Overall, however, there were many misunderstandings and struggles over the meaning and implementation of Indian control. Frustrated with the pace and direction of change, in 1988 the Assembly of First Nations (AFN) produced *Tradition and Education: Towards a Vision of the Future*, which was a rearticulation of the ideas in *Indian Control of Indian Education*. However, more than just updating and revising the original policy statement, *Tradition and Education* reflected a clear shift in thinking among First Nations leaders about the meaning of "Indian control." While *Indian Control of Indian Education* spoke about control in terms of devolving responsibility for education to Indian bands that would have authority over education similar to that of provincial school boards, *Tradition and Education* emphasized Aboriginal peoples' inherent right to self-government as the basis for control over education (Abele, Dittburner, and Graham 2000). It was argued that a constitutional amendment was needed to formally recognize and affirm this inherent right, or, at the very least, federal legislation that would ensure future dealings between First Nations and the federal government were on a government-to-government basis.

To aid in the transition process, *Tradition and Education* demanded that the government provide the funding necessary to create a new administrative structure, establish national and regional educational institutions, formulate long-term education plans, research First Nations learning styles, and develop new curriculum. Monetary issues were central to the report, as it was argued that funding was a key barrier to First Nations jurisdiction over education. For First Nations to truly take control of their education systems, funding would need to be adequate and sustainable and First Nations would need to have full and complete control over the allocation and management of resources (AFN 1988).

The government responded to *Tradition and Education* by commissioning James MacPherson to review the document. His findings were published in the *MacPherson Report on Tradition and Education: Towards a Vision of Our Future* in 1991. MacPherson reported that the federal government's Aboriginal education policy was extremely skeletal and unclear. Echoing the AFN's proposal, it was recommended that a constitutional amendment be made to provide a strong foundation for First Nations jurisdiction over education. MacPherson further recommended that the government implement a national Indian education law that would specify the role of First Nations in developing education policy, affirming their jurisdiction and control. The law would also include provisions for the establishment of a national advisory committee and a national Indian education institute that would aid in the transition to First Nations control and contribute to the development of national education policies (MacPherson 1991).

While MacPherson generally supported the AFN's proposals, Abele, Dittburner, and Graham (2000) note that the two documents differ in their understanding of the meaning of self-government. Seeking to assure the federal government and the public that self-government is not a "scary concept," MacPherson states in this report that it should not be thought of in terms of self-determination:

> We should not allow our pre-occupation with the place of Quebec in Canada or our political and legal thinking rooted in the concept and definition of federalism, to lead us to the facile, but wrong, conclusion that self-government means independence or self-determination. (MacPherson 1991, 42)

This could be understood as in contrast to the AFN's assertion in *Tradition and Education* that self-determination is central to their call for jurisdiction over education:

> The recognition and reflection of the inherent right to be and to remain distinct First Nations and to exercise local self-determination over local education programs through self-government is at the heart of this *Declaration of First nations Jurisdiction Over Education.* (AFN 1988, 38)

Furthermore, MacPherson fails to use the term "inherent right" throughout his report. Nevertheless, *Tradition and Education* and the subsequent *MacPherson Report* brought First Nations education back to the national arena.

It could be argued that the federal government attempted to respond to the recommendations of MacPherson and the AFN by including a constitutional amendment recognizing First Nations' "inherent right of self-government within Canada" in the 1992 Charlottetown Accord. However, the Accord was defeated that same year. Rather than re-opening constitutional debates, the federal government introduced a new policy in 1995 known as the Aboriginal Self-Government Policy, which officially recognized Aboriginal peoples' inherent right of self-government under section 35 of the *Constitution Act*, 1982, and established the willingness of the federal government to enter into self-government negotiations with First Nations (DIAND 1995).[4] This policy statement did not attempt to delineate uniform terms for Aboriginal self-government, but rather proposed to negotiate self-government agreements that are tailored to the needs of each First Nation with the broad guidelines that Aboriginal jurisdiction could apply to matters that are internal to their communities, integral to their distinct identities, and essential to their operation as a government. Education is explicitly listed as an area for negotiation (DIAND 1995).

While self-government agreements with education provisions had been created prior to the 1995 Aboriginal Self-Government Policy, for example the aforementioned James Bay and Northern Quebec Agreement, this policy was important because it established a new willingness on the part of the federal government to constitutionally protect the rights negotiated in self-government agreements. Rights set out in agreements that are protected by the Constitution are thus considered to be treaty rights, theoretically making them much more difficult to violate, restrict, or rescind than those established in previous agreements.

Since 1995, there have been a number of self-government agreements and agreements-in-principle signed that explicitly address jurisdiction over education. Examples of these are the Nisga'a Final Agreement (1998), the Anishnaabe Government Agreement-in-Principle (1998) and the Westbank First Nation Self-Government Agreement (2003). These agreements generally contain provisions stating that the First Nation(s) will have jurisdiction over pre-school, elementary, and secondary education, including the power to make laws with regards to education. However, as many commentators have noted, these agreements also all include at least one clause stating that the education provided by the First Nation must be comparable to that provided in the provincial system, in effect constraining the participating community's ability to truly exercise jurisdiction and control over education (McCue 1999, Morgan 1998).

British Columbia has recently begun a new approach to negotiating jurisdiction over education with First Nations in the province. Rather than negotiating jurisdictional issues with each First Nation through the self-government agreement process, a framework agreement between the province, the federal government, and First Nations in BC was signed in 2006 that outlined a process for transferring responsibility for elementary and secondary on-reserve education to First Nations in BC that decide to opt-in to the agreement. Supported by the passage of both federal and provincial legislation,[5] participating First Nations will be able to make laws with regard to education and design and deliver education programs. As part of the agreement, a First Nations Education Authority composed of all participating First Nations will act as a regulatory body for teacher certification, school certification, and the development of curriculum standards for core courses.

In terms of off-reserve education, a number of provinces have produced policy frameworks and initiatives designed to improve the quality of education provided to First Nations, Inuit and Métis students in their schools. For example, Manitoba created the *Aboriginal Education Action Plan, 2004–2007* (2004), Saskatchewan has an *Indian and Métis Education Policy from Kindergarten to Grade 12* (1995), British Columbia developed a framework for the creation of Education Enhancement Agreements, and both Ontario (2007) and Alberta (2002) have produced reports titled *First Nations, Inuit, and Métis Education Policy Framework*. All of these policy initiatives are designed to enhance Aboriginal student, parent, and community participation in provincial education structures and improve learning outcomes for Aboriginal learners. However, it is difficult to ascertain how effective these provincial initiatives have been in bringing about real change.

In the meantime, numerous reports and policy statements have reiterated the calls to recognize and work towards a comprehensive understanding of First Nations' jurisdiction over education as a key element of Aboriginal self-government. The 1996 *Report of the Royal Commission on Aboriginal Peoples* (RCAP) recommended that federal, provincial, and territorial levels of government move to recognize education as a core area of jurisdiction in self-government, placing emphasis on the importance of capacity development to the transition process.

According to the Commission, acknowledging First Nations' jurisdiction over education would involve First Nations passing their own education policies and legislation and regulating all aspects of education. To this end, the Commission proposed that Aboriginal education systems be developed consisting of multiple levels of organization, including local communities, Aboriginal nations, multi-nation organizations and Canada-wide networks.

In the federal government's response to RCAP, a report titled *Gathering Strength: Canada's Aboriginal Action Plan*, the government acknowledged that it was lacking in the area of capacity building and pledged to make capacity building a focus in the negotiation and implementation of self-government arrangements. However, the report had very little to say on the issue of education. In the space devoted to the topic, it was briefly stated that the federal government would work with First Nations to support education reform on reserves with the goal being to "improve the quality and cultural relevance of education for First Nations students; improve the classroom effectiveness of teachers; support community and parental involvement in schools; improve the management and support capacity of First Nations systems; and enhance learning by providing greater access to technology for First Nations schools" (INAC 1997, 16). Despite the clear demand in both RCAP and *Tradition and Education* that the federal government recognize education as a core element of Aboriginal self-government, *Gathering Strength* fails to include any mention of the relationship between self-government and First Nations' jurisdiction over education.

In 2000 the Auditor General issued a report on the state of First Nations education, concluding that more needed to be done to close the education gap between First Nations and other Canadian students (Auditor General of Canada 2000). In particular, the report noted that there was considerable confusion about the roles and responsibilities of the federal government in First Nations education, and a lack of information on actual education costs, appropriate performance indicators, and the state of many education funding agreements. Two years after the Auditor General's report, the Minister of Indian and Northern Affairs established the Minister's National Working Group on Education to provide strategies for improving the quality of First Nations education, and improving education outcomes for First Nations students. The group had a series of recommendations, including that the federal government commit to jurisdictional discussions with First Nations that include capacity building measures and strategies for implementation and that the federal government and First Nations work together to establish the role of Indian and Northern Affairs Canada (INAC) in First Nations education (Minister's National Working Group 2002).

Despite the strong recommendations made in these two reports, a follow-up study by the Auditor General in 2004 found that the federal government had done little to address the issues (Auditor General of Canada, 2004). In response, the department prepared a paper titled *Education Action Plan* in 2005 that outlined how they were addressing each of the concerns raised by Auditor General

(INAC, 2004). The *Action Plan* was organized around five key areas: strategy and action plan, roles and responsibilities, funding, accountability, performance measurement, monitoring, and reporting. The centerpiece of the report, however, was a First Nations Education Policy Framework and a First Nations Management Framework to be developed in partnership with First Nations. The policy framework, projected to be completed in June 2006, was to outline a strategic vision for First Nations education and clarify the roles and responsibilities of various stakeholders. The management framework was to institute performance indicators and targets, outline a new funding model and establish accountability measures, and had a projected completion date of June 2007.

To coordinate the process of developing these two frameworks in collaboration with First Nations, INAC joined with the AFN to form an education policy framework joint steering committee. The steering committee held regional dialogues with various First Nations and education organizations in 2006. However, the projected completion dates for both the policy framework and management framework have long since passed and, to date, nothing has been produced. Further, the AFN reports that INAC halted the collaborative process in 2007 and has been proceeding alone (personal communication 2008).

While a clear national policy on First Nations education has not been produced,[6] efforts have been made in recent years to atone for the wrongs of the past. In May 2006, the Indian Residential Schools Settlement Agreement (IRSSA) was formally approved by all parties involved. Under the terms of the agreement, former residential school students were provided monetary compensation in the form of a "common experience payment" along with additional compensation based on their years of attendance at a residential school. The agreement also established an Independent Assessment Process for former students to pursue claims of sexual and physical abuse, provided $125 million for the Aboriginal Healing Foundation to continue their healing programs, granted additional funding to support local and national commemoration projects, and included provisions for the establishment of a five-year Truth and Reconciliation Commission. Furthermore, in June 2008 the federal government finally issued a formal apology for its role in the creation and operation of the residential school system.[7] For the thousands of former residential school students who are no longer living, however, the apology and compensation has come far too late. For many, the hope now is that the truth and reconciliation commission will bring a renewed focus on education, a commitment to improving education for all First Nations learners, and the impetus to continue taking meaningful steps towards First Nations control of First Nations education.

Endnotes

1 We have chosen to use the words in the language of the day to identify people and groups, thus terms such as 'Indian', 'tribe' and 'Native' have been employed. As nomenclature shifts over history we will shift our language as well.

2 For more information on abuse in residential schools see Knockwood,1992, Haig-Brown 1988, and Miller 1996.

3 The "North" is being used here to refer to the area encompassing present day Yukon, Northwest Territories, Nunavut, and Northern Quebec.

4 The policy is also known as the Inherent Right of Self-Government Policy.

5 Federally, Bill C-34, titled the *First Nations Jurisdiction over Education in British Columbia Act*, received royal assent in December 2006. In British Columbia, Bill 46, *The First Nations Education Act*, received royal assent in November 2007.

6 The department of Indian and Northern Affairs Canada has recently unveiled their own plan, referred to as the Reforming First Nation Education Initiative. This initiative consists of two new programs: the Education Partnerships Program (EPP) and the First Nation Student Success Program (FNSSP), details of which were released in December 2008 (INAC 2008, INAC 2008a). The EPP is designed to encourage and support tripartite partnership agreements between regional First Nation organizations, provincial ministries of education and Indian and Northern Affairs Canada (INAC). The partnerships are to improve coordination between First Nation and provincial schools and promote the sharing of expertise and service provision among partners. The FNSSP provides First Nation regional organizations or band-operated schools with funding to develop school success plans, implement student learning assessments, and adopt a performance measurement system.

7 The churches involved in operating residential schools also issued formal apologies. The United Church of Canada was the first to apologize in 1986. Following suit, in 1991 the Anglican Church, the Canadian Conference of Catholic Bishops, and the Missionary Oblates of Mary Immaculate offered their apologies. The Presbyterian Church apologized in 1994.

References

Abele, F., C. Dittubrner and K.A. Graham. 2000. "Towards a Shared Understanding in the Policy Discussion about Aboriginal Education." In M.B. Castellano, L. Davis and L. Lahache (Eds), *Aboriginal Education: Fulfilling the Promise*. Vancouver: UBC Press. 3–24.

Aboriginal Healing Foundation. 2005. *Reclaiming Connections: Understanding Residential School Trauma Among Aboriginal People. A Resource Manual*. Ottawa: Aboriginal Healing Foundation.

Aboriginal Healing Foundation. 2007. *A Directory of Residential Schools in Canada*. Ottawa: Aboriginal Healing Foundation.

AFN. 2005. *First Nations Education Action Plan*. Ottawa: Assembly of First Nations.

AFN. 1988. *Tradition and Education: Towards a Vision of Our Future, A Declaration of First Nations Jurisdiction Over Education*. Ottawa: Assembly of First Nations.

Auditor General of Canada. 2000. "Chapter 4: Indian and Northern Affairs Canada—Education and Secondary Education." In *Report of the Auditor General of Canada to the House of Commons*. Ottawa: Office of the Auditor General of Canada. 30.

Auditor General of Canada. 2004. "Chapter 5: Indian and Northern Affairs Canada—Education Program and Post-Secondary Student Program." In *Report of the Auditor General of Canada to the House of Commons*. Ottawa: Office of the Auditor General of Canada.

Barman, J., Y. Hébert and D. McCaskill. 1986. "The Legacy of the Past: An Overview." In J. Barman, Y. Hébert and D. McCaskill (Eds), *Indian Education In Canada. Volume 1: The Legacy*. Vancouver: University of British Columbia Press. 1–22.

Burns, G.E. 1998. "Factors and Themes in Native Education and School Boards / First nations Tuition Negotiations and Tuition Agreement Schooling." *Canadian Journal of Native Education*. 22(1): 53–66.

Caldwell, G. 1967. *Indian Residential Schools: A Research Study of the Child Care Programmes for Nine Residential Schools in Saskatchewan.* Prepared for the Department of Indian Affairs and Northern Development. Ottawa: Canadian Welfare Council.

Carney, R. 1995. "Aboriginal Residential Schools Before Confederation: The Early Experience." *Historical Studies: Canadian Catholic Historical Association.* 61: 13–40.

Chalmers, J.W. 1972. *Education Behind the Buckskin Curtain.* Edmonton: University of Alberta.

Chrisjohn, R. and C. Belleau. 1991. "Faith Misplaced: Lasting Effects of Abuse in a First Nations Community." *Canadian Journal of Native Education.* 18(2):161–197.

Coates, K.S. 1986. "A Very Imperfect Means of Education: Indian Day Schools in the Yukon Territory, 1890–1955." In J. Barman, Y. Hébert and D. McCaskill (Eds), *Indian Education In Canada. Volume 1: The Legacy.* Vancouver: University of British Columbia Press. 132–149.

Coates, K.S. 1991. *Best Left as Indian: Native-White Relations in the Yukon Territory, 1840–1973.* Montreal: McGill-Queen's University Press.

DIAND. 2005. *Basic Departmental Data, 2004.* Ottawa: Department of Indian Affairs and Northern Development.

DIAND. 1995. *The Government of Canada's Approach to the Implementation of the Inherent Right and the Negotiation of Aboriginal Self-Government.* Ottawa: Department of Indian Affairs and Northern Development.

Grant, A. 1996. *No End of Grief: Indian Residential Schools in Canada.* Winnipeg: Pemmican Publications Inc.

Haig-Brown, C. 1988. *Resistance and Renewal: Surviving the Indian Residential School.* Vancouver: Tillacum Library.

Hawthorn, H.B. (Ed.). 1967. *A Survey of the Contemporary Indians of Canada: A Report on Economic, Political and Educational Needs and Policies.* Volume II. Ottawa: Indian Affairs Branch.

INAC. 2005. "Chapter 5: Education Action Plan: In Response to the Auditor General's Observations and Recommendations." *November 2004 Report.* Ottawa: Indian and Northern Affairs Canada.

Jaenen, C. J. 1986. "Education for Francization: The Case of New France in the Seventeenth Century." In J. Barman, Y. Hébert and D. McCaskill (Eds), *Indian Education In Canada. Volume 1: The Legacy.* Vancouver: University of British Columbia Press. 45–63.

Knockwood, I. 1992. *Out of the Depths: The Experiences of Mi'kmaw Children at the Indian Residential School at Shubenacadie, Nova Scotia.* Lockeport, Nova Scotia: Roseway Publishing.

Longboat, D. 1986. "First Nations Control of Education: The Path to Our Survival as Nations." In J. Barman, Y. Hébert and D. McCaskill (Eds), *Indian Education In Canada. Volume 2: The Challenge.* Vancouver: University of British Columbia Press. 22–42.

MacPherson, J. 1991. *MacPherson Report on Tradition and Education: Towards a Vision of Our Future.* Ottawa: Department of Indian Affairs and Northern Development.

Macpherson, N.J. 1991. *Dreams and Visions: Education in the Northwest Territories from Early Days to 1984.* Yellowknife: Department of Education, Government of the Northwest Territories of Canada.

Magnuson, R. 1992. *Education in New France.* Montreal: McGill-Queen's University Press.

McCue, H. 1999. *Self-Government Agreements and Jurisdiction in Education.* Ottawa: Assembly of First Nations.

Miller, J.R. 1996. *Shingwauk's Vision: A History of Native Residential Schools.* Toronto: University of Toronto Press.

Miller, J.R. 2000. *Skyscrapers Hide the Heavens: A History of Indian-White Relations in Canada.* 3rd Edition. Toronto: University of Toronto Press.

Milloy, J.S. 1999. *A National Crime: The Canadian Government and the Residential School System, 1879 to 1986.* Winnipeg: University of Manitoba Press.

Minister's National Working Group on Education. 2002. *Our Children: Keepers of the Sacred Knowledge.* Ottawa: Indian and Northern Affairs Canada.

Morgan, N.A. 1998. *Legal Mechanisms for Assumption of Jurisdiction and Control Over Education by First Nations.* Prepared for the First Nations Education Steering Committee, British Columbia.

National Indian Brotherhood. 1972. *Indian Control of Indian Education.* Ottawa: National Indian Brotherhood.

Nock, D.A. 1988. *A Victorian Missionary and Canadian Indian Policy: Cultural Synthesis vs Cultural Replacement*. Waterloo: Wilfred Laurier University Press.

Royal Commission on Aboriginal Peoples. 1996. *Report of the Royal Commission on Aboriginal Peoples* (Vols. 1–5). Ottawa: Canada Communication Group Publishing.

Sluman, N. and J. Goodwill. 1982. *John Tootoosis: A Biograhpy of a Cree Leader*. Ottawa: Golden Dog Press.

Vick-Westgate, A. 2002. *Nunavik: Inuit-Controlled Education in Arctic Quebec*. Calgary: University of Calgary Press.

Wilson, Donald J. 1986. " 'No Blanket to be Worn in School': The Education of Indians in Nineteenth-Century Ontario." In J. Barman, Y. Hébert and D. McCaskill (Eds), *Indian Education In Canada*. Volume: The Legacy. Vancouver: University of British Columbia Press. 64–87.

Wilson, J.B. 2007. "First Nations Education: The Need for Legislation in the Jurisdictional Gray Zone." *Canadian Journal of Native Education*. 30(2): 248–256.

3

Formal Educational Attainment of Inuit in Canada, 1981–2006

Chris Penney

Strategic Research and Analysis Directorate
Indian and Northern Affairs Canada

Introduction

A good education is generally considered a cornerstone for getting a good job and building financial security. For many Inuit, however, the education system is another southern institution that has only recently taken hold in their lives. Inuit live in Canada's north, primarily in one of four regions: the Inuvialuit region of the Northwest Territories, the Territory of Nunavut, the Nunavik region of northern Quebec, and the Nunatsiavut region of northern Labrador. Collectively, these regions are known as Inuit Nunaat, or "the land where Inuit live." With land claim agreements signed in all regions of Inuit Nunaat, there are increasing opportunities for Inuit to take a role in the future of their communities and regions, but poorer educational attainment puts these possibilities out of reach for many. In this chapter we will use Census data from 1981 to 2006 to look at the educational attainment of Inuit over time. An analysis of Inuit educational attainment poses several problems, including the difficulty we have had identifying the Inuit population from Census to Census over the past 25 years. However, it is clear that no matter how one defines the Inuit population, Inuit educational attainment, particularly post-secondary education, has remained far below that of the rest of Canada.

Background

Inuit have lived in the northern region of what we now call Canada for over 5,000 years, living a traditional nomadic lifestyle of hunting and fishing. It has only been recently that Inuit have moved into permanent settlements, and have become engaged in southern Canadian (European-style) social structures, such as the wage-based economy and formal education. Indeed, there are Inuit alive today that were born on the land and lived a traditional nomadic lifestyle for the first part of their lives.

Traditionally, knowledge transmission in Inuit culture was based on shared experiences, where elders and parents would show young Inuit what they need to know in terms of life skills, such as living out on the land or domestic tasks.

Table 3.1: Residential School Attendance for the Inuit Identity Population aged 15 Years and Over, by age group, Canada, 2001

N=3,380	Total 15 and over	15–34	35–44	45–54	55 and over
Attended Residential School	13.0%	4.0%	15.5%	43.7%	29.7%

The Inuit identity population includes those people who reported identifying as Inuit (either as a single response or in combination with North American Indian and/or Métis). Data are for the non-reserve population only. They do not include the small number of Inuit who live on Indian reserves, nor those living in institutions.

Source: Statistics Canada, Aboriginal Peoples Survey, 2001

Teaching was done by demonstration, and learning came from practice. At the same time, Inuit youth would also learn about traditional Inuit culture, values, and traditions. This traditional Inuit knowledge is known as Inuit Qaujimajatuqangit, or IQ. This is characterized by life-long learning through an individual's different life stages (i.e. child, youth, young adult, adult, and elder) and encompasses all aspects of learning, including people, culture, land, and environment (Canadian Council on Learning 2007).

It has only been two or three generations of Inuit who have experienced living in permanent settlements, and as a part of this European influence, the formal education system. For many of the first Inuit to go to western schools, the experience was far from a positive one. The residential schools legacy has directly affected many Inuit, as it has First Nations and Métis throughout Canada. The first federally regulated residential school in the north started in 1951, and through 1960, Inuit attendance at residential schools totalled almost 7,000 (King 2006).[1] From the point of view of the government, these were designed to prepare Inuit for the expansion of the southern economy into the North, by giving Inuit a southern education. While the experiences of Inuit attendees of residential schools vary between the positive and the abusive, all Inuit attending these schools suffered from a disconnection from their families, communities, and culture. Although Inuit residential school attendees were not strictly forbidden to speak Inuktitut in all schools, the federal government refused to allow Inuit elders to teach students traditional knowledge, further cementing the break from the traditional Inuit education methods of the past (King 2006).This legacy is believed to contribute to an entrenched mistrust of the education system, where Inuit parents do not fully support their children's education (Simon 2007).

Table 3.1 shows the proportion of Inuit who report having attended a federal residential school. The highest proportion is for the 45 to 54 year age group, where over 40% reported having attended residential school. Although regional statistics must be interpreted with caution, since the presence of residential schools varied by region, residential school attendance was highest in the Northwest Territories, with over 25% of all Inuit attending. Labrador reported the lowest attendance, at just over 8%.[2]

Defining the Inuit Population in Census Data

The Census of Population has modified and adjusted how it measures the Aboriginal population of Canada from 1981 through to the most recent Census in 2006. In order to use all of these data, our analysis is divided into two parts, based on the changing definitions of the Inuit population. The first part of this analysis will look at the Inuit ancestry population in the Census from 1981 to 2001. The second part will look at the Inuit identity population from 1996 to 2006.

Since the 1996 Census, Statistics Canada has included a question on Aboriginal identity that has become the standard definition of the Aboriginal population used in most studies of Census data. The identity concept depends on respondents self-identifying with one or more of the three Aboriginal groups described in the Constitution: First Nations (referred to as North American Indians by Statistics Canada), Métis and Inuit. This personal perception of ones ethnic and cultural affiliation does not require any specific formal membership or registry with a recognized group (for example membership in one of the four recognized Inuit land claim organizations). The Aboriginal identity concept, however, was not asked on the Census prior to 1996, making it impossible to do any time-trend analysis before that year. In order to look at data from 1981 forward, the first part of this study will include all people who report at least some Inuit "ancestry," as it is possible to have ancestors from multiple ethnic or cultural groups.

The Inuit ancestry population is based on a question which Statistics Canada has used for the entire period from 1981 to 2001, though the question has undergone changes over time. In 1981, multiple responses were not encouraged by the wording or the layout of the question on ethnic origins. In 1986, the question referred to ancestral groups in the plural, and instructed respondents to give as many responses as needed. This had the effect of drastically increasing the number of individuals who reported Inuit ancestry in combination with other ethnic groups, from 12,380 in 1981 to 18,270 in 1986. Including respondents with multiple reported ancestries also has the effect of changing the socio-economic characteristics of the study population—those with mixed Inuit and other ancestry are less likely than those reporting only Inuit ancestry to speak an Inuit language, and they are more likely to live in the south, be employed, and have better incomes (see INAC/ITK 2006a).

As seen in **Table 3.2**, the Inuit population captured by the Census has more than doubled from 1981 to 2001. While the Inuit population is one of the most fertile in Canada (Statistics Canada 2008a), these changes can be explained partly by non-demographic factors. For example, in 2001, 63% of the Inuit population in the Atlantic region were of mixed ancestry. Given that the 1981 questionnaire did not encourage multiple ethnicity answers, the doubling of the Inuit population of

Table 3.2: Inuit Ancestry Population, Canada and Regions, 1981–2001

Region	1981	1986	1991	1996	2001	% Change 1981–2001	% Change 1996–2001
Canada	24,290	36,045	48,890	49,630	56,190	131	13
Atlantic	2,005	4,620	7,655	8,220	9,220	360	12
Quebec	4,220	7,335	8,470	9,430	10,725	154	14
Nunavut	13,045	15,195	17,640	20,510	22,610	73	10
Northwest Territories	2,480	2,900	3,615	4,220	4,130	67	-2
Ontario/ Western Canada	2,450	5,930	11,345	7,140	9,300	280	30

Source: Statistics Canada, Census of population, 1981–2001 in INAC and ITK 2006b

the Atlantic region between 1981 and 1986 should therefore be considered largely an artifact of changing collection methodology. The Inuit ancestry population in Ontario/Western Canada in 1991 was over four and a half times the population in 1981. This is undoubtedly caused by people reporting Inuit ancestry in 1991 who didn't in the past, rather than actual demographic growth. The negative population growth in the Northwest Territories between 1996 and 2001 is due largely to the net under coverage in the territory in 2001.[3]

In order to include data from the 2006 Census, and to provide context for these data, the second part of this analysis will look at data from 1996 to 2006 using the Inuit single identity population. As stated above, the Census has collected information on an individual's self-reported Aboriginal identity since 1996. Although it is possible to look at all individuals who reported Inuit identity, this report will include only those Inuit who reported a single Aboriginal identity, and will exclude those that reported Inuit identity in combination with North American Indian (i.e. First Nations) or Métis identity. While this has the effect of slightly reducing the study population,[4] this is the population that has been adopted by most researchers (see for example Statistics Canada 2008a). As noted above, using a wider definition of Inuit, such as one based on any Inuit ancestry, will lead to improved socio-economic traits in the study population. Looking at the Inuit single identity population will therefore likely lead to poorer education statistics relative to the 1981 to 2001 data from the first part of the analysis.

Education Variables and Definitions

For the years 1981 through 2001, education data from the Census was fairly consistently collected, with little change to the questionnaire content over this period. These questions were based on a respondents "highest level of schooling," which included cases of completed as well as incomplete schooling. The categories for highest level of schooling based on the Census content for the years 1981 through 2001 are:

- Less than grade 9
- Incomplete high school
- High school certificate
- Incomplete post-secondary
- Completed trades
- Completed college
- Completed university
    (Statistics Canada 2002)

Although these indicators have been used over several Censuses, Statistics Canada has identified several weaknesses over time. These categories did not allow analysts to track respondents' different education paths, especially in cases of multiple instances of incomplete post-secondary education. In the Aboriginal populations we often see incomplete high school and then some form of post secondary training. Analytical categories often made several hierarchical assumptions, such as the idea that incomplete post-secondary was "higher" than a high school certificate, even though it is possible for individuals to receive some post-secondary education without having a high school certificate (Hull 2006).

Beginning with the 2006 Census, Statistics Canada changed the education module on the questionnaire to one primarily based on the attainment of credentials, which is considered more important when looking at how a person's education subsequently helps them in the labour market. The revised content is also expected to allow researchers to look at multiple post-secondary credentials in greater detail. There are, however, downsides to these changes. For example, it is no longer possible to study those that have completed their education without obtaining a credential (Hull 2006).[5]

In reviewing the 2006 Census data on education, we look at the following categories under "Highest degree, certificate, or diploma":

- No degree, certificate, or diploma
- High school diploma or equivalent only
- Trades/apprenticeship certificate or diploma only
- Other non university certificate or diploma
- University certificate below bachelor level
- University degree (including certificate above bachelor level)
    (Statistics Canada 2007)

Although the data between the old and new Census content are similar, analysis and comparison between the two are ongoing. For the present study we will compare one variable that is identical for the two series: completed university degree (Statistics Canada 2008b).

Based on the differences both in defining the Inuit population (see above), and in the education content of the Census over time, this chapter will present data

Table 3.3: Highest level of Schooling, Inuit Ancestry and Reference Populations, Canada, 1981 to 2001

	Highest Level of Schooling	Percentage				
		1981	1986	1991	1996	2001
Total with Inuit Ancestry	Less than grade 9	60.5	49.8	33.3	28.8	23.5
	Incomplete high school	20.1	25.2	24.0	27.9	29.3
	High School certificate	3.2	5.1	6.9	6.5	7.3
	Incomplete post-secondary	6.3	8.6	13.8	14.8	15.6
	Completed post-secondary					
	Completed trades	6.0	6.2	11.5	11.1	11.4
	Completed college	2.2	3.7	6.9	8.5	9.7
	Completed university	1.6	1.3	3.6	2.4	3.3
	Total (n)	14,500	22,085	30,240	29,930	34,765
Reference Population	Less than grade 9	20.0	17.2	13.9	12.0	9.8
	Incomplete high school	27.9	27.1	24.3	22.7	21.4
	High School certificate	13.0	12.8	14.8	14.3	14.1
	Incomplete post-secondary	14.0	15.7	15.9	16.2	16.8
	Completed post-secondary					
	Completed trades	9.9	9.3	10.3	9.9	10.2
	Completed college	7.2	8.3	9.4	11.5	12.2
	Completed university	8.0	9.6	11.4	13.3	15.4
	Total (n)	18,594,785	19,612,015	21,274,455	22,598,995	23,866,595

Source: Statistics Canada, Census of Population 1981–2001, in INAC and ITK 2006c

in two different series. The first includes the total Inuit ancestry population from 1981 through 2001, and looks at a variety of education variables over this period. The second series is based on the Inuit single identity population, and will feature recent data from the 2006 Census. For each group, the reference population will be other Canadians. Specifically, this refers to those who did not report Inuit ancestry, or identity.[6] In order to place this most recent year of data into context, we will look at those having completed a university degree from 1996 and 2001, the other two years which measured the Inuit identity population. Although these two series can provide a picture of Inuit formal education over the last 25 years, they are not comparable in the traditional sense, due primarily to the changes in the study populations described above.

Educational Attainment of the Inuit Total Ancestry Population in Canada 1981-2001

Table 3.3 shows the results of educational attainment for the Inuit ancestry and reference populations from 1981 to 2001. During this time period, Inuit education levels improved, according to most indicators. The proportion of Inuit with less than a grade 9 education fell dramatically from over 60% in 1981 to less than 25% in 2001. Those with a high school diploma more than doubled (from 3% in 1981 to over 7% in 2001). Another considerable improvement occurred among those completing college: from just over 2% in 1981 to almost 10% in 2001. Completion of university also doubled from 1981 to 2001, although the actual increase was fairly small, from just over 1.5% to over 3%. The proportion of Inuit having completed university actually peaked at over 3.5% in 1991, though this is likely an artefact of how the Inuit population was identified, as we discussed above (see also INAC and ITK 2006a).

Although Inuit made gains in all indicators of educational attainment during this period, the reference population were making gains at the same time. In particular, the proportion of non-Inuit with less than a grade 9 education was just under 10% in 2001, less than half the proportion in 1981 of 20%. The proportion with a university education in 2001 was about 15%, up from less than 10% in 1981.

In comparison with other Canadians, gains made by the Inuit ancestry population give mixed messages. On one hand, the proportion of people with less than a grade 9 education shows steady improvement over the twenty year period of study, where the gap between Inuit and other Canadians has steadily narrowed. The proportion of the Inuit ancestry population reporting a high school education has also risen, more than doubling over that time period. On the other hand, while the gap has narrowed, the proportion is still fairly low, at around half that of the reference population, which has remained more or less constant. In terms of post-secondary schooling, the proportion of the Inuit ancestry population reporting a completed trades education, which had lagged behind that of other Canadians in 1981, was slightly above that of the reference population by 2001.

Statistics for other post-secondary indicators, which indicated improvement for the Inuit ancestry population, did not translate into a narrowing of the gap between them and the reference population. The proportion of Inuit ancestry population with a college education increased considerably, though the gap narrowed only modestly, due to gains among other Canadians. The proportion of the Inuit ancestry population completing a university education doubled between 1981 and 2001, although the absolute increase was quite small. In the reference population

Figure 3.1: Highest Level of Schooling, Total Inuit Ancestry Population, Northern and Southern Canada, 2001

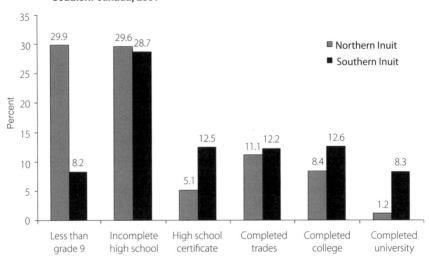

a steady increase occurred throughout the period of study, so that the absolute gap has actually increased since 1981.

We can also look at the educational attainment of Inuit living in Inuit Nunaat, compared to those living in the rest of Canada. Note, however, that Inuit regional land claim areas were not incorporated into Census geography before 2006, so the present analysis looks at the "North," defined here as the Northwest Territories, Nunavut, the Nunavik region of northern Quebec, and Labrador. The "South" is defined as the rest of Canada. An examination of the differences in educational attainment between these two areas highlights some of the challenges facing Inuit in the North. Inuit in the North are much more likely to have less than grade 9, and are much less likely to have completed high school, college, or university (**Figure 3.1**).

There are several possible explanations for why Inuit education levels in the North are poorer than those in the South. Inuit living in the South enjoy greater access to post-secondary education that is simply not available in many northern communities. Not only does this mean that Inuit in the North do not have the same educational opportunities, there is the possibility that those in the North who do leave home to further their education may remain in the South in order to take advantage of greater economic opportunities.

Looking at differences in educational attainment between males and females, each were equally likely to have less than a grade 9 education, or to have a high school certificate. Males, however, were more likely to have an incomplete high school education, but were much more likely to have a completed trades certificate. Females were more likely to have completed college or university (**Figure 3.2**).

Figure 3.2: Highest Level of Schooling, Total Inuit Ancestry Population Aged 15 and Over, by Sex, Canada, 2001

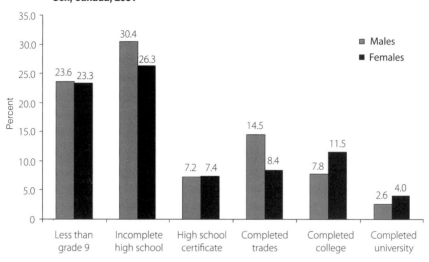

Educational Attainment of the Inuit Identity Population in Canada 1996–2006

As stated above, educational attainment on the 2006 Census is based on a respondent's highest completed degree or credential. Looking at **Figure 3.1**, the Inuit identity population lags behind the educational attainment of other Canadians[7] for all levels of qualification, and is over two and a half times more likely to have no qualification at all. Moreover, the proportion of the Inuit identity population with a trades/apprenticeship certificate or diploma was slightly below the level of the reference population, which was a category for which the Inuit ancestry population reported a higher proportion than did other Canadians in 2001. As the gap between the two is still narrow, this difference is likely an artifact of the changes in data collection and concepts discussed above.

As we noted, it is not possible to present a direct comparison of 2006 data to that from 1981 to 2001. One variable that is constant over time is the proportion of respondents having completed a university degree. **Figure 3.4** looks at the percentage of the total Inuit ancestry population and the Inuit single identity population with a completed university degree. If the Inuit single identity population is considered the more reliable definition of the Inuit population, using the identity population from 1996 and 2001 can help us compare the two populations.

The data from the Inuit single identity population demonstrates the expected trend that the total Inuit ancestry population tends to overestimate the education attainment of Inuit. Although the numbers are too small to be included here, this gap between the two populations can be explained by regional variations on the Inuit identity and ancestry populations. As discussed earlier, there have

Figure 3.3: Highest Degree or Credential, Inuit and Reference Population Aged 15 and Over, Canada, 2006

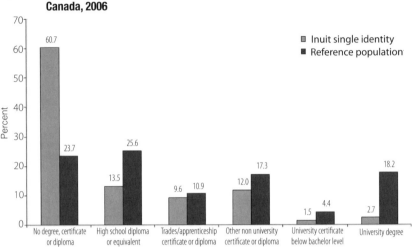

historically been issues with the Aboriginal data collected in southern Canada, and in particular Ontario, where a large number of respondents in 1986 and 1991 reported all four Aboriginal ancestry categories (Inuit, North American Indian, Métis and non-Aboriginal). In addition, a regional comparison shows that the number of respondents who report Inuit ancestry but not Inuit identity is higher in Quebec and Newfoundland & Labrador, and much smaller in Nunavut and the Northwest Territories. Indeed, looking at the territories, Nunavut and the Northwest Territories show neither the "bump" in the 1991 data, nor the gap between the ancestry and identity series as seen in the national figures here. These inconsistencies indicate the value of using the Inuit single identity population as currently defined to study the Inuit population.

Discussion

It is clear from the data presented above that Inuit educational attainment has been improving since 1981, though gains in the reference population, particularly in terms of post-secondary education, mean that the overall gap between Inuit and the rest of Canada has remained large and even increased in some attainment categories. Data from 2006 confirm that there is still a considerable disparity between the Inuit identity population and other Canadians. Although the trades category is an exception, the increasing gap in university education indicates that Inuit are not fully participating in higher education, whether through a lack of preparation from secondary school, or simply the lack of availability in isolated northern communities. The decrease in the number of Inuit with less than a grade 9 education is encouraging, but this must translate into more Inuit continuing on to further study.

Figure 3.4: Completed University, Inuit and Reference Populations aged 15 and over, 1981 to 2006, Canada

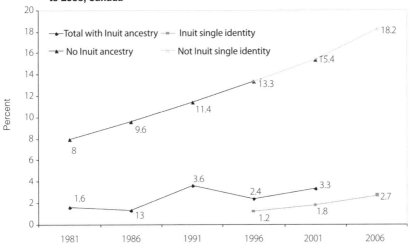

If the switch to using the Inuit identity population as the population of analysis lowers the overall proportion of Inuit with a university degree, it is likely that other indicators are similarly overestimated. The difference in the percentage of Inuit with a completed university degree underlines the importance of using an appropriate study population. Nevertheless, the message is essentially the same for either population: modest increases in the proportion of Inuit with a university degree are being outstripped by the gains in university education in the rest of the Canadian population.

The low proportion of Inuit benefitting from a formal education has made it difficult for Inuit to fully participate in the new economic and cultural opportunities offered by the transition to a wage-based economy in the North, where Inuit increasingly have their own public and Aboriginal government institutions with which to help shape their destiny.

With land claims settled in the four Inuit regions of Canada, Inuit are pushing for more direct involvement in these government institutions, and mainstream Canadian society. The Government of Nunavut has stated a goal of hiring Beneficiaries of the Nunavut Land Claim Agreement (Inuit peoples) to match their proportion of the total Nunavut population. As of 2007, Inuit made up about 50% of the total public service, as opposed to around 85% of the total population, and this number was heavily weighted toward the administrative support section, where 92% of positions were filled by beneficiaries. Higher paying positions tended to be staffed with more non-Inuit than beneficiaries. Inuit were underrepresented in senior management positions (28%), middle management positions (24%) and professional positions (25%) (Government of Nunavut 2007). Although there are no similar statistics available for the other Inuit regions, based on the national levels of schooling statistics, we can assume the situation is likely similar across the country. Education is the key to preparing Inuit for skilled positions in government, as well as the private sector.

In 2006, a landmark report by Thomas Berger looked at this issue of Public Service representation by Inuit in Nunavut, and the role education must play in allowing Inuit to compete for these jobs. Berger tackles the question "what has to be done to qualify the Inuit for employment in all occupational groupings and grade levels in their own government?"(Berger 2006).

At the heart of the issue, Berger contends, is the lack of high school graduates. The education system in Nunavut is designed to teach younger students in Inuktitut until around grade 3 or 4, after which instruction is exclusively in English. This is creating a situation where Inuit do not have strong enough English skills to make this transition, making progression in the middle and later grades ever more challenging. Inuktitut, the dominant language of Nunavut, is also not taught at an advanced level, so that neither aspect of the system is successful (Berger 2006). Another factor that comes into play here is that all Inuit do not speak the same dialect, and there are multiple writing systems, using either syllabic symbols or the Roman alphabet. This can make learning a new language even more difficult, and the variation across Inuit Nunaat means that Inuktitut reading materials have to be specifically produced for different groups. Whether or not the challenges of instituting a bilingual education program are key to improving the situation, as Berger contends, it is clear that high school graduation rates must increase, as this is the primary requirement for post-secondary schooling and access to employment.

Beyond secondary school, the gap in university education must ultimately be closed. Many agree that such education is required so that Inuit can participate in the higher levels of public and Aboriginal government, and ultimately occupy more positions of authority and decision making.

Gender equality is also an issue here. Men are underrepresented among those involved in college and university education. To allow all Inuit to compete for positions at the management level this needs to be addressed. Further research is necessary to determine how the education path of Inuit males tends to differ from that of females.

Conclusion

Inuit have been latecomers to the formal education system in Canada, and data from 1981 to the present indicates relatively low levels of Inuit education compared to other Canadians. Looking in particular at post-secondary education, the gap between Inuit—however defined—and non-Inuit is increasing, despite the absolute gains made by Inuit. These gaps might be explained in part by a history of residential schools, and a legacy that leaves many wary of the education system, but the changing economic environment in Inuit Nunaat underscores the need for Inuit to succeed in their formal schooling endeavours if they are to assume a greater role in their economic and political future.

Endnotes

1 There were several boarding schools in Labrador, including at Northwest River and Nain, where past attendees have related stories of mistreatment and abuse, but as these were not federally regulated institutions, they are not officially considered federal residential schools (CBC 2008).

2 Statistics Canada asked whether respondents had attended a federal residential school. Although there were no federally run schools in Labrador, eight percent of Inuit in Labrador reported attendance, so it is possible that some respondents did not make the distinction between federally run schools and other residential schools.

3 The Census does not capture everyone in the population. Each Census they calculate the number of people that are missed by the census (undercoverage) as well as the percentage counted twice, or the overcoverage. The net undercoverage (undercoverage − overcoverage) is added to the census count to get a censal estimate for use in the population estimates program. The rate of undercoverage in the Northwest Territories is about 8%, compared to 3% for all of Canada in 2001.

4 Looking at the 2006 Census, the Inuit single identity population was 32,775, compared to the total Inuit identity population of 33,620, a difference of 845 individuals.

5 The Inuit Human Development Index project (Senécal, et al. 2007), as well as other similar studies used completion of grade 9 as a proxy for functional literacy, an indicator which is no longer collected in the Census.

6 For each definition of the Inuit population, therefore, the reference population will be slightly different, but these changes are not large enough to affect the statistics.

7 The reference population of "other Canadians" is slightly different here than for the total Inuit ancestry population, though there is no actual difference in data for either group.

References

Berger, T. 2006. *The Nunavut Project*. Conciliators Final Report for the Nunavut Land Claims Agreement Implementation Contract Negotiations for the Second Planning Period 2003–2013. Vancouver.

Canadian Broadcasting Corporation. 2008. "Harper Apology Leaves Labrador's Former Students in Cold: Innu, Inuit." <**www.cbc.ca/canada/newfoundland-labrador/story/2008/06/12/labrador-apology.html?ref=rss&loomia_si=t0:a16:g2:r1:c0.11764**>. Last updated June 11, 2008. Accessed July 2008.

Canadian Council on Learning. 2007. "Inuit Holistic Lifelong Model." <**www.ccl-cca.ca/CCL/Reports/RedefiningSuccessInAboriginalLearning/RedefiningSuccessModelsInuit.htm**>. Last updated September 2007. Accessed July, 2008.

Government of Nunavut. 2007. *2006–2007 Public Service Annual Report*. Iqaluit: Government of Nunavut.

INAC and ITK. 2006a. *Determining the Inuit Population: Definitional Issues and Differences*. Indian and Northern Affairs Canada and Inuit Tapirit Kanatami. Ottawa: Minister of Public Works and Government Services.

INAC and ITK. 2006b. *Inuit in Canada: Regional Distribution and Demographic Changes from 1982 to 2001*. Indian and Northern Affairs Canada and Inuit Tapirit Kanatami. Ottawa: Minister of Public Works and Government Services.

INAC and ITK. 2006c. *Gains Made by Inuit I Formal Education and School Attendance, 1981–2001*. Indian and Northern Affairs Canada and Inuit Tapirit Kanatami. Ottawa: Minister of Public Works and Government Services.

King, D. 2006. *A Brief Report of the Federal Government of Canada's Residential School System for Inuit*. Aboriginal Healing Foundation. Ottawa.

Simon, M. 2008. "Remarks to Delegates at the Summit on Inuit Education." April 15, 2008, Inuvik. Available at <**itk.ca/200804-Toward-a-National-Inuit-Education-Strategy.html**.> Accessed July 2008.

Statistics Canada. 2002. *2001 Census Dictionary*. Catalogue No. 92-378-XIE. Ottawa: Ministry of Industry.

Statistics Canada. 2007. *2006 Census Dictionary*. Catalogue No. 92-566-XWE. Ottawa: Ministry of Industry.

Statistics Canada. 2008a. *Aboriginal Peoples in Canada in 2006: Inuit, Métis and First Nations, 2006 Census*. Catalogue No. 97-558-XIE. Ottawa: Ministry of Industry.

Statistics Canada. 2008b. *Education Reference Guide, 2006 Census*. Catalogue No. 97-560-GWE2006003. Ottawa: Ministry of Industry.

4

Métis Educational Attainment

Piotr Wilk, Jerry P. White and Éric Guimond

Introduction

Education is considered an essential tool for securing a good job and building financial security (Penney 2008). To the Aboriginal population, achieving higher levels of post-secondary education can provide increased opportunities for employment (Hull 2004). And, once Aboriginal individuals complete post-secondary education, research has indicated that they can enjoy similar labour market outcomes as their non-Aboriginal counterparts.

The objective of this chapter is to examine educational attainment of the Métis ethnic identity population. The first part of this chapter will look at the recent data from the 2006 Census to examine educational attainment of the Métis population. The second part will explore cross-sectional trends in university attainment by analyzing the changes in the proportion of the Métis population that completed a university certificate or degree from 1996 to 2006. In both parts, we will compare the Métis ethnic identity group with non-Aboriginal Canadians. The following section outlines the data source and some of the methodological challenges faced in this study.

Source of Data and Definitions

Data

The Census is considered to be the primary source of data on the educational attainment of Aboriginal people in Canada, including the Métis ethnic identity group. In this study, we rely on the 2006 Census data to provide an up-to-date educational profile of the Métis population, while the cross-sectional trends in university attainment will be assessed using Census data from 1996, 2001, and 2006. The indicators of educational attainment presented in this study are based on data from the custom tabulations prepared for Indian and Northern Affairs Canada (INAC).

Assessment of educational attainment of Métis people poses several methodological problems related to the identification of the Métis population in the Census data and to the inconsistencies in measurement of educational attainment over time. Both of these challenges are discussed in further detail below.

Métis Population

Statistics Canada has modified and adjusted census questions that measure ethnic and cultural affiliation of Canadians. Since the 1996 Census, Statistics Canada has been asking a question on Aboriginal identity that allows respondents to self-identify themselves with one or more of the three Aboriginal groups in Canada: First Nations (North American Indian), Métis, and Inuit. Respondents are able to choose more than one identity and, as a consequence, may have multiple Aboriginal or mixed identity affiliation. The primary disadvantage to the use of the Aboriginal identity concept as a measurement tool for ethnic and cultural affiliation is that the Census did not collect information on self-reported Aboriginal identity before 1996, making it impossible to do any time-trend analysis that would include pre-1996 data (Penney 2008).

The results presented in this study are based on the Métis who reported a single Aboriginal identity. Thus, individuals who reported Métis identity in combination with another Aboriginal or non-Aboriginal identity are excluded. Even though this adjustment has the potential to slightly impact the study population, it has been adopted by most researchers (Penney 2008). Non-Aboriginal Canadians, the reference group, is comprised of individuals who did not report belonging to any of the three Aboriginal ethnic identity groups.

As Guimond (2003) has pointed out, the Aboriginal population has increased much more rapidly than that of other Canadians over the last few decades. Some of this increase in population can be explained through higher fertility rates. However, it is clear that a substantial portion of this demographic growth cannot be explained by births, deaths, migration or quality of data. Guimond (2003) points out that the residual growth can only be explained utilizing the concept of "ethnic mobility," a phenomenon by which individuals and families experience changes in their ethnic affiliation.

With the increased urbanization and intermarriage Canada has experienced in the past four decades, there has been a rapid growth in the number of children of mixed ethnocultural backgrounds. Once they are adults, these children may "choose" their ethnic affiliation, and such a choice may vary depending on the circumstances. The choice to self-identify with a particular Aboriginal group is effected by many things, not the least of which are social issues and their media coverage, both contributing to restoring Aboriginal people's pride. Moreover, higher court decisions over the past two decades have drawn many people with mixed ancestries to self-identify as Aboriginal. The Métis, given their mixed roots, have been the primary recipient of this ethnic drift. These changes in ethnic affiliation had and will continue to have an important impact on the measurement and monitoring of educational and other socio-economic outcomes of the Métis over time.

Table 4.1: Highest Degree or Credential, Métis Identity Population and the Non-Aboriginal Population Aged 15 and Over, Canada 2006

Highest Degree of Credential	Métis	Non-Aboriginal
No degree, certificate, or diploma	34.59	23.10
High school diploma or higher	65.41	76.90
High school diploma or equivalent only	25.60	25.66
Post-secondary certificate or degree	39.81	51.24
Trades/apprenticeship or other non-university	30.01	28.21
Trades/apprenticeship certificate or diploma	13.12	10.84
Other non-university certificate or diploma	16.89	17.37
University	9.80	23.03
University certificate below bachelor level	2.76	4.48
With degree	7.04	18.55
Bachelor's degree	5.90	14.38
Master's degree	0.98	3.47
Earned doctorate	0.16	0.71

Education Variables in Census

Before the 2006 Census, Statistics Canada was fairly consistent in collecting data on educational attainment. The question regarding "highest level of schooling" allowed individuals to chose one of the following categories: (1) Less than grade 9, (2) Incomplete high school, (3) High school certificate, (4) Incomplete post-secondary, (5) Completed trades, (6) Completed college, and (7) Completed university. Since this hierarchical variable had serious shortcomings, for the 2006 Census, Statistics Canada changed the educational attainment indicator to actually record the educational credential attained. The question regarding "highest degree, certificate, or diploma" now includes the following categories: (1) No degree, certificate, or diploma, (2) High school diploma or equivalent only, (3) Trades/apprenticeship certificate or diploma only, (4) Other non-university certificate or diploma, (5) University certificate below bachelor level, and (6) University degree (including certificate above bachelor level). As a result of these changes, methodological problems exist due to inconsistencies in the measurement of educational attainment. The only category that is comparable across time is the "Completed university degree" category. As a consequence, our examination of cross-sectional trends in Métis educational attainment is limited to the analysis of changes in the proportion of Métis that completed a university certificate or degree from 1996 to 2006.

Figure 4.1: Highest Degree or Credential, Métis Identity Population and the Reference Population Aged 15 and Over, Canada, 2006

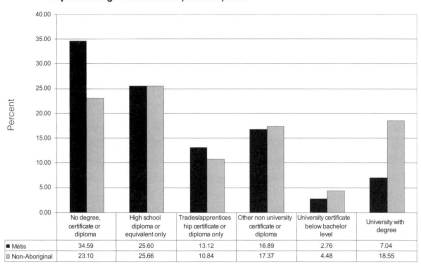

	No degree, certificate or diploma	High school diploma or equivalent only	Trades/apprenticeship certificate or diploma only	Other non university certificate or diploma	University certificate below bachelor level	University with degree
■ Métis	34.59	25.60	13.12	16.89	2.76	7.04
▤ Non-Aboriginal	23.10	25.66	10.84	17.37	4.48	18.55

Results

Educational Attainment in 2006

This section provides an overview of educational attainment among the Métis single identity population based on the recent data from the 2006 Census. Specifically, it examines the relationships between education attainment and gender, age, and geographic location.

Highest Degree or Credential in 2006.

Table 4.1 and **Figure 4.1** present the highest degree or credential attained by Métis and by non-Aboriginal individuals. **Table 4.1** displays a more detailed educational profile for each population by showing percentages for all categories and sub-categories of educational outcomes, from failing to attain a high school diploma to earning a university certificate or degree. **Figure 4.1** presents a subset of these results, focusing on the main educational indicators. Census data indicate that in 2006 individuals who reported Métis identity were less successful in earning a certificate, diploma (including a high school or equivalent diploma), or degree, as compared to non-Aboriginal individuals. As displayed in **Table 4.1**, only 65.4% of Métis obtained a high school diploma or any post-secondary certificate, diploma, or degree, as compared to 76.9% of non-Aboriginals. It should also be noted that the levels of high school completion for non-Aboriginals in younger age groups is close to 90%. The overall numbers are pulled down by the large group of persons over 55 years old (see **Table 4.3**).

Table 4.2: Degree or Credential by Sex, Métis Identity Population and the Reference Population Aged 15 and Over, Canada, 2006

Highest Degree or Credential	Métis		Non-Aboriginal	
	Male	Female	Male	Female
No degree, certificate, or diploma	37.00	32.27	23.37	22.85
High school diploma or higher	63.00	67.73	76.63	77.15
High school diploma or equivalent only	24.33	26.82	24.44	26.81
Post-secondary certificate or degree	38.68	40.90	52.19	50.34
Trades/apprenticeship or other non-university	30.65	29.40	29.64	26.85
Trades/apprenticeship certificate or diploma	16.81	9.57	14.24	7.62
Other non-university certificate or diploma	13.83	19.84	15.41	19.23
University	8.03	11.50	22.55	23.49
University certificate below bachelor level	2.08	3.40	3.90	5.03
With degree	5.94	8.09	18.65	18.46
Bachelor's degree	4.70	7.06	13.83	14.89
Master's degree	1.04	0.91	3.82	3.13
Earned doctorate	0.21	0.12	1.00	0.43

The disparity in educational attainment between Métis and non-Aboriginal individuals is quite pronounced when considering post-secondary educational outcomes. Overall, in 2006 more non-Aboriginal individuals (51.2%) reported earning any post-secondary certificates, diplomas, or degrees, as compared to only 39.8% of Métis individuals. On the positive side, a slightly higher percentage of Métis individuals earned a post-secondary certificate or diploma below the university level than did non-Aboriginals (30% and 28.2% respectively). In particular, when considering non-university educational attainment, the Métis were more likely to earn trades/apprenticeship certificates or diplomas (13.23%) than non-Aboriginals (10.8%) who instead were more likely to obtain other non-university post-secondary credentials. Despite achieving equivalence in the area of non-university post-secondary education, the Métis were much less likely to obtain university level education. The percentage of non-Aboriginal individuals that attended university (with or without a degree) is much higher than the percentage of Métis individuals by a factor of 13.2% (23% versus 9.8%). The gap between the Métis and non-Aboriginal populations is the most pronounced when considering the proportion of individuals who graduate from university with a degree; only 7% of Métis reported having graduated with a degree, as compared to 18.5% of non-Aboriginals. Thus, the low rates of university completions observed in the Métis population are a major contributor to the overall gap in post-secondary educational outcomes between the two identity groups.

Highest Degree or Credential in 2006 by Sex.

Table 4.2 and corresponding **Figure 4.2** compare the highest degree or credential attained for Métis men and women, also considering non-Aboriginals as the

Figure 4.2: Highest Degree or Credential by Sex, Métis Identity Population and the Reference Population Aged 15 and Over, Canada, 2006

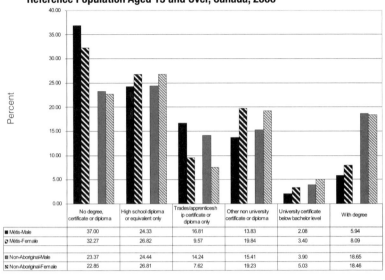

	No degree, certificate or diploma	High school diploma or equivalent only	Trades/apprenticesh ip certificate or diploma only	Other non university certificate or diploma	University certificate below bachelor level	With degree
■ Métis-Male	37.00	24.33	16.81	13.83	2.08	5.94
▨ Métis-Female	32.27	26.82	9.57	19.84	3.40	8.09
▥ Non-Aboriginal-Male	23.37	24.44	14.24	15.41	3.90	18.65
▨ Non-Aboriginal-Female	22.85	26.81	7.62	19.23	5.03	18.46

reference population. As illustrated in **Figure 4.2**, there were some substantial differences in the attainment of certificates, diplomas, and degrees between Métis men and women. In general, more Métis females attained higher levels of education, as compared to their male counterparts. **Table 4.2** shows that Métis females were more likely than Métis males to earn a certificate, diploma, or degree (67.7% and 63% respectively). In contrast, when considering non-Aboriginals, there was no gender gap as approximately the same percentage of men and women earned certificates, diplomas, and degrees (76.6% and 77.1% respectively).

Figure 4.2 indicates that, compared to Métis males, Métis females excelled in all categories of post-secondary education, except for trades/apprenticeships. A much higher proportion of Métis women (19.8%) received other non-university certificates or diplomas, as compared to Métis men (13.8%) and they were much more likely (11.5%) to attend university, as compared to Métis males (8.0%). When considering accreditation in trades, the gender gap is reversed, as 16.8% of Métis males reported receiving a trades/apprenticeship certificate or diploma, compared to only 9.6% of females with the same ethnic identity. Similar gender gaps and differences in educational outcomes were observed in the non-Aboriginal population with the exception of attainment of university credentials. When analysing statistics related to post-secondary education at the university level, **Figure 4.2** illustrates that substantially more Métis women (8%) reported earning a university degree, as compared to Métis men (5.9%). However, the same gender gap was not observed in the non-Aboriginal population where, in 2006, slightly more males (18.7%) received a university degree than females (18.5%). For Canada in general it is recognized that in earlier generations women were not

Figure 4.3: Post-secondary Certificate or Degree, Métis Identity Population and the Non-Aboriginal Population Aged 15 and Over, Canada, 2006

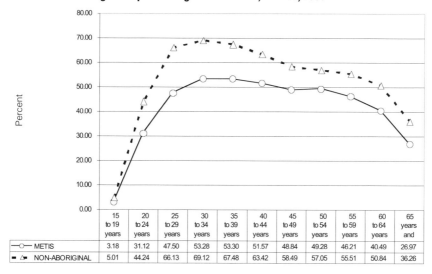

	15 to 19 years	20 to 24 years	25 to 29 years	30 to 34 years	35 to 39 years	40 to 44 years	45 to 49 years	50 to 54 years	55 to 59 years	60 to 64 years	65 years and
—○— METIS	3.18	31.12	47.50	53.28	53.30	51.57	48.84	49.28	46.21	40.49	26.97
▪ △▪ NON-ABORIGINAL	5.01	44.24	66.13	69.12	67.48	63.42	58.49	57.05	55.51	50.84	36.26

encouraged to attend university. This cultural norm has changed dramatically in the last two decades.

Highest Degree or Credential in 2006 by Age.

Figure 4.3 displays the percentages of Métis and non-Aboriginal individuals of the different age groups that attained any post-secondary certification, including trades/apprenticeship certificates or diplomas, non-university certificates and diplomas, as well as university certificates and degrees by various age groups.

Figure 4.3 illustrates that, looking at the Metis population, 31.12% of individuals in the 20–24 years of age group attained post-secondary certification, as compared to 53.3% of individuals in the 35–39 years of age group—an increase of more than 20%. In fact, the 35–39 years of age group had the highest percentage of individuals that obtained a post-secondary certificate or degree. The proportion of the population with a post-secondary education is the lowest for the older age groups, particularly for those 65 years of age and older (27%). In general, the same relationship between level of educational attainment and age is observed in the non-Aboriginal population; however, as indicated before, the rates of post-secondary education for this population are much higher.

It is important to point out that in the non-Aboriginal population, the highest percentage of individuals with post-secondary education was reported for the 30–34 years of age group (69.1%), compared to 35–39 years of age group in the Métis population. In addition, the gap between the Métis and non-Aboriginal identity populations in the percentage of individuals with a post-secondary certificate, diploma, or degree is the largest among individuals in the 25–29 years

Table 4.3: Highest Degree or Credential by Age, Métis Identity Population and the Non-Aboriginal Population Aged 15 and Over, Canada, 2006

	Highest Degree or Credential	15-19	20-24	25-29	30-34	35-39	40-44	45-49	50-54	55-59	60-64	65 +
Métis	No degree, certificate, or diploma	72.80	25.38	20.76	19.79	22.52	24.77	27.22	28.57	33.87	44.79	60.14
	High school diploma or higher	27.20	74.62	79.23	80.21	77.46	75.22	72.76	71.43	66.11	55.21	39.86
	High school diploma or equivalent only	24.02	43.50	31.73	26.95	24.18	23.67	23.92	22.15	19.90	14.73	12.92
	Post-secondary certificate or degree	3.18	31.12	47.50	53.28	53.30	51.57	48.84	49.28	46.21	40.49	26.97
	Trades/apprenticeship or other non-university	2.96	22.78	33.03	38.35	40.09	41.25	38.13	37.12	34.19	31.29	21.21
	Trades/apprenticeship certificate or diploma	1.61	7.68	11.67	14.16	15.65	18.25	17.18	18.24	17.98	17.91	13.19
	Other non-university certificate or diploma	1.36	15.10	21.36	24.19	24.45	23.00	20.94	18.89	16.21	13.38	8.01
	University	0.22	8.35	14.45	14.93	13.19	10.32	10.73	12.16	12.02	9.20	5.73
	University certificate below bachelor level	0.16	2.23	2.98	2.97	3.64	3.34	3.46	4.05	3.63	2.83	2.30
	With degree	0.06	6.11	11.47	11.96	9.54	6.95	7.24	8.09	8.39	6.33	3.46
	Bachelor's degree	0.06	6.00	10.48	10.42	8.30	5.53	5.95	6.06	6.17	4.02	2.45
	Master's degree	0.00	0.05	0.93	1.24	1.03	1.30	1.16	1.78	1.84	1.87	0.83
	Earned doctorate	0.00	0.05	0.07	0.30	0.20	0.10	0.13	0.26	0.37	0.48	0.13
Non-Aboriginal	No degree, certificate, or diploma	64.33	12.55	10.21	9.79	10.75	12.84	15.48	16.28	19.31	26.47	42.26
	High school diploma or higher	35.67	87.45	89.79	90.21	89.26	87.16	84.52	83.72	80.69	73.53	57.74
	High school diploma or equivalent only	30.66	43.21	23.66	21.09	21.77	23.74	26.03	26.67	25.18	22.69	21.48
	Post-secondary certificate or degree	5.01	44.24	66.13	69.12	67.48	63.42	58.49	57.05	55.51	50.84	36.26
	Trades/apprenticeship or other non-university	4.40	27.06	32.89	33.63	34.17	35.48	33.70	31.72	30.06	28.22	21.84
	Trades/apprenticeship certificate or diploma	1.56	7.38	10.22	10.53	11.84	13.28	13.25	12.90	13.03	13.11	10.91
	Other non-university certificate or diploma	2.85	19.68	22.67	23.10	22.33	22.21	20.44	18.82	17.03	15.12	10.93
	University	0.61	17.19	33.24	35.49	33.31	27.94	24.80	25.32	25.45	22.61	14.42
	University certificate below bachelor level	0.43	3.89	4.51	4.73	4.99	4.94	4.86	5.11	5.57	5.73	4.50
	With degree	0.17	13.30	28.73	30.76	28.32	23.00	19.94	20.22	19.88	16.88	9.92
	Bachelor's degree	0.17	12.73	24.40	24.36	22.05	17.51	14.99	14.99	14.46	11.67	7.05
	Master's degree	0.00	0.51	4.06	5.64	5.36	4.55	4.10	4.35	4.47	4.02	2.04
	Earned doctorate	0.00	0.06	0.27	0.76	0.91	0.94	0.84	0.87	0.94	1.19	0.83

Figure 4.4: Highest Degree or Credential by Region of Canada, Métis Identity Population Aged 15 and Over, Canada, 2006

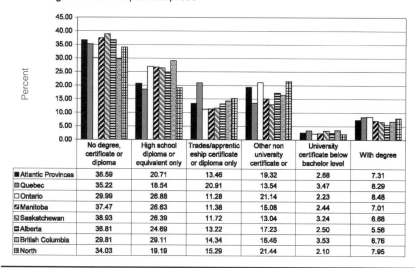

	No degree, certificate or diploma	High school diploma or equivalent only	Trades/apprenticeship certificate or diploma only	Other non university certificate or	University certificate below bachelor level	With degree
■ Atlantic Provinces	36.59	20.71	13.46	19.32	2.68	7.31
▤ Quebec	35.22	18.54	20.91	13.54	3.47	8.29
☐ Ontario	29.99	26.88	11.28	21.14	2.23	8.48
▨ Manitoba	37.47	26.63	11.38	15.08	2.44	7.01
◩ Saskatchewan	38.93	26.39	11.72	13.04	3.24	6.68
▤ Alberta	36.81	24.69	13.22	17.23	2.50	5.56
▥ British Columbia	29.81	29.11	14.34	16.46	3.53	6.76
⊞ North	34.03	19.19	15.29	21.44	2.10	7.95

of age group (18.6%). The gap then decreases to 14.2% for individuals in the 35–39 years of age group. These statistics indicate that a large proportion of Métis students continue to pursue post-secondary education into their late 30's, This likely reflects a trend that Métis students are moving through the school system at a slower rate than non-Aboriginal students and/or are coming to want more education later in life.

Finally, **Table 4.3** presents highest degree or credential attained by Métis and non-Aboriginal individuals belonging to different age groups. This table shows a more detailed educational profile for each population and for each age group by displaying percentages for all categories and sub-categories of educational outcomes. However, these statistics are not discussed in this chapter.

Highest Degree or Credential in 2006 by Geographic Location

Geography affects educational attainment because it reflects such factors as regional and local differences in educational systems and the labour market. Literature also suggests that proximity to colleges and universities has an effect on levels of educational attainment (Hull, 2004). The present study examines geographic location in several ways. First, differences among provinces or regions are explored. In this analysis, the four Atlantic Provinces have been grouped and are indicated as such, and Nunavut, the Northwest Territories, and Yukon Territory have also been combined and are listed as Northern Canada Region. Second, it looks at differences in levels of educational attainment in four areas of residence: urban Census Metropolitan Area (CMA), urban non-CMA, rural, and on-reserve.

Table 4.4 and **Figure 4.4** illustrate the differences in educational attainment for the Métis living in different provinces and regions of Canada. In 2006, "only"

Table 4.4: Highest Degree or Credential by Region of Canada, Métis Identity Population and the Non-Aboriginal Population Aged 15 and Over, Canada, 2006

	Highest Degree or Credential	Atlantic	Quebec	Ontario	Manitoba	Saskatchewan	Alberta	British Columbia	North
Métis	No degree, certificate, or diploma	36.59	35.22	29.99	37.47	38.93	36.81	29.81	34.03
	High school diploma or higher	63.45	64.78	70.02	62.52	61.08	63.18	70.19	65.82
	High school diploma or equivalent only	20.71	18.54	26.88	26.63	26.39	24.69	29.11	19.19
	Post-secondary certificate or degree	42.74	46.25	43.13	35.91	34.68	38.50	41.08	46.63
	Trades/apprenticeship or other non-university	32.78	34.45	32.43	26.47	24.77	30.44	30.80	36.73
	Trades/apprenticeship certificate or diploma	13.46	20.91	11.28	11.38	11.72	13.22	14.34	15.29
	Other non-university certificate or diploma	19.32	13.54	21.14	15.08	13.04	17.23	16.46	21.44
	University	9.96	11.79	10.71	9.43	9.92	8.06	10.29	10.04
	University certificate below bachelor level	2.68	3.47	2.23	2.44	3.24	2.50	3.53	2.10
	With degree	7.31	8.29	8.48	7.01	6.68	5.56	6.76	7.95
	Bachelor's degree	6.38	6.75	6.72	6.29	5.98	4.77	5.23	7.05
	Master's degree	0.66	1.34	1.52	0.65	0.58	0.73	1.24	0.60
	Earned doctorate	0.23	0.22	0.24	0.06	0.12	0.06	0.28	0.30
Non-Aboriginal	No degree, certificate, or diploma	28.83	24.77	21.95	26.38	27.65	22.34	19.07	15.33
	High school diploma or higher	71.17	75.23	78.05	73.62	72.35	77.66	80.93	84.69
	High school diploma or equivalent only	23.93	22.34	26.82	27.54	27.48	26.47	27.99	23.70
	Post-secondary certificate or degree	47.23	52.88	51.23	46.08	44.88	51.20	52.94	60.98
	Trades/apprenticeship or other non-university	29.37	31.37	26.33	25.43	26.68	28.99	27.55	31.91
	Trades/apprenticeship certificate or diploma	11.48	15.27	7.96	9.87	11.47	10.86	10.78	10.21
	Other non-university certificate or diploma	17.88	16.10	18.37	15.56	15.22	18.13	16.77	21.70
	University	17.87	21.51	24.90	20.65	18.19	22.21	25.39	29.04
	University certificate below bachelor level	3.66	4.89	4.16	4.23	4.35	4.09	5.52	4.04
	With degree	14.21	16.62	20.74	16.42	13.85	18.12	19.88	25.04
	Bachelor's degree	11.16	12.80	15.94	13.48	11.37	14.50	15.22	19.66
	Master's degree	2.52	3.17	4.04	2.29	1.92	2.94	3.84	4.88
	Earned doctorate	0.52	0.66	0.76	0.65	0.56	0.67	0.81	0.48

about thirty percent of the Métis in Ontario or British Columbia (30% and 29.8% respectively) did not obtain certificate, diploma, or degree (including high school or equivalent diploma). This figure increases when moving to other regions of Canada and it was the highest for the Métis in Saskatchewan (38.9%). Despite having the lowest proportion of individuals who failed to receive certificates, diplomas and degrees, in "relative terms," the Métis living in Ontario and British Columbia still lagged non-Aboriginals living in these two provinces as only 22% of non-Aboriginals in Ontario and 19.07% in BC reported having no certificate, diploma, or degree. As a consequence, the gap between the two ethnic identity populations in Ontario (8%) and in British Columbia (10.8%) was still substantial (national average gap was 11.5%). It is important to note that the gap between the two identity groups was the largest in the Northern Canada Region (18.9%); however, this gap is primary due to very high percentage of non-Aboriginals in the Northern Canada reporting to have received certificates, diplomas and degrees. This high number probably reflects the occupational distribution of those non-Aboriginal peoples in the North.

Table 4.4 indicates that more Métis living in Quebec (46.3%) and in the Northern Canada Region (46.7%) earned a post-secondary certificate, diploma, or degree, as compared to the Métis living in the other provinces, regions, and territories. Manitoba (35.9%) and Saskatchewan (34.7%), on the other hand, reported the lowest percentages. When comparing the Métis to non-Aboriginals, the smallest gap in the rates of obtaining post-secondary credentials was observed in the Atlantic Provinces (4.5%) and in Quebec (6.6%), while the biggest gap was observed in the Northern Canada Region (14.4%).

There were some interesting between-province differences with regard to the prevalence of different types of post-secondary credentials. For example, Quebec and Ontario reported similar rates of non-university post-secondary educational attainment (Quebec, 34.5%; Ontario, 32.4%). However, as many as 20.9% of Métis living in Quebec attained a trades/apprenticeship certificate or diploma while the percentage in Ontario was much lower (11.3%). The situation is reversed when considering the percentage of individuals with other non-university certificates or diplomas, as fewer Métis in Quebec (13.5%) reported having a non-university certificate or diploma than Métis living in Ontario (21.1%). Similarly, more Métis living in the Northern Canada Region (21.4%) and the Atlantic Provinces (19.3%) reported having a non-university certificate or diploma, exceeding the national average of 16.9%. These differences may reflect diversities in provincial educational systems.

In 2006, there were no substantial regional differences with regard to university degree attainment. Ontario and Quebec boasted slightly higher levels (8.48% and 8.3% respectively), as compared to the other provinces, regions, and territories of Canada. The gap in attainment of a university degree between the two identity populations was the highest in Northern Canada Region (17.1%) where 8% of Métis reported having a university degree, as compared to 25% of the

Figure 4.5: Highest Degree or Credential by Area of Residence, Métis Identity Population Aged 15 and Over, Canada, 2006

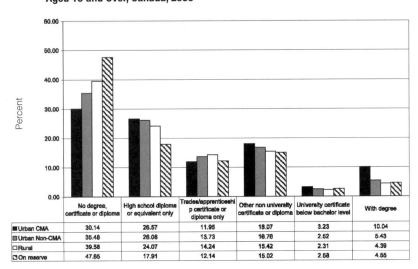

	No degree, certificate or diploma	High school diploma or equivalent only	Trades/apprenticeship certificate or diploma only	Other non university certificate or diploma	University certificate below bachelor level	With degree
■ Urban CMA	30.14	26.57	11.95	18.07	3.23	10.04
▩ Urban Non-CMA	35.48	26.08	13.73	16.76	2.62	5.43
☐ Rural	39.58	24.07	14.24	15.42	2.31	4.39
▨ On reserve	47.65	17.91	12.14	15.02	2.58	4.55

non-Aboriginals. The gap was the smallest in the Atlantic Provinces (6.9%) and Saskatchewan (7.2%); however, these low numbers can be attributed to the relatively low rate of university degree attainment among the non-Aboriginal population in these two provinces.

Figure 4.5 displays the highest degree or credential for the Métis identity population by area of residence, which includes four categories: urban Census Metropolitan Areas, urban non-CMA area, rural area, and on-reserve. **Table 4.4** presents a more detailed set of statistics for this relationship, as well as the percentages for the non-Aboriginal population.

In 2006, 30.1% of Métis living in urban CMAs reported having no certificate, diploma, or degree, as compared to 35.5% of Métis living in urban non-CMAs and 39.5% living in rural areas. Close to half of Métis living on-reserve (47.7%) reported having no educational credentials, signifying potential challenges and barriers to attaining post-secondary education.

Census data indicate that the Métis living in highly populated areas (CMAs) attained higher levels of education. For example, 43.3% of the Métis living in urban CMAs reported earning either a post-secondary diploma or degree, as compared to 38.4% of the Métis living in urban non-CMAs, 36.4% living in rural areas, and 34.3% living on reserves. Similarly, the Métis living in urban CMAs were more likely to obtain a university degree (10%), as compared to the Métis living in other areas (urban non-CMA, 5.4%; rural, 4.4%; on reserve, 4.6%). Thus, it appears that the size of a community one lives in is positively related to her or his chances of obtaining a high school diploma or any post-secondary education. A similar trend was observed in the non-Aboriginal population. However, it is inter-

Table 4.5: Highest Degree or Credential by Area of Residence, Métis Identity Population and the Non-Aboriginal Population Aged 15 and Over, Canada, 2006

Highest Degree or Credential	Urban CMA	Urban Non-CMA	Rural	On Reserve
	Métis			
No degree, certificate, or diploma	30.14	35.48	39.58	47.65
High school diploma or higher	69.86	64.52	60.42	52.20
High school diploma or equivalent only	26.57	26.08	24.07	17.91
Post-secondary certificate or degree	43.29	38.44	36.36	34.29
Trades/apprenticeship or other non-university	30.02	30.48	29.66	27.16
Trades/apprenticeship certificate or diploma	11.95	13.73	14.24	12.14
Other non-university certificate or diploma	18.07	16.76	15.42	15.02
University	13.27	7.95	6.69	7.13
University certificate below bachelor level	3.23	2.52	2.31	2.58
With degree	10.04	5.43	4.39	4.55
Bachelor's degree	8.22	4.78	3.73	4.10
Master's degree	1.56	0.55	0.57	0.30
Earned doctorate	0.25	0.11	0.09	0.00
	Non-Aboriginal			
No degree, certificate, or diploma	20.14	27.50	29.55	24.10
High school diploma or higher	79.86	72.50	70.45	75.92
High school diploma or equivalent only	25.59	26.47	25.20	26.34
Post-secondary certificate or degree	54.27	46.02	45.25	49.58
Trades/apprenticeship or other non-university	26.54	31.20	31.37	31.99
Trades/apprenticeship certificate or diploma	9.24	13.28	14.24	14.46
Other non-university certificate or diploma	17.31	17.93	17.13	17.56
University	27.73	14.82	13.87	17.54
University certificate below bachelor level	5.05	3.55	3.33	4.24
With degree	22.68	11.27	10.54	13.33
Bachelor's degree	17.34	9.28	8.55	10.61
Master's degree	4.43	1.69	1.66	2.27
Earned doctorate	0.92	0.30	0.33	0.45

esting to note, when assessing the gap between the two identity populations, that the Métis living in urban non-CMAs and in rural areas were comparatively better off than those living in urban CMAs, as the gap between Métis and non-Aboriginals was only 5.8% in urban non-CMAs and 6.2% in rural areas, compared to 12.6% for CMA urban areas.

Change in Completed University—1996–2006

The second part of this chapter examines cross-sectional trends in completion of a university certificate or degree from 1996 to 2006. As discussed previously, due

Figure 4.6: Completed University, Métis Identity Population and the Reference Population Aged 15 and Over, Canada, 1996-2006

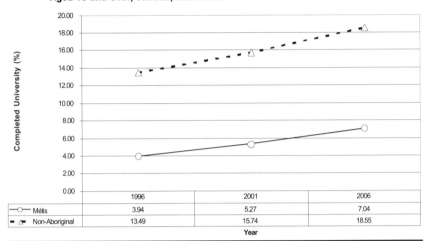

	1996	2001	2006
—○— Métis	3.94	5.27	7.04
▪ ⊿▪ Non-Aboriginal	13.49	15.74	18.55

Year

to changes in data collection procedures for education attainment in 2006, the 2006 Census data cannot be directly compared to data collected in 1996 and 2001. The only educational attainment category that remained constant over time is the category measuring the proportion of respondents having completed a university degree. Thus, only data on obtained university degrees at the Bachelor's level and higher can be compared across time. Therefore, we examine data on university degree attainment from 1996 to 2006 for the Métis and non-Aboriginal populations.

Figure 4.6 displays changes in university certificate or degree attainment from 1996 to 2006 for the Métis and non-Aboriginal identity populations, 15 years of age and over. For both populations, the proportion of individuals that attained a university degree increased during this time period. For the Métis identity population, the reported rate of obtaining a university certificate or degree nearly doubled between 1996 and 2006, increasing from 3.9% to 7%. Similarly, the proportion of non-Aboriginals that attained a university certificate or degree also increased, from 13.5% in 1996 to 18.6% in 2006. Thus, over the ten-year time period from 1996 to 2006, increases in attainment of university credentials observed in the Métis population were not as substantial as the increases experienced by the non-Aboriginals. As a consequence, the gap between the Métis and non-Aboriginals in achieving a university certificate or degree has increased over that time period, from 9.6% in 1996, to 10.5% in 2001, to 11.5% in 2006.

Another way to examine the underlying trend in educational attainment over time is to assess the nature of change for a younger age group. Educational attainment, including completion of a university certificate or degree, is related to age. In general, younger individuals tend to have higher levels of educational attainment than do older individuals. Specifically, we decided to examine change in the

Figure 4.7: Completed University, Métis Identity Population and the Non-Aboriginal Population Aged 30–34, Canada, 1996–2006

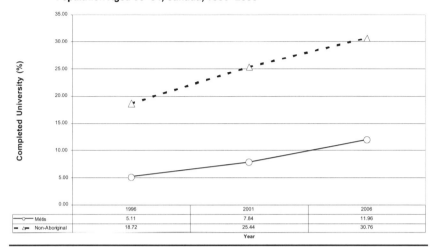

	1996	2001	2006
Métis	5.11	7.84	11.96
Non-Aboriginal	18.72	25.44	30.76

Year

rate of university degree attainment for the 30–34 years of age group. This age group was chosen because they were the most likely to have attained a university certificate or degree.

Figure 4.7 illustrates that the percentage of the Métis 30–34 years of age that obtained a university certificate or degree more than doubled, from 5.1% in 1996 to 12% in 2006. The rate of university completion also increased among the non-Aboriginal population, from 18.7% in 1996 to 30.8% in 2006. When comparing the gap in university degree attainment between Métis and non-Aboriginals 30–34 years of age (**Figure 4.7**) with the gap between the total population for each group 15 years of age and older (**Figure 4.6**), the gap for the 30–34 year olds is much wider and increases. Specifically, in 1996 the gap was 13.6% while by the year 2006, it increased to 18.8%.

Change in Completed University by Age Groups

Figures 4.8a and **4.8b** depict the proportion of the population with a university certificate or degree by age group and for the Census periods 1996, 2001, and 2006, separately for each identity group. They indicate substantial increases in the attainment of university certificates and degrees for all age groups and for both identity groups during this ten-year time period. For the non-Aboriginal population, **Figure 4.8b** shows that the younger age groups (25–19 and 30–34 years of age) had consistently the highest proportion of individuals with a university certificate or degree. **Figure 4.8a** illustrates that the distribution of educational attainment by age is slightly different for the Métis population. Specifically, in 1996, the 45–49 years of age group was the group with the highest rate of university completion (6.2%). However, by 2001, young Métis in the 25–29 years of age group represented the group with the highest proportion with a university

Figure 4.8a: Completed University by Age, Métis Identity Population Aged 30–34, Canada, 1996–2006

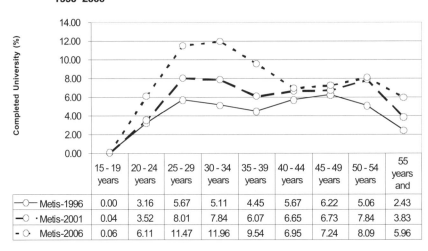

	15 - 19 years	20 - 24 years	25 - 29 years	30 - 34 years	35 - 39 years	40 - 44 years	45 - 49 years	50 - 54 years	55 years and
Metis-1996	0.00	3.16	5.67	5.11	4.45	5.67	6.22	5.06	2.43
Metis-2001	0.04	3.52	8.01	7.84	6.07	6.65	6.73	7.84	3.83
Metis-2006	0.06	6.11	11.47	11.96	9.54	6.95	7.24	8.09	5.96

certificate or degree (8%), narrowly outperforming individuals in the 50–54 years of age group (7.8%). In 2006, young Métis in the 25–29 (11.5%) and 30–34 (12%) years of age groups comprised the highest proportions with a university certificate or degree.

Although the level of university attainment among the Métis is not as high as for the non-Aboriginal population, progress has been achieved over the ten-year time period between 1996 and 2006. For instance, the proportion of the Métis 30–34 years of age that reported having attained a university certificate or degree has increased from 5.1% in 1996, to 7.9% in 2001, to 12% in 2006. The rate of increase in university attainment for the Métis in this age group is higher than the rate of increase for 30–34-year-old non-Aboriginals.

Change in Completed University by Sex

Figure 4.9 depicts change in the proportion of Métis and non-Aboriginal males and females that reported having either a university certificate or degree for the ten-year time period from 1996 to 2006, illustrating that the number of Métis males and females that reported obtaining a university-level education increased from 1996 to 2006. In 1996, 3.4% of Métis males reported having obtained a university certificate or degree. This figure increased to 4.6% in 2001 and to 5.9% in 2006. Many more Métis females completed either a university certificate or degree, with rates increasing from 4.5% in 1996, to 5.9% in 2001, and to 8% in 2006.

Although the proportions of Métis men and women that completed university with a degree or certificate increased during the ten-year time period, so too did the proportions of non-Aboriginal males and females. As a consequence, for females, the gap between Métis and non-Aboriginals increased from 8% in 1996

Figure 4.8b: Completed University by Age, Non-Aboriginal Population Aged 30–34, Canada, 1996–2006

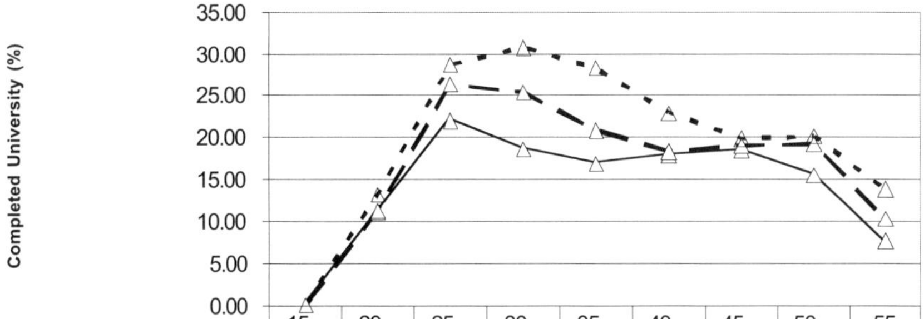

	15 - 19 years	20 - 24 years	25 - 29 years	30 - 34 years	35 - 39 years	40 - 44 years	45 - 49 years	50 - 54 years	55 years and
Non-Aboriginal-1996	0.10	11.23	22.11	18.72	17.00	17.95	18.59	15.61	7.77
Non-Aboriginal-2001	0.12	11.42	26.37	25.44	20.93	18.42	19.12	19.22	10.36
Non-Aboriginal-2006	0.17	13.30	28.73	30.76	28.32	23.00	19.94	20.22	13.99

Figure 4.9: Completed University by Sex, Métis Identity Population and the Reference Population Aged 30–34, Canada, 1996–2006

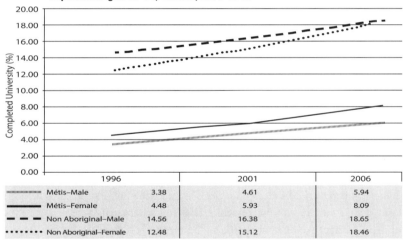

	1996	2001	2006
Métis–Male	3.38	4.61	5.94
Métis–Female	4.48	5.93	8.09
Non Aboriginal–Male	14.56	16.38	18.65
Non Aboriginal–Female	12.48	15.12	18.46

to 9.2% in 2001 and to 10.4% in 2006. Similarly, the gap for males increased from 11.2% in 1996 to 11.8% in 2001 and 12.7% in 2006.

Figure 4.9 also illustrates that, in 1996, within the non-Aboriginal population, men had a higher rate of university completion than women. By 2006, both genders achieved parity; the 2.6% gap from 1996 had almost disappeared. If the same trend continues, non-Aboriginal women should outperform men by the next Census date. In the Métis population, however, women were reporting higher rates of university completions throughout the 1996–2006 period. In fact, the gender gap in the Métis population has been growing from 1.1% in 1996 to 1.3% in 2001 and to 2.2% in 2006.

Conclusion

As the data indicates, there is a substantial gap between Métis identity persons and rest of the Canadian population. We can see this gap exists throughout the educational attainment levels with fewer Métis completing high school than other Canadians (65.4% vs 76.9 %). Fewer Métis gaining post secondary training (39.8% vs 51%) and substantially lower numbers securing university degrees (7% vs 18.5%). These patterns repeat themselves for both men and women although we see Métis women outperforming Métis men particularly at the higher levels of education (except in trades).

Have the gaps been closing? The short answer is "no." Although there appears to be a positive movement toward gaining post-secondary trades and apprenticeship training. This would be important to capitalize on from a policy perspective. The gap in high school completion continues to widen and the gap between Métis and non-Aboriginals in achieving a university certificate or degree has increased over the last three census periods, from 9.6% in 1996, to 10.5% in 2001, to 11.5% in 2006.

Those in cities do better than those in rural areas and the largest cities are better than the non-CMA areas. Younger Métis are seeking higher education but at a rate still less than the non-Aboriginal groups. Interestingly, a large proportion of the Métis students continue to pursue post-secondary education into their late thirties. This could mean that that Métis students are moving through the school system at a slower rate than non-Aboriginal students or it may mean they are coming to want more education later in life.

Lastly we see that the Western Prairie provinces of Manitoba and Saskatchewan, along with the North, represent particularly difficult situations. We see the gap between Métis and others in the major urban CMAs is larger, but across the board the Métis in the CMAs do better than their identity population cohorts in the smaller urban, rural, and northern areas. This may reflect that there is a negative social capital effect (see Chapter 10), or there may be other factors we are not tapping.

Despite the gaps that exist, the Métis have better achievement levels than other Aboriginal identity groups. Particularly they do better than on-reserve First Nations and Inuit. Why? It is clear that the vast majority of Métis utilize the provincial public and private school systems; they do not have developed school systems of their own. As such, the Métis have been able to encourage the provincial systems to include more Aboriginal content in the school systems. It could be that the level of integration with the wider Canadian society is greater for those identifying as Métis than for other Aboriginal groups. This raises many issues about what the way forward may be.

References

Guimond, E. 2003. "Changing Ethnicity: The Concept of Ethnic Drifters." In *Aboriginal Conditions: Research as a Foundation for Public Policy*. J.P. White, P. Maxim, and D. Beavon (eds). Vancouver: UBC Press. 91–107.

Hull, J. 2004. *Post-Secondary Education and Labour Market Outcomes Among the Aboriginal Population of Canada, 2001*. Ottawa: Indian and Northern Affairs Canada, Strategic Research & Analysis Directorate.

Statistics Canada. 2008a. *Aboriginal Peoples in Canada in 2006: Inuit, Métis and First Nations, 2006 Census*. Catalogue 97-558-XIE. Ottawa: Ministry of Industry.

Statistics Canada. 2008b. "Education Reference Guide, 2006 Census." Catalogue 97-560-GWE2006003. Ottawa: Ministry of Industry.

5

University Attainment of the Registered Indian Population, 1981–2006: A Cohort Approach

John Clement

Introduction

The trends in university attainment for the Registered Indian population from 1981 to 2006 are presented in the article below. Given our understanding that the Registered Indian population generally has the poorest educational outcomes of all of the Aboriginal groups in Canada, we are particularly interested in seeing if efforts to encourage post-secondary studies are bearing fruit. We chose a cohort approach to the analysis in which age cohorts are treated as birth cohorts and tracked through time to examine trends in the educational attainment of the Registered Indian population in Canada with appropriate comparisons to the same progress made by other Canadians. Finally, both cross-sectional and cohort approaches are employed to quantify the gap or differential in university degree attainment between Registered Indians and other Canadians. This allows us to assess the policy implications of the current situation.*

Background

It is well documented that educational and labour market outcomes for Aboriginal people in Canada lag behind those of non-Aboriginal Canadians (Hull 2005, Mendelson 2006). In terms of educational attainment, Aboriginal peoples have experienced some progress in increasing their levels of high school and post-secondary completions in the last decade (Maxim and White 2005). Additionally, it has been shown that those Aboriginal people who complete their university degrees enjoy similar labour market outcomes as their non-Aboriginal counterparts, with improved unemployment rates and higher levels of employment income, which all contributes to an improved economic well-being. Unfortunately, these educational improvements for Aboriginal Canadians have not kept pace with the increasing educational attainment experienced by non-Aboriginal Canadians. In particular, relatively few Aboriginal Canadians have completed university degrees, which is quite contrary to the situation for non-Aboriginal Canadians.

---

* This introduction was written by the editors.

This situation is of particular importance given Canada's, and other OECD countries', increasing concern over the educational outcomes of children and youth. Education policy goals articulated by Canada and other organizations have been to encourage youth to attend university and higher education programs in greater numbers than in the past in order to engage and reap benefits in an increasingly competitive and global knowledge-based economy. So far, the populace has taken note of this policy push with recently published data describing the increasing numbers of individuals enrolling in university programs at Canadian universities (Statistics Canada, 2005). However, this policy shift has the potential to be a double-edged sword. Some researchers have stated that this drive to pursue post-secondary credentials is out of sync with the realities of the labour force (Côté and Allahar 2007). Unreasonably high education credentials may be needed for entry-level or junior white collar positions simply because employers can now demand it. But a more insidious effect of this change could be its ability to further disadvantage those individuals who choose not to pursue post-secondary education or those groups who have experienced less success in the Canadian educational system.

One of these groups is Aboriginal Canadians, who face considerably more social and economic barriers to educational success than other Canadians due to their lower socio-economic status. Research indicates that educational outcomes are highly correlated with social economic status where one finds higher educational success for children in families with higher levels of education and income (Goran, Fitz, and Taylor 2001). Additionally, precursors such as health status and emotional and behavioural disorders have been shown to be related to social economic status where both adults and children of lower socio-economic levels suffer poorer health and are more likely to experience emotional and behavioural distress than families in higher social and income levels (Brownell, Roos, and Fransoo 2006). Unfortunately, Aboriginal Canadians also suffer poorer rates of health and lower life expectancy than non-Aboriginal Canadians.

The interaction between the Canadian educational system and Aboriginal Canadians in the past has not been a positive one. Historically, the residential school system, formerly a part of the federal governments' assimilationist education policy, has left Aboriginal people a legacy of mistrust and alienation for pursuing higher education, particularly at the post-secondary level (Canada Millennium Scholarship Foundation 2004). Despite these various points, researchers and educators have not remained silent on suggesting measures to improve the academic success and persistence towards higher education for Aboriginal peoples. Some researchers have gone as far as to ask the question "how much do schools contribute to the problem?" and suggest more cultural and mutually accommodating environments in which schools and universities can respect and acknowledge Aboriginal cultures, languages, traditions and contributions made to Canadian society (Kirkness and Barnhardt 1991, MacKay and Myles 1995). However, at the same time, there has been very little empirical evidence linking

Aboriginal cultural and language accommodation to an improvement in academic achievement and other educational outcomes such as retention and persistence.[1]

All of this said, this article has several objectives. First, the cross-sectional trends in university attainment of the Registered Indian population are examined from 1981 to 2006. Registered Indians are a sub-group within the Aboriginal population defined by the *Indian Act* (1985) and generally have the poorest educational outcomes of all of the Aboriginal groups in Canada. Second, a cohort approach in which age cohorts are treated as birth cohorts and tracked through time is utilized to examine trends in educational attainment of the Registered Indian population in Canada with appropriate comparisons to the same progress made by other Canadians. Finally, both cross-sectional and cohort approaches are employed to quantify the gap or differential in university degree attainment between Registered Indians and other Canadians to determine its growth over time.[2]

Before we move to the presentation of results, the following sections outline the data sources, the variables used to identify the Registered Indian population, and their limitations for tracking and measuring university educational progress.

Sources of Data on Aboriginal Educational Outcomes

Overall, a reliable and consistent data source to compare and track progress of educational attainment of various ethnic groups is the Census of Canada. The Census contains detailed questions on the highest level of education attained by individuals, which remained essentially unchanged until the 2006 Census of Canada was undertaken.[3] These same questions also recorded whether an individual attended a post-secondary educational program even if a degree or diploma was never achieved. This is no longer the case for any Census conducted from 2006 and onward. Only actual educational credentials obtained, such as high school certificates and post-secondary degrees and diplomas, are to be recorded. No longer will any educational attainment below a high school certificate be recorded nor will any studies which did not result in the completion of a post-secondary degree or diploma. One serious implication of this new accounting method for the highest level of schooling is the continuity of current educational indicators over time and also their comparability before and after the 2006 Census. In some cases, these Census changes have rendered some educational indicators invalid, such as university participation and completion rates, which rely on the numbers of all individuals who attended university regardless if they completed their degree. In other cases, new and more refined data will result from the new Census educational questions such as further details on trades and community college degrees. For the purposes of this article, the impact of this change on the university attainment counts of Registered Indians is minimal as will be discussed at length in the next section.

The Census is not without its inherent limitations (Census Technical Report 2001). The Census does not collect at any qualitative depth data that may explain the associated reasons or factors for emerging trends or gaps in educational attainment amongst various ethnic groups. However, some post-censal surveys and qualitative studies are attempting to fill this policy research gap, at least for the non-Aboriginal population of Canada. For example, the 2000 Youth in Transition Survey (YITS) gathers longitudinal data on school to work transitions of two Canadian youth cohorts, one aged 15 years and the other aged 18 to 20 years. Although Aboriginal youth were included in the overall sample of this survey, the sample was too small to distinguish between Registered Indians and other Aboriginal Canadians and thus not representative of the total Registered Indian youth population in Canada.[4] Although a representative sample of Aboriginal Canadians in YITS is seen as desirable to support evidenced-based policy development in educational matters, other YITS-like qualitative studies are occurring with Indian reserves across Canada that attempt to describe the factors that support or diminish the post-secondary pursuits of their members.[5] Findings from these case studies can provide the evidence base required to create community-specific policy to maximize potential for educational and labour market outcomes.

Another source of data on Aboriginal educational outcomes comes from the federal program which serves to provide funding for qualified Aboriginal Canadians to pursue post-secondary education. The Post-Secondary Student Support Program (PSSSP), administered by Indian and Northern Affairs Canada (INAC) provides funding to Registered Indians and Inuit to pursue post-secondary education. The objective of the program is to support the increased participation and success of Registered Indian and Inuit students in recognized post-secondary programs thus affecting their employment prospects upon graduating (Vermaeten, Norris, and Buchmeier 2004). In 2002, INAC provided $285 million to support the educational pursuits of those who qualify. This funding is transferred to Indian bands and reserves across Canada who manage and set priorities for student funding within their jurisdiction. However, not all who apply receive funding from the PSSSP. Furthermore, program data collected from Registered Indian students funded through PSSSP only records a completion event when students graduate from their program of study and not for any other circumstances such as dropping out, moving out of province, or death. Therefore, tracking educational outcomes of these students is restricted to those who receive funding, with limited or no knowledge of outcomes when a student ceases to receive funding from the program. In fact, the Auditor General of Canada (Report, Chapter 5, 2004) has described the program data from the PSSSP as a "data challenge" in which there are difficulties in reporting success and outcomes from the funding program other than at the most basic level.

A Cohort Approach to Measuring Educational Progress

Despite changes in the Census educational variables and the limitations of INAC program data to track post-secondary progress, it is still feasible to examine the overall educational progress for Registered Indians using Census data and a cohort approach (Hull 2006). In terms of definitions, Registered Indians are those individuals entitled under the *Indian Act* to be registered as an Indian and thus to receive benefits and rights as outlined under the Act (*Indian Act*, 1985). Likewise, a cohort is defined as a group of individuals who share common characteristics (Glenn 2005). For this analysis, these common characteristics are that individuals are Registered Indians by birth and share a common age category. For the population not entitled to be Registered Indians, they are referred to in this analysis as the non-Registered Indian or other Canadian population and compromise the comparative population group.[6]

Between 1981 and 2006, the Census of Canada is capable of distinguishing various social and economic characteristics between the Registered Indian and other Canadian populations. Additionally in this twenty-five year period, the Census education question on the completion of a university degree has remained unchanged and comparable to previous Census periods. The stability in both of these Census variables over time allows the possibility to examine the university educational progress between the Registered and other Canadian populations for all age categories or by following specific age cohorts through several Census periods.[7]

Census Data Limitations for the Registered Indian Population

Since our focus on university educational progress is restricted to the Registered Indian population, it is first worthwhile to discuss some of the limitations associated with the Census data for this Aboriginal group.

According to the 2006 Census, just less than half of Registered Indians reside on-reserve (48%) with the majority (52%) residing off-reserve in either rural or urban areas of Canada. Not all reserves participate in the Census, particularly some larger ones located in the provinces of Ontario and Quebec (Census Technical Report 2001). The number of non-participating reserves has varied over Census periods and is documented in the Census technical literature. A consequence of what is described as "incomplete enumeration" is that the educational attributes of any non-participating Registered Indian population are not included in the overall Census counts or in any other analysis using this data. Additionally, there was no attempt at this time to control for this variation of Census non-participating reserves. Minimally, one method would be to include only a core number of

Figure 5.1: Proportion of Registered Indians and Other Canadians with a University Degree, 2006

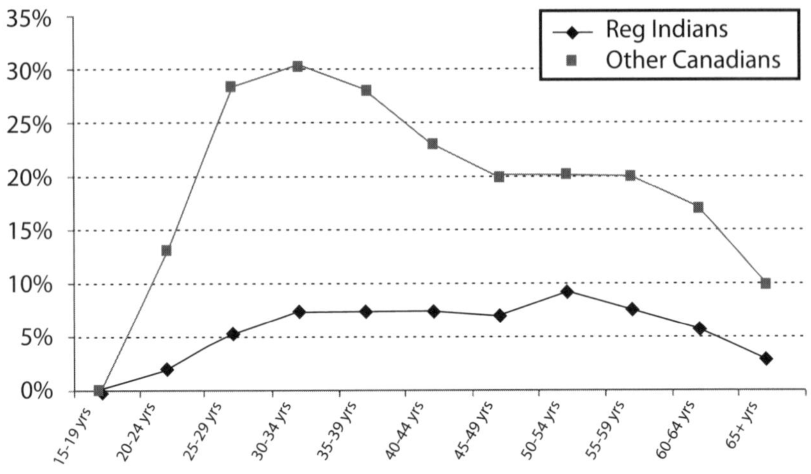

reserves that participated in all Censuses from 1981 to 2006 but at the exclusion of education data for those that participated intermittently within this period.[8]

A legislative event that has affected the overall Registered Indian population over time was the enactment of Bill C-31 in 1985. Bill C-31 removed the paternalistic tendencies of the previous *Indian Act*, allowing for the reinstatement of Registered Indian status to those who lost status previously and allowing for the registration of Indian status to their children. The population most affected by this legislative change were Registered Indian women who lost their Indian status through marriage to non-Staus men. Subsequently, one would expect to find a sharp increase in the Registered Indian population, particularly in the 1991 Census, which is the case. Basic departmental data (BDD) collected by INAC on reinstatements resulting from Bill C-31 reveal that the two years subsequent to 1985 experienced a quadrupling of the regular year-over-year increase in the Registered Indian population. The year over year increase in the Registered Indian population has since returned to similar levels prior to 1985 (INAC 2002) around 2 to 4% a year.

One issue that comes to mind as a consequence of Bill C-31 is the impact of this reinstated population on the overall educational attainment of the Registered Indian population? This is not a trivial question; the Census does not contain any variables to separate out the Bill C-31 sub-population from those who had Status prior to 1985. However, the Aboriginal Peoples Survey (APS) conducted in 1991 did include several questions to determine if respondents regained their Indian status through Bill C-31, but only on a one time basis. Preliminary analysis using the 1991 APS Public Use Microdata File (PUMF) shows that the educational characteristics of the Bill C-31 population is not that much different from that of

Figure 5.2: Proportion of Other Canadians with a University Degree by Age Category, 1981 and 2006

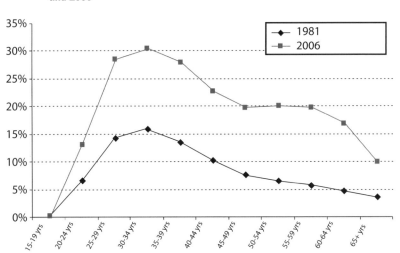

the Registered Indian population who had status prior to Bill C-31, particularly for university degree completions.[9]

Overall University Attainment of Registered Indian and Other Canadian Populations in 2006

The proportions of university degree attainment by age group of Registered Indians and other Canadians in Canada using 2006 Census data are shown in **Figure 5.1**. As discussed previously, all analysis presented is based on comparing university degree completions in previous Census periods from 1981 to 2006, which are comparable to the new definition of the highest degree, certificate or diploma (HCDC) variable used in the 2006 Census, where only data on actual obtained university degrees at the Bachelor's level and higher are counted.[10]

Age groups are organized in five year intervals for the Registered Indian and other Canadian populations aged 15 years and older starting with those aged 15 to 19, 20 to 24 and so on until the last age category of 65 years and older (65+ yrs). No analysis is provided for any age groups older than 65 years, since the likelihood of individuals in this group increasing their university attainment is greatly reduced due to increased mortality.

In 2006, the Registered Indian population had much lower overall university degree attainment (5%) than the other Canadian population (18%). For certain age groups, the proportion of the other Canadian population with a university degree is almost six times that for the Registered Indian population (20–24 and 25–29 years old). One point of interest is the age groups in which both populations possess the highest proportion with a university degree. For the Registered Indian population,

Figure 5.3: Proportion of Registered Indians with a University Degree by Age Category, 1981 and 2006

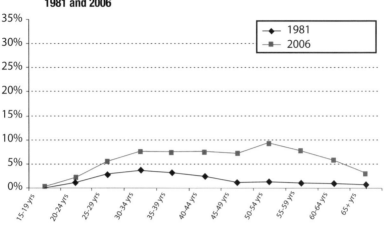

older age cohorts (30–34 to 50–55 years old) appear to possess slightly higher proportions with a university degree than younger ones. In contrast, young other Canadian cohorts possess higher proportions with a university degree.

University Attainment of the Registered Indian and Other Canadian Populations in 1981 and 2006

The Census data allow for the examination of university educational trends for both the Registered Indian and other Canadian populations in 1981 and twenty-five years later in 2006.

Figure 5.2 depicts the proportions in the other Canadian population with a university degree for the Census periods of 1981 and 2006. In 1981, 8% of the other Canadian population had a university degree, more than doubling to 18% in 2006. For both Census periods, it is the younger age groups which have the highest proportions with a university degree, with the 30–34 year olds having the highest proportion in 1981 (16%) and again in 2006 (30%). Clearly, there has been noticeable progress in the attainment of university degrees for all age groups in this twenty-five year period, except for the very young (15–19 years old). This would be reasonable given that university graduates are likely to be over 19 years old and most in this age group were still attending high school.

Figure 5.3 depicts the age group proportions with a university degree for the Registered Indian population in the Census periods of 1981 and 2006. Although university attainment for all age categories is nowhere near as pronounced as it is for the other Canadian population, some progress has been achieved over the twenty-five year period. Overall in 1981, only 2% of the Registered Indian population had a university degree, increasing to 5% in 2006. In 1981, the younger age groups exhibited the highest proportions of individuals who obtained a university

Figure 5.4: Proportion of Other Canadian Males with a University Degree by Age Category, 1981 and 2006

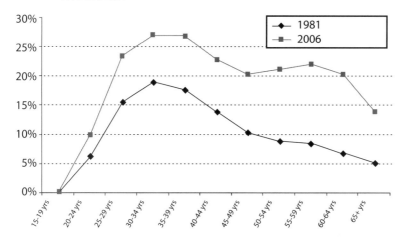

Figure 5.5: Proportion of Other Canadian Females with a University Degree by Age Category, 1981 and 2006

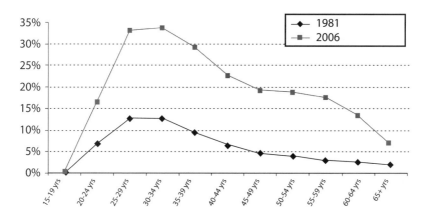

degree, although the proportions are quite small, with the highest being around 4%. However in 2006, it is the older age groups (30–34 to 55–59 years old) that have the highest proportion of individuals who have obtained their university degree. This trend, unlike that of the other Canadian population, has been noted by other researchers (Hull 2006) where it has been observed that those Aboriginal individuals who go on to complete their post-secondary educational pursuits do so at an older age than other Canadians. To date, no additional quantitative or qualitative research has been performed to explain this phenomenon to any level of detail.

Figure 5.6: Proportion of Registered Indian Males with a University Degree by Age Category, 1981 and 2006

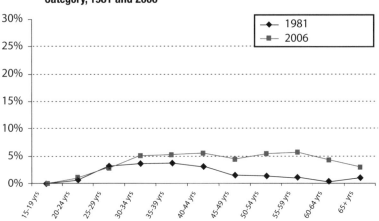

University Attainment of the Registered Indian and Other Canadian Population by Gender between 1981 and 2006

The Census also allows for the examination and comparison of educational trends in the Registered Indian and other Canadian populations from a gender perspective. **Figures 5.4** and **5.5** depict the proportions with a university degree by age groups in 1981 and 2006 for the other Canadian male and female populations respectively.

In 1981, 10% of the other Canadian male population obtained a university degree, increasing to 18% in 2006. The other Canadian male population showed progress in the proportions obtaining their university degrees in almost all age categories over the twenty-five year period. In 1981, young male other Canadian age groups of 25 to 29, 30 to 34 and 35 to 39 year olds had the highest proportions with a university degree compared to older ones. These same young male age groups, plus the middle aged group of 40 to 44 year olds, have the highest proportions with a university degree in 2006, where even higher proportions are achieved.

In 1981, 6% of the other Canadian female population obtained a university degree, tripling to 18% in 2006. The other Canadian female population experienced significant progress in obtaining their university credentials between 1981 and 2006. In 1981, young female age groups of 25 to 29 and 30 to 34 years old had the highest proportions with a university degree. In 2006, these same young female age groups had the highest proportions with a university degree (25–29 and 30–34 years old), with the distinction of having the highest proportions of any age group presented in this analysis. This supports other observations that females have been attending and completing their university studies in higher

Figure 5.7: Proportion of Registered Indian Females with a University Degree by Age Category, 1981 and 2006

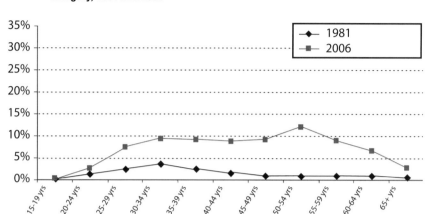

numbers than their male counterparts in the last decade or so (Statistics Canada, 2005). Other recent research has linked the gender imbalance of university attendance between males and females to the higher returns from university education obtained by females than males (Christofides, Hoy, Yang 2006).[11]

Figures 5.6 and **5.7** depict the proportions by age groups of university degree attainment in 1981 and 2006 for the Registered Indian male and female populations respectively.

Both the Registered Indian male and female populations have much smaller proportions with a university degree, overall and by age category, than their other Canadian counterparts.

In 1981, 2% of the Registered Indian male population had a university degree increasing only slightly to 4% in 2006. For Registered Indian males in age categories younger than 40 to 44 years, very little progress was made in obtaining higher proportions with university degrees between 1981 and 2006. In 1981, the younger Registered Indian male age groups had higher attainment than older cohorts. In 2006, this trend was no longer the case, with a mix of young and older male age groups (30–34 to 55–59 year olds) having the highest proportions with a university degree compared to younger ones.

Similarly, in 1981, only 1% of the Registered Indian female population had a university degree. By 2006 this had increased to 7%. Except for the youngest and oldest Registered Indian female age groups, there has been some noticeable progress for most age groups, albeit small, over the twenty-five year period between 1981 and 2006. In 1981, the highest proportions with a university degree were amongst the younger Registered Indian female age groups (35–39 years and younger). However, by 2006 older Registered Indian female age groups (40–44, to 55–59 years old) also had high relative proportions with a university degree in 2006.

Figure 5.8: Proportion of Registered Indians On-reserve with a University Degree by Age Category, 1981 and 2006

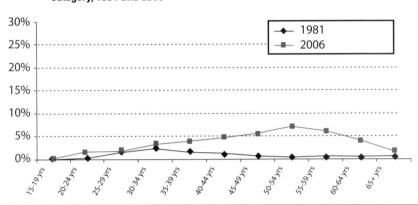

Registered Indian females exceeded the university attainment progress of their male counterparts in 2006 for all age categories. The largest gap in university degree completions between Registered Indian females and males were for 40 to 44 and 50 to 54 year olds where females in both of these age categories had between 6 to 7% more individuals in their age group populations with a university degree (9% vs. 3% and 12% vs. 5%).

University Attainment of Registered Indians Residing On- and Off-reserves in 1981 and 2006

In 2006, as mentioned previously, Registered Indians were slightly more likely to live in off-reserve locations. **Figures 5.8** and **5.9** depict the proportions by age category of university attainment for Registered Indians residing on and off-reserve.

For Registered Indians residing on-reserve in 1981, overall very few obtained a university degree (1%), increasing only slightly to 3% in 2006. Those with a university degree in 1981 were primarily in the younger age categories of 25 to 29, 30 to 34, and 35 to 39 years old, compromising about 2% of the total population in these age groups at the time. In 2006, the slight progress in university attainment is most evident in the older age categories of 45 to 49, 50 to 54, and 55 to 59 years old, at around 6% of the total population in these age groups.

Registered Indians residing in off-reserve locations fared slightly better than their on-reserve counterparts in obtaining a university degree in the same time periods. In 1981, 2% of Registered Indians residing in off-reserve locations had a university degree, increasing modestly to around 7% in 2006. In 1981, Registered Indian residing in off-reserve locations in the age groups of 25 to 29 years old to 40 to 44 years old had the highest attainment of university degrees at between 4 to 5%. In 2006, the age groups of Registered Indians residing in off-reserve locations with the highest proportions of university degree attainment was a mix

Figure 5.9: Proportion of Registered Indians Off-reserve with a University Degree by Age Category, 1981 and 2006

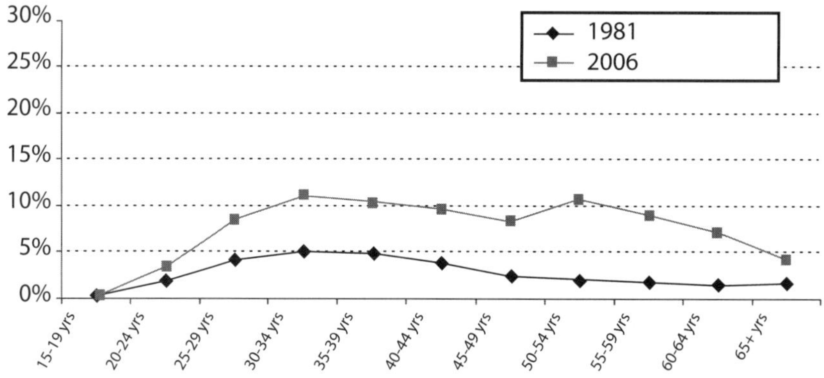

of young (30–34, 35–39 and 40–44 years old) and older age groups (50–54 and 55–59 years old).

Registered Indians residing in off-reserve locations exceeded the university attainment progress of their on-reserve counterparts in 2006 for all age categories except 15 to 19 year olds. The largest gap in progress between off-reserve and on-reserve Registered Indians by age category was for 20 to 25, 30 to 34 and 35 to 39 year olds. Off-reserve Registered Indians in these age categories had between 6 to 8% more individuals with a university degree than those Registered Indians residing on-reserve (8% vs. 2%, 11% vs 3% and 10% vs. 4%).[12]

University Attainment of Registered Indians Residing On- and Off-reserve by Gender in 1981 and 2006

Figures 5.10 and **5.11** depict the university attainment of Registered Indians residing on-reserve by gender in 1981 and 2006.

For Registered Indian males residing on-reserve in 1981, relatively few (less than 1%) had obtained a university degree. Of those that did, the age groups with the highest proportions were 25 to 29 to 40 to 44 years old, at around 2% respectively. In 2006, Registered Indian males experienced only a very slight improvement in their attainment of university degrees (to 1.8% of the population). The age groups with the highest proportions with a university degree were much older than in 1981 (45–49, 50–54 and 55–59 year olds) at around 3–4% of the cohorts, respectively.

Similarly, for Registered Indian females residing on-reserve, relatively few (1%) had obtained a university degree according to the 1981 Census. Of those that had obtained their degrees, the age groups with the highest proportions were 30 to 34 and 35 to 39 year olds with around 2% respectively. In 2006, Registered Indian

Figure 5.10: Proportion of Registered Indian Males Residing On-reserve with a University Degree by Age Category, 1981 and 2006

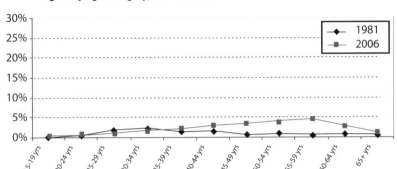

Figure 5.11: Proportion of Registered Indian Females Residing On-reserve with a University Degree by Age Category, 1981 and 2006

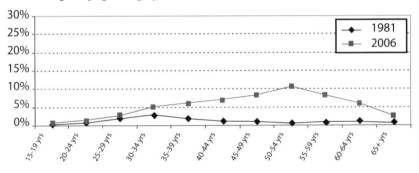

females residing on-reserve had experienced a slight but noticeable improvement in their attainment of university degrees (4%). In 2006, the age groups with the highest proportions with a university degree were older, comprised of 45 to 49 (8%), 50 to 54 (10%) and 55 to 59 (8%) year olds.

The higher educational attainment of Registered Indian females residing on-reserve, in comparison to their male counterparts, has been documented by other researchers (Hull 2006). Although the university attainment of Registered Indians in 1981, regardless of gender, was relatively low, there are some differences in 2006. Registered Indian females residing on-reserve in 2006 appear to be more successful than males in obtaining a university degree. Similarly, the data also seems to support that the Registered Indian population over the twenty-five year period have obtained their university degrees at an older age compared to other Canadians, which is a trend also observed by other researchers.

Figures 5.12 and **5.13** depict the university attainment of Registered Indians residing off-reserve, by gender, in other rural and urban areas in 1981 and 2006.

For Registered Indian males residing off-reserve in 1981, 3% of this population had a university degree, increasing slightly to 5% in 2006. In 1981, the propor-

Figure 5.12: Proportion of Registered Indian Males Residing Off-reserve with a University Degree by Age Category, 1981 and 2006

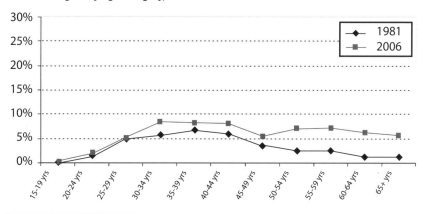

Figure 5.13: Proportion of Registered Indian Females Residing Off-reserve with a University Degree by Age Category, 1981 and 2006

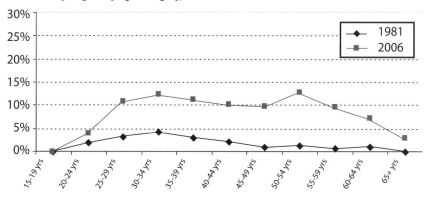

tions with a university degree are small for all cohorts of Registered Indian males residing off-reserve. The highest proportions were for those aged 35 to 39 (7%) and 40 to 44 (6%) years old. In contrast to the Registered Indian male population residing on-reserve during the same time period, these results are two to three times as large, although in general the proportions are generally small compared to other Canadian males. This result also supports other research that indicates that Registered Indians residing off-reserve experience higher educational attainment than those residing on-reserve.

Twenty-five years later, in 2006, all cohorts of Registered Indian males residing off-reserve, except for the three youngest, underwent slight increases in their proportions with a university degree. However, unlike the situation in 1981, the highest proportions with a university degree was shared amongst younger and older cohorts of 30 to 34 (8%), 35 to 39 (8%), 40 to 44 (8%), 50 to 54 (7%) and 55–59 (7%) year olds.

Similar to Registered Indian females residing on-reserve, very small proportions of Registered Indian females residing off-reserve obtained a university degree in 1981. Of those who did, the highest proportions were amongst the 25 to 29 (3%), 30 to 34 (4%), and 35 to 39 (3%) age groups. Twenty-five years later, in 2006, there was noticeable improvements in the attainment of university degrees amongst Registered Indian females residing off-reserve. The age groups with the highest proportions were shared amongst younger age groups of 25 to 29 (11%), 30 to 34 (12%) and 35 to 39 (11%) and the middle-aged age group of 50 to 54 (13%) which recorded the largest proportion with a university degree for the Registered Indian population in 2006.

Similar to the gender differences in university attainment between Registered Indian males and females who reside on-reserve, Registered Indian females residing at off-reserve locations have been more successful in earning a university degree than their male counterparts, particularly in 2006.

A Cohort Approach to Analysis

Until now, the analysis has been restricted to a cross-sectional glimpse of the Census data in 1981 and 2006, and has examined any trends in the proportion of university attainment by age groups for the two populations in question. Keeping in mind the limitations explained previously, the Census definition of the Registered Indian and other Canadian population, as well as the HLOS and HDCD variable categories for university degrees, has remained relatively stable in all the Census periods from 1981 through to the 2006.[13] Therefore, this variable consistency allows for the tracking of university attainment progress by cohorts in this twenty-five year period.

In a cohort approach to tracking progress in university degree attainment, age groups from the 1981 Census are considered as birth cohorts and are then tracked or "aged" through the five remaining Census periods until the 2006 Census is reached. Cohorts in 1981 that are of particular interest in this exercise are the 15 to 19, 20 to 24, 25 to 29, 30 to 34, 35 to 39 and 40 to 44 years old. When the university attainment proportion is tracked for these six cohorts from 1981 to 2006, these cohorts essentially become 40 to 44 to 65+ year olds, respectively at the end of this period.[14]

Table 5.1 shows the university attainment proportions of the Registered Indian population by age category using Census data from 1981 to 2006. The findings outlined in the previous sections were primarily taken from the first and last columns of this table and others which represent the cross-sectional Census data at a given point of time. By adding data series from other Census periods between 1981 and 2006, is it possible to construct cohort trend lines for university attainment by Census year from 1981 and 2006 for both the Registered Indian and other Canadian populations.

Table 5.1: Proportion of the Registered Indian Population with a University Degree by Age Category, 1981–2006

Age Category	1981	1986	1991	1996	2001	2006
15–19 yrs	**0.0%**	0.0%	0.0%	0.0%	0.0%	0.0%
20–24 yrs	1.0%	**0.6%**	0.9%	1.3%	1.5%	1.9%
25–29 yrs	2.7%	1.9%	**2.2%**	3.1%	4.5%	5.3%
30–34 yrs	3.5%	2.8%	3.0%	**3.7%**	5.6%	7.3%
35–39 yrs	3.0%	3.4%	4.3%	4.9%	**5.3%**	7.2%
40–44 yrs	**2.3%**	2.4%	4.2%	6.1%	5.3%	**7.3%**
45–49 yrs	1.2%	**1.5%**	3.5%	5.7%	7.0%	6.9%
50–54 yrs	1.0%	0.8%	**2.0%**	4.2%	6.6%	9.0%
55–59 yrs	0.9%	0.7%	1.0%	**2.7%**	4.3%	7.5%
60–64 yrs	0.7%	0.5%	1.0%	1.3%	**2.3%**	5.5%
65+ yrs	0.6%	0.2%	0.5%	0.8%	1.3%	**2.8%**

For illustrative purposes, let us focus on the Registered Indian age cohort 15 to 19 years in 1981 to construct its cohort trend line for university attainment from 1981 to 2006. This cohort is the first bolded label in **Table 5.1** under the age category column. The horizontal series of values under the six Census years gives the cross-sectional proportions of the Registered Indian population aged 15 to 19 years who possessed a university degree. It should be noted here that when we look at the university proportions for each age group horizontally, or by rows, through the Census periods, these age groups are not cohorts in the strictest sense but are different individuals in a similar age group but separated in time by a different Census period. However, if instead we follow the diagonal of university attainment proportion values beginning in 1981 through to 2006 for the 15 to 19 year old cohort, represented by the bolded and larger font proportions, this is essentially the same cohort aged over time and followed through the Census periods. By following the 15 to 19 years old Registered Indian cohort, in 1981 in this manner, in 2006 it becomes part of the 40 to 44 year age group in that Census period and is twenty-five years older.

Also highlighted in the age category column of **Table 5.1** is the 1981 Registered Indian 40 to 44 years old cohort. It is important to note that this is the last cohort to be tracked in this analysis since it is the one which ends up precisely at the 65+ year old cohort when aged over twenty-five years. Since dramatic improvements in post-secondary educational attainment are less likely to occur as one ages, it was decided not to track the progress of older age cohorts past 65 years of age but note that it does ends up being a "catch all" cohort for the cohorts 45 to 49 years and older.

Figure 5.14: Proportion of Other Canadians with a University Degree, Selected Cohorts in 1981, Aged to 2006

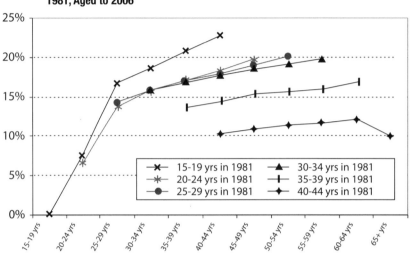

Age Cohort Trends in University Attainment for Other Canadian and Registered Indian Populations from 1981 to 2006

By tracking the progress in university attainment of six cohorts, for both the Registered Indian and other Canadian population, we can examine simultaneously trends within cohorts and amongst themselves as a group over a twenty-five year time frame. However, caution should be exercised when directly comparing the progress of one cohort over another for several reasons. The most obvious is that each of the six cohort trend lines represent individuals in different age ranges who have had varying amounts of time to complete their university degrees. For example, the 15 to 19 year old cohorts almost always show the greatest improvement in university degree completion because, for the most part, they are starting at a zero university completion proportion. Additionally, cohorts that lie between 25 to 44 years of age have a tendency to have the highest post-secondary completion rates because they have had more time to go back and complete their degrees than younger ones (Hull 2005).

Figures 5.14 and **5.15** depict the trends in university degree completion of the six age cohorts in the other Canadian and Registered Indian population through the twenty-five year time period.

For the other Canadian population, all six cohort trend lines—except the oldest—show progress in attainment of university credentials from 1981 to 2006. The youngest cohort of 15 to 19 years old experienced a large increase in the proportion of university attainment going from 0% in 1981 to 23% in 2006 when the cohort becomes 40 to 44 years olds. Slightly older cohorts of 20 to 24, 25 to 29

Figure 5.15: Proportion of Registered Indians with a University Degree, Selected Cohorts in 1981, Aged to 2006

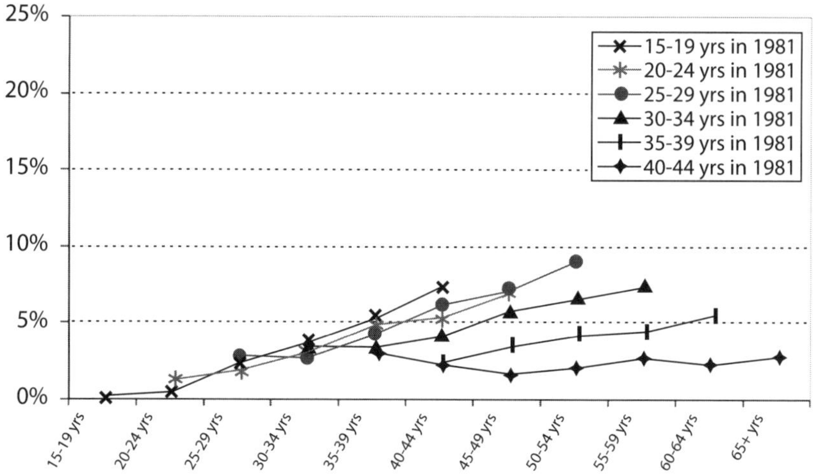

and 30 to 34 years old also experienced noticeable gains in university completion going from 7% to 20%, 14% to 20%, and 16% to 20%, respectively, in the same time period. The older cohort of 40 to 44 years old slightly increased their proportion of university completions from 10% to 12% between 1981 to 2001 but then decreased back to 10% in 2006.

For the Registered Indian population, all cohort trend lines, except for 40 to 44 years old, showed slight progress in university degree completion from 1981 to 2006. The progress of the six Registered Indian cohorts in 1981 was much less than those experienced by their other Canadian counterparts. Similar to other Canadians, the 15 to 19 years old cohort of Registered Indians in 1981 experienced an increase in their proportion with a university degree from 1981 to 2006 going from 0% to 7% in this time period. The slightly older Registered Indian cohorts of 20 to 24, 25 to 29 and 30 to 34 years old also experienced gains in university completion going from 1% to 7%, 3% to 9%, and 3% to 7%, respectively. Older Registered Indian cohorts of 35 to 39 and 40 to 44 years old only experienced marginal or no gains in their proportions in university completions from 1981 to 2006.

Gender Dimensions of Age Cohort Trends in University Attainment of Registered Indians and Other Canadian Populations from 1981 to 2006

Tracking cohort progress in university degree completion amongst the other Canadian and Registered Indian populations by gender is possible using Census data. **Figures 5.16** and **5.17** depict the trends in the proportion of university degree

Figure 5.16: Proportion of Other Canadian Males with a University Degree, Selected Cohorts in 1981 Aged to 2006

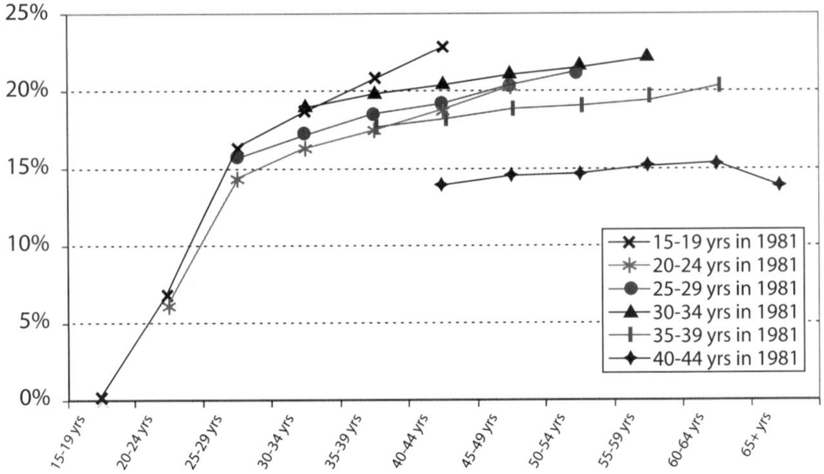

completion during this period for the other Canadian male and female populations by age cohorts respectively.

For the other Canadian male population, five of six cohort trend lines show progress in the completion of university degrees from 1981 to 2006, particularly for the two youngest cohorts of 15 to 19 and 20 to 24 years old. The other Canadian male cohort of 15 to 19 years experienced a large increase in their university degree completion in this time frame going from 0% in 1981 to 23% in 2006 when they are 40 to 44 years old. The slightly older other Canadian male cohorts of 20 to 24, 25 to 29 and 30 to 34 years old also made progress in increasing their university completions, going from 6% to 20%, 16% to 21% and 19% to 22% respectively. Smaller or marginal gains in the proportion of university degree completions were recorded for the older other Canadian male cohorts of 35 to 39 and 40 to 44 years old increasing from 18% to 20% and 14% to 14%, respectively, from 1981 to 2006.

Likewise for the other Canadian female population, all cohorts except the oldest (40–44 years) experienced gains in the proportions with a university degree over the twenty-five year period. Similar to their other Canadian male counterparts, the two youngest female cohorts of 15 to 19 and 20 to 24 years old underwent large increases in their university degree completion from 1981 to 2006, going from 0% to 23% and 7% to 19% respectively. The slightly older other Canadian female cohorts of 25 to 29, 30 to 34 and 35 to 39 years old also made progress in increasing their university completions going from 13% to 19%, 13% to 18% and 9% to 14% respectively. Only the 40 to 44 years old other Canadian female cohort showed no overall progress in this time frame, remaining at 7% in both 1981 and 2006. In comparison to their other Canadian male counterparts during this time period, the gains in university degree completions for female cohorts are lower,

Figure 5.17: Proportion of Other Canadian Females with a University Degree, Selected Cohorts in 1981 Aged to 2006

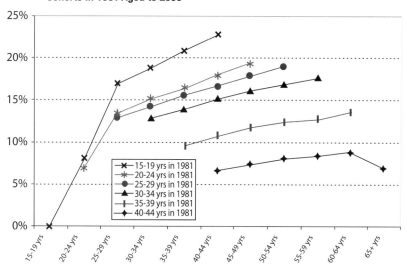

except for the two youngest of 15 to 19 and 20 to 24 years old which experienced similar gains to the male cohorts.

Figures 5.18 and **5.19** depict the trends in proportions of university degree completion from 1981 to 2006 for the Registered Indian male and female populations by age cohorts, respectively.

For Registered Indian males, the trend in progress in university degree completion from 1981 to 2006 is small for all age cohorts except those, older and including 35 to 39 years old. Similar to other 15 to 19 years old cohorts, the Registered Indian male cohort of 15 to 19 years showed a noticeable increase in the twenty-five year time period going from 0% in 1981 to 6% in 2006. However, this gain is nowhere near that of those experienced by their other Canadian 15 to 19-years-old counterparts. Some slight gains were experienced by slightly older Registered Indian male cohorts of 20 to 24, 25 to 29 and 30 to 34 years old increasing from 1% to 4%, 3% to 5% and 4% to 6% respectively. However, no gain in progress of university degree completion was experienced by the older Registered Indian cohorts of 35 to 39 and 40 to 44 years old.

It should be noted that decreases in the proportions with university degree completions occurred between the 1981 and 1986 Census periods for all Registered Indian male cohorts except for the two youngest. To date, there is no explanation to account for this decrease between these two Census years. However, it may be due to changes in the participation of First Nations reserves in the Census during different Census periods, as was mentioned previously, or the change in the Census question used to identify Registered Indians in 1981 and 1986 (see note 12).[15]

Figure 5.18: Proportion of Registered Indian Males with a University Degree, Selected Cohorts in 1981, Aged to 2006

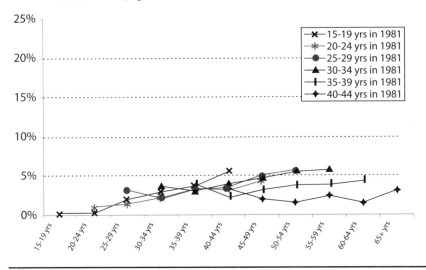

Figure 5.19: Proportion of Registered Indian Females with a University Degree by Age Category, Selected Cohorts in 1981, Aged to 2006

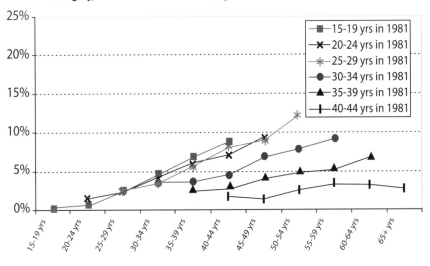

The trends in university degree completion for the six Registered Indian female cohorts from 1981 to 2006 was slightly better than their male counterparts. Similar to other 15 to 19 years old cohorts, the Registered Indian female cohort of 15 to 19 showed a noticeable increase in university degree completions, going from 0% in 1981 to 9% in 2006. This is a better result compared to the 15 to 19 years old Registered Indian male cohort. However, this increase is nowhere near the one experienced by their other Canadian 15 to 19 year old female counterparts.

Figure 5.20: Proportion of Registered Indians Residing On-reserve with a University Degree, Selected Cohorts in 1981, Aged to 2006

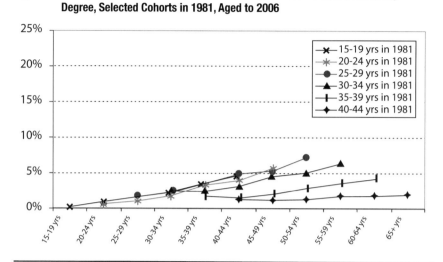

Figure 5.21: Proportion of Registered Indians Residing Off-reserves with a University Degree, Selected Cohorts in 1981, Aged to 2006

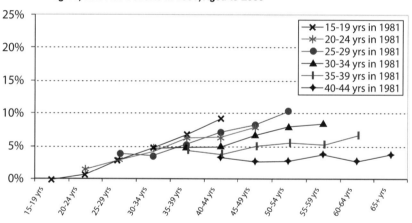

Noticeable gains in university completions were experienced by slightly older Registered Indian female cohorts of 20 to 24, 25 to 29, 30 to 34 and 35 to 39 years old increasing from 1% to 9%, 2% to 12%, 3% to 9% and 2% to 6% respectively. The older Registered Indian female cohort of 40 to 44 years old experienced a small gain in their completion of university degrees, going from 1% to 3%.

Figure 5.22: Proportion of Registered Indian Males Residing On-reserve with a University Degree, Selected Cohorts in 1981, Aged to 2006

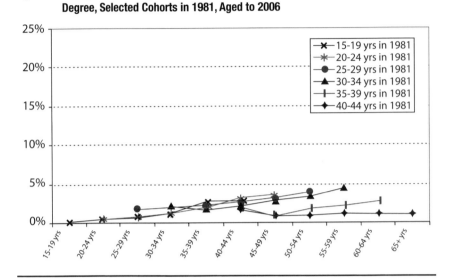

Figure 5.23: Proportion of Registered Indian Females Residing On-reserve with a University Degree, Selected Cohorts in 1981, Aged to 2006

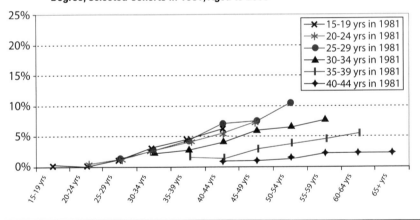

Age Cohort Trends in University Attainment for Registered Indians Residing On- and Off-reserve from 1981 to 2006

The trends in university degree completion for six age cohorts beginning in 1981 to 2006 are depicted for the Registered Indian population residing on- and off-reserve in **Figures 5.20** and **5.21**.

For Registered Indians residing on-reserve, all six age cohorts experienced only slight gains in the proportion of university degree completions from 1981 to 2006. The four youngest on-reserve Registered Indian cohorts of 15 to 19, 20 to 24, 25 to 29 and 30 to 34 increased their university completions slightly from 1981 to 2006 going from 0% to 5%, 0% to 6%, 2% to 7%, and 2% to 6%, respectively. The two older on-reserve Registered Indian cohorts of 35 to 39 and 40 to 44 years old underwent only a slight improvement in this same time period from 2% to 4% and 1% to 2% respectively.

For Registered Indians residing off-reserve, the four youngest age cohorts experienced small but noticeable gains in their proportions of university completion from 1981 to 2006. Registered Indian cohorts of 15 to 19, 20 to 24, 25 to 29, and 30 to 34 residing off-reserve increased their university credentials going from 0% to 9%, 2% to 8%, 4% to 10%, and 5% to 9%, respectively, in the twenty-five year period. The older off-reserve Registered Indian cohorts of 35 to 39 (4% to 7%) and 40 to 44 (4% to 4%) years old experienced small or no changes in this same time period. Although the gains in university degree completions for the off-reserve Registered Indian cohorts are small, they are much more pronounced in magnitude than their counterparts residing on-reserve, particularly for the early adult aged cohorts in 1981.

Age Cohort Trends in University Attainment for Registered Indians Residing On-reserve by Gender from 1981 to 2006

Trends in university degree completion for six age cohorts beginning in 1981 to 2006 are depicted for the Registered Indian population residing on-reserve by gender in **Figures 5.22** and **5.23**.

For Registered Indian male cohorts residing on-reserve, five out of six cohorts underwent only slight gains in their proportion of university degree completions from 1981 to 2006. Specifically, the on-reserve Registered Indian cohorts of 15 to 19, 20 to 24, 25 to 29, 30 to 34, and 35 to 39 years old slightly increased their proportions from 0% to 3%, 0% to 3%, 2% to 4%, 2% to 4%, and 2% to 3%, respectively. The on-reserve Registered Indian male cohort of 40 to 44 (2% to 1%) years old experienced a slight decrease in their already small proportion with a university degree between 1981 and 2006.

For Registered Indian female cohorts residing on-reserve, the situation is more promising compared to their on-reserve male counterparts. Of the six cohorts, five experienced noticeable gains in their proportions of university degree completions from 1981 to 2006, the exception being the oldest cohort. On-reserve Registered Indian female cohorts of 15 to 19, 20 to 24, 25 to 29 and 30 to 34 years old posted gains in university completions from 0% to 7%, 1% to 8%, 1% to 10%, and 2% to 8%, respectively, between 1981 and 2006. Older cohorts of 35 to 39, 40 to 44 (2% to 6%) and 45 to 49 (1% to 2%) years old experienced smaller gains over this same time period. These gains, although positive to see, are much smaller in magnitude than their other Canadian female cohort counterparts.

Figure 5.24: Proportion of Registered Indian Males Residing On-reserve with a University Degree, Selected Cohorts in 1981, Aged to 2006

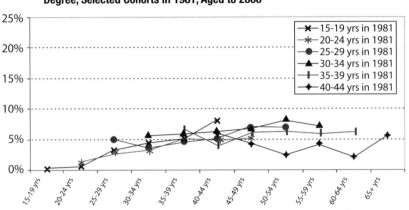

Age Cohort Trends in University Attainment for Registered Indians Residing Off-reserve by Gender from 1981 to 2006

Trends in university degree completion for six age cohorts beginning in 1981 to 2006 are depicted for the Registered Indian population residing off-reserve by gender in **Figures 5.24** and **5.25**.

Of the Registered Indian male cohorts residing off-reserve, all except the oldest cohort experienced only slight gains in their proportions with a university degree from 1981 to 2006. These gains in university degree completions are slightly better than their on-reserve male cohort counterparts. Specifically, the off-reserve Registered Indian male cohorts of 15 to 19, 20 to 24, 25 to 29, and 30 to 34 years old increased their university completions from 0% to 8%, 1% to 5%, 5% to 7%, and 5% to 7% respectively between 1981 and 2006. The older off-reserve Registered Indian male cohorts of 35 to 39 (7% to 6%) and 40 to 44 (6% to 6%) years old experienced either decreases or no changes in their progress in completing university degrees in the twenty-five year period.

It should be noted that trends in university degree completion for certain cohorts for the off-reserve Registered Indian male population has varied over time. In particular, the cohorts of 25 to 29, 35 to 39 and 40 to 44 years old experienced decreases in their proportions with a university degree between 1981 and 1986 and sometimes to 1991. To date, there is very little empirical evidence that accounts for this negative trend during this time. However, one possible explanation may be that Registered Indians with university degrees may need to migrate to other areas in Canada to work in their field, thus being subject to local and Canada-wide labour market demands.

For Registered Indian female cohorts residing off-reserve, the situation is more promising compared to their off-reserve male counterparts. All cohorts, except

Figure 5.25: Proportion of Registered Indian Females Residing On-reserve with a University Degree, Selected Cohorts in 1981, Aged to 2006

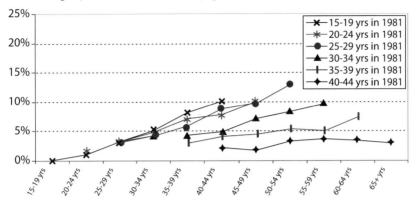

Table 5.2: Overall Proportion with a University Degree, Aged 15+

	1981	1986	1991	1996	2001	2006	Average census year over census year increase
Registered Indians	1.5%	1.32%	2.0%	3.0%	3.9%	5.1%	0.72%
Other Canadians	8.1%	9.6%	11.5%	13.4%	15.6%	18.4%	2.06%
Difference	-6.5%	-8.3%	-9.4%	-10.4%	-11.7%	-13.2%	(1981-2006)
(% Reg Ind - %Oth Can)							

Table 5.3: Overall Proportion with a University Degree, Aged 25–44

	1981	1986	1991	1996	2001	2006	Average census year over census year increase
Registered Indians	2.9%	2.53%	3.2%	4.3%	5.2%	6.8%	0.77%
Other Canadians	13.8%	15.20%	16.7%	18.6%	22.2%	27.1%	2.66%
Difference	-10.8%	-12.60%	-13.5%	-14.4%	-17.0%	-20.3%	(1981-2006)
(% Reg Ind - %Oth Can)							

for the oldest ones, experienced noticeable gains in their proportions of university degree completions from 1981 to 2006. In fact, off-reserve Registered Indian female cohorts exhibited the best progress of all the Registered Indian cohorts in university degree completion. The off-reserve Registered Indian female cohorts of 15 to 19, 20 to 24, 25 to 29, and 30 to 34 years old posted gains in university completions from 0% to 10%, 2% to 10%, 3% to 13%, and 4% to 10%, respectively, between 1981 and 2006. Older cohorts of 35 to 39 (3% to 7%) and 40 to 44

(2% to 3%) years old experienced smaller gains over this same time period. These gains, although positive to see, are much smaller in magnitude than their other Canadian female cohort counterparts.

The Gap in University Attainment between the Registered Indian and Other Canadian Populations

Albeit some progress has been made, it is apparent that the trends in the proportions of university degree completions in the Registered Indian population is much lower than that of other Canadians over the twenty-five year period from 1981 to 2006. Using the 2006 Census cross-sectional data, it is clear that all age groups in the other Canadian population have increased their proportions of university degree completion over that in 1981. In particular, young other Canadians are enrolling and completing their university degrees at much higher proportions and at an earlier age compared to the same age groups in earlier Census periods. Given this gap in university degree completions between the two populations, an additional question comes to mind: What is the magnitude of this gap, or differential, and how has it been changing over time?

Tables 5.2 and **5.3** show the proportions of university degree completions amongst the Registered Indian and other Canadian populations aged 15+ years and between 25 to 44 years in the six Census periods from 1981 to 2006.

In 1981, the difference in the proportion of university degree completion for those aged 15+ between the Registered Indians and other Canadians was -6.5%. In 2006, this gap had doubled to -13.2%. Although Registered Indians have slowly increased the number of individuals with a university degree between 1981 and 2006, the average Census-year-over-Census-year increase amounted to only 0.72%, compared to 2.06% for other Canadians. At this rate, the gap in the proportions with a university degree between the two populations is not expected to close anytime in the near future.[16]

As mentioned previously, the Highest Level of Schooling (HLOS) and the new 2006 Highest Degree, Certificate or Diploma (HDCD) census variables do not take into account the amount of time a respondent takes to complete their post-secondary or university studies. It could take four years or twenty years to complete their post-secondary studies and this makes no difference in how the HLOS/HDCD variable captures this information. However, this does affect completion rates for various post-secondary categories in which certain age groups will have better completion rates simply because they have had more time than younger ones to complete their studies. In particular, other researchers have documented this scenario for certain mid-range age groups, such as those aged 25 to 44 years. Consequently, this is of interest to examine in this analysis because previously it was shown that Registered Indians in this age range tended to have higher proportions with university degrees than their younger counterparts.

Figure 5.26: Proportion of Registered Indian and Other Canadian Populations Aged 15+, with a University Degree, 1981 to 2006

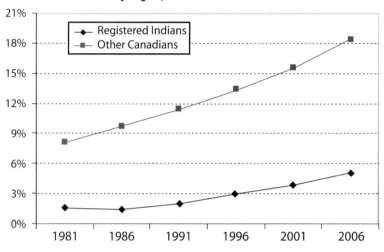

Figure 5.27: Proportion of Registered Indian and Other Canadian Population Aged 25–44 Years with a University Degree, 1981 to 2006

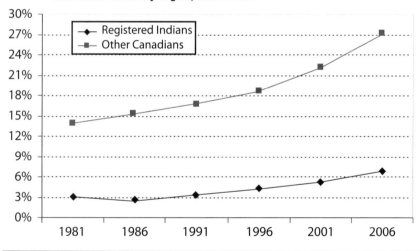

Table 5.3 focuses on the overall proportion of university degree completions amongst Registered Indians and other Canadians ages 25 to 44 from 1981 to 2006.

Unfortunately, even when we examine the proportions of university completions for the mid-range age group of 25 to 44 years old between Registered Indians and other Canadians, we see no improvement in the gap between the two populations compared to overall populations aged 15+ years. For this mid-range age group, we see a much wider gap.

More specifically, in 1981 the difference in the proportion of university degree completion for those aged 25 to 44 years between Registered Indians and other Canadians was -10.8%. In 2006, this gap had increased further to -20.3%. Both of these gaps in 1981 and 2006 are much larger for the 25 to 44 years old than for the total population aged 15+ years for Registered Indians and other Canadians. If we examine the average Census-year-over-Census-year increase in university degree completions for Registered Indians aged 25 to 44 years, it increased slightly to 0.77%, compared the same rate for the 15+ year Registered Indian population. For other Canadians aged 25 to 44 years old, their average Census-year-over-Census-year increase in proportions of university completions was 2.66%, much higher than that for the total other Canadian population age 15+ years old. Based on these rates, the gap in the proportions with a university degree between the two populations aged 25 to 44 years old is also not expected to close in the near future.

Figures 5.26 and **5.27** graphically depict the gaps or differential in the proportions of university degree completions amongst the Registered Indian and other Canadian populations from 1981 to 2006, as described above.

Five-year Trends in University Attainment for Registered Indians and the Other Canadian Population Using the Cohort Approach

In addition to looking at the cross-sectional trends of university degree completions by Registered Indian and other Canadian age groups from 1981 to 2006, we can also use the Census data to examine trends of similar cohorts in different Census periods followed over an equivalent time period. This would allow us to determine if similar cohorts, although separated by different Census periods, have improved their university attainment tracked over a similar amount of time. Unlike the previous cohort analysis, where we looked at the twenty-five year progress for six cohorts of 15 to 19 to 40 to 44 years old in 1981, the progress of all cohorts is examined except those older than 45 to 49 years old due to diminishing increases in university completions.

Tables 5.4 and **5.5** depict the change in university degree attainment by cohorts over a five-year time frame for the other Canadian and Registered Indian populations. The first column indicates the cohort in question, and the second column, the final age of the cohort after the five-year period. Since we have six periods of Census data, the following columns indicate the changes in attainment from one Census period to the next. This is simply the Census-year-over-Census-year difference between the university attainment proportions of the cohort in question.

In **Table 5.4**, for the other Canadian population, the younger cohorts of 15 to 19 and 20 to 24 years old have the highest average change in university attainment over a five-year period of 10.3% and 12.3%, respectively. Additionally, the 15 to 19 and 20 to 24 years old cohorts have been increasing their change in university attainment over consecutive Census periods, meaning that cohorts in more

Table 5.4: Change in University Degree Attainment Rate by Age Group and Time Period

Other Canadians

Initial Cohort	Final Cohort	1981– 1986	1986– 1991	1991– 1996	1996– 2001	2001– 2006	Avg Change
		Change in Attainment per Time Period					
15–19	20–24	7.4%	9.0%	11.1%	11.2%	13.0%	10.3%
20–24	25–29	7.3%	9.3%	12.8%	14.9%	17.1%	12.3%
25–29	30–34	1.5%	1.8%	1.8%	3.3%	4.3%	2.5%
30–34	35–39	1.0%	1.3%	1.2%	2.2%	2.8%	1.7%
35–39	40–44	0.7%	0.8%	0.9%	1.4%	2.0%	1.2%
40–44	45–49	0.6%	0.8%	0.8%	1.1%	1.5%	1.0%
45–49	50–54	0.4%	0.4%	0.4%	0.6%	1.1%	0.6%

Table 5.5: Change in University Degree Attainment Rate by Age Group and Time Period

Registered Indians

Initial Cohort	Final Cohort	1981– 1986	1986– 1991	1991– 1996	1996– 2001	2001– 2006	Avg Change
		Change in Attainment per Time Period					
15–19	20–24	0.6%	0.9%	1.3%	1.5%	1.9%	1.2%
20–24	25–29	0.8%	1.7%	2.2%	3.2%	3.8%	2.3%
25–29	30–34	0.0%	1.2%	1.5%	2.5%	4.5%	1.9%
30–34	35–39	-0.1%	1.5%	1.8%	1.6%	1.7%	1.3%
35–39	40–44	-0.6%	0.8%	1.8%	0.5%	2.0%	0.9%
40–44	45–49	-0.7%	1.0%	1.6%	0.9%	1.6%	0.9%
45–49	50–54	-0.3%	0.4%	0.8%	0.9%	2.0%	0.7%

recent Census periods are doing better than similar ones in later Census periods. Although the older cohorts (25–29 to 45–49 years old) have also increased their proportions of university degree completion, their average change in attainment per time period is much small than the two younger cohorts, ranging from 2.5% to 0.6%.

In **Table 5.5**, for the Registered Indian population, and unlike the other Canadian population, it is the slightly older cohorts of 20 to 24, 25 to 29 and 30 to 34 years old that have the highest average change in university degree completions over a five-year period of 2.3%, 1.9%, and 1.3% respectively. However, these average changes in university attainment are much lower than their other Canadian counterparts. Only the 15 to 19, 20 to 24, and 30 to 34 years old Registered Indian cohorts underwent a consistent increase in the change in university attainment over consecutive Census periods, indicating that more recent cohorts are doing slightly better than previous ones. Additionally, the 40 to 44 years old Registered Indian cohort underwent a similar average change to the other Canadian cohort. However, the proportion of university degree completions for the 40 to 44 years old other Canadian cohort is much higher than that for the Registered

Indian cohort. The average change only reflects those in this cohort who went on to complete their university degrees, thus adding to the overall proportion in the next Census year.

Summary and Concluding Remarks

We have presented a great deal of data in this chapter. We looked at male and female university completion on- and off-reserve and compared that to all other Canadians. We looked at these same comparisons for different age cohorts and even examined them over time.

To summarize, analysis of cross-sectional Census data from 1981 to 2006 show that even though the Registered Indian population has slightly increased their overall (15+ years) and age group specific proportions of individuals with university degrees, the other Canadian population has also done so but at much greater rates. By focusing on the progress of specific age groups for both populations, we find that higher proportions of university degree completions are found with older age groups for the Registered Indian population. This is contrary to the situation for other Canadians, where we find that younger age groups are increasing their proportions of university degree completions and exceeding the progress of similar age groups in earlier Censuses. Very little supportive research has been performed to adequately explain these different pathways to university (or other post-secondary education) between the Registered Indian and other Canadian populations. However, one possible hypothesis is that it is embedded in the different social and economic characteristics of the two populations. It is well-known that Registered Indians have much lower levels of high school diploma completions than other Canadians due to high dropout rates (White et al. 2002, Maxim and White 2006). Coupled with the fact that a high school diploma is usually a prerequisite to be considered for admission into a post-secondary program, other social and economic factors may work to delay the few that do go back to complete high school. This group that continues on to post-secondary studies does so at a later age than other Canadians.

Examining the cross-sectional data from 1981 to 2006 revealed some interesting trends in the proportions of university degree completions amongst the Registered Indian and other Canadian populations along gender dimensions. For female other Canadians, large gains in the proportions of university degree completions were experienced from 1981 to 2006. In fact, these gains significantly exceed those made by their male counterparts. In 2006, the female other Canadian 25 to 29 and 30 to 34 years old age groups have the highest levels of university completions. This female gender trend is somewhat paralleled in the Registered Indian population, albeit at lower rates of completion overall. Female Registered Indians have improved their proportions of university degree completions between 1981 and 2006, exceeding the progress of their male counterparts. However, it is the older or mid-range female Registered Indian age groups that possess the highest proportions with a university degree.

For the Registered Indian population, university degree attainment patterns varied according to on- or off-reserve location. Generally, Registered Indians residing on-reserve had the lowest proportions with a university degree overall and by age groups. Even after twenty-five years, the increase in university degree completions for on-reserve Registered Indians was only slight. However, the scenario was brighter for off-reserve Registered Indian population, who had modest but noticeable gains in their proportions with a university degree from 1981 to 2006. These results support findings from other researchers who have noted that overall education outcomes for the on-reserve Registered Indian population are poorer than their off-reserve counterparts.

Examining the proportions of university degree completions for the on- and off-reserve Registered Indian population by gender revealed that male Registered Indians residing on-reserve underwent very little progress in university degree completions from 1981 to 2006. In fact, they showed the lowest progress of any population subgroup in this analysis. Little is known that would explain this lack of progress, but it clearly warrants further investigation to determine if any specific policy interventions should, or could be put in place to provide opportunities for on-reserve male Registered Indians to pursue and complete their university studies, if they choose to do so. Similar to the overall gender results, on-reserve female Registered Indians showed improvement in their proportions with a university degree from 1981 to 2006, which exceeded those of their male counterparts. For some age groups, the proportion of university degree completions for on-reserve females was over double that of their male counterparts. For the off-reserve Registered Indian population, males showed slight progress in university degree completions from 1981 to 2006. However, again their results were exceeded by off-reserve females who had the greatest gains in their proportions with a university degree from 1981 to 2006 for the Registered Indian population.

Using the cohort approach to analyzing progress in university attainment, the 15 to 19 years old cohort for the other Canadian population underwent a large gain in university degree completions from 1981 to 2006. In 2006 this group was 40 to 44 years old. This is to be expected, as they are starting essentially from zero because their age would have precluded finishing a degree. The mid-range age cohorts for the other Canadian population also experienced noticeable gains in their proportions of university degree completions. The older cohorts of 40 to 44 and 45 too 49 years old experienced marginal gains in university degree completions, but this was not unexpected, given they were over 65 by the 2006 Census. For Registered Indians, all cohorts except—for the two oldest—experienced gains in university attainment but on a much smaller scale than that of their other Canadian counterparts, particularly for younger cohorts. The cohort approach also confirmed some of the results gathered from the cross-sectional analysis. In particular, Registered Indian female cohorts have been more success-ful in improving their university degree attainment over the twenty-five years than their male counterparts. In fact, the cohort approach confirms that this trend started sometime after 1981 and continued to 2006. The progress in university attainment for Registered Indian males is almost non-existent for those residing on-reserves. And finally, Registered Indian female cohorts residing off-reserve underwent the largest gains in university attainment from 1981 to 2006 of all Registered Indian cohorts tracked in this analysis.[17]

Upon quantifying the gap or differential in the progress of university degree completions between the Registered Indian and other Canadian populations from 1981 to 2006, it is established that the gap is wide and has increased substan-tially in this period, regardless of the gains made by Registered Indians. When we restrict this analysis to the population age group of 25 to 29 years old, who typically have higher post-secondary completion rates than younger age groups, we find that the situation is not better but slightly worse. If we hypothesize that even though the Registered Indian population may have more long-term success in going back to complete their university degrees at an older age than other Canadians, the numbers are not enough to close the gap, which in part has been fuelled by the success and earlier completions by younger other Canadians.

Using a cohort approach in examining the five-year trends of university degree completions for similar aged cohorts, but in different Censuses, we find that the two young other Canadian cohorts of 15 to 19 and 20 to 24 years old had the highest average change in proportions of university completions. For Registered Indians, slightly older cohorts of 20 to 24, 25 to 29, and 30 to 34 years old held this distinction but at much lower average rates than their other Canadian coun-terparts. Some progress has been noted in similarly aged young Registered Indian cohorts in the more recent Census. We see slightly better five-year improvement rates, which means more recent cohorts are doing slightly better than previous ones. But again, this progress is not enough to close or even maintain the gap with the progress experienced by their other Canadian counterparts.

This analysis has focused primary on university degree attainment. Increasing numbers of young Canadians are pursuing and completing their university studies to compete and maintain a competitive edge in the global market, with the expec-tation of an increased standard of living or well-being. However, there are other kinds of post-secondary education that are just as important in the work force. Not everyone will want or have the ability to pursue a university education pathway, including those in the other Canadian population. Findings from the 2006 Census have shown that Registered Indians and Aboriginal Canadians in general have had more success in completing college and trades programs. This has led to interest-ing policy options articulated by various organizations and governments which describe the young Aboriginal population as a potential and under-utilized human resource to fill shortages in the skilled labour force and the jobs being vacated by the aging baby-boomer generations who are quickly facing their retirement years.

Given the youthfulness of the Registered Indian population and of Aboriginal Canadians in general, ever increasing numbers will be of workforce age in the next decade and onward. While these populations must increase their levels of education and training in order to perform in these occupations, the growing rate of completion in college and trade programs offers promise in increasing Aboriginal and Registered Indian labour force participation. However, the same cannot be said for occupations requiring a university degree. Given the pace of attainment set by non-Aboriginal Canadians, Registered Indians and any others who are not able or willing to pursue this educational path are at risk of jeopardizing or stalling any progress made in their overall economic well-being.

Endnotes

1 Editor's note: Alternative arguments have been advanced that it is less the schools and curriculum that are to blame and more the social, economic, demographic, and geographic settings of the communities that are negatively influencing the outcomes. See the introduction of this book and the introduction to White, Beavon, and Spence (2008) *Aboriginal Well-being*.

2 The author wishes to be on record that other forms of post-secondary education are important and needed in the labour market; however, there is clear evidence that indicates that university education has a major positive impact on Aboriginal peoples in terms of income and related outcomes. See White et al., 2007.

3 Statistics Canada has recommended that only the university degree completion categories are comparable from the 2006 Census to previous Census periods. Any other comparisons are not recommended due to the total reformulation of the Census education questions that were implemented in the 2006 Census.

4 Editor's note: Strictly speaking the YITS only captured a sample of Aboriginal youth that were in the cities. It did not sample First Nation youth living in their communities or on-reserve. The YITS did have some 800+ Aboriginal respondents and their experience was assessed by an Aboriginal Policy Research Consortium study by Maxim and White (2006).

5 A reserve is a tract of land set apart for the use and benefit of an Indian or First Nation Band as defined by the *Indian Act*. Many First Nations now prefer the term 'First Nation community.' See **<www.ainc-inac.gc.ca/pr/pub/wf/trmrslt_e.asp?term=31>**.

6 Readers should take note that the "other Canadian" population is comprised of both Aboriginal and non-Aboriginal people in Canada. The common characteristic in this definition is that no one in the other Canadian population group is a Registered Indian under the *Indian Act* (1985).

7 Unfortunately, this is not the case for other Aboriginal groups such as the Métis and non-Status Indians, for reasons described later in this chapter.

8 This is a complex issue. An attempt was made to determine if reserves that did not take part in the 1996 Census of Canada were significantly different (outliers) to those that did participate. This was done by going back to previous Census data where the target reserves were enumerated. The analysis showed no significant patterns of differences between participants and non-participants for that particular Census. See Maxim and White, 2000.

9 Beginning with the 1996 Census and onward, it is possible to identify other Aboriginal populations using the Aboriginal identity questions (including those individuals who are Métis, Inuit and North American Indian or have multiple Aboriginal identities). However, a cohort approach to analyzing the educational progress for these groups over several Census periods is not encouraged for several reasons. First, there is a limited amount of Census periods for which this data would be available resulting in a very short trend. However, a second and more serious limitation exists. The growth rates for these groups as measured using Census data exceed what is theoretically possible and explainable using what is known about fertility and mortality (Guimond 2003). The phenomenon of "ethnic mobility" has been used to explain the extraordinary growth rates for these Aboriginal groups, in which one changes their ethnic affiliation over time, which in turn is reflected in the Census figures. Without any clear method to control for such changes in ethnic affiliations, no analysis by the Aboriginal groups affected by this phenomenon is presented in this discussion.

10 In the 2006 Census, the highest level of schooling variable is called the "Highest Degree, Certificate or Diploma" (HCDC) variable, which was known in previous Censuses as the "Highest Level of Schooling" (HLOS) variable.

11 Editor's note: Given that these are percentages/proportions, it could be that we see a pent-up demand releasing for women, since they had lower proportions before and now are active as partners in most occupational categories. This is most likely giving us a look at the effect of social change concerning women over the last quarter century.

12 The problems in educational attainment of Registered Indians residing on-reserve in comparison to counterparts off-reserve has been documented by other researchers such as White et al., 2002.

13 For the 1981 Census, Registered Indian status was collected through an ethnic-origin-based question. However in 1986, Registered Indian status was collected through an "Aboriginal identity"-based question. This data collection change, in conjunction with the incomplete enumeration of reserves during this time explains, the overall difference in Registered Indian population counts from the 1981 and 1986 Censuses.

14 These are not the only cohorts arising from the six cross-sectional Census periods. There are also five other 15-19 year old cohorts which arise in the 1986, 1991, 1996, 2001 and 2006 Census periods as well as the older cohorts of 45-50 to 65+ year olds in the 1981 Census. We do not track the younger cohorts after 1981 because they are not in existence for all five census periods. This results a period of tracking that is not the same as the 15-19 year olds in 1981. Secondly, given the oldest category is 65+, tracking of the older 1981 cohorts is meaningless. As well, changes in university attainment for this group is minimal.

15 Editor's note: These are not likely to provide a full explanation, given that Registered Indian women still showed improvement.

16 As a speculative exercise, if the other Canadian university degree proportion and the average Census-year-over-Census-year increase for Registered Indians remained at 2006 levels, it would take the Registered Indian population 92 years to close the university attainment gap.

17 Editor's note: The gains for females off-reserve may provide us with some understanding about what contributes to success. It raises the hope that there are potentials for real gains.

References

Brownell, M. et al. 2006. "Is the Class Half Empty? A Population-Based Perspective on Socio-Economic Status and Educational Outcomes." *Institute for Research on Public Policy*. 12(5): 3–30.

Christofides, L.N., M. Hoy, and L. Yang. 2006. *The Gender Imbalance in Participation in Canadian Universities (1997–2003)*. Department of Economics, University of Guelph Working Paper.

Côté, J. and A. Allahar. 2007. *Ivory Tower Blues: A University System in Crisis*. Toronto: University of Toronto Press.

Council of Ministers of Education and Statistics Canada. 2005. *Education Indicators in Canada: Report of the Pan-Canadian Education Indicators Program, 2005*. Ottawa: Statistics Canada.

DIAND. 2001. Overview of Department of Indian and Northern Development (DIAND) Program Data: Education, Information Management Branch, 2001. <**www.ainc-inac.gc.ca/pr/sts/ridex_e.html**>

Glenn, Norval D. 2005. *Cohort Analysis*. 2nd Ed., Thousand Oaks, CA: Sage Publications.

Guimond. E. 2003. "Changing Ethnicity: The Concept of Ethnic Drifters." In *Aboriginal Conditions: Research as a Foundation for Public Policy*. J.P. White, P.S. Maxim and D. Beavon (eds). Vancouver: UBC Press. 91–107.

Hanson/Mcleod Institute, June 2005. *Evaluation of the Post-Secondary Education Program*. Ottawa: Indian and Northern Affairs Canada, Departmental Audit and Evaluation Branch.

Hull, J. 2005 (June 15). *Post-secondary education and labour market outcomes Canada, 2001*. Ottawa: Minister of Indian Affairs and Northern Development.

Hull, J. 2006 (June). *Aboriginal Youth in the Canadian Labour Market*. Research and Analysis Directorate. Ottawa: Indian and Northern Affairs Canada.

Indian Act, R.S.C, 1985. <**http://laws.justice.gc.ca/en/showdoc/cs/I-5///en?page=1**>

INAC. 2002. *Basic Departmental Data, 2002*. Ottawa: Indian and Northern Affairs Canada. <**www.ainc-inac.gc.ca/pr/sts/index_e.html**>.

Kirkness, V.J. and R. Barnhardt, 1991. "First Nations and Higher Education: The Four Rs – Respect, Revelence, Reciprocity and Responsibility." *Journal of American Indian Education*. 30(2): 1–15.

Lambert, M. et al. 2004. "Who Pursues Post-Secondary Education, Who Leaves and Why: Results from the Youth in Transition Survey." Research Paper, Culture, Tourism and the Centre for Education Statistics Division. Ottawa: Statistics Canada.

Mackay, R. and L. Myles, 1995. "A Major Challenge for Education System: Aboriginal Retention and Dropout", In *First Nation Education in Canada: The Circle Unfolds*. M. Battiste and J. Barman (eds). Vancouver: UBC Press. 157–178.

Maltest, R.A. and Associates. 2004. *Aboriginal Peoples and Post-Secondary Education: What Educators Have Learned*. Montreal: Canadian Millennium Scholarship Foundation.

Maxim, P. and J.P. White. 2006. "School Completion and Workforce Transitions among Urban Aboriginal Youth." *Aboriginal Policy Research: Moving Forward, Making a Difference, Volume III*. Toronto: Thompson Educational Publishing. 33–52.

Maxim, P. and J. White. 2000. "The Impact of Underenumeration of First Nations Communities." Ottawa: Indian and Northern Affairs Canada.

Mendelson, M. 2006. "Aboriginal Peoples and Post-Secondary Education in Canada." Ottawa: Caledon Institute of Social Policy.

Office of the Auditor General of Canada. 2004 (November). "Report of the Auditor General of Canada to the House of Commons, Chapter 5." Ottawa: Office of the Auditor General.

Statistics Canada. 2001. *Census Technical Report*. Ottawa: Statistics Canada. <**www12.statcan.ca/english/census01/Products/Reference/tech_rep/index.cfm**>.

Statistics Canada. 2003. "University Tuition Fees, 2003–4." *The Daily*, August 12. Ottawa: Statistics Canada.

Statistics Canada. 2005. "University Enrolment, 2003–4." *The Daily*. October 11. Ottawa: Statistics Canada.

Stastics Canada. 2007. *2006 Census Dictionary*. Ottawa: Statistics Canada, Census Operations Division. <**www.statcan.gc.ca/bsolc/olc-cel/olc-cel?catno=92-566-X&lang=eng**>.

Statistics Canada. 2002. *2001 Census Dictionary*. Ottawa: Statistics Canada Census Operations Division.

Vermaeten, A. et al. 2004. "Educational Outcomes of Students Funded by the Department of Indian Affairs Canada: Illustration of a Longitudinal Assessment with Potential Application to Policy Research." In *Aboriginal Policy Research: Setting the Agenda for Change, Volume 1*. Toronto: Thompson Educational Publishing. 205–230.

White, J.P., D. Beavon and N. Spence. 2007. *Aboriginal Well-being : Canada's Continuing Challenge*. Toronto: Thompson Educational Publishing.

White, J.P., P. Maxim and N. Spence. "An Examination of Educational Success." In *Aboriginal Policy Research: Moving Forward, Making a Difference, Volume I*. White et al. (eds). Toronto: Thompson Educational Publishing. 129–148.

Part Two:
Causes, Costs, and Possible Solutions

6

Aboriginal Education: Current Crisis and Future Alternatives

Julie Peters and Jerry P. White

Current Policy Proposals

In this chapter, we present an overview of two seemingly contradictory proposals for moving forward on educational reform. For lack of a better nomenclature we have labeled the work of John Richards and the C.D. Howe Institute as a "free market" approach. We did this because at the core of the argument on how to improve educational performance in First Nations schools is the creation of choice for parents. Giving parents the opportunity to choose the school their children attend is considered key to forcing schools to improve student outcomes, or risk losing their students. On the other side of this contradiction is the Assembly of First Nations (AFN), whose position we have labeled as a "nationalist" approach. We chose this label because the AFN's core argument is that First Nations should have control over the school system through an expanded self-government model. The AFN sees education as critical to the preservation of culture and well-being.

Free Market Approach

John Richards of the C.D. Howe Institute is one of the key proponents of a free market approach to schooling. In *Creating Choices: Rethinking Aboriginal Policy*, Richards lays out four policy alternatives for improving Aboriginal education off-reserve: 1) create separate schools controlled by Aboriginal peoples within a community; 2) enhance student mobility by relaxing school boundaries, allowing parents to choose where to enroll their children; 3) designate magnet schools that will concentrate on Aboriginal studies; and 4) enrich certain schools by providing them with extra resources to be used to aid Aboriginal students. Among the four alternatives, Richards clearly favours the second option: enhance student mobility, which is more commonly referred to as the "school choice model." In this system funding follows pupils to whichever school they choose to attend. The other three options are also carefully considered and provided a degree of endorsement, but it is clear that these are seen as options that can enhance the school choice model and serve to appease those who argue for more culturally appropriate Aboriginal education.

To substantiate the assertion that enhanced student mobility can improve Aboriginal educational outcomes, Richards argues that for many Aboriginal families, their neighbourhood school often fares poorly in academics based on provincial standardized test scores (Richards 2006; Richards and Vining 2004). Therefore, requiring that Aboriginal parents send their children to their neighbourhood school means that many of these children will have to attend schools with poor academic standards. In support of this contention, Richards provides statistics from British Columbia's Foundation Skills Assessment[1] showing that Aboriginal students are overrepresented in schools that perform poorly and that there is a greater gap between the scores of Aboriginal and non-Aboriginal students in low performing schools than in schools in the top ranks. By relaxing school boundaries, Richards argues that parents can decide to enroll their children in better performing schools in other neighbourhoods where it is assumed that they will receive a higher quality education and thus have improved educational outcomes.

Parents, from this perspective, are seen as informed consumers of education who choose from among a range of competing products. For parents to be informed consumers in the education marketplace, they must receive relevant performance data with which to compare various schools. Having publicly available school achievement results thus becomes central to a market-based approach to education. Accordingly, proponents of market-based reforms, such as the Fraser Institute, advocate for and actively work towards the publication of school-by-school performance indicators for Aboriginal students attending institutions both on- and off-reserve (Cowley and Easton 2004; Cowley and Easton 2006).

With regard to on-reserve schooling, Richards recently produced a policy piece on Aboriginal educational attainment in which he advocated for the creation of professionalized First Nations school authorities responsible for administering on-reserve educational institutions (Richards 2008). This idea was also briefly discussed in his book, *Creating Choices,* as a mechanism for improving on-reserve education and, based on the few details provided, it is consistent with the free market approach. While the proposal is not thoroughly discussed in either publication, it is clear that the aim of Richards' plan is not to give more control over education to First Nations communities, but rather to remove control from local bands and centralize authority. The need to develop bodies and organizations that can provide support services to First Nations schools has been well documented (Mendelson 2008; McCue 2006). However, it seems that the main function of a centralized school authority as Richards envisions it is to establish curriculum and testing that is in line with the provinces (Richards 2006). As with his plan for off-reserve schooling, increasing accountability through standardized tests that can be used to inform parental decisions regarding schooling is a main element of the on-reserve proposal.

One of the key assumptions underlying the free-market approach is that the combination of school accountability (based on the publication of school assessment results) and parental choice will lead to overall school improvement by encouraging competition among schools. Drawing on economic theory, the argument is that when monopolies exist, as is the case when school board districts determine which school each student attends based on geographic area of residence, the quality of services provided will be lower. Educational institutions will have no incentive to provide information on their performance or to improve their performance, as underperforming schools will not be held accountable (Guillemette 2007). When parents are provided with school performance data and are able to choose from among schools, so the theory goes, they will tend to send their children to better performing institutions. Thus, schools that have weaker academic results will face declining enrolments and will be compelled to find ways to improve the education they provide, or risk closure.

However, if school performance is determined by ranking schools against one another, as is currently the case, there will always be low-performing schools, and these schools will very likely continue to be found in low-income neighbourhoods. This can have harmful implications for these schools. For example, school choice could lead to an even greater difficulty in attracting good teachers and administrators to low-income schools since this model assumes that low test scores are in large part a reflection of the quality of the teaching and administrative staff.

Furthermore, critics have argued that school choice models lead to academically successful schools becoming more selective of students based on academic and social characteristics. When operating in a competitive system, schools will choose those students that provide the greatest return on investment and increase the prestige of their school. This is especially detrimental to special needs students, whose education tends to be more costly and who may be perceived as lowering a school's performance results (Whitty 1997).

Contrary to the suggestion that school choice would lead to greater First Nations cultural programming and more diverse forms of educational delivery, Whitty (1997) suggests that school choice actually reinforces existing school hierarchies based on social class and academic performance. That is, the schools that are privileged in this system are those that conform most closely to the traditional education model, rather than those that attempt to innovate and provide culturally relevant education.

The economic theory that underlies this model is based on assumptions that simply do not have universal applicability. First, the model expects students have unimpaired mobility. This is clearly not the case in either rural or urban communities. In cities school choice could not be supported by school bus service, therefore the students with restricted ability to travel (low family income, for example) would be "stuck" in their neighbourhoods, while those with more mobility would leave the local school and further disadvantage it. Furthermore, for many First Nations communities, geographic remoteness precludes the possibility of real school choice.

The second flaw in this argument relates to the form of the advertising or information that allows rational choice to be made. Simply stated, provincial standardized test scores are not a good public measure for school evaluation (see White and Peters, Chapter 7). Finally, rational choice models work under certain limited assumptions: when the information is accessible to all making the choice and the choice is possible to make. That means those making decisions need to know their options and must be able to exercise the option. These assumptions do not hold up in the case of many Aboriginal peoples.

Nationalist Approach

First Nations have been demanding greater control over education for decades. Noting the destruction and harm wrought by federally run educational institutions as well as fundamental differences in the cultural values and educational philosophy of First Nations peoples, it is argued that First Nations should have full sovereignty over the education of their children. Furthermore, from the nationalist perspective, control over education is considered a key element of Aboriginal self-government

While there are many proponents of this approach, the AFN has played an important role in bringing it into the public arena. As outlined in Chapter 2, in 1972 the National Indian Brotherhood (NIB), the predecessor of the AFN, produced a paper titled *Indian Control of Indian Education*, which was a comprehensive philosophical and policy statement on the need for greater involvement of First Nations in education. After abandoning the 1969 White Paper on abolishing the *Indian Act*, the federal government accepted *Indian Control of Indian Education* in principle as its national policy statement on Aboriginal education. Centered on the concepts of parental responsibility and community control, *Indian Control of Indian Education* clearly stated that while the federal government remained financially responsible for providing the resources needed for Aboriginal education, authority over the delivery of education should be devolved to band councils. While *Indian Control of Indian Education* was not explicitly nationalist, it laid the groundwork for future work by the AFN.

In the decade following the adoption of *Indian Control of Indian Education* a number of band councils began to either partly or completely operate their own schools. However, it also became clear there were considerable disagreements over the meaning and scope of "Indian control" (Abele, Dittburner, and Graham 2000). Frustrated with the lack of progress being made, in 1988 the AFN produced *Tradition and Education: Towards a Vision of Our Future* in 1988, which advanced the main ideas expressed in *Indian Control of Indian Education*. While maintaining the call for Aboriginal control over education, it is here that we see the AFN's first clear articulation of a nationalist perspective on education, marking a turning point in how control was defined and understood.

The AFN's latest proposal for education, 2005's *First Nations Education Action Plan*, emphasizes jurisdiction and sustainability as the two central concepts necessary for transformative change in education (AFN 2005). Jurisdiction reflects the continued call for the acknowledgement of First Nations jurisdiction over all levels of education and for relations between First Nations and federal and provincial authorities to be on a government to government basis. The second key concept, sustainability, is central due to the recognition that First Nations jurisdiction cannot become a reality without secure, stable, and adequate long-term funding.

From these reports, we can glean the key elements of the nationalist proposal for Aboriginal education. First and foremost, it is argued that First Nations must have full and total control over education based on their inherent right to self-government. This is to include the power to develop education policies, control finances, create curriculum, and administer education services, as well as the jurisdiction to negotiate tuition agreements and culturally appropriate programs with provincial school boards where desired. Thus, it is argued that the education of First Nations students both on- and off-reserve at all levels should fall under the jurisdiction of First Nations themselves.

A second key element of the nationalist approach is the conceptualization of education as a transmitter of culture. From the nationalist perspective, education is not merely about attaining credentials or skills to be used in the marketplace. Rather, education is seen as part of a holistic learning experience that should affirm students' Aboriginal identity and give them the opportunity to learn their language and history.

Finally, nationalist approaches to education call for funding arrangements that can support the transition to First Nations–controlled education as well as the continued administration and development of education once the transfer has taken place. Burns (2001) points out that the devolution of education from the federal government to First Nations has been accompanied by a loss of the education infrastructure that was previously provided by the Department of Indian and Northern Affairs (DIAND), without the provision of adequate resources to develop this infrastructure for themselves. According to the AFN,

> First Nations must have the opportunity to design and develop appropriate institutions to deliver essential professional and administrative support to their schools and communities in areas such as curriculum development, specialized services, assessment, and other second- and third-level education services. (2005)

Thus, it is argued that for First Nations to successfully run their own education systems, the government must provide ample resources and support. However, it is also firmly maintained that while the federal government is obliged to fulfill its financial obligations to First Nations, this does not give the federal government the right to control or interfere in First Nations education.

Beyond these key elements, there are numerous ideas regarding how to conceptualize and implement education systems founded on Aboriginal self-government. The AFN has envisioned taking a leading role in negotiating recognition of First Nations jurisdiction over education at a national level and securing adequate and sustainable funding (AFN 2005). The AFN also calls for the establishment of First Nations education assessment systems at the local, regional, and national level to assist First Nations in developing effective education programs. However, they argue that the use of funds and the actual form that education systems take within communities needs to be decided upon by the communities themselves.

Wilson (2007) argues that the AFN's proposals are inadequate for bringing about First Nations jurisdiction over education because they fail to include the accountability measures needed to move beyond mere administrative control of education. Lacking these accountability measures, it is said that educational practice is decided arbitrarily by the political order of the day rather than truly controlled by First Nations peoples. He calls for the establishment of First Nations education acts at band, regional, and provincial levels that are developed by the First Nations themselves.

Conclusion

On the surface, Richards' recommendations appear to be closely aligned with those of the AFN. Both advocate for the creation of First Nations education systems that are supported by regional and provincial organizations and both argue for the development of assessment systems to improve the effectiveness of First Nations educational institutions. However, Richards' proposal is very different in one important aspect: it is driven by a market-based model of school choice. That is, while the AFN proposes to develop culturally appropriate assessment systems that can be used to empower First Nations to improve their school systems, Richards argues that schools should use standardized provincial assessment systems that allow parents to choose an appropriate school for their children. In Richards' plan, implementing educational assessments and developing regional education organizations are part of market-driven reforms designed to increase the accountability of schools to individual parents. School improvement, in this model, will come about through market mechanisms in which schools compete for student enrolment. If there are no students, there can be no school; therefore, it is argued that if a school is not meeting the expectations of its consumers (parents and students) the school will be forced to demonstrate improvements to attract students and avoid closure. For the AFN, the purpose of implementing educational assessments and creating regional education organizations is to help First Nations take greater control of their educational institutions while also improving the quality and cultural relevance of schooling.

In the midst of these proposals for policy change, the Department of Indian and Northern Affairs Canada (INAC) has recently unveiled their own plan, referred to as the Reforming First Nation Education Initiative. This initiative consists of two new programs: the Education Partnerships Program (EPP) and the First Nation Student Success Program (FNSSP), details of which were released in December 2008 (INAC 2008a; INAC 2008b). The EPP is designed to encourage and support tripartite partnership agreements between regional First Nations organizations, provincial ministries of education, and INAC. The partnerships are to improve coordination between First Nations and provincial schools and promote the sharing of expertise and service provision among partners. The FNSSP provides First Nations regional organizations or band-operated schools with funding to develop school success plans, implement student learning assessments, and adopt a performance measurement system.

Examining the government's new policy initiative in light of the free market and nationalist proposals for education, it is clear that while the government does not strictly follow either approach, their current direction is more inline with the free market approach. This is evident in both the guidelines of the two INAC new programs, as well as in the discourse surrounding the initiative. In terms of the programs, elements of the free market approach are evident in the emphasis on implementing provincial standardized assessment systems and the push for greater alignment with provincial schools. Although INAC does not call for the publishing of results nor do they advocate using results to track schools so that parents can choose which school their children should attend. Furthermore, the program guidelines for the EPP state that only regional First Nations organizations are eligible recipients of funding and FNSSP program guidelines state that priority will be given to regional organizations over individual band councils, in effect pushing First Nations to professionalize the administration of their schools. The discourse surrounding the initiative is also somewhat more inline with the free market approach, with the impetus for the program being framed in terms of the need to increase accountability, get greater value for money, and improve First Nation students' human capital. Nowhere in the government's discussion of the initiative is there mention of First Nations' jurisdiction over education or the relationship between education and self-government, and there is very little reference to the role of education in strengthening and supporting First Nations' languages, cultures, and knowledge.

If we look at the trajectory of the federal government's education policy overtime, as outlined in Chapter 6, it seems that this current initiative is very much inline with the government's position since 1973, which has been to formally accept and support "Indian control of Indian education" in theory, but to interpret "control" as primarily administrative. The new policy initiative is a continuation of this path, and represents further moves to align the First Nations system more closely with the provincial system, in effect also off-loading more responsibility to the provinces.[2]

Endnotes

1 The Foundation Skills Assessment (FSA) is a standardized achievement test in reading, writing, and numeracy that is administered province-wide in British Columbia. British Columbia is the only province that provides public data on the test results of the Aboriginal population.

2 It is also important to note that governments in Canada have also committed themselves to the nationalist approach in theory, negotiating a number of land claims and Self-Government Agreements with First Nations that either include or specifically refer to jurisdiction over education. Examples of these are the Nisga'a Final Agreement, the Mi'kmaq Education Act, and the James Bay and Northern Quebec Agreement. While the terms and scope of the agreements vary, educational jurisdiction is consistently limited by "meet or beat" clauses that mandate that First Nations governments must meet or exceed current provincial standards in education. This is a clear departure from the AFN's conception of an inherent right to jurisdiction over education.

References

Abele, F., C. Dittburner and K.A. Graham. 2000. "Towards a Shared Understanding in the Policy Discussion About Aboriginal Education." In *Aboriginal Education: Fulfilling the Promise*. M.B. Castellano, L. Davis and L. Lahache (Eds). Vancouver: UBC Press. 3–24.

AFN. 2005. *First Nations Education Action Plan*. Ottawa: Assembly of First Nations.

AFN. 1988. *Tradition and Education: Towards a Vision of Our Future, A Declaration of First Nations Jurisdiction Over Education*. Ottawa: Assembly of First Nations.

Burns, G.E. 1998. "Factors and Themes in Native Education and School Boards/First Nations Tuition Negotiations and Tuition Agreement Schooling." *Canadian Journal of Native Education*. 22(1): 53–66.

Cowley, P. and S. Easton. 2004. *Report Card on Aboriginal Education in British Columbia, 2004 Edition*. Vancouver: Fraser Institute.

Cowley, P. and S. Easton. 2006. *Report Card on Aboriginal Education in British Columbia, 2006 Edition*. Vancouver: Fraser Institute.

Guillemette, Y. 2007. *Breaking Down Monopolies: Expanding Choice and Competition in Education*. C.D. Howe Institute Backgrounder. No. 105. Toronto: C.D. Howe Institute.

INAC. 2008a. *Education Partnerships Program Guidelines*. Ottawa: Indian and Northern Affairs Canada.

INAC. 2008b. *First Nation Student Success Program Guidelines*. Ottawa: Indian and Northern Affairs Canada.

McCue, H. 2006. *First Nations 2nd & 3rd Level Education Services*. A Discussion Paper for the Joint Working Group INAC–AFN.

Mendelson, M. 2008. *Improving Education on Reserve: A First Nations Education Authority Act*. Ottawa: Caledon Institute of Social Policy.

Morgan, N.A. 1998. *Legal Mechanisms for Assumption of Jurisdiction and Control Over Education by First Nations*. Prepared for the First Nations Education Steering Committee (West Vancouver).

National Indian Brotherhood. 1972. *Indian Control of Indian Education*. Ottawa: National Indian Brotherhood.

Richards, J. 2006. *Creating Choices: Rethinking Aboriginal Policy*. C.D. Howe Institute Policy Study 43. Ottawa: Renouf Publishing Company Limited.

Richards, J. 2008. *Closing the Aboriginal/Non-Aboriginal Education Gaps*. C.D. Howe Institute Backgrounder. No. 116. Toronto: C.D. Howe Institute.

Richards, J. and A. Vining. 2004. *Aboriginal Off-Reserve Education: Time for Action*. C.D. Howe Institute Commentary. No. 198. Toronto: C.D. Howe Institute.

Whitty, G. 1997. "Creating Quasi-Markets in Education: A Review of Recent Research on Parental Choice and School Autonomy in Three Countries." *Review of Research in Education*. 22: 3–47.

Wilson, J.B. 2007. "First Nations Education: The Need for Legislation in the Jurisdictional Gray Zone." *Canadian Journal of Native Education*. 30(2): 248–256.

7

Enhancing Educational Attainment for First Nations Children

Jerry P. White, Julie Peters, and Dan Beavon

Introduction

Education has been targeted as a key issue for both federal and provincial policy for the coming years. After the November 2005 meeting of First Ministers and Aboriginal leaders, a statement was released in which participants pledged to eliminate the gap in K–12 educational attainment by 2016.[1] This policy decision is based on research foundations that document First Nations students as having patterns of lower educational achievement than the student population at large (King 1993, White and Maxim 2002). This lower attainment has been shown to be correlated with lower income (Maxim, White, and Beavon 2001), reduced well-being (Beavon and Cook 2003) and lower rates of labour force participation (White and Maxim 2002). Targeting education is also predicated on research indicating that there are real social and economic returns to improvements in human capital (White and Maxim 2003).

This report is aimed at developing a proposal for using incentives to improve the use of diagnostics in basic skills learning by First Nations children. Our thinking is that if the acquisition of the basic academic skills is problematic, then the problems of attainment, particularly at the high school level, may be explicable. Through encouraging the use of standardized testing of First Nations students, the problems and successes in skills transfer will be exposed. This may lead to improvements in both teaching methods and curriculum content over time.

This report has six aims:

1. To clearly present the problem First Nation students face in terms of educational attainment based on recent research presented at the Aboriginal Policy Research Conference.

2 To develop a review of relevant North American literature on dialogues and studies of performance-based assessment and standards-based reform of Aboriginal education.

3 To present a proposal that moves Canada closer to a full performance-based assessment of nationally recognized and culturally sensitive content standards as a basis for funding the growth of educational achievement. This will include a rationale for transferring funds to First Nations' communities, based on the number of students who train for and take provincial standardized tests. A

mechanism will be proposed for determining how the funds can be delivered and their criteria for transfer.

4 To outline the procedures and standard assessment tools used provincially in Canada.

5 To project a potential cost for a financial incentive program to encourage First Nations schools to enter into the standardized testing processes of the provinces. Scenarios will be developed that estimate the probable costs of the transfer under selected assumptions (annual vs. multi-year) and finally we will assess the possible returns from such a program (principally income and labour force participation).

6 To outline the future research and development that must be done to enhance the success of the proposed program.

The Problem of Attainment

Both older reviews and recent studies indicate that there is a gap in educational attainment between First Nations students and other Canadian students. Older reviews point to certain patterns of underachievement. First, high school completion rates are considerably lower among the First Nations population than among the rest of the population. In a study of First Nations students in Ontario schools, MacKay and Myles (1989) report that while the enrolment of students increased in the 1980s, the overall graduation rate from high school for Registered Indians remained considerably lower than the non-Aboriginal population. In the grade 9 cohorts that they studied, the graduation rate for Registered Indian students was between 33% and 55%, compared to reported completion rates for non-Aboriginal students of more than 70% in all districts (MacKay and Myles, 1989). Armstrong, Kennedy, and Oberle (1990) found, using 1986 national data, that only 25% of Registered Indians completed high school as compared with one-half of the non-Indian population. In 1986, Aboriginal people were also 2.2 times more likely not to complete high school than non-Aboriginal people. By 1996, that relationship was measured at 2.6 times more likely to have not completed high school (Tait, 1999).

A second significant pattern relates to post-secondary attainment. Siggner (1986) found that in 1971, less than 3% of the First Nations out-of-school population had attained any post-secondary education. Encouragingly, by 1981 that proportion had risen to 19%, but this was still less than half the national average. Only 23% of Aboriginal high school completers were going on to university by the early 1990s (King 1993).

Early studies also pointed to differences in levels of attainment on- and off-reserve. Generally speaking, First Nations people residing off-reserve have been shown to have greater educational attainment than people living on-reserve (McDonald 1991, Canada 1991). Census data from 1986 and 1991 showed that Registered Indians living on-reserve were almost twice as likely to have less than a grade 9 education than those living off-reserve. Status Indians living on-reserve were also less likely to complete high school (Canada 1995).

More recent studies have shown signs of incremental improvements. Between 1996 and 2001 the percentage of young Aboriginal adults (15+) with less than a high school diploma dropped from 54% to 48%. Those whose highest level of education was a high school diploma rose from 9% to 10% while those with any form of post-secondary credentials rose from 26% to 29%. However, the number of Aboriginal persons holding a university degree actually dropped from 5% in 1996 to 4% in 2001, although it should be noted that the proportion of non-Aboriginal peoples with university credentials also dropped by one percentage point during this time period (Mendelson 2006).

For most levels of educational attainment, the gap between Aboriginal and non-Aboriginal attainment narrowed between 1996 and 2001. However, if we look only at those aged 20–24 we find that differences stayed the same or actually widened in regards to having some post-secondary education, non-University post-secondary education and University post-secondary education. Furthermore, high school non-completion rates remain alarmingly high in this age group, with 43% of the Aboriginal population age 20–24 attaining less than a high school diploma in comparison to 16% of the non-Aboriginal population (Mendelson 1999).

In a 2002 study, White and Maxim looked at three non-traditional measures of educational attainment among Aboriginal students living on-reserve: graduation rates, withdrawal rates, and age appropriateness for the grade the students were in. Using 1995–1996 data, the graduate rate among the sample averaged 19.8 % and the withdrawal rate was 17.8%.[2]

For the third measure of educational attainment, the age-appropriate rate, it was found that Aboriginal students living on-reserve lagged behind the general population with approximately 46% of the grade 12 and 13 students being age appropriate for their grade. This was approximately 78% behind the non-Aboriginal population's age-appropriate numbers. These findings are supported by British Columbia studies, which indicated that 61% of Aboriginal students compared to 23% of non-Aboriginal students did not complete high school in six years and that Aboriginal students are behind age-grade level norms in every grade in every district examined (British Columbia 2000a, 2000b). White and Maxim also found that the age-appropriate rate was much higher among younger students than older students, with the rate among students in grades 9 or lower being 90.8% but dropping significantly to 55.4% in the high school grades.

White and Maxim also examined differences between band students who attend provincially operated schools and those who attend band-operated schools for the 1995–1996 and 2000–2001 school years. They found that band students who chose to go to provincially operated schools had a higher age-appropriate rate than those in band-operated schools, but that the students tended to withdraw in larger numbers from the provincially operated schools. Before grade 9, the age-appro-

Figure 7.1: The HDI Educational Index

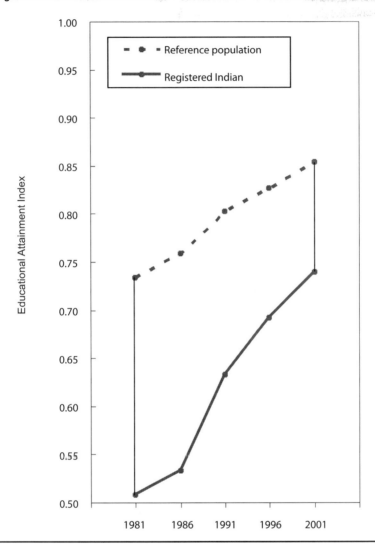

priate rate for students in provincial schools was 92.8%, while in band schools it was 86%. After grade 9, the age-appropriate rate drops to 62% for provincial schools and 43.8% for band schools. The withdrawal rate for provincial schools, however, is 18.2% compared to 11.8% for band schools. It was noted that provincial schools do not have a statistically significant different effect on graduate rates or withdrawal rates than band schools

In an update of this study, White, Maxim and Spence (2004) found significant improvements in the age-appropriate rate in both provincial and band operated schools over the five year period from 1995–1996 to 2000–2001. For provincial schools, the age-appropriate rate among school leavers increased from 49.2% to

Figure 7.2: Proportion of Registered Indians with a University Degree, 1991, 1996, & 2001

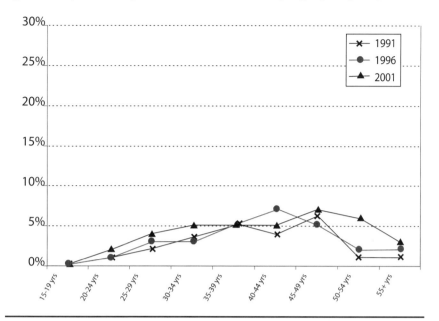

73.2% while the rate increased from 45.4% to 61.3% in band schools. Changes in the withdrawal rate by type of school were not calculated, but analysis showed that the overall withdrawal rate fluctuated yearly, decreasing from 41.1 in 1995–1996 to 30.3 in 2000–2001.

Identifying Accurate Trends Overtime

The studies discussed above indicate that there is a pattern of lower educational attainment among Aboriginal peoples. However, we are not able to clearly identify educational trends over time, as the studies used different population samples, different data sources, and different levels of attainment. Therefore, Census data on education for the Registered Indian population and the other Canadian population is presented here to enable analysis of changes in educational attainment over time.

Figure 7.1 is an examination of the educational component of the HDI measure developed by White, Beavon and Cooke (See Beavon and Cooke 2003, White and Beavon forthcoming). The HDI educational index is created using two measures. The first measure is the proportion of the population that has completed grade 9, and the second measure is the proportion of the population that has completed grade 12. The non-Aboriginal population is used as the reference population.

Looking at **Figure 7.1**, we first see that the Registered Indian population has shown tremendous improvement from 1981 to 2001. However, while significant progress has been made, a large gap remains between the Registered Indian

Figure 7.3: Proportion of Other Canadian Population with a University Degree, 1991, 1996 & 2001

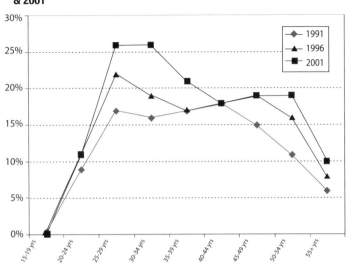

population and the non-Aboriginal population. We also see that as of 2001, the Registered Indian population is at the same level on the education index as the non-Aboriginal population was in 1981. Thus, the gap in grade 9 and grade 12 completions between the Registered Indian and non-Aboriginal population is closing, but very slowly.

We can also examine trend data for post-secondary attainment. **Figures 7.2** and **7.3** show the proportion of Registered Indians and other Canadian population, respectively, with a university degree for the years 1991, 1996, and 2001. The data is further broken down by age category. Looking at **Figure 7.2** alone we see that since 1991, the Registered Indian population has shown only modest increases in university-level attainment. When we compare this to other Canadians, shown in **Figure 7.3**, it is clear that the other Canadian population has seen significant increases in university attainment during this same time period, especially in the 25–29 and 30–34 years old age groups. This suggests that the gap in university attainment between the Registered Indian population and other Canadians has actually widened from 1991 to 2001 (Clement, 2007).

Figure 7.4 also looks at post-secondary attainment in a different way, presenting data on the percentage of the other Canadian population 15 and over who achieved a university degree for the years 1951 to 2001, along with the 2001 percentage for the Registered Indian population. This graph more starkly highlights the disparity in university-level attainment, showing that, as of 2001, the percentage of the Registered Indian population with a university degree was roughly equal to the 1951 attainment levels of the other Canadian population.

Figure 7.4: Proportion of the Population with a University Degree

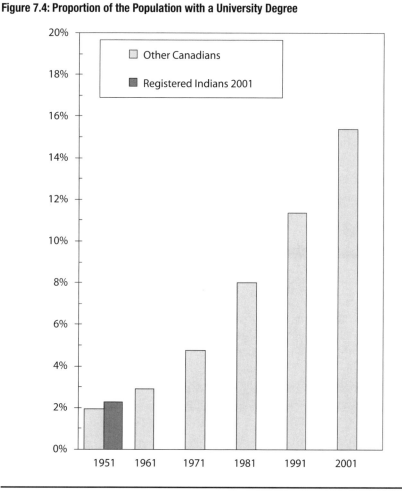

This trend data is important in that it demonstrates that while there has been success in reducing disparity at the lower levels of attainment, this has not been followed by a significant increase in university-level attainment among the Registered Indian population. Canada has a knowledge-based economy which increasingly demands ever higher levels of education for economic prosperity. Therefore, increasing high school graduation rates is positive but it also needs to be accompanied by improving university enrolment and completion rates, which does not appear to be happening.

The Importance of Increasing Educational Attainment

While the previous studies revealed attainment difficulties and gaps in achievement between Aboriginal students and non-Aboriginals, the returns to education for Aboriginal students who do succeed are dramatic. Hull (2000, 2005) has shown that higher levels of educational attainment among the Aboriginal population are correlated with significant increases in labour force participation, employment, and income, and with lower unemployment levels. The largest gains are made at two key benchmarks: completion of high school and achieving a post-secondary degree or certification. This indicates that formal education is a major factor in the First Nations population achieving economic parity with the rest of the country.

Educational attainment has also been linked to improved health and well-being. Aboriginal individuals with less than a high school education are far more likely to report being unhealthy than are individuals with a high school or post-secondary education (Wilson and Rosenberg, 2002). An individuals' educational attainment also has an impact on their child's well-being. According to the Aboriginal Peoples Survey, children of a parent with a university degree are far more likely to report having very good or excellent health than are children whose parent completed elementary school or less (Turcotte and Zhao 2004).

One of the brightest rays of hope lies in the finding that there are community correlates with educational achievement. The most promising is that as the average education increases in the parental population, there are incremental gains in students' levels of achievement. Spence, White and Maxim (forthcoming) have found that the level of education among the adults in a community is an important factor related to a higher age-appropriate rate and graduation rate and a lower withdrawal rate. Furthermore, Turcotte and Zhao (2004) have found that the higher a parent's education, the less likely it is that their child will ever repeat a grade. This indicates that as we make improvements in the achievement of this cohort and the next generation of students, these improvements will trigger even greater positive consequences in later generations.

Where Do We Go From Here?

While it is clear that there is a gap in educational attainment between Aboriginal youth and other Canadian youth, and that education can have an impact on employment, income, health, well-being, and community development, it is less clear exactly why such differences in attainment exist and what can be done to close the gap. The gap may be due to curriculum, instruction quality, social factors or a range of other issues. For the most part, there is also a lack of information regarding which specific areas Aboriginal students excel in, and in which they have greater difficulties.

Implicitly, this report argues that it is necessary to have some external device to assess the nature of these problems. More specifically, it suggests that provincial standardized tests could serve this purpose. But more important, this evaluation mechanism is proposed as an incentive system that transfers needed dollars while encouraging the development of better learning and improved achievement. We propose that a financial incentive be given to the bands, linked to educational issues only, based on the bands' having their students engage in the provincially administered standardized tests. The students from the First Nations communities that choose to attend the public schools are already subject to the standardized assessment programs. They can act as a crude control for comparative purposes between band-school-educated students and those who leave.[3]

We are not alone in recognizing this need. The Northern Aboriginal Education Circle, a group composed of educators in provincial and First Nations schools in Northern Ontario, encourages First Nations schools in Ontario to take part in provincial testing so that educators can get a baseline of how students are performing, targets can be set for improvements, and schools who are doing well can share best practices. Increasing data gathering, analysis, and setting targets for improvement is one of four key goals of the group's work plan. The Assembly of First Nations (AFN) has also identified information gathering and analysis as a key requirement needed to improve First Nations education. Without this information, they argue that First Nations are at a disadvantage in terms of identifying successes and failure and improving educational practices (AFN 2005).

One of the strongest advocates of the use of assessment systems for improving Aboriginal education has been Chief Nathan Mathew of the North Thompson Indian Band in British Columbia. Mathew believes that the data provided by standardized testing can prove to be a valuable tool in communicating needs to government bodies, educational authorities, parents, and the public. He argues that it is only by knowing how students are faring in different areas that meaningful dialogue about improving education for Aboriginal students can take place (Bell, et al. 2004).

In a report detailing case studies of success in Aboriginal schooling, Bell, et al. (2004) identify a strong link between the use of assessment data and performance. They note that the provinces that have assessment programs and use the data for improvement planning have shown the largest gains in Aboriginal education (321). Thus, they recommend that all First Nations schools measure, track, and report on student performance in part by participating in provincial assessments (324).

Furthermore, while band operated schools do not currently have to participate in provincial standardized testing, some schools have already chosen to do so. Two examples are Chalo School on the Fort Nelson Reserve in BC and Peguis Central School on the Peguis Reserve in Manitoba. Educators in these schools are said to have positive attitudes towards provincial standardized testing and believe that it provides them with useful information about their students (Bell, et al. 2004).

The inadequacy of current funding for Aboriginal education is also well known. The AFN has stated that First Nations are currently facing an education funding crisis which is hindering meaningful progress from being made in improving education outcomes for Aboriginal students. Over the last eight years, there has been a 2% funding cap for First Nations education which has contributed to the current underfunding. This funding cap can be contrasted with the provincial education systems, which have received on average a 3.4% increase per year during the same time period. The AFN (2006) estimates that over the next five years there will be a $1.2 billion funding shortfall for elementary/secondary schools. The Auditor General has also called attention to the inadequacy of current funding arrangements (2000, 2004). In a 2004 report, the Auditor General points out that the funding formula currently used to allocate core funding to band-operated schools, which has not been updated since it was created in the 1980s, is outdated.

This proposal aims to infuse much needed finances into education while developing benchmarks for future measurement and the assessment of possible improvement. This scheme would lay the first structures for performance-based funding and empirical studies of core strengths and weaknesses. The proposal is consistent with approaches being used in other jurisdictions. As we point out in a later section of this report, however, there are some very serious and important issues to confront in the medium term. These include the involvement of the First Nations, including parents, in the development of better test instruments and in the development of a long-range strategic plan for enhancing the educational attainment of First Nations students. In the next section we review the research done on standardized testing and standardized curricula, as it applies to First Nations.

The Scientific Literature and Research around Assessment, Standards, and Incentives

This review is directed at studies and discussions that have centred on the assessment of Aboriginal children in North America, and the issues surrounding standards-based reform and assessment. By standards-based reform we refer to the attempt to improve the core of what is taught in schools through a standardized testing mechanism.

The US Experience

Over the past few decades, the United States has been moving increasingly towards the use of national testing as an accountability mechanism—an assessment of student, school, district, and state performance—and a way of improving and standardizing school curriculum. The impetus for a national program came from research findings indicating that American students were lagging behind their peers in other countries around the world (Jennings, 1998). This problem was even more pronounced among disadvantaged and minority students, including the American Indian and Alaska Native populations. Thus, in an effort to improve the educational performance of American students, the US government has been trying to establish certain basics that all in the US students need to know, along with the level at which students should be able to perform the basic skills.

Through *Goals 2000: The Educate America Act* (1993) and the *Improving America's Schools Act* (1994), states were required to bring in new content standards and assessment systems. In 2001, the standardized testing regime was strengthened with the *No Child Left Behind Act* (NCLB). This Act mandates that all states must administer standardized tests in reading and math to students in grades 3 through 8 and at least once during high school. Testing in science must be carried out at least once in grades 3 to 5, grades 6 to 9 and grades 10 to 12. Previously, states would often administer different tests to students who performed at a lower level. A key change under the NCLB is that all students within a state, including students in the 184 schools administered by Bureau of Indian Affairs (BIA), are required to write the same test. States must submit assessment plans and results to the secretary of education and annual report cards for individual districts and schools are released to the public.

The act also mandates that each state must define the Adequate Yearly Progress (AYP) that is necessary in order to reach the goal of every student scoring at the proficient level in reading/language arts and mathematics by the 2013–2014 school year. AYP must be defined and met for all students as a whole, as well as for four subgroups: economically disadvantaged students, students from major racial and ethnic groups in the state, students with disabilities, and students with limited English proficiency. States, districts, and schools are required by law to meet AYP targets. For schools who fail to meet AYP for more than two consecutive years there are strong punitive measures, such as replacing school staff, restructuring, or state-takeover. Meeting the requirements of NCLB is also tied to Title 1 funding, which is the largest single federal funding source for education. Non-compliance with NCLB results in the withholding of Title 1 funds.

Implementation of the NCLB in Bureau schools has been a challenging process, as the BIA struggles with many of the same issues facing Indian and Northern Affairs Canada (INAC) in Canada with regard to educational attainment (BIA 1988). American Indian and Alaska Native students score lower on National Assessment of Educational Progress reading and mathematics assessments, score lower on the SAT exam, have higher rates of absenteeism, are more likely to drop out of school, and are less likely to enrol in college or university than the non-Indigenous population (Freeman and Fox 2005). Acknowledging the special challenges that BIA schools face in meeting the requirements of the NCLB, an executive order was signed in 2004 to study and report on the achievement and progress of American Indian and Alaska Native students and to establish an Inter-agency Working Group to oversee the implementation of the legislation.

While initially the BIA was to develop its own assessment system and targets to meet the requirements of the NCLB, this was later revised such that Bureau schools must now adopt their state's standards. This was done because when the requirement for new assessment systems was first mandated under the *Goals 2000 Act*, the Bureau of Indian Affairs decided to formulate its own national curriculum, standards, and assessment that all tribes would follow, but most Bureau schools chose to adopt the standards of the state in which they were located. Individual tribal school boards can develop alternative progress standards, but they must be approved by the secretary of education (Bureau of Indian Affairs, 2005). At the present time, most BIA schools use the content standards and assessment systems of the state in which they are located.

Fox (2001) has noted that the adoption of state content standards by BIA schools holds promise for three reasons. First, they encourage more common curricula among schools within states and clearer learning expectations across states. This is potentially helpful to Indian educators in meeting the needs of the students who transfer between schools. Because the BIA's schools have chosen to adopt the state standards in which they are located, the public and Indian schools have much more in common. Second, the content standards drive the curriculum; therefore educators, parents, and students can refer to them to provide increased focus on teaching and learning. Lastly, the new content standards encourage instruction improvement.

There is very little, if any, evidence that reliably assesses the outcomes of these changes in the US system. There are some very interesting observations, however, that have arisen in the process of implementation of these changes. A series of hearings and consultation sessions involving American Indian and Alaska Native educators, administrators, leaders, parents, and students brought forth many negative aspects of the NCLB legislation's affect on Indian education. In a preliminary report produced by the National Indian Education Association (NIEA), it is stated that while the majority of witnesses believed that greater accountability among schools and districts is a positive aspect of the NCLB, they did not believe that the legislation was having the desired effect and many felt that the legislation was actually leaving Native children behind (Beaulieu, Sparks and Alonzo 2005). A key problem appears to be that mandated assessment has not been accompanied with adequate funding. This has meant that districts and schools may have poor testing scores, but are not provided with the resources to improve performance.

This underfunding has also led schools to focus their existing resources on teaching to the test at the expense of liberal arts and Native language and cultural programming. In terms of the learning environment, the high stakes attached to assessment results and the pressure to achieve the mandated Annual Yearly Progress has created a climate in which students and teachers feel as though they are blamed for poor results, leading to higher dropout rates and higher teacher turnover. Concern was also voiced over the focus on annual school results, as opposed to individual student improvement. Finally, many argued that the NCLB is far too rigid and was constructed without consultation with Native peoples (Beaulieu, Sparks, and Alonzo 2005).

One positive result of NCLB that was discussed in the report was the increased data available on the performance of Native students (Beaulieu, Sparks, and Alonzo 2005). Under NCLB, the BIA must now publish a Bureau-wide annual report card as well as individual report cards for each BIA school. The report cards provide detailed information on student performance such as test results for language arts, reading and mathematics, as well as average daily attendance rates, graduation rates, and dropout rates. The student data is broken down by male/female and by Special Education and Limited English Proficiency groups. Data on educators is also provided, such as the number of teachers, teacher turnover, average school principal tenure and the number of core area teachers who incorporate culture or language into classes (See Appendix 2).

The 2005–2006 Bureau-Wide Report Card shows that 47.5% of students in BIA schools are performing at the Proficient or Advanced levels in language arts, 36.7% are doing so in reading and 29.8% in mathematics. Scoring below proficient is considered failing. These figures represent decreases in achievement from the 2004–2005 school year in reading and mathematics, with language arts remaining roughly the same. The report card also shows that less than one third of BIA schools are meeting AYP (Bureau of Indian Affairs, 2006).

While the high stakes testing regime ushered in by the NCLB is widely criticized, the US experience can provide insight into the uses and dangers of a large-scale assessment system. Standardized testing is not a panacea and cannot be thought of as the definitive determinant of a student's academic performance, but rather as one measure which can provide useful information regarding students' progress at the individual, school, and regional levels. The US practice of publishing individual school test results, mandating specific increases in achievement, expecting large results in a short amount of time, and tying results to high stakes penalties are seen by many to be having negative consequences. It is also important to keep in mind recent research findings showing a link between neighbourhood social capital and performance on standardized testing (Berthelot, Ross, and Tremblay 2001). In light of this information, it may be important to consider school performance within the neighbourhood context and to determine student and school progress based on individual improvement rather than in comparison with other schools or on the basis of a regionally mandated target.

The whole debate over testing, assessment, and standards is fascinating and can provide interesting perspectives for understanding the implications and potential flashpoints in the process. We will touch on a very few key issues in the literature.

The Limitations and Uses of Standardized Tests

The term "standardized testing" often carries a negative connotation among educators and in academic circles. Many of the concerns raised by those who oppose standardized testing are valid and should be considered. However, rather than dismiss standardized testing outright, these criticisms point to important precautions that need to be taken when implementing an assessment system. The following are five of the main criticisms that have been put forth in opposition to standardized testing.

Teaching to the Test

A common criticism of standardized testing is that it leads educators to "teach to the test" (Mehrens and Kaminski 1989, Wright 2002, Neil 2003). This term is used to denote a narrowing of curriculum, such that an excessive amount of time is spent preparing students to take the test at the expense of subjects such as physical education, music, art, and social studies, which are not tested. As Wright (2002) argues, the preoccupation with teaching to the test also leads to drilling students on basic skills rather than focusing on broader learning and higher order thinking.

The pertinent question here is "Will the effect of testing be to force teachers to cut non-core teaching, such as cultural programs, and concentrate on core competencies?" The answer has been that, yes, in some cases this has occurred when high stakes are attached to test results, such as when results are highly publicized and it is used as a competitive process to garner funding and prestige. However, there is no evidence that this need be so when the purpose is diagnostic. In fact, a US study showed that testing with low to moderate stakes did not result in teachers significantly changing what was taught in classrooms; that is, teachers were not found to be "teaching to the test" (Firestone, Mayrowetz, and Fairman 1998).

This also raises the issue of aligning testing and curriculum. Standardized tests need to be constructed in consultation with educators such that they accurately reflect what students should know. Thus, teachers should not need to spend an inordinate amount of time preparing students for the test. Rather, the test should reflect basic skills that are already part of the curriculum. Of course, the diagnosis may mean that math skill teaching appears substandard and that would hopefully lead to a shift in priorities.

Cultural and Language Bias

Bordeaux (1995) argues that standardized tests based on general population norms and using multiple-choice questions are culturally biased. This is because standardized, norm-referenced tests are "normed" based on dominant culture student populations and will therefore tend to miss-measure minority and low-income students. Research presented by FairTest (1995) indicates that performance on standardized, norm-referenced tests is highly correlated with socio-economic status. Very early studies such as McDiarmid (1972) discussed the role that poverty, health, and nutrition, social conflict, language, and test motivation play in the interpretation of test data. These issues have remained problems into the new millennium (Fox 2001). Green and Griffore (1980) argue that standardized testing is often culturally biased because the people who choose the test content and wording of tests, as well as the students used to "try out" the test, are often white and middle class. Thus, success on the test often assumes, and requires, knowledge of white, middle-class culture (FairTest 1995).

Language skills are also correlated with test outcomes (Fortune 1985, Brescia and Fortune 1988). Students who have any structurally limited use of English, such as any group whose first language is not English, are known to be at a disadvantage in standardized testing (Fox and La Fontaine 1995). This disadvantage appears when we rank students or try and use psychometric approaches to determine the student's ability to learn. On the other hand, using the testing process as a diagnostic tool, to determine deficits that may restrict First Nations from full participation in the economy, makes this a less critical issue.

These problems are particularly relevant to the First Nations population in Canada. As we noted earlier, First Nations students are more likely to come from low socio-economic households and may have non-standard English backgrounds. This raises the concern that First Nations students in reserve schools may score lower on provincial standardized tests more because of cultural mismatch than because of a lack of knowledge of basic skills. Therefore, it will be important to ensure that testing instruments are culturally appropriate. Apthorp (2002, 13), in a recent review of the literature on standards-based practices for Native American students, concludes with a set of recommendations that place the issues of cultural appropriateness in an easy-to-understand framework. She says that success in school settings depends on "developing and/or adapting curriculum and learning materials that incorporate every day and culturally specific knowledge in ways that connect with content-area knowledge and skills" that you want the student to acquire (Apthorp 2002,13–14).

Negative Psychological Effects on Students

The Canadian Psychologist's Association (CPA) makes an interesting point that public comparison and ranking of schools in Canada places a serious stressor on students and teachers. It raises the spectre of losing status within and between communities, and they note that such stress has led to problems across the US (CPA 2002). It has also been suggested that standardized testing can lead to increased dropout rates among low-scoring students. This has primarily been in relation to high-stakes testing, such as when students are not able to move on to the next grade unless they pass the test. In the US, instances of students being encouraged to drop out in order to increase schools' test scores are noted (Amrein and Berliner 2002).

The CPA proposal advocates that no ranking be done and only specific results be published. Care must also be taken in how test results are communicated to both teachers and students. Emphasis should be placed on understanding what the test scores do and do not convey, as well as how the new information can be used for improvement. While instances of increased dropout rates have been under high-stakes testing regimes, special attention should be paid to rates of non-completion.

Improper Comparisons

The first issue of concern is the potential problem of improper comparison across student populations. The results of tests for minorities, cultural subgroups and structurally disadvantaged persons, it is argued, cannot be compared with norms for general populations. This is primarily an issue in norm-referenced testing. Norm-referenced testing is when students are scored relative to their peers (e.g., a student may score in the top 5 percent) (Volante 2004). By definition, there will always be students whose performance will be considered poor by virtue of being in the bottom 5 or 10% of scores. As was discussed previously, students from lower socio-economic backgrounds have consistently been found to score lower on standardized tests. Therefore, it is likely that low-income students would continually be labelled as poor performers regardless of any improvements they may have made. The alternative to this is criterion-referenced testing, which is proposed here. Criterion-referenced testing involves clearly defining and articulating expectations so that students, parents and teachers know exactly what is expected at each level (Taylor 2001).

Another criticism of standardized testing is that results are often used to rank schools, as is done by the Fraser Institute in Canada. Comparison across schools, provinces or nations is seen as problematic (Canadian Teacher's Federation 2003a, 2003b, Fox 2001, Forbes 2000, FairTest 1995, Mcdiarmid 1972). This is because studies have shown that as much as 70% of the variation in student test scores is due to factors beyond a school's control, such as student, family and community level factors (Ungerleider 2006). For example, a school located in a low-income neighbourhood may have innovative, positive teaching strategies but appear to be performing poorly when ranked against other schools in higher-income neighbourhoods. Different schools also have different human and financial resources available to them. Therefore, focus should be on individual student and school improvement, and any broader comparisons should take contextual factors into account.

Assimilation and Forced Integration

The final major issue has to do with assimilation and forced integration. This is a very complex question. On the one hand the existence of a "test" that is common across large populations, such as a standardized process like the one we are exploring in this proposal, implies that the subject content of the test has been taught. The curriculum of the school is then somewhat determined and there is a pressure to conform to the dominant methods rather than addressing the roots of students' problems or the specific needs they have for specialized curricula (Canadian Teacher's Federation, 2003b). This has implications for the use of schools to maintain cultures and traditions among the First Nations peoples (Bordeaux, 1995). The issue of First Nations control of their curriculum therefore has to be addressed in the development of the plan to begin testing. However, as Demmert (2001) and Apthorp (2002) both point out, the core content is teachable in many ways. The job of the teachers and schools is to transfer the basic numerical, scientific, and literacy skills to the students in a way that they can relate to and understand.

Pewewardy (1998) argues that testing should not be permitted to curtail the Indian educators and parents from developing appropriate educational materials and strategies. The inability to do that can be a contributor to a system of forcing integration and resurrecting the past feelings and realities around forced assimilation. Deyhle and Swisher (1997) point out that the commonly held and espoused maxim was that "tradition is the enemy of progress" and that educators, often with the best intentions, argued that assimilation into the mainstream would be the best solution to poor performance at school and in the job market. Angela Willeto (1999) is one of many researchers (see also Rindone 1988, Platero 1986) who draw quite the opposite conclusions based on empirical research. She found that Navajo students with the highest participation rates in traditional activities and who spoke Navajo language, scored the highest on achievement tests. Coggins et al. (1997) and Cummins (1996, 2000) also come to the conclusion that maintaining traditional languages and cultures is not related to poor educational achievement. We can conclude that the issue is not what is taught, nor specifically how it is tested. The issue is how do we make schools places of both basic skills acquisition and culturally appropriate learning?

Uses of Standardized Testing

While there have been many criticisms of standardized testing, the literature points to many ways in which test data can be used effectively. The following are four common uses of standardized tests.

Identify Strengths and Weaknesses

Identifying strengths and weaknesses involves using standardized testing as a diagnostic tool. As a diagnostic tool, test results can point out areas where schools or classes are doing particularly well. In these cases, best practices can be identified that are contributing to success in the content area. It is hoped that successful schools can share their best practices with others. Testing can also point to areas where schools or classes are not seeing the desired results. In these cases, the test results identify a problem to be further examined. As Buly and Valencia (2002) have shown, a failing score on a standardized test can be due to many different underlying reasons. Therefore, it is important that the test score not be seen as the answer, but as an indicator of an issue that needs to be further explored.

Motivate Change

Building on the use of testing as a diagnostic tool, once a diagnosis has been made it can motivate change. Schools and teachers may realize that a particular approach is not working and they need to try something new, or that a special program may be needed for certain students who are having a particularly difficult time with the material.

The data provided by standardized testing can not only motivate instructional change, but also change among students. According to Natriello and Dornbusch (1984), when students are held to higher standards through testing it generally leads to higher class attendance and increased student effort. Bishop (1995) found that external examinations challenge students to do their best and encourages them to become more actively engaged in the learning process. Bishop also observed that in Canadian provinces with examination systems, parents were more likely to talk with their child about what they were learning in school.

Measure Change

Testing can and has been used to track trends over time. Depending on the frequency of testing, the results can be used to track change for an individual student, for a school, a region or the entire country. Testing can also be used to examine the effects of relevant government, school or community changes on performance. For example, the effectiveness of new educational programs or curriculum reform could be examined using trend data.

Supplemental Resource Allocation

Finally, standardized testing can also be used for resource allocation. There are different ideas and models of how this can take place. For example, Popham (2001) suggests that testing data can be used to allocate supplemental resources to low-performing schools. This money could be used for professional development, new educational materials, or for the development of educational programs to improve performance. Alternatively, supplemental funding could be allocated to those schools that show improvement as an incentive to improve performance.

Content Standards and Testing are Linked

The proposal to employ standardized test has two major anticipated outcomes. The first is diagnostic. We aim to determine what underlies the decreasing achievement between elementary and high school by first looking at the basic preparation of elementary level students. The second is to develop the skills and ability of First Nations students so they can redeem the rewards that better education gives the general population. Testing identifies weaknesses and strengths: policy change can build on the strengths and ameliorate the weaknesses. Conceptually, this is simple; however, it implies that the content of Aboriginal education will change. The content will be pushed to a higher (or different?) standard.

The testing process will simply help identify the weaknesses and strengths. It should encourage, through material incentive, a striving for better results in the classroom. The key to those better results is, according to much of the litera-ture, revamping what is taught and how it is taught by involving the Aboriginal community (Apthorp 2002, Fox 2000, 2001, Demmert 2001, Butterfield 1991, Charleston, et al. 1991). We cannot, nor should we, comment on how to fix problems and capitalize on strengths. That will be determined by the educators, those being educated, and the communities themselves.

The First Nations students will, on average, get lower test results than the general population. As Shields (1997) has noted, the common response will be denial and defensiveness:

> Denial frequently focuses on the inappropriateness of standardized tests as a measure of student performance and ultimately leads to a call for a total rejection of all standardized testing. The argument emphasizes the fact that test bias makes it difficult for children from other than the mainstream culture to achieve the test norms. There is no doubt that test bias must be factored into both expectations and interpretations of test scores for students from specific contexts; however, because the bias of the tests remains constant, scores on standardized tests may provide useful information regarding overall performance trends within a school or a particular district. (103)

She continues

> While denial rejects the validity of the tests as well as teacher responsibility, defensiveness emphasizes once again the nature of the students in the school—students with many of the characteristics that identify them as members of the "at-risk" population—low socio-economic status, single parent families, home alcoholism, illiteracy, health problems. This stance situates the "problem" in the students, their homes, and their community, rather than in the institutions and practices of schooling. (104)

Shields argues that it is the knowledge that there is a public stigma potential from the test that discourages students and causes the problems. If she is correct, this would help to account for persistent research findings that the school achievement of Native American children declines dramatically after the fourth grade (Coleman 1966, Deyhle 1983, McShane 1983).

> Deyhle's perception was that as Native American students understood the significance of poor performance on tests, and they "tried to approach tests seriously, their efforts seemed futile. It was at this point that the Navajo students seemed to 'give up'" (1983:77). Overcoming both the defensiveness and the denial are important steps to changing from an assessment that legitimizes (or delegitimizes) to one that empowers. (Shields 1997, 106)

This raises an important issue that much of the critique of the assessment process has to do with public comparisons made of students, schools, and communities, and the stigma attached with those comparisons. This indicates that the usefulness increases for testing when there is a private process of assessment and no public competition over results. Even where we see the effects of cultural bias, there are important consistencies with these effects, which can be assessed when interpreting the results.

The purpose of this paper is to propose standardized testing, outline a potential costing estimate, and point out the advantages that are potential to the successful increase in educational attainment. It should be understood as such and not as a test of ability to learn.

Understanding Testing in a Different Framework

Many of the issues raised in the review of the literature are tangential to the plan being explored in this paper—for example, the issue of cultural and language appropriateness for the standardized tests. It is true that the science of testing tells us that there may be inappropriate or culturally difficult references in the tests. These may put First Nations students with poor English language skills at a relative disadvantage if the aim of the test is ranked competition with the general population. However, the proposal to test the First Nations students should be understood as a process to see how well the First Nations students are acquiring basic skills that will be needed in order to participate in the wider Canadian economy. If the testing indicates there is a deficit in English language literacy, then that is what we want to find out, so we can develop those skills among the students. From that perspective, we are interested in discovering which of the basic skills have the lowest acquisition and which are better developed.

Future Research

Michael Marker (2000) makes the point in the *Canadian Journal of Native Education* that it is going to be necessary to conduct qualitative studies of settings where First Nations enter into collaboration with dominant mainstream institutions. This would include looking at the situations where students chose between reserve schools and public schools to ascertain the differences in experience and achievement. Currently, the First Nations Cohesion Project at the University of Western Ontario is conducting such a pilot study.

Apthorp (2002) calls for a large scale multi-site research project on educational experience and outcomes, and Fox (2000) notes we need to study the range of assessments and tests that could be used and developed. These are going to be helpful, but we need not stay our quest for improvement while we wait for more data. We can proceed with the tools we have.

Standardized Testing of First Nations Students: The Alberta Experience

The Province of Alberta has monitored the results of testing for First Nations students in grades 3, 6, and 9 from 1998–99 to 2000–2001. In their vision statement, Aboriginal Policy Framework (September 2000), they point out that they are seeking ways to improve the success rates of Aboriginal students in the province, and decrease the dropout rates.

One diagnostic tool they wished to use is the success rates of First Nations students on the grade 3, 6 and 9 standardized tests given to all Alberta students.

They note that the data are limited, as they can identify only "those First Nations students who live on reserve or who have previously lived on reserve." These students attend either a band school or have a tuition fee agreement with the school authority.

They report data for these students broken down into four subgroups. These include:

1 Band School Only: Students attend one or more band-operated schools.

2 Tuition Fee Agreement Only: Students have a tuition fee agreement with one or more school authorities outside the band.

3 Mixed: Students who attended a band school for part of the year and an outside school authority for part of the year.

4 Other: Students who had previously attended a band school or had a tuition agreement but not in the data gathering years. These are assumed to be living off-reserve.

Table A (see Appendix 3) indicates grade-specific levels of participation for the province. Alberta reports that the identified First Nations participation was 76.7% in grade 3, 71% in grade 6, and 53.3% in grade 9. The participation rate for all students was reported to be slightly more than 90% (Alberta 2003, 2). It is interesting to note that the rates decline as we move into the higher grades, driven particularly by absences from school on test days. Overall, First Nation students have a lower participation rate at all levels. The Alberta Learning Ministry notes in its assessment that the participation varies by school with some band schools at more than 90%. This would lend support to the argument that there are schools seeking to use the tests and be involved in the assessment process.

Table B (see Appendix 3) gives us a breakdown of the participation by type of school attendee. The same pattern observed in **Table A** holds, where First Nations students have lower rates of participation as we move higher in the grades. We can also see that the band school attendees have the lowest participation across the grades and the mixed category. This latter group includes part-year band school students who have the next lowest rates of participation.

Tables C and **D** (see Appendix 3) illustrate the results of the tests. **Table C** indicates the percentage of First Nations students meeting the "acceptable standard" according to Alberta Learning. Alberta notes (2003, 3) that 85% of the general student population are expected to achieve this acceptable standard. This was the case in most grades for most exams. However, in 2001, the general population scored 74.5% acceptable in grade 9 math, 79.7% in grade 9 science and 81.1% in grade 9 social studies. **Table D** breaks down the First Nations student population into subgroups based on where they take their schooling.

The tables illustrate that performance was much lower among the First Nations students. Again the pattern emerges that the success level declines as grade level advances. The best achievement among First Nations students was in grade 3, where slightly over one-half of the students met acceptable levels; by grade 9, those rates drop closer to 25% in many categories. It is also noteworthy that the students do best in the English Language Arts exam and worst in science and math.

The subgroups follow the same patterns of achievement as we saw in the participation rates. Band school students are the lowest achievers. The strongest group was the "other" category, which is those assumed to be living off-reserve and attending non-band schools. These students are often two or three times more successful.

The last two tables look at the achievement at the top of the spectrum. **Table E** reports the First Nations Students who met a "Standard of Excellence," and **Table F** breaks down the First Nations students who wrote and achieved the excellence designation by the school they attended. The Province of Alberta reports that approximately 15% of the general student population in any year on any test might be expected to meet the standard of excellence (2003, 5). Such was the case for 2001, except in math where 13.2% met the excellence standard.

Very few of the First Nations students met the standard of excellence. In many categories there were no students who met the standard, in many others it was less than 1%. When we examine **Table F** we can see that Grade 3 Tuition Fee Agreement students and "other" students did better on math. We can see a pattern where the students in the "other" category were generally the strongest, followed by the tuition fee students. Other students may well be attending private schools or the like but what is clear is that the lowest performers are those who attend band schools for a part year or full year. Finally, we provide a case study of a band-operated First Nations school that is currently administering Ontario's EQAO exams to demonstrate some of the challenges and benefits of standardized test taking as experienced by one First Nations school (see Appendix 1).

The next section outlines the guiding principles of the proposal to encourage standardized test taking, we then outline the projected costs that would be associated with the several different models for funding the proposal.

The Proposal and Some Guiding Principles

The proposal has several practical aspects:

1 Offer funding on a per student basis for each student who writes the provincial standardized test for their appropriate grade. The funding will be for every band member, in elementary or high school, whether they go to a band school or to a public/Catholic school near the community. This provides an incentive to have the students write and infuses cash into the educational system to fund improvements, regardless of the results.

2 The band will be responsible for securing the exam results from the public/ Catholic school boards and transferring the results to Indian Affairs. This should be possible given the tuition arrangements between INAC and the

provinces.

3 The test results will not be used to determine all funding, nor will communities be publicly ranked or have their test results released publicly. The models propose several scenarios. We have built in an additional sum that would be given for each student who meets minimum standards. This will encourage the bands to use the money to improve achievement without creating adverse community results. The models are based on varying the amounts paid to write and to succeed, and offer the possibility for making changes in these amounts to increase the emphasis on achievement over time. For example the transfer for writing could be reduced and the success payment increased over time. The models give policy-makers the option of beginning with public school only or doing the high school program as well. Other models can be developed where year-to-year improvements receive rewards, or that reward the public schools and band schools differently.

4 The results will be evaluated by teams of trained individuals specific to each province. The aim will be to diagnose the strengths and the deficiencies in basic skills acquisition.

5 Teachers and educators in the First Nations communities will be given the results of these tests and asked to make improvements based on the diagnosis. INAC will develop a plan and policies based on its assessment of the results. This could include the promotion of curriculum development projects, advisors for band education officials, or a range of other options.

6 The proposal is developed with potential problems in mind. For example, if INAC were to reward only band school attendees this could cause social disruption, where bands exert pressure on families to use the band school and not send children off-reserve.

The proposal can be divided into different options. For example, it may be possible to begin with the primary school populations first and move to secondary schools in the future. There is a basic and reasonable method of creating controls that have built-in norms based on First Nations populations. There are many communities where the students choose between the band school and the public school near the reserve. This allows us to compare the band school attendees with the public school attendees. It could be argued that developing a solid diagnosis at the primary level will permit the building of a foundation at that level on which to build.

The bands will be given funding for every student who writes the standardized tests. Therefore, the public school attendees will have to have the results passed from the public school to INAC through the band. This provides potential diagnostic possibilities concerning content of curricula in the two systems.

Models for Funding Participation in Standardized Tests

Generating Cost Models

For this analysis, two basic costing models are constructed. The first is based on test administration within elementary schools only; hence, only grades 3 and 6 are included. The second model assumes that tests are administered in grades 3, 6 and 9. These grades have been selected since they represent the typical grades in which standardized tests are administered in most provinces.[4]

Within each model, two elements or parameters are considered. The first element is based on a per student allocation for each student who writes a standardized test. The access to funds would have to be made equitable, which would mean developing mechanisms to deal with intra-provincial variations in testing regimes.

The second element is an amount provided for each student who achieves or exceeds the provincial "bar" or expectation for the exam.[5] While standards vary from province to province, we have chosen to use the norms and achievement rates from the province of Alberta as a basis for constructing the models. A single province was selected as the basis of analysis in order to simplify the analysis. Detailed, province-by-province figures could be used, but a preliminary investigation suggested that such an exercise only increases the complexity of the analysis without changing the results substantially.

Alberta provides a good example case for several reasons. Its expectations for performance on standardized tests are not inconsistent with those of the other provinces. Furthermore, not only does Alberta have a substantial First Nations population, it is one of the few jurisdictions that has provided an analysis of Registered Indian students separate from the general school population.

The first phase of the model is relatively simple. We will assume that a nominal amount—say, $100—is provided for each student writing the standardized test. The second phase will provide a more substantial amount for each Registered Indian student equalling or exceeding the base score for acceptability.

Table 7.1 summarizes the number of Registered Indian students in grades 3, 6, and 9, enrolled in either a band school or off-reserve school across Canada in the year 2000. Assuming a 100% participation rate, the cost for the test writing incentive (based on a fee of $100 per student) is listed in **Table 7.2**.

In Alberta, the proportion of Registered Indian students writing the test is less than 100%, particularly in the on-reserve schools. Thus, these figures might be considered the "maximum exposure" for the program based on the current population of students. Using the estimated rates of writing from Alberta—about 40–71% for on-reserve schools and 65–81% for off-reserve schools—the actual amount would be approximately $573,000 less for the elementary grades only and $845,000 less for all three grades.[6]

Table 7.1: Number of Registered Indian Students in School

	On-reserve	Off-reserve	Total
Grade 3	6,072	2,586	8,658
Grade 6	5,064	2,510	7,574
Grade 9	4,467	3,746	8,213
Total	15,603	8,842	24,445

Table 7.2: Cost of Writing Test Incentive by Grade

	On-reserve	Off-reserve	Total
Grade 3	$607,200	$258,600	$865,800
Grade 6	$506,400	$251,000	$757,400
Total elementary	$1,113,600	$509,600	$1,623,200
Grade 9	$446,700	$374,600	$821,300
Total all grades	$1,560,300	$884,200	$2,444,500

Table 7.3: Estimated Number of Student Attaining Acceptable Results

	On-reserve	Off-reserve	Total
Grade 3	1,214	1,552	2,766
Grade 6	1,013	1,506	2,519
Grade 9	893	1,236	2,130
Total	3,121	4,294	7,414

Estimating the cost of the program component for students achieving or exceeding expectations requires slightly more consideration. This comes about because the per student amount we wish to provide the schools is substantially larger and, under current conditions, the proportion of Registered Indian students passing the provincial norm is substantially lower than the average for the overall population. While the figures for Alberta vary across grade and year of testing, approximately 20% of the on-reserve elementary school students achieve or exceed the expected bar. This is also the situation with grade 9 students attending on-reserve schools.

The figures are substantially different, however, for students not attending band schools. About 60% of the Registered Indian students in both grades 3 and 6 exceed the provincial norms, while only about 33% of the grade 9 students do so. Extrapolating this pattern nationally, we would expect about 7,400 of the total 24,500 students to achieve an acceptable score. Broken down by grade and type of school this would work out as listed in **Table 7.3**.

Assuming an award of $2,500 per student, the cost of this component of the program would be as indicated in **Table 7.4**. Combining this amount with the $100 writing fee would result in the costs listed in **Table 7.5**.

Table 7.4: Estimate Cost for Students Achieving Acceptable Standard

	On-reserve	Off-reserve	Total
Grade 3	3,036,000	3,879,000	6,915,000
Grade 6	2,532,000	3,765,000	6,297,000
Total elementary	5,568,000	7,644,000	13,212,000
Grade 9	2,233,500	3,090,450	5,323,950
Total all grades	7,801,500	10,734,450	18,535,950

Table 7.5: Total Estimated Cost for Students Writing Exams Based on $100+$2,500 Model

	On-reserve	Off-reserve	Total
Grade 3	3,643,200	4,137,600	7,780,800
Grade 6	3,038,400	4,016,000	7,054,400
Total elementary	6,681,600	8,153,600	14,835,200
Grade 9	2,680,200	3,465,050	6,145,250
Total all grades	9,361,800	11,618,650	20,980,450

Table 7.6: Estimated Amounts Available per Student Achieving Acceptable Standard Based on Program Ceilings

Elementary Grades Only				Grades 3, 6, and 9			
		Program cost ceiling				Program cost ceiling	
Percent meeting standards	Expected number of Students	$15 million ($13.4 m available)	$30 million ($28.4m available)	Percent meeting standards	Expected number of students	$15 million ($12.6m available)	$30 million ($27.6m available)
30	4870	$2747	$5827	0.3	7334	$1712	$3757
40	6493	$2060	$4371	0.40	9778	$1284	$2818
50	8116	$1648	$3496	0.50	12223	$1027	$2254
60	9739	$1374	$2914	0.60	14667	$856	$1879
70	11362	$1177	$2497	0.70	17112	$734	$1610
80	12986	$1030	$2185	0.80	19556	$642	$1409

Thus, for the elementary schools, the total cost would be about $14.8 million while for all three grades the total cost would be about $21.0 million.

Should the incentives provided by this program succeed, the expected number of students achieving the provincial standards ought to increase substantially. In Alberta, the expectation for the general population is that 85% of the students will meet or exceed the bar. If the Registered Indian students achieved this overall success rate, the total cost for the two elementary grades would be approximately $36.1 million, and $54.4 million for the three grades combined.

To limit the liability of the program, it might be considered prudent to place a cap on the total amount available. Such a cap can not only be justified on the basis of limiting exposure, it also makes programmatic sense since it is likely that the incremental resources needed per student to achieve higher success rates is greater with smaller rather than larger percentages of students exceeding the norms. Furthermore, the larger per student amount provided at the lower rates of success will likely provide a greater incentive to help the students improve their performance.

For illustrative purposes, total program caps of $15.0 million and $30.0 million have been imposed. Assuming that $100 will still be paid for each student writing (at 100% participation), this would leave $13.4 million and $28.4 million available respectively for the elementary grades only.[7] Providing incentives for grades 3, 6 and 9 would result in $ 12.6 million and $27.6 million being available for distribution.

Table 7.6 shows the estimated number of eligible students and the amount available per student for overall success rates ranging from 30% of the student population to the general norm of 85% of the student population. Thus, for a total program cap of $15 million and considering elementary grades only, $2,700 would be available per student if only 30% of the students achieved the expected standard. This amount would decrease to $970 per student with 85% of the students achieving the standard. The corresponding amounts would be $1,700 and $600 per student if all three grades are included in the program.

One factor that has not been considered in this modelling exercise is the impact of increasing numbers of students. First Nations communities have a higher than average birth rate which is resulting in a rapidly increasing student population relative to the rest of Canada. This would clearly result in the amount of monies available per student decreasing over time under a "capping" scenario. Similarly, we might expect the retention rate to increase slightly among the grade 9 students given the economic incentives to increase the number of students writing the exams and to do well. The program also allows for adjustments for inflation and population change.

Concluding Comments

This program proposal is an incentive. It is designed to create the positive conditions for First Nation students, schools, and educational structures, at the band level, to achieve increased successes through better programs of education.

How might the program act as an incentive and what might be accomplished? At the base of this proposal is a material incentive. We can see from the Alberta data presented earlier that the numbers of students who absent themselves from the standardized testing process is quite high. The transfer that is based on each student who writes creates a positive incentive to increase the student participation. The second level of incentive relates to achievement. Given that the transfers of funds increase rapidly, with increases in the students who reach minimum acceptable levels, there is a positive incentive to build programs for success.

The key element here is that the levers for change stay in the community, with the parents, teachers and band. These stakeholders can use the funds in a variety of ways that are community sensitive with regards to aims within their cultural and social goals. The basic shape of the incentive system itself sets participation and achievement as the goal but the road to those achievements can vary widely depending on the community needs.

Funds can be directed to building teacher resources. The hiring of teachers, retention of teachers and/or the employment of tutors and educational assistants are all possible. We noted in an earlier section that parent involvement is highly correlated with success according to studies in other jurisdictions. Funds could be used to encourage greater parent-teacher and parent-school interaction. Elder involvement programs could also be developed. The issue of cultural survival and cultural appropriateness could be addressed. Funds could be used to develop curriculum materials that address these issues. Whereas in some jurisdictions, teaching Aboriginal languages have had to be limited, new programs could be funded. Weekend schooling in specialized subjects could be started. The potential is really limited only by the imagination and the needs of the community themselves.

The incentives program we propose here has the advantage of having built-in measurement systems and cost containment. Given that the models allow one to forecast maximum exposure financially, there are protections against overruns. Most importantly, given the standardized testing system, both INAC and the community themselves can see what the results of the program really are. Very successful initiatives can be popularized through the sharing of best practices which will help all communities. This focus on the positive is also a major issue with First Nations that see the negatives reported too often.

This proposal cannot be a panacea, but it has tremendous potential. It avoids costly creations of new structures that are divorced from the First Nations communities themselves. It is relatively easy to administer and puts the majority of any transfer payments into the hands of the people working on the problems.

Appendix 1

While First Nations schools are not required to participate in standardized assessments in most provinces, a number of schools have chosen to do so. These schools provide an opportunity to examine the issues that arise when implementing and administering provincial assessment systems in band-operated schools. In what follows, we examine the use of Education Quality and Assessment Office (EQAO) exams in one First Nations school in Ontario. While this is only one school's experience, it can provide insight into the issues, benefits and problems that can result from administering standardized testing in First Nations schools.

Methods

Semi-structured qualitative interviews were conducted with twelve teachers and one school administrator in April 2008, at a First Nations school in Ontario. The teachers interviewed taught grades 2 through 8, with the exception of one language teacher and two resource teachers. Five of the teachers were male and eight were female. Approximately half of the interview participants were Aboriginal. The majority of the respondents had experience with administering the EQAO testing, while for a few EQAO was relatively new and unknown.

Interviews lasted approximately 45 minutes and were conducted in a private room in the school during school hours. The interviews were recorded and then transcribed. Transcribed interviews were mailed to participants to give participants the opportunity to confirm the accuracy of the transcript and to add or clarify any points. The verified interview transcripts were then analyzed following Strauss and Corbin's (1990) coding process. This involved beginning by coding interview data into relatively open categories, progressively building more specific coding schemes and eventually developing more selective categories, showing the relations among categories, and validating the relationships with the data.

Teaching to the Test, Emotional Distress and Cultural Bias: Assessing Common Criticisms of Standardized Testing

Teachers were familiar with the common criticisms of standardized testing and had clearly thought about many of the issues before being asked in the interview setting. Below, we outline teachers' responses to and feelings about three of the common criticisms of standardized testing: teaching to the test, emotional distress, and cultural bias.

Teaching to the Test

Teaching to the test generally refers to spending a disproportionate amount of classroom time focusing on the subjects and content that will be covered on the exam at the expense of other areas, and using the format of the test as a model for teaching. In the case of the EQAO exams, the subjects tested are reading, writing and math, and questions are generally in a multiple-choice and short-answer formats.

Teachers interviewed noted, positively, that since implementing EQAO, learning had become more integrated, in that basic skill development was included in all subject areas. For example, many teachers discussed working to include reading and writing strategies in subject areas such as science, social studies, and drama. In this way, some teachers argued that teaching to the test was not an issue as instruction time on non-tested areas did not decrease. However, the majority of teachers stated that a concern for doing well on the testing and the need to cover a lot of curriculum before administering the test necessarily leads to an increased focus on the subjects and subject content that they know will be covered on the exam. This was particularly the case in grade 3 and 6 classrooms, where teachers felt pressure to ensure that the curriculum content included on the test had been fully covered in class prior to the administration of the exam in May.

While literacy and mathematics are seen as important subjects, focusing on them to the exclusion of areas such as science, social studies, drama, music, and art was argued to take away from the fun, creative elements of schooling and to be particularly disadvantageous for students who excel in these areas. As one teacher stated:

> That's the fun of school and sometimes that's the only level playing field that some kids have is to be, you know, if they are good in art, they just feel so proud that they can do something better than anyone else in the class. And a lot of times it's the ones that are lower levels of EQAO, they are struggling in school and this is where they excel and we are almost taking it away or discounting its importance.

The majority of teachers felt that there needed to be more balance in the amount of classroom time spent on different subject areas, though it was clear that the reality of the testing for grade 3 and grade 6 teachers made this a difficult task.

Testing and Emotional Distress

Standardized tests are often argued to be a significant source of stress and anxiety for both teachers and students. For the teachers interviewed who had observed students taking the EQAO exams, most noted that some students would become upset and anxious before and while writing the test. However, many teachers pointed out that this was not specific to the EQAO exam, but that some students would experience test anxiety with a math, language or science test as well. That is, some students will experience nervousness and anxiety regardless of the type of test being administered. The degree of emotional distress experienced by students often has more to do with how the test is framed and explained than due to the actual content of the test itself. One teacher explained:

> I really focus on making it as stress free as possible, as far as building up to it. It is like "aw, guys it's just an hour in the morning and then we are going to have fun the rest of

the day." And they don't get that stressed out about it, building up to the tests. There is definitely nervousness, but I think that's always going to be there, but I try and really actively attempt to diffuse it as well as I can, to make it no big deal.

Teachers felt that not making a "big deal" out of the test could help to reduce students' stress and nervousness. Further, some noted that ensuring students were well prepared and understood the purpose of the test was also important to easing anxiety and making the experience as minimally stressful as possible.

In terms of the anxiety that standardized testing creates for teachers, the majority of the teachers who taught grades in which the testing is administered found testing to be a very stressful time. While they appreciated that the testing had recently been relabeled the "primary test" and "junior test" as opposed to the "grade 3 test" and "grade 6 test" in recognition that preparing students was a collaborative effort, they still experienced stress and pressure in their desire for their students to succeed. Positively, none of the teachers administering the testing felt external pressure from administration, the board, or other teachers to improve students' scores and did not feel that they would face negative repercussions if the test results were poor. Rather, many teachers noted that the school worked as a whole to develop strategies to improve on areas where test results showed weakness, as opposed to promoting test taking strategies or encouraging teachers to teach to the test.

Test Format and Questions: Culturally Biased?

Teachers had mixed views about the cultural appropriateness of EQAO exams for their students. While some felt that recent improvements in the test had removed any concern about cultural bias, others stated that the wording of certain questions and the format of the test itself can sometimes disadvantage First Nations learners. Test questions deemed to be problematic were those that involved references to aspects of urban living, such as riding a subway, reading a bus schedule, or walking down a sidewalk, as well as questions that included ethnically diverse names. Students can often get "stuck" on these questions, and given that teachers are not allowed to offer any assistance—for example a teacher would not be able to tell the student that the unfamiliar word is a name—the student can lose time or answer a question incorrectly because of a trivial element of the test question. However, almost all teachers who talked about biased test questions pointed out that this was not a concern only for First Nations students, but was more of a socio-economic or urban/rural issue. It was also noted that there are typically only a couple of problematic questions any given year, and that test bias such as this does not completely determine test results.

In terms of the format of the exam itself, concerns were raised that the way in which the test is administered conflicted with the style of teaching that is currently being encouraged. One teacher articulated this particularly well:

My big problem with EQAO is the fact that good teaching practice these days is group experience. Kids working to explore, find answers, critical thinking, working with everything from whole groups to pairs, triads, these sorts of things. And when EQAO rolls around, it is, ok, everybody at their own desk, dividers, no one is allowed to talk, no one is allowed to discuss anything. The test goes against everything we are being taught on how to teach these guys. It's the exact opposite style of what we are doing on a daily basis.

Thus, there is seen to be a large disconnect between current "best practice" teaching methods and the format of the EQAO assessment. It was also noted that First Nations students often demonstrate their knowledge better in hands-on activities and by exploring and finding answers as opposed to the paper and pencil format of EQAO. Participants did not see any clear solutions to these issues, as many acknowledged that it would be difficult to administer a standardized exam that reflected the current teaching practice of using group work and that involved more hand-on activities.

It is important to note that even participants that felt that there was some cultural bias in the EQAO assessments did not feel that the testing should be stopped for this reason or that it was creating cultural bias in their teaching practices. While the core content that is taught in classrooms may need to be similar to the public school system due to the testing, the way in which the content is taught can and needs to be culturally relevant:

> So a lot of people don't understand the importance or results of that standardized test and they think, oh that's just a biased test, and our kids don't need to know that. Well, they are not going to learn the same way, they are not going to learn the information the same way as everybody else, I'm going to teach it to them in a way they understand it . . . using the strategies that they are comfortable with to get them up to the next level. And I think a lot of parents, and maybe some teachers I guess, think well that's not for our students. We don't need to do that. I think we need to do it, we are just going to do it in a different way to get there.

Administering a standardized exam presupposes that certain curricular content has been taught. However, as this teacher suggests, the testing does not have to determine how students are taught this content on a day-to-day basis. Teachers can adapt the curriculum and teach it in a way that is appropriate for their students.

One idea that has been considered is to develop a test specifically for First Nations students. When participants were asked whether this would be a positive development, responses were mixed. A few teachers did not want a test devised specifically for First Nations, noting the great cultural diversity among First Nations themselves, as well as a concern that parents may see it as a second rate test. However, about half of the participants felt that the possibility of creating a test specifically for First Nations schools that would better reflect their students' cultural backgrounds should be explored. For the time being, the school does not have the resources necessary to create and administer their own standardized assessment that is personalized to their student community and it is not immediately clear what body or organization could take on such a task.

Benefits of Testing

Over the course of the interviews, many positive aspects of administering the EQAO testing emerged. These benefits have been lumped into three main categories: increased resources and funding, improved classroom instruction, and better preparation for high school.

Increased Resources and Funding

By far the most often cited benefit of using EQAO was the extra resources and funding that administering the test has accrued to the school. Given the widespread under-funding of First Nations elementary institutions, schools such as this one need to battle for funding year after year and be creative in how they seek out resources. Both teachers and administrators argued that administering EQAO gives the school administration hard data that is recognized by provincial and federal authorities that can demonstrate the schools' needs. This data can be used to show that the school requires extra support services and to lobby for additional educational resources. The year-over-year results also provide a mechanism to demonstrate the improvement that the extra resources are making, which helps in turn to garner further resources and funding. That is, the school can show funding agencies that they are putting the extra dollars to good use and that future funding will be put to good use as well.

For this school, the ability to clearly demonstrate the needs of their students through EQAO has meant extra educational assistants; additional time with speech pathologists, counsellors, and other specialized second-level services; more professional development for teachers; and a new developmental reading assessment program that includes a book room and a literacy coach that works with the primary teachers. One teacher noted that they now had a full time educational assistant in math, which was desperately needed, because of the test results. Reflecting the feelings voiced by the administration and many of the teachers, one participant commented:

> I think the results have been an eye opener, that we can say, ok, see we need a speech pathologist, we need EAs in our classrooms, we need counselling, we need all these other specialized services. So it's been used as a tool to get funds, to get people, to get help for our students. So that's what I think the main positive thing is as a result of doing these tests ... We can completely show these are our scores, this is what we need. It's all concrete.

In the current reality of unstable funding and continually battling for resources, the test results are being used as a means to garner additional funds to meet the schools' needs. For many of the teachers, it is these types of benefits that make participating in the testing most worthwhile.

Improved Classroom Instruction

Another positive aspect of administering EQAO cited by many teachers was that it had improved their classroom instruction techniques and strategies. It was argued that participating in EQAO and working to prepare students for the test has helped to keep teachers current with the curriculum and with best teaching practices. For example, one teacher noted that the leveling EQAO uses to grade responses had encouraged them to teach students how to build better answers in steps. According to this teacher:

> It [EQAO] helped us to understand I think as teachers, how to get the kids to communicate better, but in stages, as opposed to saying 'ok, this is the perfect sentence and this is a perfect paragraph,' and never really showing them how to build up to that.

By teaching students new literacy skills in stages, students can better understand the process of building upon elementary skills to improve their oral and written communication.

Classroom instruction has also been improved through the professional development that has accompanied the implementation of EQAO. Due to EQAO, teachers of grades 3 and 6 have been sent to professional development days with a local provincial school board to learn more about the testing and how to ensure students are well prepared. One teacher in particular noted that this had led them to adjust their teaching style:

> I have [had to adjust my style of instruction] but I think for the better. I think a lot of the things I have learned through professional development and speaking with others is really best practice ... I think the things I do in the classroom aren't necessarily for EQAO, I think it helps the kids overall. It's best teaching practice, but it's come about because of EQAO.

Thus, EQAO had led to additional professional development that has kept grade 3 and grade 6 teachers current on new teaching strategies and best practices. Whether and how this gets filtered to other teachers in the school is unclear, but ideally the best practices would be shared with and discussed amongst the teachers who did not receive the professional development as well.

In addition to the best practices learned from EQAO focused professional development, administering EQAO has helped to provide both individual staff, and the school as a whole, direction and goals to work towards. The test results are used by many teachers to see where students are having difficulties and where instruction needs to be improved. While few reported that they used EQAO test scores to assess where individual students excelled or needed improvement, teachers were more likely to look at the schools' overall results and use these to focus on areas where students had done poorly.

At the school level, this has been translated into division-wide long-term literacy planning in the primary grades, a key area where EQAO has shown students are struggling. A literacy coach works with the teachers to develop a cohesive plan to improve students' literacy. These meetings and the planning has also led to improved consistency among the grades in terms of what is being taught from year to year. Primary teachers reported that they are working towards teaching the same literacy units at the same time, which will ensure that students can build upon what they have learned year after year and will allow teachers to work together and draw on each other as they go through units simultaneously. While this has been a positive development, a number of teachers noted that they would like to see even more done with the test results in terms of school and division-wide strategizing and planning.

Better Preparation for High school

As in many First Nations communities, there is no high school on the reserve where this elementary school is located. Therefore, students will have to attend a nearby provincial high school outside of their community after they graduate. About half of the teachers interviewed raised this issue and felt that administering EQAO helped to better prepare their students for attending high school off-reserve. One element of this was a recognition that once students reach high school, they will have to write an EQAO mathematics assessment in Grade 9 and a literacy test in Grade 10, which they will need to pass to graduate. By using the EQAO testing in elementary school, it is thought that the students will be familiar with the testing and will be more likely to have the skills necessary to do well on the secondary school assessments. One teacher explained:

> It [EQAO] has been a positive experience, because we're tired of hearing about how our kids are going into the city and failing. That really concerns us, when they hit high school and they don't have these skills, a lot of them are dropping out. We want to prepare them and have them meet the province, you know, head on, and have the skills that everybody else does to survive in that environment.

Administering EQAO has been one way to equip students with some of the skills that will be necessary for success in the provincial high school system. That is, by using EQAO, students at this school become familiar and more comfortable with both the format and content of this type of assessment. A few teachers reported that these feelings have been echoed by parents, who are worried about whether their children will be fully prepared to integrate into the provincial school system. With EQAO, parents can now see how their child fares on a test that is taken by all students in Ontario and can see that their child is learning comparable skills to those taught in the provincial school system.

Additionally, it was noted that since implementing EQAO communication and resource sharing between the school and the local provincial school board has increased. The grade 8 teachers at this school now meet with teachers and administrators from the local high school along with other grade 8 teachers from feeder schools to talk about EQAO math results and discuss areas to focus on and strategies to prepare students for the grade 9 EQAO math assessment.

Challenges

Implementing and administering EQAO assessments in this First Nations school was certainly not an easy undertaking. Both teachers and administrators noted that the in the beginning, the testing created a lot of problems and negative feelings in the school. This was likely in large part due to the way the testing was implemented, as it was sprung on teachers, students, and parents with little advance warning by a previous administration. Teachers did not have time to understand the process or prepare students and it generated a lot of confusion and anger. While this was a unique situation, the school's experience can illuminate some of the challenges that First Nations schools may face when introducing and using a provincial assessment system.

Low Initial Test Scores

When EQAO was first implemented at this school, the test scores were alarmingly low. Not only did this hurt teacher morale, it also caused both parents and the education council to question the effectiveness of the administration and the school as a whole. While the administration of the day was let go, the current administration has also faced a lot of heat over the test scores. According to one participant, there were "bitter, bitter battles for the first two years." This can be a very trying situation and could lead to a desire to abandon the testing completely. Participants noted that there needs to be a strong administration in place that can withstand the criticism and questioning and can use the results for planning.

One positive benefit of the low initial scores, however, was that it united parents and the community and promoted action to improve the education students were receiving. For example, after the initial test results came in, the community offered additional funding to get extra supports in place to assess and assist students. Thus, when test scores are initially low, it can be quite challenging for the school, but the low scores can also motivate action and change.

Finally, participants noted that test scores have to be put into perspective. There are other types of learning and knowledge that need to factor in to an assessment of a student's performance or the overall quality of a school, especially for First Nations schools where the EQAO tests clearly do not measure all aspects of schooling that are important to First Nations communities. As one teacher stated, the testing is not the "be all, end all." Rather, test results need to be understood as one measure among many that can be used to assess student and school performance in the areas that are tested. Reflecting this understanding, teachers often used the term "snap-shot" when discussing EQAO scores, suggesting that test scores are understood to be an indicator of performance on selected measures at one point in time.

Publication of Assessment Results

Since 2003, the Fraser Institute has been publishing an annual "School Report Card" for elementary and secondary schools in Ontario. The report involves ranking all schools in Ontario based on their EQAO results, including the few First Nations schools that administer the testing. While some teachers were not aware of the Fraser Institute's report, for those that were, the publication of the school's test results and its inclusion in the rankings was viewed as a challenging aspect of administering EQAO testing. Since implementing the testing, the school has been ranked quite low and these results often get picked up by both national and local media outlets, bringing negative attention to the community. Commenting on this, participants stated:

> That's been very difficult for the community to hear and see the comparisons. I think this is one of the, the main point or stress areas for a First Nations community with EQAO, is the community doesn't want to be compared to others.

> When you get your reputation bandied about across the radio waves, why would they want to put themselves in that position? So it does take a brave stand to do it.

These comments suggest that the very fact that First Nations schools are included in the report and ranked against other schools can discourage a school from participating in the testing. At this school, the rankings have led both parents and band council to question the quality of the education being provided at the school and some felt that it was also discouraging for both teachers and students to see their school ranked poorly compared to other schools in Ontario.

An understanding of the various factors that can affect standardized test scores is important in these situations. It has been shown that aside from the quality of the school itself, factors such as socio-economic status and language skills can have a large impact on standardized test scores. In First Nations schools where English is not the first language of many students and/or where many of the students come from low socio-economic backgrounds, comparisons with other schools can be invalid and unfair. Thus, many teachers felt that the school should primarily be concerned with comparing their own results to results from previous years.

Participants also pointed out a number of problems with the Fraser Institute's rankings themselves. Firstly, First Nations schools did not begin administering the EQAO testing until significantly after it was begun in the rest of Ontario. Test results are bound to be lower as teachers and students become accustomed to the testing and learn from and respond to previous test results. Comparisons with schools that have been administering the test for far longer are therefore seen as unfair and invalid. Secondly, participants noted that the ranking of schools also masks the real improvements that are being made within the school. Finally, many felt that because the school purchases the test, they should have ownership over the results and should be able to control where, when, and to whom the school's test scores are released.

Conclusion

Due to the challenges that First Nations schools can face when implementing a provincial assessment system, participants felt that having a strong, stable school administration and stable community leadership were essential to successfully implementing and using standardized testing in a First Nations school. It was also argued the administration needs to have the support and trust of teachers, parents, the school council, and the entire community. It is up to the administration to ensure that these stakeholders understand why the testing is being implemented, how the scores should be interpreted and how the results can be used. This is especially vital for teachers, as many participants noted that having all teachers onboard, working together and having continuity throughout the grades in terms of what is being taught are important elements of making the testing a positive experience for the school, and is something that this school was continuing to work towards. It is important to note that many of the participants stated that they were initially against the use of the testing in their school, but as they came to better understand the process and saw how it was being used they began to appreciate its role as an instructional tool.

While there is certainly an uneasiness, among about half of the teachers, about the testing and its appropriateness for a First Nations school, the majority still felt that despite these issues, administering the testing has been a positive experience. Through administering EQAO assessments, the school has been able to use the results to lobby for and receive additional funding and resources, to inform classroom, division, and school-wide planning, and to prepare students for their EQAO exams in high school. Using a provincial standardized exam may not be the ideal situation, but since the school does not have the resources or supports necessary to develop and administer a more culturally appropriate test and because the school has been able to use the testing to garner much needed resources, in the current climate it is accruing benefits to the school that would not otherwise be realized.

Appendix 2

U.S. Bureau of Indian Affairs
Office of Indian Education Programs
Bureau-Wide Annual Report Card
2005 – 2006

Enrolment

	All Students		LEP		Special Ed	
	Male	Female	Male	Female	Male	Female
Total	22,872	22,115	8,405	7,551	4,914	2,498
M/F		44,987		15,956		7,412

Average Daily Attendance Rate, Graduation Rate and Dropout Rate

	All Students	LEP	Special Ed
Avg. Daily Attendance Rate K–8	91.00%	90.93%	89.77%
Avg. Daily Attendance Rate 9–12	84.45%	85.04%	85.05%
Graduation Rate (High School)	50.69%	48.94%	47.84%
Dropout Rate (High School)	10.35%	12.61%	10.31%

Student Achievement

Language Arts

	Number of Students	Participation Rate	Basic %	Proficient %	Advanced %	Proficient + Advanced %
All Students	1532	99.61%	52.49%	37.48%	10.03%	47.51%
Males	728	99.59%	57.66%	34.90%	7.45%	42.34%
Females	804	99.63%	47.82%	39.83%	12.36%	52.18%
Race and Ethnicity						
Native American	1532	99.61%	52.49%	37.48%	10.03%	47.51%
Other Groups						
IEP	429	60.84%	80.08%	15.71%	4.21%	19.92%
Limited English Proficient	978	99.90%	52.81%	36.85%	10.34%	47.19%

Two-Year Trend in Language Arts

	Number of Students	Participation Rate	Basic %	Proficient %	Advanced %	Proficient + Advanced %
2005-2006	1532	99.61%	52.49%	37.48%	10.03%	47.51%
2004-2005	16288	93.21%	52.81%	43.84%	3.35%	47.19%

Reading

	Number of Students	Participation Rate	Basic %	Proficient %	Advanced %	Proficient + Advanced %
All Students	23423	96.72%	63.26%	33.95%	2.79%	36.74%
Males	11767	96.61%	67.71%	29.90%	2.39%	32.29%
Females	11656	96.83%	58.78%	38.02%	3.20%	41.22%
Race and Ethnicity						
Native American	23423	96.72%	63.26%	33.95%	2.79%	36.74%
Other Groups						
IEP	4600	93.35%	85.21%	13.88%	0.91%	14.79%
Limited English Proficient	8851	96.64%	75.12%	23.52%	1.36%	24.88%

Two-Year Trend in Reading

	Number of Students	Participation Rate	Basic %	Proficient %	Advanced %	Proficient + Advanced %
2005-2006	23423	96.72%	63.26%	33.95%	2.79%	36.74%
2004-2005	24196	97.31%	61.60%	35.24%	3.16%	38.40%

Math

	Number of Students	Participation Rate	Basic %	Proficient %	Advanced %	Proficient + Advanced %
All Students	23796	96.89%	70.18%	25.96%	3.86%	29.82%
Males	11898	96.70%	71.49%	24.66%	3.85%	28.51%
Females	11898	97.08%	68.87%	27.26%	3.87%	31.13%
Race and Ethnicity						
Native American	23796	96.89%	70.18%	25.96%	3.86%	29.82%
Other Groups						
IEP	23796	96.89%	70.18%	25.96%	3.86%	29.82%
Limited English Proficient	23796	96.89%	70.18%	25.96%	3.86%	29.82%

Two-Year Trend in Math

	Number of Students	Participation Rate	Basic %	Proficient %	Advanced %	Proficient + Advanced %
2005-2006	23796	96.89%	70.18%	25.96%	3.86%	29.82%
2004-2005	24335	97.45%	65.21%	30.80%	3.99%	34.79%

High-Quality Teachers

A1	Full-time teaching positions available in the current school year:			3838
	Full-time teachers new to the school:			537
	Unfilled vacancies for full-time teachers:			83
	Total Number of Teachers:			3755
A2	Teachers at the end of last SY:			4010
	Not offered contracts: 172 Teachers retired: 106			
	Teachers returning:			3451 (86.06%)
B	Number of core area teachers:			3227
	Highly qualified core area teachers:			3019 (93.55%)
C	Average school principal tenure (years):			4.28571428571429
D	Number of core area classes taught:			7944
	Core area classes taught by highly qualified teachers:			6739 (84.83%)
	Teachers receiving high-quality professional development:			3903
	Core area teachers' qualifications in the sue of technology for instruction			
		Basic	678 (21/0%)	
		Proficient	1715 (53.15%)	
		Advanced:	834 (25.84%)	
E	Full-time paraprofessionals employed:			1548
	Fully qualified paraprofessionals employed:			1394

Appendix 3

Table A: **Average Participation of First Nations Students in the Grades 3,6, and 9 Achievement Testing Program 1998-99 to 2000-2001***

	Grade 3		
	1998/99	**1999/00**	**2000/01**
# Enrolled	1472.5	1607.0	1657.0
# Writing	1198.5	1257.5	1270.5
% Writing	81.4	78.3	76.7
% Excused	6.3	7.2	6.0
% Absent	12.3	14.5	17.3
	Grade 6		
	1998/99	**1999/00**	**2000/01**
# Enrolled	1392.5	1409.8	1465.8
# Writing	978.0	1077.8	1077.8
% Writing	70.2	76.4	71.0
% Excused	7.6	7.5	5.0
% Absent	22.2	16.1	24.0
	Grade 9		
	1998/99	**1999/00**	**2000/01**
# Enrolled	1259.3	1241.3	1342.3
# Writing	649.5	783.5	715.3
% Writing	51.6	63.1	53.3
% Excused	5.7	8.1	12.5
% Absent	42.8	28.8	34.3

*The data represent the average across the subjects within each grade.

Source: Alberta Learning: Government of Alberta 2002

Table B: Average Participation of First Nations Students in Grades 3, 6, and 9* Achievement Testing Program 1998/99–2000/01 by Subgroup

			Subgroup									
		1. Band School Only			2. Tuition Fee Agreement Only			3. Mixed			4. Other		
		1998/99	1999/00	2000/01	1998/99	1999/00	2000/01	1998/99	1999/00	2000/01	1998/99	1999/00	2000/01
Grade 3	# Enrolled	628.0	694.0	752.0	552.0	659.5	567.5	80.0	112.0	94.0	212.5	141.5	243.5
	# Writing	494.0	497.0	536.0	463.5	559.5	457.0	60.5	88.5	70.0	180.5	112.5	207.5
	% Writing	78.7	71.6	71.3	84.0	84.8	80.5	75.6	79.0	74.5	84.9	79.5	85.2
	% Excused	3.8	5.0	1.7	8.4	8.6	10.6	10.0	4.5	4.3	6.8	13.8	9.4
	% Absent	17.5	23.3	27.1	7.6	6.6	8.9	14.4	16.5	21.3	8.2	6.7	5.3
Grade 6	# Enrolled	521.0	542.8	601.5	568.0	623.0	508.5	59.0	80.5	99.0	244.5	163.5	256.8
	# Writing	324.5	392.3	358.0	437.8	494.0	411.3	35.8	59.5	61.8	180.0	132.0	209.5
	% Writing	62.3	72.3	59.5	77.1	79.3	80.9	60.6	73.9	62.4	73.6	80.7	81.6
	% Excused	3.7	3.2	1.4	10.0	10.9	7.8	10.2	4.0	2.3	9.6	10.2	9.1
	% Absent	34.0	24.6	39.1	12.9	9.8	11.3	29.2	22.0	35.4	16.8	9.0	9.3
Grade 9	# Enrolled	480.0	528.0	560.3	497.0	484.8	491.3	83.0	97.3	83.3	199.3	131.3	207.5
	# Writing	193.3	318.5	225.5	316.3	337.3	317.0	22.5	45.5	35.8	117.5	82.3	137.0
	% Writing	40.3	60.3	40.2	63.6	69.6	64.5	27.1	46.8	42.9	59.0	62.7	66.0
	% Excused	2.7	4.2	9.8	5.8	11.4	16.7	4.2	7.5	9.0	13.2	12.2	11.0
	% Absent	57.1	35.5	49.9	30.6	19.0	18.8	45.8	45.8	48.0	27.9	25.1	23.0

* The data represent the average across the subjects within each grade

Source: Alberta Learning: Government of Alberta 2002

Table C: The Percentage of First Nations Students Who Wrote the Test and Met the Acceptable Standard*

	Grade 3		
	1998/99	**1999/00**	**2000/01**
English Language Arts	55.3	57.4	53.6
Mathematics	48.9	52.6	50.2
Science	–	–	–
Social Sciences	–	–	–
	Grade 6		
	1998/99	**1999/00**	**2000/01**
English Language Arts	38.6	41.2	38.7
Mathematics	34.8	38.4	35.5
Science	39.8	38.6	40.1
Social Sciences	33.4	35.5	35.9
	Grade 9		
	1998/99	**1999/00**	**2000/01**
English Language Arts	47.0	46.7	46.4
Mathematics	22.5	20.5	21.2
Science	27.0	21.5	23.7
Social Sciences	31.4	25.0	30.6

*85% of Alberta students writing achievement tests are expected to meet the acceptable standard.

Source: Alberta Learning: Government of Alberta 2002

Table D: The Percentage of First Nations Students Who Wrote the Test and Met the Acceptable Standard 1998/99–2000/01* by Subgroup

			Subgroup										
			1. Band School Only			2. Tuition Fee Agreement Only			3. Mixed			4. Other		
			1998/99	1999/00	2000/01	1998/99	1999/00	2000/01	1998/99	1999/00	2000/01	1998/99	1999/00	2000/01
Grade 3	English Language Arts		41.7	42.2	31.7	65.3	68.0	68.9	57.6	55.2	50.0	65.4	72.1	76.2
	Mathematics		41.1	43.3	36.2	53.0	58.5	62.1	48.4	44.4	37.8	59.9	71.9	65.6
Grade 6	English Language Arts		22.1	24.6	22.5	45.5	50.1	46.5	31.3	31.0	29.3	51.4	59.5	54.2
	Mathematics		15.0	20.9	20.1	44.0	47.8	40.8	30.6	27.1	30.5	48.3	60.2	53.3
	Science		28.0	24.6	28.0	44.3	44.7	43.6	30.8	26.2	37.3	52.2	63.4	54.2
	Social Studies		19.2	21.4	22.9	40.5	43.1	41.6	22.2	21.7	27.0	45.4	56.4	49.3
Grade 9	English Language Arts		23.8	21.8	28.3	55.2	63.7	52.1	40.0	39.5	35.3	57.3	66.2	62.5
	Mathematics		6.8	9.8	8.6	29.2	29.1	24.8	20.0	6.4	7.9	31.8	35.4	38.8
	Science		10.5	7.5	12.8	34.6	33.7	28.0	8.3	16.0	2.6	40.5	35.7	37.8
	Social Studies		12.7	11.2	11.8	40.1	34.2	38.4	23.1	21.3	15.2	42.4	41.9	47.4

* 85% of Alberta students writing achievement tests are expected to meet the acceptable standard.

Source: Alberta Learning: Government of Alberta 2002

Table E: The Percentage of First Nations Students Who Wrote the Test and Met the Standard of Excellence* 1998/99–2000/01

	Grade 3		
	1998/99	**1999/00**	**2000/01**
English Language Arts	1.3	1.5	1.7
Mathematics	4.2	4.2	3.9
Science	–	–	–
Social Sciences	–	–	–
	Grade 6		
	1998/99	**1999/00**	**2000/01**
English Language Arts	1.7	1.3	0.8
Mathematics	1.7	1.2	1.5
Science	2.5	2.1	2.2
Social Sciences	1.6	1.4	0.9
	Grade 9		
	1998/99	**1999/00**	**2000/01**
English Language Arts	1.0	0.7	1.6
Mathematics	1.0	0.8	1.6
Science	0.8	0.2	0.7
Social Sciences	1.0	0.9	0.7

*15% of Alberta students writing achievement tests are expected to meet the standard of excellence.

Source: Alberta Learning: Government of Alberta 2002

Table F: The Percentage of First Nations Students Who Wrote the Test and Met the Standard of Excellence 1998/99–2000/01* by Subgroup

		Subgroup											
		1. Band School Only			2. Tuition Fee Agreement Only			3. Mixed			4. Other		
		1998/99	1999/00	2000/01	1998/99	1999/00	2000/01	1998/99	1999/00	2000/01	1998/99	1999/00	2000/01
Grade 3	English Language Arts	0.4	0.4	0.0	2.4	1.8	2.2	0.0	0.0	1.5	1.1	6.3	4.9
Grade 3	Mathematics	2.0	2.0	1.6	6.2	5.0	5.6	3.2	2.2	1.4	5.5	11.4	7.2
Grade 6	English Language Arts	0.0	0.3	0.3	2.1	1.2	0.5	0.0	1.7	1.7	4.0	4.6	2.0
Grade 6	Mathematics	0.3	0.0	0.3	2.3	1.4	1.2	0.0	0.0	0.0	3.4	4.5	4.8
Grade 6	Science	0.3	0.3	0.5	3.4	2.5	2.3	0.0	0.0	1.5	4.9	6.9	5.1
Grade 6	Social Studies	0.3	0.0	0.3	2.3	2.2	1.0	0.0	0.0	0.0	2.7	3.8	2.3
Grade 9	English Language Arts	0.0	0.0	1.0	0.9	0.9	1.0	0.0	0.0	0.0	2.4	2.6	4.4
Grade 9	Mathematics	0.0	0.0	0.4	1.3	0.6	1.3	0.0	0.0	0.0	1.8	4.9	4.5
Grade 9	Science	0.0	0.0	0.4	1.6	0.3	0.0	0.0	0.0	0.0	0.0	1.2	2.8
Grade 9	Social Studies	0.0	0.0	0.0	0.9	0.6	0.0	0.0	0.0	0.0	3.2	5.8	3.7

* 15% of Alberta students writing achievement tests are expected to meet the standard of excellence

Source: Alberta Learning: Government of Alberta 2002

Appendix 4

Provincial Standardized Testing Programs

Province-Wide Assessment Programs		
Location	**Grade Tested**	**Type of Test**
British Columbia	4,7 & 10	Provincial Learning Assessment Program (PLAP)
	4,7 & 10	Foundation Skills Assessment (split off from PLAP)
	12	Provincial Examination Program
Alberta	3,6 & 9	Provincial Achievement Testing Program
	12	Diploma Exams
Saskatchewan	Varies with core curricula (random sample testing)	Curriculum Evaluation Program
	5, 8, & 11 (random sample testing)	Program Learning Assessment Program
	12	Provincial Diploma Exams
Manitoba	6 (optional school division may implement)	Standards Test
	Senior 1, grade 9 (optional school division may implement)	Standards Test
	Senior 4, grade 12 (compulsory)	Standards Test
	12	Provincial Examinations (beginning 2000-01, replaced with standards test)
Ontario	3	EQAO , Reading, Writing and Mathematics Assessment
	6	EQAO Grade Assessment
	9	EQAO Mathematics Assessment
	10	EQAO Test of Reading, Writing Skills
Quebec	Elementary 6 & Secondary III	Compulsory Examinations
	Secondary I & IV	Uniform Ministry Examinations
	Elementary 3 & 6 (secondary level: optional for school boards & private schools.)	Complementary Examinations

	3 & 5	Provincial Assessments
New Brunswick (English)	8 (also; 10 not successful on 1st attempt & 11 not successful on 2nd attempt	Provincial Assessments
	12	Provincial Assessments
	11	Provincial Diploma Examination
New Brunswick (French)	4 & 8	Programme d'évaluation Provinciaux
	10, 11, & 12	Examens de fin d'études secondaires (EFES)
Nova Scotia	6	Program of Learning Assessment for Nova Scotia (PLANS)
	12	Program of Learning Assessment for Nova Scotia (PLANS)
Prince Edward Island	12 (students taking designated courses)	Grade 12 Exams
Newfoundland/Labrador	3, 6 & 9	Criterion-referenced Tests (CRT)
NFL & Lab. Cont'd	12	Atlantic Provinces Education Foundation (APEF) Chemistry Exam
	4,7,10, & 12	Canadian Test of Basic Skills (CTBS)
Northwest Territories	12	Diploma Exams (Alberta)
	10, 11, & 12 (with knowledge of an Aboriginal language may apply)	Aboriginal Challenge Exam
Yukon	4 - 7	Canadian Test of Basic Skills (CTBS)
	9 & 11	Yukon Territorial Exams
	12	Provincial Exams (BC)
	11 & 12	Language Proficiency Index

Courtesy of the Canadian Teachers Federation

Endnotes

1 We have also seen the release of the Ontario First Nation, Métis and Inuit Educational Framework (2007) and the new BC Aboriginal Education Enhancement Agreement (2008).

2 The graduate rate was the proportion of grade 12 and 13 students in a band who are included on nominal roles and graduated in the 1995/1996 school year. The withdrawal rate was measured by those students who were 16 years of age and older on the nominal rolls who withdrew from school.

3 For this to be possible the provinces that do not currently have a record of whether a student is Aboriginal would have to collect that information.

4 Appendix 4 outlines the province by province breakdown of which grades are subject to standardized testing.

5 In the previous section on the Alberta experience with testing, these achievement levels are reported.

6 The proportion of students writing annually from 1998/99 to 2000/01 remained fairly constant. Substantial variations exist, however, by grade and type of school. On band schools, the percentage of students writing is about 71, 60, and 40% for grades 3, 6 and 9 respectively. In the non-band schools, the percentage of students writing is 81, 81, and 65% for grades 3, 6 and 9.

7 That is, $15.0 million minus $1.6 million and $30.0 minus $1.6 million for test writing, leaving residuals of $13.4 million and $28.4 million respectively.

References

Alberta, Province of. 2000. "Aboriginal Policy Statement." Edmonton: Alberta Learning.

Alberta, Province of. 2003. "Participation and Results for First Nations Students: Grade 3, 6 and 9 Achievement Tests." Edmonton: Learning Assessment Branch.

American Indian Education Committee. 1994. "American Indian Frameworks Curriculum." St. Paul, MN: Minnesota State Board of Education

Amrein, A.L. and D.C. Berliner. 2002. "An Analysis of Some Unintended and Negative Consequences of High-Stakes Testing." Michigan: The Great Lakes Center for Education Research & Practice.

Apthorp, H.S., E. DeBassige D'Amato, and A. Richardson. 2003. *Effective Standards-Based Practices for Native American Students: A Review of the Literature.* Aurora, CO: Mid-continent Research for Education and Learning.

Armstrong, R., J. Kennedy and P.R. Oberle. 1990. *University Education and Economic Well Being: Indian Achievement and Prospects.* Ottawa: Indian and Northern Affairs Canada, Quantitative Analyses and Socio-Demographic Research, Finance and Professional Services.

AFN. 2005. *First Nations Education Action Plan.* Ottawa: Assembly of First Nations.

AFN. 2006. *Securing Our Future: First Nations Agenda for the 2007 Federal Budget. A Submission to the House of Commons Standing Committee on Finance.* Ottawa: Assembly of First Nations.

Bancroft, B.A. 1989. "Beyond the Single Standardized Test Score as an Indicator of Pupil and School Progress: a Review of Literature in Support of the Development of a Monitoring and Evaluation System that Utilizes Varied Measures to Determine Pupil Progress and Program Performance in BIA School." A paper presented to the National Bureau Effective Schools Team. Okemos, MI.

Beaulieu, D. 1991. A Concluding Prospectus on Change and Development for Native Education. Washington, DC: US Department of Education, Indian Nations at Risk Task Force. ERIC Document Reproduction Service No. ED 343 774.

Beaulieu, D., L Sparks, and M. Alonzo. 2005. *Preliminary Report on No Child Left Behind in Indian Country.* Washington, DC: National Indian Education Association.

Beavon, D. and M. Cooke. "An Application of the United Nations Development Index to Registered Indians in Canada." In J. White, P. Maxim and D. Beavon (eds). *Aboriginal Conditions: The Research Foundations of Public Policy.* Vancouver: UBC Press.

Bell, D., K. Anderson, T. Fortin, J. Ottoman, S. Rose, L. Simard, and K. Spencer. 2004. "Sharing Our Success: Ten Case Studies in Aboriginal Schooling." Kelowna: Society for the Advancement of Excellence in Education.

Berg, P., and J. Ohler, 1991. *Strategic Plans for use of Modern Technology in the Education of American Indian and Alaska Native Students*. Washington, DC: US Department of Education. ERIC Document Reproduction Service No. ED 343 765.

Bernardoni, L.C. 1967. "The Testing of Bicultural Children." *Sharing Ideas*. (4): 1–5. ERIC Document Reproduction Service No. ED 077 977.

Berthelot, J., N. Ross, and S. Tremblay. 2001. "Factors Affecting Grade 3 Student Performance in Ontario: A multilevel analysis." *Education Quarterly Review*. 7(4): 25–36.

Bishop, J.H. 1995. "The Impact of Curriculum-Based External Examinations on School Priorities and Student Learning." *International Journal of Education Research*. 23(8). 653–752.

Black, P. and D. William. 1998. "Inside the Black Box: Raising Standards through Classroom Assessment." Phi Delta Kappan. October.

Black-Branch, J. 1993. "O Canada, Our Home on Native Land: Aboriginal Self-Government, Not the Canadian Charter of Rights and Freedoms, May Be the Key to Educational Reform." *The Canadian Journal of Native Studies*. 13(2): 280–289

Boloz, S.A. and R. Varrati. 1983. "Apologize or Analyse: Measuring Academic Achievement in the Reservation School." *Journal of American Indian Education*. 23(1): 23–28

Bordeaux, R. 1995. "Assessment for American Indian and Alaska Native Learners." ERIC Digest. Charleston, WV. ERIC Clearinghouse on Rural Education and Small Schools. ERIC Document Reproduction Service No. ED 385 424.

Bowker, A. 1992. "The American Indian Female Dropout." *Journal of American Indian Education*. 31(3): 3–20.

Brandt, E.A. 1992. "The Navajo Area Student Dropout Study: Findings and Implications." *Journal of American Indian Education*. 31(2): 48–63.

British Columbia Ministry of Education, Aboriginal Education Branch. 2000a. "How are we doing: An Overview of Aboriginal Educational Results 2000–2001." <**www.bced.gov.bc.ca./abed/results**>.

British Columbia Ministry of Education, Aboriginal Education Branch. 2000b. "Aboriginal Education Improvement Agreements." <**www.bced.gov.bc.ca/abed/agreements/**>.

Browne, D.B. 1984. "WISC-R Scoring Patterns Among Native Americans of the Northern Plains." *White Cloud Journal*. (3): 3–16.

Buly, M.R. and S.W. Valencia. 2002. "Below the Bar: Profiles of Students who Fail State Reading Assessments." *Educational Evaluation and Policy Analysis*. 24(3): 219–239.

Bureau of Indian Affairs. 1998. *Report on BIA Education: Excellence in Indian Education through the Effective School Process*. Washington, DC: US Department of the Interior.

Bureau of Indian Affairs. 2005. "Implementation of the *No Child Left Behind Act* of 2001: Final Rule." *Federal Register*. 70(81): 22178–22222.

Bureau of Indian Affairs. 2006. *Bureau-Wide Annual Report Card, 2005–2006*. Bureau of Indian Affairs. Office of Indian Education Programs.

Butterfield, R.A. 1991. "Blueprint for Indian Education: Improving Mainstream Schooling." ERIC Digest. ERIC Clearing House on Rural Education and Small Schools. Charleston, WV. ERIC Document Reproduction Service No. ED 372 898.

Butterfield, R., and F. Pepper. 1991. "Improving Parental Participation in Elementary and Secondary Education for American Indian and Alaska Native Students." Washington, DC: US Department of Education, Indian Nations at Risk Task Force. ERIC Document Reproduction Service No. Ed 343 763.

Canada. 1995. *Highlights of Aboriginal Conditions, 1991, 1986: Demographic, Social and Economic Characteristics*. Ottawa: Indian and Northern Affairs Canada.

Canada, House of Commons Standing Committee on Aboriginal Affairs. 1989. *A Review of the Post-secondary Student Assistance Program of the Department of Indian Affairs and Northern Development*. Ottawa: Queen's Printer.

Canada, Secretary of State. 1991. *Canada's Off-reserve Aboriginal Population: A Statistical Overview*. Ottawa: Social Trends Analysis Directorate, Department of the Secretary of State.

Canadian Psychological Association and the Canadian Association of School Psychologists. 2002. "A Joint position statement on the Canadian Press-coverage of Province-Wide Achievement Test Results." <**www.cpa.ca/docujents.join_position.html**>.

Canadian Teachers Federation. 2003a. "Assessment and Evaluation: National Testing." <**www.ctf-fce.ca/e/assessment/testing-main.htm**>.

Canadian Teachers Federation. 2003b. "Assessment and Evaluation: National Testing." <**www.ctf-fce.ca/e/assessment/high-stakes.htm**>.

Cahape, P. 1993. "Blueprints for Indian Education: Research and Development Needs for the 1990's." ERIC Digests. Charleston WV. ERIC Clearinghouse on Rural Education and Small Schools. ERIC Document Reproduction Service No. ED 357 908.

Cantrall, B., L. Pete, and M. Fields. 1990. "Navajo Culture: A Bridge to the Rest of the World." Paper presented at the Annual Meeting of the American Educational Research Association. Boston, MA: ERIC Document Reproduction Service No. ED 342 163.

Cawelti, G. 1995. *Handbook of Research on Improving Student Achievement.* Arlington, VA: Educational Research Service.

Charlie, L. 1997. "Understanding the Rules of Culture to Improve your Classroom Practice." *Snap Shots: A Journal of Classroom Practice.* 6(2). School District 79 (Cowichan Valley).

Charleston, G., and G. Knight. 1992. "Foreword." In *Indian Nations at Risk: Listening to the People.* P. Cahape and C. Howley (eds.). Charleston, WV: ERIC Clearinghouse on Rural Education and Small Schools. ERIC Document Reproduction Service No. ED 339 588. 7–12.

Charleston, G., and G.L. Knight. 1991. "Indian Nations at Risk Task Force: Listen to the People." Washington, DC: US Department of Education, Indian Nations at Risk Task Force. ERIC Document Reproduction Service No. ED 343 763

Clement, J. (forthcoming in 2009). "The University Attainment of the Registered Indian Population in Canada, 1981–2001: A Cohort Approach." In *Aboriginal Education: Current Crisis and Future Alternatives.* J.P. White, D. Beavon, J. Peters, and N. Spence (eds). Toronto: Thompson Educational Publishing.

Coggins, K., and N. Radin. 1997. "The Traditional Tribal Values of Ojibwa Parents and the School Performance of their Children: An Exploratory Study." *Journal of American Indian Education.* 36(3): 1–15.

Coleman, J. 1988. "Social Capital and the Creation of Human Capital." *American Journal of Sociology.* 94(3): S95–S120.

Coleman, J.S., et al. 1966. *Equality of Educational Opportunity.* Washington, DC: US Government Printing Office.

Coles, R. 1989. *The Call of Stories: Teaching and the Moral Imagination.* Boston, MA: Houghton-Mifflin.

Commission on Instructionally Supportive Assessment. 2001. *Building Test to Support Instruction and Accountability: A Guide for Policy Makers.* Washington, DC: National Education Association et al.

Cotton, K. 1994. "Fostering Intercultural Harmony in Schools: Research Findings." Topical Synthesis. No. 7. Portland, OR: Northwest Regional Educational Laboratory.

Cummins, J. 2000. *Language, Power and Pedagogy: Bilingual Children in the Crossfire.* Clevedon, UK: Multilingual Matters.

Cummins, J. 1996. *Negotiating Identities: Education for Empowerment in a Diverse Society.* Ontario, CA: California Association for Bilingual Education.

Cummins, J. 1997. "Minority Status and Schooling in Canada." *Anthropology and Education Quarterly.* 28(3): 411–430.

Cummins, J. 1992. "The Empowerment of Indian Students." In *Teaching American Indian Students.* J. Reyhner (ed.). Norman: University of Oklahoma Press. 1–22.

Cummins, J. 1989. "Empowering Minority Students: A Framework for Intervention." *Harvard Educational Review.* 56(1): 18–36.

Cummins, J. 1984. *Bilingualism and Special Education: Issues in Assessment and Pedagogy.* San Diego: College Hill.

Demmert, W.J. Jr. 2001. *Improving Academic Performance Among Native American Students: A Review of the Research Literature.* Charlston, WV: ERIC Clearinghouse on Rural Education and Small Schools.

Deyhle, D. 1992. "Constructing Failure and Maintaining cultural Identity: Navajo and Ute School Leavers. *Journal of American Indian Education.* 31(2): 24–47.

Deyhle, D. 1989. "Pushouts and Pullouts: Navajo and Ute School Leavers." *Journal of Navajo Education*. 6(2): 36–51.

Deyhle, D. 1986. "Success and Failure: a Micro-ethnographic Comparison of Navajo and Anglo Students' Perceptions of Testing." *Curriculum Inquiry*. 16(4): 365–389.

Deyhle, D. 1983. "Measuring Success and Failure in the Classroom: Teacher Communication about Tests and the Understandings of Young Navajo Students." *Peabody Journal of Education*. 61(1): 67–85.

Deyle, D., and K. Swisher. 1997. "Research in American Indian and Alaska Native Education: From Assimilation to Self-Determination." In *Review of Research in Education. Vol. 22*. M.W. Apple. (ed). 113–194.

Drost, H. 1994. "Schooling, Vocational Training and Unemployment: the Case of Canadian Aboriginals." *Canadian Public Policy*. 20(1): 52–65.

Educational Testing Service (ETS). 1982. "Tests for American Indians." Princeton: ETS. ERIC Document Reproduction Service No. ED 227–995.

Epstein, J.L. 1988. "How Do We Improve Programs for Parent Involvement?" *Educational Horizons*. (Winter): 58–59.

Epstein, J.L. 1987. "Parent Involvement: What Research Says to Administrators." *Education and Urban Society.* (February): 119–136.

Estrin, E.T., and S. Nelson-Barber. 1995. "Bringing Native American Perspectives to Mathematics and Science Teaching." *Theory into Practice*. 34(3): 174–185.

ERIC. 2001. "Gender Differences in Educational Achievement within Racial and Ethnic Groups." *ERIC Digests 164*. New York: ERIC Clearinghouse on Urban Education. ERIC Document Reproduction Service No. ED 455 341.

FairTest. 1995. *Implementing Performance Assessments: A Guide to Classroom, School and System Reform*. Cambridge, MA: National Center for Fair and Open Testing.

FairTest. 1999. "Newsletter Articles of FairTest: the National Center for Fair & Open Testing." *FairTest Examiner*. 13(4): 1–8.

Fase R. 1989. *Dropout Rates in the US: 1988*. National Centre for Education Statistics US Department of Education, Washington D.C., US Government Printing Office.

Firestone, W.A., D. Mayrowetz and J. Fairman. 1998. "Performance-Based Assessment and Instructional Change: The Effects of Testing in Maine and Maryland." *Educational Evaluation and Policy Analysis*. 20(2): 95–113.

Forbes, J.D. 2000. "The New Assimilation Movement: Standards, Tests, and Anglo-American Supremacy." *Journal of American Indian Education*. 39(2): 7– 28.

Fortune, J.C. 1985. *Choctaw Comprehensive School Study*. Philadelphia, MS: Choctaw Heritage Press.

Fox, S.J. 2000. "Standards-based Reform and American Indian/Alaska Native Education." American Indian/ Alaska Native Research Agenda Conference. Albuquerque, NM.

Fox, S.J. 2001. "American Indian/Alaska Native Education and Standards-Based Reform." *ERIC Digest*. Charleston, WV: ERIC Clearinghouse on Rural Education and Small Schools. ERIC Document Reproduction Service No. ED 459 039.

Fox, S. and V. LaFontaine. 1995. "A Whole Language Approach to the [sic] Communication Skills." In *Teaching the Native American*. H. Gilliland. (ed). Dubugue, IA: Kendall/Hunt Publishing.

Freeman, C. and M. Fox. 2005. *Status and Trends in the Education of American Indians and Alaska Natives. (NCES 2005-108)*. U.S. Department of Education, National Center for Education Statistics. Washington, DC: U.S. Government Printing Office.

Giroux, H.A. 1985. "Critical Pedagogy, Cultural Politics and the Discourse of Experience." *Journal of Education*. 167(2): 22–41.

Government of Alberta. 2001. *Satisfaction with Learning in Alberta: A Quantitative Report*. Edmonton: Government of Alberta.

Government of British Columbia. 2000. "Interpreting CTBS Test Results." Victoria: Ministry of Education.

Government of Manitoba. 2002. "Policies and Procedures for Standardized Testing?" Winnipeg: Manitoba Education, Training and Youth.

Government of Ontario. 2002. "Ontario Provincial Report on Achievement 2001–2002, English Language Schools." Education Quality and Accountability Office. Toronto: Queens Printer.

Graysol, D.A., and M.D. Martin. 1990. "Gender/Ethnic Expectations and Student Achievement (GESA)." *Teacher Handbook*. Earlham, IA: Graymill Publications.

Green, R.L. and R.J. Griffore. 1980. "The Impact of Standardized Testing on Minority Students." *The Journal of Negro Education*. 49(3): 238–252.

Guerin, G.R., and A.S. Maier. 1983. *Informal Assessment in Education*. Palo Alto, CA: Mayfield Publishing Co.

Guilment, G.M. 1983. "The Inappropriateness of Standardized Testing in a Culturally Heterogenous Milieu: A Navajo Example. Los Angles: University of California. ERIC Document Reproduction Service No. ED 261 830.

Haney, W. 1991. "We Must Take Care: Fitting Assessment to Functions." In *Expanding Student Assessment*. V. Perrone (ed). Alexandria, VA: Association for Supervision and Curriculum Development. 142–163.

Harcey, D.W., and B.R. Croone. 1993. *White-Man-Runs-Him*. Evanston, IL: Evanston Publishing Co.

Hatch, J. 1991. *American Indian and Alaska Native Adult Education and Vocational Training Programs: Historical Beginnings, Present Conditions and Future Directions*. Washington, DC: US Department of Education. ERIC Document Reproduction Service No. ED 343 773.

Herman, J.L., P.R., Aschbacher, and L. Winters. 1992. *A Practical Guide to Alternative Assessment*. Alexandria, VA: ASCD Publications. ERIC Document Reproduction Service No. ED 352 389.

Hull, J. 2000. "Aboriginal Post-Secondary Education and Labour Market Outcomes Canada 1996." Ottawa: Department of Indian Affairs and Northern Development.

Hull, J. 2005. "Post-secondary Education and Labor Market Outcomes: Canada, 2001." Ottawa: Indian and Northern Affairs Canada.

Hunter, J.E. 1983. "Fairness of the General Aptitude Test Battery: Ability Differences and Their Impact on Minority Hiring Rates." Users Test Research Report No. 46. Sacramento: California State Department of Employment Development. ERIC Document Reproduction Service No. ERIC Document Reproduction Service No. ED 537 534.

Indian Nations at Risk Task Force. 1991. "Indian Nations at Risk: An Educational Strategy for Action, Final Report." Washington, DC: ERIC Document Reproduction Service No. ED 339–587.

James, K., E. Chavez, F. Beauvais, R. Edwards, and G. Oetting. 1995. "School Achievement and Drop-out Among Anglo and Indian Females and Males: A Comparative Examination." *American Indian Culture and Research Journal*. 19(3): 24–30.

Jankowski, W. and B. Moazzami. 1995. "Returns of Education Among Northwestern Ontario's Native People." *Canadian Journal of Native Studies*. 15(1): 104–111.

Jennings, J. 1998. *Why National Standards and Test? Politics and the Quest for Better Schools*. Thousand Oaks: Sage Publications.

Jerald, C.D. 2000. "The State of the States." *Education Week*. January 13. 62–65.

Kaulback, B. 1984. "Styles of Learning Among Native Children: A Review of the Research." *Canadian Journal of Native Education*. 11(3): 27–37.

Kerman, S., T. Kimball, and M. Martin. 1980. *Teacher Expectations and Student Achievement: Coordinator Manual*. Bloomington, IN: Phi Delta Kappa.

King, C. 1993. "The State of Aboriginal Education in Southern Canada." Ottawa: RCAP, Public Policy and Aboriginal Peoples 1965–1992.

Kirkness, V. and S. Selkirk Bowman. 1992. *First Nations and Schools: Triumphs and Struggles*. Toronto: Canadian Education Association.

Kleinfeld, J., G.W. Mcdiarmid, S. Gurbis, and W. Parrett. 1991. "The Effects of High Stakes Testing on Achievement: Preliminary Findings about Generalization across Tests." Paper Presented at the Annual Meeting of the American Education Research Association. Chicago. April.

Kober, N.. 2001. *It Takes More Than Testing: Closing the Achievement Gap*. Washington, DC: Center on Education Policy.

Koretz, D.M., G.F. Madeus, E. Haertel, and A.E. Beaton. 1992. National Educational Standards and Testing: A Response to the Recommendations of the National Council on Educational Standards and Testing (Congressional Testimony). Santa Monica, CA: Rand Institute for Education and Training.

Koretz, D.M., R.L. Linn, S.B. Dunbar, and L.A. Shepard. 1991. "The Effects of High Stakes Testing on Achievement: Preliminary Findings about Generalization Across Tests." Paper Presented at the Annual Meeting of the American Education Research Association. Chicago, IL. April.

Kunisawa, K. 1988. "A Nation in Crisis: the Dropout Dilemma." *NEA Today*. 6(6): 61–78.

Ledlow, S. 1992. "Is Cultural Diversity An Adequate Explanation for Dropping Out?" *Journal of American Indian Education*. 31(3): 21–36.

Leveque, D.M. 1994. "Cultural and Parental Influences on Achievement Among Native American Students in Barstow Unified School District." Paper presented at the National Meeting of the Comparative and International Educational Society, San Diego, California, March, 1994.

Lofthouse, N. 1999. "Effective schools research British Columbia Ministry of Education. Aboriginal Education Branch." <**www.bced.gov.bc.ca/abed/research/esr/**>.

MacKay, R. and L. Myles. 1989. *Native Student Dropouts from Ontario Schools*. Toronto: Ontario Ministry of Education.

MacPherson, J.C. 1991. *Report on Tradition and Education Towards a Vision of our Future*. September. Ottawa: Indian Affairs and Northern Development.

Madeus, G., and A.G.A. Tan. 1993. " The Growth of Assessment." In *Challenges and Achievements of American Education*. G. Cawelti (ed). Alexandria: Association for Supervision & Curriculum Development.

Marker, M. 2000. "Economics and Local Self-determination: Describing the Clash Zone in First Nations Education." *Canadian Journal of Native Education*. .24(1): 30–38.

Marzano, R.J. 1990. "Standardized Tests: Do they Measure Cognitive Abilities?" NASSP Bulletin. No, 74: 93–101.

Maxim, P., J. White and D. Beavon. 2003. "Dispersion and Polarization of Income among Aboriginal and non-Aboriginal Canadians." In *Aboriginal Conditions: The Research Foundations of Public Policy*. J. White, P.S. Maxim and D. Beavon (eds). Vancouver: UBC Press.

McBride Management. 2001. *Over-representation of Aboriginal Students Reported with Behaviour Disorders*. Victoria: British Columbia Ministry of Education, Special Programs Branch.

McDiarmid, G.L. 1972. "The Hazards of Testing Indian Children." Las Cruces, NM: ERIC/CRESS. ERIC Document Reproduction Service No. Ed 055 92

McDonald, R.J. 1991. "Canada's Off Reserve Aboriginal Population." *Canadian Social Trends*. (Winter): 2–7.

McShane, D. 1985. "Explaining Achievement patterns of American Indian Children: A Transcultural and Developmental Model." *Peabody Journal of Education*. 61(1): 34–48.

McShane, D.A., and J.M. Plas. 1982. "Wechsler Scale Performance patterns of American Indian Children." *Psychology in the Schools*. 19(1): 8–17.

McWhorter, J. 2000. *Losing the Race: Black Americans and Intellectual Self-sabotage*. New York: Free Press.

Mehrens, W.A., and J. Kaminski. 1989. "Methods for Improving Standardized Test Scores: Fruitful, Fruitless, or Fraudulent?" *Educational Measurement: Issues and Practices*. 8(1): 14–22.

Ministry of Education 2007. "Ontario First Nation, Métis and Inuit Educational Framework." Toronto: Aboriginal Education Office, Ministry of Education.

Ministry of Education (B.C.) 2008. *Aboriginal Education Enhancement Agreement*. Victoria: Ministry of Education.

Mishra, S.P. 1981. "Relationship of WISC-R Factor Scores to Academic Achievement and Classroom Behaviours of Native American Navajos." *Measurement and Evaluation in Guidance*. 14(1): 26–30.

Natriello, G. and S.M. Dornbusch. 1984. *Teacher Evaluative Standards and Student Effort*. New York: Longman.

Neil, M. 2003. "High Stakes, High Risk: The Dangerous Consequences of High-Stakes Testing." *American School Board Journal*. 190(2): 18–21.

Nelson-Barber, S., and E.T. Estrin. 1995. *Culturally Responsive Mathematics and Science Education for Native Students*. San Francisco: The Far West Laboratory for Educational Research and Development.

Nichols, R. 1991. "Continuous Evaluation of Native Education Programs for American Indian and Alaska Native Students." Washington, DC: US Department of Education, Indian Nations at Risk Task Force. ERIC Document Reproduction Service No. ED 343 760.

Office of Educational Research and Improvement. 1997a. *Assessment of Student Performance*. Washington, DC: Department of Education.

Office of Educational Research and Improvement. 1997b. *School Reform and Student Diversity*. Washington, DC: Department of Education.

Office of Indian Education Programs. 1993. *Annual Report: FY 1992*. Washington, DC: Bureau of Indian Affairs. ERIC Document Reproduction Service No. ED 371 929.

Ogbu, J.U. 1992. "Understanding Cultural Diversity and Learning." *Educational Researcher*. 21(8): 5–14.

Olson, J.F. 1997. *The Inclusion of Students with Disabilities and Limited English Proficient Students in Large-scale Assessment: A Summary of Recent Progress*. Washington, DC: National Center for Education Statistics.

Ontario Elementary Teachers Federation. 2002. "Assessment and Accountability: Why Standardized Testing is the Wrong Answer." <**www.etfo.on.ca**>.

ORBIS Associates. 1998. *American Indian Content Standards*. Washington, DC: Bureau of Indian Affairs.

ORBIS Associates. 1998. "American Indian Standards for Arts Education." Bureau of Indian Affairs. Washington, DC: ERIC Document Reproduction Service No. ED 420–478.

Paul, A. 1991. "Early Childhood Education in American Indian and Alaska Native Communities." Washington, DC: US Department of Education. ERIC Document Reproduction Service No. ED 343 761.

Pewewardy, C. 1998. "Our Children Can't Wait: Recapturing the Essence of Indigenous Schools in the United States." *Cultural Survival Quarterly*. 22(1): 29–34.

PL 103-227 *Goals 2000*: *Educate America Act*. 1994. Washington, DC: Government Printing Office.

Popham, W.J. 2001. "The Uses and Misuses of Standardized Tests." NASSP Bulletin 2001. 85; 24. DOI: 10.1177/019263650108562204.

Portes, A and J. Sennsenbrenner. 1993. "Embeddedness and Immigration: Notes on the Social Determinants of Economic Action." *American Journal of Sociology*. 98(6): 1320–1350.

Preston, V. 1991. "Mathematics and Science Curricula in Elementary and Secondary Education for American Indian and Alaska Native Students." Washington, DC: US Department of Education, Indian Nations at Risk Task Force. ERIC Document Reproduction Service No. ED 343 767.

Reyhner, J. 2001. "Family, Community, and School Impacts on American Indian and Alaska Native Students' Success." 32nd. Annual National Indian Education Association Annual Convention. <**jan. ucc.nau.edu/~jar/AIE/family.html**>.

Reyhner, J. 1991. "Plans for Dropout Prevention and Special School Support Services for American Indian and Alaska Native Students." Washington, DC: US Department of Education. ERIC Document Reproduction Service No. ED 343 732.

Richardson, C. and N. Blanchet-Cohen. 2000. "Adult Education and Indigenous Peoples in Canada." In *International Survey on Adult Education for Indigenous Peoples. Country Study: Canada*. L. King (ed). Hamburg: UNESCO Institute for Education.

Sack, W.H., M. Beiser, G. Clarke, and R. Redshirt. 1987. "The High Achieving Sioux Indian Child: Some Preliminary Findings From the Flower of Two Soils Project." *American Indian and Alaska Mental Health Research*. 1(1): 37–51.

Shepard, L.A. 1989. "Why We Need Better Assessments." *Educational Leadership*. 46(7): 4–9.

Shields, C.M. 1997. "Learning About Assessment From Native American Schools: Advocacy and Empowerment." *Theory into Practice*. 36(spring): 102–109.

Shields, C.M. 1996. "Creating a Learning Community in a Multicultural Settings: Issues of Leadership." *The Journal of School Leadership*. 6(1): 47–74.

Shields, C.M. 1995. "Context, Culture, and Change: Considerations for Pedagogical Change in a Native American Community." *Planning and Changing*. 26(No. ½): 2–24.

Shields, C.M., and P.A. Seltzer. 1995. "Conflict, Culture, and Difference: Towards a Deeper Understanding of Community." A Paper Presented at the Annual Meeting of the University Grand Council for Educational Administration. Salt Lake City, UT: October.

Shindell, R. 2001. "What is the Real Purpose of Standardized Testing?" *Teacher Magazine*. 14(1): 9.

Shutt, D.L. "Family Participation in the Psychological Evaluation of Minority Children." Paper presented to the Southwestern Orthopsychological Association Meeting. Galveston, TX: ERIC Document Reproduction Service No. ED 071 830.

Siggner, A. 1986. "The Socio-demographic Characteristics of Registered Indians." *Canadian Social Trends* (Winter): 2–9.

Sleeter, C.E. 1990. "Staff Development for Desegregated Schooling." *Phi Delta Kappan*. 72(1): 133–140.

Snipp, C. 1990. *American Indians: The First of this Land*. New York: Russel Sage Foundation.

Snipp, C and G. Sandefur. 1988. "Earnings of American Indians and Alaskan Natives: the Effects of Residence and Migration." *Social Forces*. 66(4): 994–1008.

Spence, N., J. White and P. Maxim. (Forthcoming). "Modeling Educational Success of First Nations Students in Canada: Community Level Perspectives."

Sperling, D.H. 1994. *Tiospa Zina Tribal School—Student Handbook*. Agency Village, SD: Sisseton Wahpeton School Board.

Sperling, D.H. 1994. "Assessment and Reporting: A Natural Pair." *Educational Leadership*. 52(2): 10–13.

Tait, H. 1999. "Educational Achievement of Young Aboriginal Adults." *Canadian Social Trends*. 52 (Spring): 6–10.

Tonemah, S. 1991. "Gifted and Talented American Indian and Alaska Native Students." Washington, DC: US Department of Education. ERIC Document Reproduction Service No. ED 343 769.

Toohey, K. 1980–81. "English as a Second Language for Native Canadians." *Canadian Journal of Education*. 10(3): 275–293.

Turcotte, M. and J. Zhao. 2004. "Well-being of Off-reserve Aboriginal Children." *Canadian Social Trends*. 75(Winter): 22–27.

Ungerleider, C. 2006. "Reflections on the Use of Large-Scale Student Assessment for Improving Student Success." *Canadian Journal of Education*. 29(3): 873–883.

Upshur, J.A. and J. Fata (eds). 1967. "Problems in Foreign Language Testing: Proceedings of a Conference Health at the University of Michigan." Ann Arbor, MI: University of Michigan Research Club in Language Learning. ERIC Document Reproduction Service No. ED 022 162.

Urion, C. 1993. "First Nations Schooling in Canada: A Review of Changing Issues." In *Contemporary Educational Issues, 2nd ed.* L.L. Stewin and S.J.H. McCann (eds). Toronto: Copp Clark Pitman Ltd.

Villegas, A.M. 1991. "Culturally Responsive Pedagogy for the 1990's and Beyond." Trends and Issues paper No. 6. Washington, DC: ERIC Clearinghouse on Teacher Education. ERIC Document Reproduction Service No. ED 339 698.

Volante, L. 2004. "Teaching To the Test: What Every Educator and Policy-maker Should Know." *Canadian Journal of Educational Administration and Policy*. Issue 35.

Wagstaff, L., and L. Fusarelli. 1995. "The Racial Minority Paradox: New Leadership for Learning in Communities of Diversity." Paper presented at the Annual Meeting of the University of Council for Educational Administration, Salt Lake City, UT.

Wang, M.C., G.D. Haertel and H.J. Walberg. 1998. *Educational Resilience*. Philadelphia: Temple University Centre for Research in Human Development and Education, Laboratory for Student Success. 98(11).

Wang, M.C., G.D. Haertel and H.J. Walberg. 1997. "Fostering Educational Resilience in Inner-city Schools." Philadelphia: Temple University Centre for Research in Human Development and Education, Laboratory for Student Success. 97(4). <**www.temple.edu/lss/htmlpublications/publications/pubs97-4.htm**>.

Wang, M.C., G.D. Haertel and H.J. Walberg. 1997. "Revitalizing Inner Cities: Focussing on Children's Learning." Philadelphia: Temple University Centre for Research in Human Development and Education. Laboratory for Student Success. 97(7).

Ward, C. 1995. "American Indian High School Completion in Rural Southeastern Montana." *Rural Sociology.* 60(3): 416–434.

Ward, C. 1998. "Community Resources and School Performance: the Northern Cheyenne Case." *Sociological Inquiry.* 68(1): 83–113.

Warner, L.S. and J. Hastings. 1995. "A Research Study to Determine Perceptions of Job-Related Stress by Bureau of Indian Affairs Education Employees." *Journal of American Indian Education.* 35(1): 16–29.

Webb, M. 1990. "Multicultural Education in Elementary and Secondary Schools." ERIC Digest. No. 67. New York: ERIC Clearinghouse on Urban Education. ERIC Document Reproduction Service No. ED 327 613.

White, J. 2002. "Aboriginal Women and the Economy" 2002 Aboriginal Policy Research Conference, Ottawa, Nov. 26–28.

White, J., D. Beavon and Paul Maxim. 2003. *Aboriginal Conditions: The Research Foundations of Public Policy.* Vancouver: UBC Press.

White, J. and P. Maxim. 2002. "Correlates of Educational Attainment in First Nations Communities." 2002 Aboriginal Policy Research Conference, Ottawa , Nov. 26–28.

White, J., P. Maxim and N. Spence. 2004. "An Examination of Educational Success." In *Aboriginal Policy Research: Setting the Agenda for Change, Volume 1.* J. White, P. Maxim and D Beavon (eds). Toronto: Thompson Educational Publishing. 128–148.

White House Conference on Indian Education. 1992. *White House Conference on Indian Education: Final Report—Executive Summary.* Washington, DC: White House.

Wilkinson, R.G. 1997. "Comment: Income, Inequality and Social Cohesion." *American Journal of Public Health.* 87(9): 1504–1506.

Willeto, A.A. 1999. "Navajo Culture and Family Influences on Academic Success: Traditionalism is not a Significant predictor of Achievement Among Young Navajos." *Journal of American Indian Education.* 38(2): 1–21.

Williams, B, and K. Gross. 1990. "English Proficiency Test and Classroom Application." Paper Presented at the 16th Annual Alaska Bilingual Multicultural Education Conference. Anchorage, AK. ERIC Document Reproduction Service No. ED 324 156. February.

Wilson, K. and M. Rosenberg. 2002. "Exploring the Determinants of Health for First Nations Peoples in Canada: Can Existing Frameworks Accommodate Traditional Activities?" *Social Science and Medicine.* 55(11): 2017–2031.

Work in Progress. 1994. "Content Standards and Assessment." A Paper Offered to Goals 2000 Participants. Washington, DC: US Department of Education. May.

Worthen, B.R. 1993. "Critical Issues that will Determine the Future of Alternative Assessment." *Phi Delta Kappan.* 74(6): 444–454.

Wright, B. 1991. "American Indian and Alaska Native Higher Education: Toward a New Century of Academic Achievement and Cultural Integrity." Washington, DC: US Department of Education. ERIC Document Reproduction Service No. ED 343 771.

Wright, W.E. 2002. "The Effects of High Stakes Testing in an Inner-City Elementary School: The Curriculum, the Teachers, and the English Language Learners." *Current Issues in Education.* 5(5). Available at: <**cie.ed.asu.edu/volume5/number5/**>.

Zessoules, R., and H. Gardner. 1991. "Authentic Assessment: Beyond the Buzzword and into the Classroom." In *Expanding Student Assessment.* V. Perrone (ed). Alexandria, VA: Association for Superviion and Curriculum Development. 47–71.

8

Exploring the Influence
and Community Relati
the Performance of .
Students in British Colum...
Public Schools

Cheryl Aman*

Introduction

In the province of British Columbia, only 49% of Aboriginal[1] students, in contrast to 83% of all British Columbia students, complete high school[2] (British Columbia Ministry of Education 2008). Remedial efforts by educators, the provincial government, and leaders of First Nations communities are focused on academic performance and school retention of Aboriginal students. At this time, there is cause for some guarded optimism. The *How Are We Doing? Demographics and Performance of Aboriginal Students in BC Public Schools* series indicates that over a nine-year period, the Aboriginal school completion rate has increased from 37% in the 1998/99 to a high of approximately 50% in the 2004/05 and 2005/06 school years. In contrast, the increase for non-Aboriginal students has been more modest (from 76% in the 1998/99 year to the most recent 83% rate). Over this same time the BC Ministry of Education reports Aboriginal participation and performance rates in grades 4, 7 and 10 for reading, writing, and numeracy components of the Foundation Skills Assessment (FSA)—a standardized test administered province-wide—have improved.

The Aboriginal Education Enhancement branch of the BC Ministry of Education articulates policies regarding the education of Aboriginal students. In recent years the Ministry of Education has been pursuing formal Enhancement Agreements (EAs), or partnerships, with First Nations people province-wide. EAs now exist between thirty-six school boards and Aboriginal communities, and they are being negotiated in most of the other twenty-two school districts. The goals of the EAs are to improve the relationships between Aboriginal communities and schools and to improve academic achievement and graduation rates of Aboriginal students. The guiding policies behind these agreements make evident a desire to improve the climate of schools for Aboriginal parents and students by sharing decision making and establishing cultural and language programs. As well, the EAs set the

---

* The author would like to thank Fernando Cartwright, who assisted with the HLM6 analysis in this study.

...at there will be close monitoring of the performance of Aboriginal ...th the intent to use these data to set local school and school-district ... continuous improvement. FSA results and the school completion rates ... of the key indicators used to determine whether Aboriginal students have ...nced educationally (see Chapter 7 for a discussion of standardized testing).

It is not clear how well these district-level initiatives are presently working across the radically different school and community contexts that exist across British Columbia. Nor are the lessons one can draw from the successes of Aboriginal students explicit. There remains a challenge to understand whether general improvement has occurred, whether or not the gap between Aboriginal students and their non-Aboriginal peers has decreased over time, and most importantly, what factors facilitate or impede the educational progress of Aboriginal students.

Recent literature devoted to Aboriginal education has focused on a narrow set of variables in accounting for Aboriginal students' poor school outcomes and for schools' poor performance with Aboriginal students. This study begins with an understanding that there are variables that have not been addressed that might be helpful in explaining the gap between Aboriginal and non-Aboriginal students in British Columbia. Those variables may include the relative proportions of Aboriginal and non-Aboriginal students in the school, the proportion of on-reserve or off-reserve Aboriginal students in the school, the size of the community in which the school is located, the socio-economic conditions of the community, and the interrelationships of these variables. We wish to contextualize the BC Ministry of Education school performance data utilizing these variables in order to explore their relationship to Aboriginal school completion rates.

Overview of the Chapter

There are six sections to this chapter. First, there is a review of literature related to factors that may be associated with school attainment of Aboriginal students, Kindergarten to Grade 12 (K–12). Second, there is a brief description of the context of Aboriginal education in the province of British Columbia. Third, there is an overview of research methods and data issues. Fourth, there is a presentation of descriptive findings related to disparities between the Aboriginal student group and the non-Aboriginal student group across the province. Fifth, the results of our HLM analysis are presented, modeling how school demographics, as well as the economic and health profiles of communities in which schools are situated, influence the completion rates of Aboriginal students. The modeling results reinforce the descriptive findings regarding the relationship between lower socio-economic conditions, student mobility, and Aboriginal school completion. Finally, in the sixth section, policy implications are outlined. We point out the importance of taking student-level characteristics, such as student mobility, into consideration when making comparisons between school-level results and when making public policy.

Section One: School Attainment and Aboriginal Students

While much research has investigated broad issues of school completion (also referred to in the research literature as graduation, attainment, attrition, and dropout) for K–12 students, a limited number of studies have been conducted that seek to identify determinants of school attainment of Aboriginal students. This is a brief summary of research in this area, where a variety of approaches and perspectives are evident. These studies provide valuable insights to both individual experiences and larger school and societal issues that may influence school completion of Aboriginal students. The studies represent varied approaches and diverge both from each other and from the large scale analysis of school records done for this chapter. Cumulatively, this body of work contributes to an emerging and provocative body of work focused on Aboriginal schooling.

Individual Aboriginal Students: What Makes the Difference in K–12 School Completion?

Researchers have explored the cases of individuals through surveys and interviews in order to understand the experiences of individuals with school systems and have sought to uncover factors that may assist or act as barriers for Aboriginal students. Studies may also attempt to uncover factors that differentiate Aboriginal students who complete high school from those who do not. For example, in British Columbia, van der Woerd and Cox (2003) link student health-related characteristics such drug and alcohol addiction with school "at risk" status for Aboriginal students in Alert Bay, British Columbia. In another British Columbia example, Aboriginal students self-report that literacy skills are a barrier (First Nations Education Council 1997). Bazylak (2002) stresses the prominence of issues such as family, personal supports, as well as self-identity, that are evident through the narrative accounts of successful female Aboriginal students in Saskatoon, Saskatchewan. Kanu (2002) identifies the use of culturally appropriate learning styles in classrooms and supportive classroom environments as prominent themes in a Manitoban study.

A similar line of inquiry appears in US studies investigating the low high school completion of Native American students. Bowker (1992) interviewed Native women in three US states and noted that pregnancy and uncaring teachers were factors identified by Native women who did not complete school in her sample, while personal support was a factor for students who did complete school. Similarly, uncaring teachers (negative) and lack of parental support are factors identified by those who did not complete school in Coladarci's study (1983). In a case study of three Native students in an urban alternative school presented by Jeffries, Nix, & Singer (2002), students indicated that the impersonality of large schools and teachers created a sense of disconnection to school. Other American studies of Native American students examine self-perception related to academic performance (House 2003) and family connectedness (Machamer & Gruber 1998). This research contributes depth at understanding individual-level experiences of school completion and complements individual-level factors identified in the school attrition literature of other student groups, albeit leaving broad school differences and socio-economic and community differences unexplored.

School Structure Issues and Aboriginal Students

There are several studies on the effects of school organization factors and K–12 school completion (Bryk & Thum 1989, Lee, Bryk & Smith 1993, Reihl 1999, Rumberger 1995, and Wehlage & Rutter 1987). McLaren (1980) notes that personal problems of students such as access and transportation issues, pregnancy, and the need to provide care for family members, simply are not accommodated by most schools. Such perspective encourages us to consider whether students actually independently drop out of school or if they are "pushed" out by systemic and school-structure factors. In contrast to identifying student factors associated with poor or successful educational outcomes, some researchers examine how the structures and dynamics of school institutions create challenges and problems for some students or some student groups in particular. Fine (1986, 1991) discusses how schools discourage and exclude certain minority groups and poor students from full participation. Based on ethnographic work, Dehyle (1989, 1992, 1995) details how Native students are systemically marginalized at the schools they attend. Levin (1992), in an examination of curriculum, argues that existing school structures actively create dropouts and that program changes would benefit Aboriginal students and others. In a review of school-based causes and solutions to school drop out of Native students in the US, Reyhner (1992) urges change in the practices of teachers, counselors, and school administrators. They call for large impersonal schools to restructure, schedule longer class blocks, and resist testing regimes that result in student grade retention. While this work begins to address school-level interventions, empirical research that identifies or measures the effects of specific school structures or school practices has yet to occur.

Schools and Larger Social Issues for Aboriginal Students

Many scholars concerned with inequity of performance among student groups look at the dynamics of racism, forced assimilation, problems with integration, and segregation of minority groups in the school context. Some minority groups, it is argued, resist school as an institution in order to maintain their own unique cultural identities (LeCompte 1987). This is a provocative theoretical lens and is helpful in understanding how student group membership might influence individuals. Ogbu (1992) presents the different political relationships minority groups have to the dominant political structure as an explanation of educational attainment differences in minority groups. In his typology, Aboriginal students occupy an "involuntary minority" status and are disadvantaged by a politically entrenched exclusion. Cummins (1997) has used Ogbu's framework in discussing Aboriginal students and current and historical power relations in the Canadian context. However, Marker (2000) notes that Aboriginal groups are very distinct from other visible minorities. As descendents of the first people, they have a profoundly different relationship to local place, as well as different historical and economic relationships to non-Aboriginal settlers. Marker also argues these distinctions regarding Aboriginal people are ignored or poorly understood by educators and education policy makers.

Schools and Aboriginal Culture

There is a substantial body of work that posits that experiences in public schools create cultural discontinuity for Aboriginal students. Many scholars and advocates for improved Aboriginal school performance argue that the aspirations, learning styles, discourses and value systems, worldviews, and histories of Aboriginal cultures are devalued in schools or eradicated by colonialist agendas (Chisholm 1994, Hampton & Roy 2002, Kanu 2002, Perley 1993, Robertson 2003, Stairs 1995, Wall & Madak 1991). Schools are discussed as negative and destructive locations for Aboriginal students. Yet, for some researchers, the relationship of identity and school is not necessarily so direct; the strength of cultural identity developed within individual Aboriginal students may support (rather than hinder) their academic performance in public schools (Brade, Duncan, and Sokal 2003, Dehyle 1992).

There are numerous calls for schools to support and enhance the cultural strength of Aboriginal students (e.g., Archibald 1995) and many Aboriginal people urge a deep and meaningful integration of Aboriginal cultures into school cultures. For example, teachers should explicitly utilize the worldviews of Aboriginal peoples as a teaching strategy (MacIvor 1995, Smith 1999, Stairs 1995). Calls have been made for anti-racist curriculum, culturally relevant curriculum, and Aboriginal language courses (e.g., see, Calliou 1995, Labercane & McEachern 1995, Leavitt 1995, Sterling 1995, Vallerand & Menard 1984). There is also a strong call from many Aboriginal educators and researchers that Aboriginal people should have jurisdiction over their own education systems to insure strong cultural ties and healthy identities (Hookimaw-Witt 1998, Kirkness 1998, Siggner 1986, Tsuji 2000). As with school-level interventions suggested by the previously mentioned literature, the impact of these changes are not easily determined empirically. Future research will have to look at these measurement problems in order to verify the proposals.

Student Outcomes and Schools in Broader Socio-economic Context

Following the seminal Coleman Report in the US (Coleman et al. 1966), researchers have attempted to determine and account for differences in school achievement of student populations by collecting and evaluating data pertaining to students, school structures, and social and economic conditions of locations. Conducting such large-scale comparative studies of schools is difficult for methodological, logistical, and financial reasons. Such studies are data-driven, and it is difficult to secure measures that mean the same thing across different contexts. The data are multi-level (student, school, family, community, district, state/province) and there are few models of how interrelationships occur (Rumberger & Thomas 2000). Another issue is the lack of common understandings and utilization of concepts. For example, when school completion (or student dropout) is a school outcome of interest, the lack of standard definitions of these terms problematicizes analyses, since difference in students outcomes become confounded with differences in definition of terminology (LeCompte and Goebel 1987, Rumberger 1987).

Research focused on understanding Aboriginal school outcomes, such as school completion, does not escape these methodological challenges. MacKay and Myles (1995) note in their survey on the causes of Aboriginal student dropout that locating even basic statistical data is "surprisingly difficult" (1995,158). Swisher et al. (1991) and Swisher and Hoisch (1992) describe the difficulty in reaching meaningful conclusions, given that existing studies are localized, dispersed across multiple school systems, and utilize multiple ways of calculating attrition rates. Brady (1996) notes that federal data pertaining to Native peoples are difficult to obtain, and there are additional difficulties posed to researchers by shifting definitions of peoples such as Status Indian, non-Status Indian, Inuit and Métis. Data are also complicated by issues of identity, both given and chosen, as Guimond (2003) has indicated. Ledlow (1992), who evaluates the research of dropout and American Indians in terms of cultural discontinuity studies versus ecological or "macro level" explanations, notes similar difficulties created where school attendance, attrition, or completion are not systematically measured in the same way across jurisdictions.

However, a few small-scale studies have been attempted that examine socio-economic factors and school structural factors in terms of Aboriginal students. Cameron (1990) has connected school performance data of secondary schools with school demographic data to examine Aboriginal school attainment in British Columbia. In the United States, Ward (1995, 1998) explores the interactions of schools and communities with Indian students in rural settings, and compares school context and cultural differences of Native communities in another rural setting. She observes how effects of multi-level factors vary by school.

Situating this Study

While the literature on factors that may be associated with school attainment of Aboriginal students informs this research presented in this chapter, the focus here was on examining available administrative data in terms of demographic characteristics of students, schools, and the broader socio-economic conditions of communities. Our objective in this study was to explore variables that could be derived from a very large sample of students (all students enrolled in the British Columbia public school system over thirteen years) in addition to community socio-economic measures. An in-depth analysis of school record data would contribute significantly to the quantitative evidence explaining the school completion differences between Aboriginal and non-Aboriginal students in British Columbia. The scope and comprehensive nature of the data created an unparallel opportunity to examine this issue across an entire provincial student population.

The variables initially explored include the relative proportions of Aboriginal and non-Aboriginal students in the school, the proportion of on-reserve (Status) or off-reserve (non-Status) Aboriginal students in the school, the size of the school, the size of the community in which the school is located, the socio-economic conditions of the community, as well as the relationships among these variables. An objective was to contextualize school performance data derived from the individual student school histories in order to uncover patterns that may exist across diverse school locations and explore their influence on the school completion rates of Aboriginal students.

Section Two: The Context of Aboriginal Education in British Columbia

This is a brief description of the education governance structure, school accountability initiatives and the school/community context of Aboriginal students living in the province of British Columbia.

In the province of British Columbia, the provincial Ministry of Education is responsible for the education of K–12 students. However, the federal government of Canada, and more specifically its Department of Indian and Northern Affairs (INAC), currently has jurisdiction over the education of Aboriginal students living on-reserve and attending band-operated schools nation-wide.[3] Band-operated schools are attended by less than 10% of K–12 Aboriginal students in the province of British Columbia (Postl 2005). The large majority of Aboriginal students in British Columbia are enrolled in provincially operated public schools. As of the 2006 academic year, approximately 565,500 students attend public schools in British Columbia; 55,000 (nearly 10% of the total public school student population) of these students self-identify as Aboriginal. In this research, the outcomes of Aboriginal students enrolled in British Columbia public schools are the focus, rather than a comparison of school completion rates in the two different schooling systems. The school outcomes of Aboriginal students attending Band-operated schools is not examined. Studies of band schools are hampered by the lack of consistant data.

In the province of British Columbia, data associated with performance monitoring have been available and published at the school, school district, and province-wide level for seven years, with the objective of serving school accountability and public transparency agendas. British Columbia is unique in Canada in that data associated with the Aboriginal student population are reported at the school, school district and province-wide level. (Other student groups for which results are available at these levels are male, female, English as a second language, French immersion, special education and gifted.) While this reported information appears to convey trends in improvement over time for this student group (at least at the provincial level), it also invites superficial and misleading comparisons between student populations, schools, and school districts from year to year. The public information establishes mainly that (a) Aboriginal students typically have lower achievement than their non-Aboriginal peers; and (b) there is wide variation across the province, and within school districts. For example, to illustrate the degree of variation that exists, Vancouver School District (a very large urban school district) reports Aboriginal school completion rates that range from 14% to 31% across schools over the five school years reported.[4] In this particular district, 3% of students identify as Aboriginal. In contrast, another district in central British Columbia with 14% of the students self-identifying as Aboriginal reports Aboriginal completion rates that range from 40% to 54%[5] over the same period. The factors that influence this variation in performance have not been identified.

Extensive differences exist in the geographic, community, and school contexts of high schools and school districts across British Columbia. Many schools are located in large urban centres in the Lower Mainland of British Columbia. Others are located in northern or otherwise remote areas of the province. The neighbourhoods where the schools are situated vary widely in terms of social, educational, and economic conditions. There are smaller schools with just over 100 high school students enrolled and large schools where several thousand attend. Unemployment rates vary in the locations of these schools from 25% to 4%. Some schools are 8–12 schools; others are 11–12 schools. The proportion of Aboriginal students ranges from less than 5% to greater than 50%. Many major population centres across the province are large enough to have more than one high school where sizable populations of Aboriginal students are enrolled. Given the wide range of school contexts that exist and that these high schools are nested within a wide range of community contexts, the exercise of drawing comparisons between schools in order to identify patterns (and possibly exemplars) of Aboriginal school completion is intricate and imperfect.

Section Three: Data and Methodological Issues of this Study

The subjects of this study are each student enrolled in the provincial public school system in British Columbia throughout the school years 1991/92–2003/04. These are the earliest cohorts for whom data has been systematically collected and retained by the BC Ministry of Education. The main school outcome explored in this study is school completion of Aboriginal students. School completion is defined as grade 12 school completion within six years of beginning grade 8. There were over 1.5 million student records associated with enrolled students over this time period available for analysis. The British Columbia Ministry of Education released this information for the purposes of this study and ensured that the identification of individual students was impossible through dummy encrypted personal identification codes. From these 1.5 million individual student-level records, eight cohorts of students starting grade 8 were constructed. In other words, all students who were enrolled in grade 8 for the first time in the provincial system were grouped together as a single cohort by school year. The cohorts ranged over time from the 1991/92 school year to the 1998/99 school year. Therefore, each student was assigned to a single cohort and was only counted as part of this cohort whether or not grade repetition or school-leaving occurred. Further, this study was able to disaggregate Aboriginal students into two Aboriginal subgroups (on-reserve and off-reserve Aboriginal students). The first objective was to examine school trajectories of cohorts progressing through the high school grade levels. The existence of several cohorts for study meant that recent cohorts could be also be compared to preceding cohorts in order to determine if changes, hopefully improvements, had occurred over time in basic school outcomes in the British Columbia public system.

From the school records, it could be calculated whether a student's school completion had occurred within six years of enrolling in grade 8 for the first time. In order to analyze patterns associated with students at the school level (such as demographic composition of the cohort), in addition to outcomes at the student level (such as high school completion), variables were aggregated to the school level in order to look at ecological relationships between schools. The aggregation was performed for each of the eight cohorts. Variables associated with school curriculum (such as Aboriginal support programs) or school district policies (such the district status regarding Aboriginal EAs), were not formally examined because policy and practices associated with these is subject to wide variation across school locations. Another limitation to analyzing such conditions is the paucity of consistent and comprehensive data associated with these characteristics. Thus, the only information used to characterize schools was based on aggregations of individual level student-records.

Data from the 2001 Census was utilized to describe the socio-economic context for each high school. These data were available for the two-mile radius surrounding each high school in the province. The socio-economic variables were (1) rate of educational attainment less than high school, (2) unemployment rate, (3) proportion of families earning under $20,000 a year, and (4) average family income. These variables do not perfectly reflect conditions associated strictly to school catchment areas and particular demographic groups residing within the area, nor may they be accurate over the entire time period examined; however, as proxy socio-economic indicators, the information was drawn from the Census data was comprehensive and salient.

Over the reference period of this study (1991–2005), many schools opened, closed, changed their names, transformed their grade structures, or altered their service delivery structure (to alternative programs or distance education, for example). In addition, the provincial education system underwent a process of school district amalgamation, during which many schools were reassigned to new school districts. These factors provided a caution in interpretation of some results: it cannot be assumed what was identified as a given "school" was stable.

A critical observation was that grade 8 cohorts at many schools did not remain stable in terms of student composition over time. Typically, differences analyses of schools in which students were enrolled *in their first (grade 8) year of high school* were conducted. However, analyses of relationships between school cohort composition and school outcomes associated with the schools students attended *in their fifth (grade 12) year of school* were also conducted. These analyses addressed the possible impact of changes in school structures that occurred in the six-year span in which students were completing high school, and the effects of student mobility and drop-out in those six years. The recognition that student demographics in schools change across and during school years allowed the pursuit of questions: In what way had the cohort composition changed due to student mobility or student attrition? How many new Aboriginal students had joined the original Aboriginal cohort? Had Aboriginal students moved to other schools in the community, the school district, or across the province?

The number of school changes that occurred at the student-level in the six-year time frame of high school was calculated. The school records allowed for further categorization of school changes as occurring within-district or between-districts.[6] School change (student mobility) emerged as important variable at the student-level with respect to school completion for Aboriginal students.

As a cautionary note, it is not known to what degree data management practices, reporting practices, and graduation policies account for observed improved outcomes in the data over time. Therefore, dependable inferences regarding the causes of the improved outcomes cannot be based solely on these data. In response, there is a statistical control (by considering schools longitudinally) for the temporal variability in completion rates in the model described in Section Five of this chapter.

Section Four: Disparity and Variability of Aboriginal School Outcomes Across British Columbia

In this section, descriptive information regarding the variability and disparity of school completion rates and related school outcomes is presented. As previously public-domain school information indicated, there was a high degree of disparity and variability in the six-year school completion rate for Aboriginal students in public schools in British Columbia. Analysis of student grade trajectories confirms that numerous differences exist in school careers of Aboriginal students and non-Aboriginal students broadly, and at the majority of high schools province-wide.

Grade to Grade Progression and School Interruption

There are substantial differences in the percentage of students progressing from one grade level to the next as early as the transition from grade 8 to grade 9. For Aboriginal students, there is a 10% attrition rate (or rate of not progressing to the next grade) after each secondary grade level. In contrast, the rate in the non-Aboriginal student group is 2%. This finding is consistent with White et al. (2004), which found that there were higher levels of school leavers at the transition to grade 9 from grade 8. As well, there is a higher rate of absence from the school system over secondary grade levels associated with Aboriginal students. The data also show that 15% of Aboriginal students have left the BC school system for one or more years in their secondary trajectories, returning to the school system after this absence. This rate of school interruption is 2% in the non-Aboriginal students.

"Secondary Ungraded" Classification

Both schools and school districts vary in the rate of students classified as "secondary ungraded"—a school program categorization in which students are no longer in the regular graded program. In other words, secondary ungraded students are not considered to be in a program associated with a secondary grade level (grade 8, 9, 10, 11 or 12). Practices regarding which students are categorized in this manner and the individualized education programs they receive are at the discretion of the school districts. Aboriginal students are invariably categorized as secondary ungraded at higher rates than non-Aboriginal students. Province-wide, approximately 11% of Aboriginal students were categorized in this way (as opposed to fewer than 2% of non-Aboriginal students). The completion rate for Aboriginal students categorized as secondary ungraded is low (8%). Therefore on average more than 90% of those students in this category never complete.

Variability Associated with School Completion of Aboriginal Students

By the expected grade 12 year, a substantial proportion of Aboriginal students have left the school system altogether (13%), nearly three times the number of non-Aboriginal students leaving (5%). These students, by definition, do not complete school. Additionally, there is a high proportion of Aboriginal students in the school system that do not graduate within 6 years, though they are present in the school system. These school completion rates differed between on-reserve Status Indian (also referred to as band-status) students attending public schools and those who are non-Status (or non-band) Aboriginal students. As well, we saw improvements in the completion rates for both groups. School completion rates for Aboriginal students with band status increased from 24% to 31%, and non-band status Aboriginal school completion rates from 29% to 48% over the eight cohort years examined.[7] Across the 103 high schools where Aboriginal cohorts were typically greater than eight students, Aboriginal school completion rates ranged from 14% to 78%. (School completion rates of Aboriginal band students ranged from 0% to 67%.) Year-to-year Aboriginal school completion rates at each school also varied dramatically. To illustrate this, a school with a long-run "average" or typical completion rate might have rates ranging from 33% to 90% over eight years. Another school with a typical long-run average might have year-to-year rates ranging from 8% to 70%. The pattern of variability from year to year can be observed in nearly all high schools. Adding complexity, band student completion rates can vary considerably from non-band student rates within the same school and the same year. This within-school variability calls into question any inference that that continuous improvement is occurring broadly at a school and hence renders accountability-driven targets based on trends problematic.

School Mobility

Finally, there are observable differences in the completion rate of Aboriginal students who changed schools in the six-year window given for school completion. To illustrate, in one cohort (starting grade 8 in the 1998/99 school year), approximately one third of the Aboriginal students did not change schools. However, 57% of Aboriginal students who did not change schools completed school within six years. This is a much higher percentage than the overall 42% completion rate reported for Aboriginal students province-wide. An estimated 18% of the Aboriginal cohort changed schools once due to grade progression, such as in cases where students are enrolled at middle schools (grade 6–grade 8) or junior high schools (grade 8–grade 10). The completion rate of these students is comparable (at 58%) to Aboriginal students who had never changed schools. Approximately one third of the province's 1998/99 Aboriginal cohort changed schools between districts. These Aboriginal students' six-year completion rate is nearly identical to the completion rate of students who change schools within districts. Approximately 30% of these Aboriginal students complete school. There is one more categorization of school change—school change within a school district. An estimated 20% of the 1998/99 Aboriginal cohort experienced within-district school change. The completion rate of these students is substantially lower than that of their peers who remain in the district and do not change schools, or alternately change schools due to grade progression. Students who change schools within district in this cohort had a 28% completion rate. We therefore suggest that disruptive school change, or student mobility, is a significant factor in both student-level and school-level school completion for Aboriginal students. However, when school change is associated with grade progression and hence is experienced by all students in a given grade level, it does not appear to have the same negative impact on student outcomes.[8]

Section Five: Modeling the Interaction of School Context, Socio-economic Community Context and Aboriginal Cohort School Completion

As described above, for each high school, there were eight cohort years in which school-completion outcomes and student composition variables were constructed. Data was merged in order to identify schools by name and by location with the data provided by Statistics Canada regarding the socio-economic status of the population living within a two-mile radius of high schools according to six-digit postal code geography information. Using information on the student records, a multilevel database that nested students-within-cohorts and cohorts-within-schools was produced. Thus, for any particular school, this database could be used to estimate the long-run average completion rate for Aboriginal students, the completion rate for any given cohort, and whether or not any single student had completed in any given cohort. This data was used in the second stage of analysis to identify the contributions of different levels of context on Aboriginal student school completion.

In the second stage of analysis, the available demographic, school context, and community socio-economic variables were used to provide a sense of the relationships these could have with individual school completion of Aboriginal students. Implicitly, the collection of certain variables by the Ministry of Education suggests the hypothesis that these variables are related to the quality or equity of students' learning conditions and experiences. Nevertheless, these variables were used to test the general hypothesis that student characteristics, schools, and community influence school-completion of Aboriginal students. A multi-level analysis was conducted using the software HLM6 to estimate the relative influence of each of these contexts, as well as identify specific variables within each context that might explain its influence.

The process of modeling the relationships had four stages. The purpose of the first stage was to establish the baseline Aboriginal completion rate and partition the variance in completion between the three levels of analysis (student, year, and school). The purpose of the second stage was to identify student-level features which might explain some of the difference in probability of completion between Aboriginal and non-Aboriginal students. The purpose of the third stage was to identify year-specific school-level characteristics, such as student composition and school size, that explained variation in either average cohort completion rates or the difference in probability of graduating between Aboriginal and non-Aboriginal students in a particular cohort. The purpose of the final stage was to identify possible permanent school-context variables that might explain either the variation in school-cohort completion rates or persistent, cross-cohort differences in the probability of completion between Aboriginal and non-Aboriginal students in a school. Parsimony in building this statistical model is achieved by backward deletion.[9]

Table 8.1: Null Model of Non-Aboriginal, Aboriginal and Band-Status Student Likelihood of School Completion

	Probability of school completion	(s.e)	s.d. (across cohorts)	s.d. (across schools)
Non-Aboriginal status	0.73	(0.01)	0.04	0.15
Aboriginal status relative to non-Aboriginal status	-0.24	(0.01)	0.07	0.10
Band status relative to non-band status	-0.15	(0.01)	0.10	0.09

Null Model Results

The first model presented below (see **Table 8.1**) or null model, contains no variables that explain the outcomes of interest. In the null model, the outcome is simply whether or not a student has completed school. The predictor variables are whether a student has ever had Aboriginal status and whether a student has ever had band status. (All students with band status also have Aboriginal status.) In a sense, the null model attempts to explain how much of the variation in the dependent variable can be explained by simply the clustering within Level 2 (school) units. Intraclass coefficients describing the relative proportions of variance of the main effects (in the leftmost column of **Table 8.1**) at the cohort and school levels can be obtained by taking the ratio of the variances of the effects at these levels. The variances can be obtained by squaring the standard deviations presented in the two rightmost columns of **Table 8.1**.

Variation in school completion rates occurs primarily between schools, not between years. The estimate presented in the first row of **Table 8.1** indicates that the overall school completion rate of non-Aboriginal students is 0.73, indicating that just over seven in ten non-Aboriginal students are expected to graduate. From year to year, the standard deviation of this estimate was 0.04, suggesting that non-Aboriginal school completion rates were fairly consistent over time. In contrast, the standard deviation of this estimate across schools was 0.15, suggesting that cohorts within schools tend to be relatively consistent in school completion rates relative to the differences in school completion rates between schools.

On average, school completion rates of Aboriginal students tend to be lower (-0.24) than that of non-Aboriginal students. This standard deviation of this effect across cohorts is 0.07, suggesting that the effect of Aboriginal status on probability of school completion is relatively unstable across cohorts.[10] The results for band-status students across cohorts are similar to those for Aboriginal students. Furthermore, since band students are a subset of Aboriginal students, the instability due to small within-cohort sample size is even greater than that of Aboriginal students generally in the student population. The ratio of the school-level variance to cohort-level variances for school completion rates of non-Aboriginal students is 0.93, indicating that variation in school completion rates occurs primarily between schools, not between years. Similarly, the variability of the effect of Aboriginal status on school completion is greater across schools (s.d. = 0.10), than across years (s.d. = 0.07), although the ratio is much smaller (0.51). In contrast to the non-Aboriginal and Aboriginal student groups, the variability of the effect of band status on school completion rates between cohorts (0.10) and between schools (0.09) is almost the same, suggesting that the average effect of band status is equally unstable across cohorts and schools.

The main interpretation from these null model results is that the variability of school completion rates *across schools* is much greater than *over time* and both Aboriginal and band students appear to be at greater risk of non-completion than of their non-Aboriginal peers. Moreover, there are relatively large variations in effect of Aboriginal and band status indicators over cohorts and schools. Given that these effects are in reference to the non-Aboriginal group, these variations indicate that the school completion outcomes in Aboriginal students tend to be far more variable than for non-Aboriginal students at all levels of analysis.

Explanatory Model Results

The full model presented below (see **Table 8.2**) describes the final model that was fit to the data in this study. Variables from the original data are not presented here if their effect is insignificant in the context of the other variables in the model. One such insignificant variable (number of Aboriginal students in a school) was left in the model for illustrative purposes. The significant variables are (1) secondary ungraded status, (2) mobility across school districts status, (3) Aboriginal status, (4) the proportions of families living with low income within a two-mile school radius, (5) the proportion of Aboriginal students in school, and (6) band status.

The explanatory model suggests that expected school completion of non-Aboriginal students who have never had secondary ungraded status, who do not attend schools with Aboriginal classmates, and have no low-income families in their communities, in British Columbia high schools is 0.87. If students are Aboriginal, the expected school completion drops by 0.17 to approximately 0.70. If the Aboriginal student has band status, the expected school completion drops further to approximately 0.54.

This explanatory model provides information about patterns that are associated with the cohort composition and student group completion rates at the school level. High school cohorts where there are no Aboriginal students are expected to have a 0.87 school completion rate. Where school cohort compositions have increasing Aboriginal and band students, associated school completion rates decline by 0.04 for each incremental change of 10% in the school student population. However, this association cannot be interpreted as causal. It is much more likely to be indicative that high proportions of Aboriginal students are correlated with community conditions associated with poorer student outcomes for all students.

Table 8.2: Explanatory Model

Description of effect	Probability of school completion	s.d. (across years)	s.d. (across schools)
School completion rate of non-Aboriginal students in schools with no mobility and no Aboriginal students	0.87	0.04	0.10
The adjustment to the school completion rate for every 10% increase in the percentage of Aboriginal students in the school	-0.04	-	-
The adjustment for every additional Aboriginal student in the school	0.00	-	-
The adjustment based on if the student has ever been assigned to secondary ungraded status	-0.39	-	-
The adjustment based on if the student has changed school districts between grades 8 and 12	-0.16	-	-
The unexplained difference in school completion between Aboriginal and non-Aboriginal students	-0.17	0.07	0.08
The change in the Aboriginal school completion difference associated with every 10% increase in the number of families living in low income in the surrounding community	-0.05	-	-
The change in the Aboriginal school completion difference associated with every 10% increase in the percentage of Aboriginal students in the same school class	0.02	-	-
The unexplained additional difference in school completion associated with band status	-0.16	0.09	0.09
The adjustment in band-status school completion rate difference associated with a 10% increase in the proportion of the surrounding community who are Aboriginal	0.02	-	-

Note: Only individual main effects were specified as variables across years and schools.

The model indicates that Aboriginal school completion is diminished where there are higher proportions of low-income families in school neighbourhoods. Wherever there is a 10% increase of families living on low incomes in the school neighbourhood, school completion rates diminish by 0.05. In other words, Aboriginal students are not uniformly distributed across communities in British Columbia.

The model illustrates the effect of mobility on the expected school completion rate of student groups. Mobility that involves a change of school districts in high school grade levels diminishes the expected probability of school completion by 0.16.

Finally, a very interesting Aboriginal cohort effect emerges from the explanatory model. Results here indicate the hypothetical difference between probability of an Aboriginal student's completing school in two otherwise similar classes, one with no other Aboriginal students and one with all Aboriginal students, is 0.21 (The change in the Aboriginal school completion rate difference associated with every 10% increase in the percentage of Aboriginal students in the same school class is 0.02) However, higher proportions of Aboriginal students are linked to increases in Aboriginal school completion and Aboriginal band student school completion at the school level.[11] An interpretation of this finding could be that although Aboriginal students tend to live in less advantaged communities, the school completion difference compared to non-Aboriginal students appears to be ameliorated somewhat wherever there are increases in the proportion of their classmates who are also Aboriginal. In a similar way, where there is increasing Aboriginal representation in the community, there is a higher probability of graduating for band-status students.

The modeling confirms that in British Columbia public high schools there are significant differences in student populations in terms of school completion. This model confirms the hypothesis that student characteristics, schools, and community influence school completion of Aboriginal students. The results of the null model indicate that the 51% of the variation in Aboriginal school completion rate differences across different schools and cohorts can be attributed to school-level factors. With the simple model presented in this study, the residual standard deviation of the Aboriginal school completion rate difference at the school level in the explanatory model was 0.08, representing a 36% decrease in variance, explained primarily by the socio-economic context of schools. While not a complete explanation of the problem, this result is not trivial and highlights the influence of context in exacerbating inequities between individual students. The explanatory model confirms that factors associated with student populations (Aboriginal status, between-district mobility), and school communities (socio-economic conditions) explain some of the differences in school completion rates across British Columbia over the time period that was the focus of this study.

Section Six: Policy Implications

What conditions are associated with the smallest and greatest disparities between Aboriginal and non-Aboriginal students when system-wide administrative data is available for examination? This study demonstrates that school completion differences are generally greater in school contexts where less favourable socio-economic conditions prevail, and where the student composition includes band students and highly mobile Aboriginal (band and non-band) students.

For those educators, researchers, and policy-makers interested in addressing the equity issue of school outcomes of Aboriginal students, both an understanding of the socio-geographic pattern of inequities and an understanding of student characteristics associated with vulnerability to poor school outcomes should be of more value than examining school-level performance rates. Comparisons of school rates of Aboriginal school completion or any other school-related measure by year or across schools can be very misleading because *fundamentally different populations of students may exist each year or in each school.* The study indicates that data must be analyzed in a manner that makes student demographic features evident before comparisons are made, particularly where comparisons are aimed at evaluation of school improvement or program success

It's hoped that studies of this kind can assist advocates, educators, and policymakers to understand and consider some of the macro-level factors that may be related to school completion by Aboriginal students. Data related to school context and community context are valuable and should be systematically gathered and shared. Such data allows for insights regarding the system-wide variability in school performance and the influence of factors within and beyond the control of individual schools.

It is hoped the identification of mobility as a significant factor in the educational careers of Aboriginal students does not persuade school officials that the problem rests with the mobile students and their families or lead them to absolve schools of any responsibility. Quite the opposite, this observation should prompt schools to think differently about their responsibility to such students.[12]

The personnel, programs, policies, and practices at the school level may contribute significantly to the variability in Aboriginal school success. While this study is a large-scale quantitative analysis, more qualitative and ethnographic work located at schools would provide refined information on current school practices that promote school completion. The qualification, experience and attitudes of teachers may play a role. Further, instructional variables such as program design, lesson activities, curriculum, and classroom structure and climate might influence Aboriginal academic success. These might include funding and resource allocation, school structure, leadership style, disciplinary climate, and homework policies. Much of the qualitative work focusing on Aboriginal issues in education suggests the importance of these factors. At a higher level, community conditions, dynamics, and available support services should be examined using information more relevant to local contexts, rather than generic socio-economic descriptors. It is our hope that research focusing on Aboriginal school outcomes will continue in order to provide information that influences positive and appropriate responses within education systems.

Endnotes

1 In this paper the term Aboriginal refers to students who have self-identified as being of Aboriginal ancestry on the annual British Columbia Ministry of Education student data collection form (Form 1701). These students may include First Nations, Status Indians, non-Status Indians, Métis or Inuit. The authors recognize that the definition of these terms is contested. Students voluntarily declare themselves Aboriginal, but may choose not to do so consistently every year. For the purpose of this analysis, we considered students who had ever declared themselves to be Aboriginal on Form 1701.

2 In British Columbia, the Ministry of Education makes a distinction between the terms "graduation" and "six-year completion." Graduation rates describe the proportion of students enrolled in Grade 12 in September who graduated in the same school year. In contrast, a six-year completion rate tracks the proportion of students who graduated within six years of starting Grade 8. In this paper, we use the term "school completion" in keeping with the Ministry of Education definition.

3 In this paper the term on-reserve student indicates a Status Indian student who is associated with a reserve or band. We use this term interchangeably with band student. These students are provided federal education funding whether they enroll in band schools or provincial public schools. For the purpose of this analysis, we considered students who had ever received federal funding as an On-Reserve student. It is important to note that in British Columbia, approximately 70% of K–12 students who identify as Aboriginal are not living as Status Indians and are not affiliated with a particular band. For these self-identified non-Status Aboriginal students, as well as for the band students attending a provincial public school, the province of British Columbia allocates an additional $950.00 per student, per school year beyond the per-pupil allocation. This additional funding ($45 million per, school year) is provided in order to address the inequity faced by Aboriginal students and is used to fund Aboriginal language and culture programs in the school system, Aboriginal academic support programs, and other localized Aboriginal programs. See www2.news.gov.bc.ca, "New Agreement to Help Aboriginal Students Succeed" regarding funding allocation.

4 See <**www.bced.gov.bc.ca/reports/pdfs/sd_perf/039.pdf**>

5 See <**www.bced.gov.bc.ca/reports/pdfs/sd_perf/073.pdf**>

6 It should be noted that students both changed high schools within their original district or within their destination district, and changed schools across districts during their high school grades. (For the purposes of this analysis, if a district change occurred between grade 8 and the fifth year of high school, the students were included in the between-district school change category.)

7 Editor's note: While improvement in both categories varies between schools, and within schools, it is interesting to note that the non-band status group improved significantly more in most of the schools studied.

8 Editor's Note: This could mean that the change is schools is not accompanied by a change in living residence. The shift therefore is not in neighbourhood, but just school of attendance. All students progressing would shift, so social capital built up in the cohort is not lost to either Aboriginal or non-Aboriginal students. See White et al. 2006.

9 At each stage, the model is specified using all predictors available at that level. Then, one-by-one, we remove variables with no statistically significant effects from the model. The remaining variables with non-zero effects are then each tested for stability by comparing the coefficients of the other variables with and without each variable included in the model. Variables whose coefficients are co-dependent (i.e., which have effects of equal magnitude but in opposite direction that only non-zero when both are included in the model) are removed from the model. When each step is finalized, the model specification is fixed at that level and the same process is repeated for modeling the next level of data.

10 We suspect that the smaller numbers of Aboriginal students in each school relative to non-Aboriginals make the year-to-year estimates more susceptible to sampling error and cohort effects. Thus, the cohort level of analysis is more likely to produce unstable results for Aboriginal students.

11 The author does acknowledge that notwithstanding, these higher proportions may be more likely to occur in schools in where poor socio-economic conditions prevail.

12 Editor's note: Policy and program aimed at encouraging new transferees to become integrated, helping with the replacement of social capital networks, and reaching out to the families of these students etc., may have greater effects on helping improvement in completion rates.

References

Archibald, J. 1995. "Locally Developed Native Studies Curriculum: An Historical and Philosophical Rationale." In M. Battiste and J. Barman, (eds.). *First Nations Education: The Circle Unfolds.* Vancouver: UBC Press. 288–312.

Bazylak, D. 2002. "Journeys to Success: Perceptions of Five Female Aboriginal High School Graduates." *Canadian Journal of Native Education.* 26(2): 134–151.

Bowker, A. 1992. "The American Indian Female Drop Out." *Journal of American Indian Education.* 31(3): 3–17.

Brade, C., K.A. Duncan, and L. Sokal. 2003. "The Path to Education in a Canadian Aboriginal Context." *Canadian Journal of Native Education.* 27(2): 235.

Brady, P. 1996. "Native Dropouts and Non-Native Dropouts in Canada: Two Solitudes or a Solitude Shared?" *Journal of American Indian Education.* 35(2): 10–20.

British Columbia Ministry of Education. 2007. "Aboriginal Report 2006/07: How Are We Doing? Demographics and Performance of Aboriginal Students in BC Public Schools." Retrieved June 22, 2008 from <**www.bced.gov.bc.ca/abed/perf2007.pdf**>.

Bryk, A.S. and Y.M. Thum. 1989. "The Effects of High School Organization on Dropping Out: An Exploratory Investigation." *American Educational Research Journal.* (26) 353–383.

Calliou, S. 1995. "Peacekeeping Actions at Home: A Medicine Wheel Model for a Peacekeeping Pedagogy." In M. Battiste and J. Barman (eds). *First Nations Education: The Circle Unfolds.* Vancouver: UBC Press. 47–72.

Cameron, I. 1990. "Student Achievement Among Native Students in British Columbia." *Canadian Journal of Native Education.* 17(1): 36–43.

Chisholm, S. 1994. "Assimilation and Oppression: The Northern Experience." *Education Canada.* 34(4): 28–34.

Coladarci, T. 1983. "High School Dropout Among Native Indians." *Journal of American Indian Research.* 9(3): 1–9.

Coleman, J. S., E.Q. Campbell, C.J. Hobson, J. McPartland, A.M. Mood, F.D. Weinfeld, and R.L. York. 1966. *Equality of Educational Opportunity.* Washington, D.C: US Government Printing Office.

Cummins, J. 1997. "Minority Status and Schooling in Canada." *Anthropology and Education.* (28): 411–430.

Dehyle, D. 1989. "Pushouts and Pullouts: Navajo and Ute School Leavers." *Journal of Navajo Education.* 6(2): 36–51.

Dehyle, D. 1992. "Constructing Failure and Maintaining Identity: Navajo and Ute School Leavers." *Journal of American Indian Education.* 31(2): 24–47.

Dehyle, D. 1995. "Navajo Youth and Anglo Racism: Cultural Integrity and Resistance." *Harvard Educational Review.* (65): 403–444.

Fine, M. 1986. "Why Urban Adolescents Drop into and out of Public High School." *Teachers College Record.* (87): 393–409.

Fine, M. 1991. *Framing Dropouts: Notes on the Politics of an Urban Middle School.* New York: State University of New York Press.

First Nations Education Council School District No. 73 (Kamloops/Thompson). 1997. "Improving School Success for First Nations Students: First Nations Education Study." Retrieved February 3, 2006 from <**www.bced.gov.bc.ca/abed/readings/iss/improving.htm**>.

Guimond, E. 2003. "Changing Ethnicity: The Concept of Ethnic Drifters" in *Aboriginal Conditions: Research as a Foundation for Public Policy.* J.P. White, P. Maxim and D. Beavon. (eds). Toronto: UBC Press.

Hampton, M. and J. Roy. 2002. "Strategies for Facilitating Success of First Nations students." *Canadian Journal of Higher Education.* 32(3): 1–28.

Hookimaw-Witt, J. 1998. "Any Changes Since Residential School?" *Canadian Journal of Native Education*. 22,(2): 159–171.

House, D.J. 2003. "A Longitudinal Assessment of Cognitive-motivational Predictors of the Grade Performance of American Indian/Alaskan Native Students." *International Journal of Instructional Media*. 30 (3): 303–315.

Jeffries R. N., M. Nix, and C. Singer. 2002. "Urban American Indians 'Dropping' Out of Traditional High Schools: Barriers and Bridges to Success." *High School Journal*. 85(3): 38–47.

Kanu, Y. 2002. "In their own Voices: First Nations Students Identify Some Cultural Mediators of their Learning in the Formal School System." *Alberta Journal of Educational Research*. 48(2): 98–121.

Kirkness, V.J. 1998. "Our People's Education: Cut the Shackles; Cut the Crap; Cut the Mustard." *Canadian Journal of Native Education*. 22(1): 10–16.

LeCompte, M.D. 1987. "The Cultural Context of Dropping Out: Why Remedial Programs Don't Solve Problems." *Education and Urban Society*. (19) 232–249.

Lee, V.E., A.S. Bryk, and J.B. Smith. 1993. "The Organization of Effective Secondary Schools." In L. Darling-Hammond (ed.), *Review of Research in Education, 19*. Washington, DC: American Education Research Association. 171–267.

Levin, B. 1992. "Dealing with Dropouts in Canadian Education." *Curriculum Inquiry*. 22(3): 257–270.

Labercane, G. and W. McEachern. 1995. "Striving for Success: First Nations Education in Canada." *Education*. 115(3): 322–331.

Leavitt, R. 1995. "Language and Cultural Content in Native Education." In *First Nations Education: The Circle Unfolds*. M. Battiste and J. Barman (eds). Vancouver: UBC Press. 124–138.

Ledlow, S. 1992. "Is Cultural Discontinuity an Adequate Explanation for Dropping Out?" *Journal of American Indian Education*. 31(3): 21–36.

Machamer, A. and E. Gruber. 1998. "Secondary School, Family, and Educational Risk: Comparing American Indian Adolescents and their Peers." *Journal of Educational Research*. 91(6): 357–370.

MacIvor, M. 1995. "Redefining Science Education for Aboriginal Students. In *First Nations Education: The Circle Unfolds*. M. Battiste and J. Barman (eds). Vancouver: UBC Press. 73–98.

MacKay, R. and L. Myles. 1995. "A Major Challenge for the Education System: Aboriginal Retention and Dropout. In *First Nations Education: The Circle Unfolds*. M. Battiste and J. Barman (eds). Vancouver: UBC Press. 157–178.

McLaren, P. 1989. *Cries from the Corridor: The New Suburban Ghettos*. Toronto: Metheun.

Marker, M. 2000. "Lummi Identity and White Racism: When Location is a Real Place." *International Journal of Qualitative studies in Education*. 24(1): 401–414.

Ogbu, J. 1992. "Understanding Cultural Diversity and Learning." *Educational Researcher*. (21): 5–14.

Perley D.G., 1993. "Aboriginal Education in Canada as Internal Colonialism." *Canadian Journal of Native Education*. 20(1): 118–128.

Postl, B. 2005. *British Columbia First Nations Schools Funding Analysis (Revised): 2003/2004 School Year*. Ottawa: Indian and Northern Affairs Canada.

Reihl, C. J. 1999. "Labeling and Letting Go: An Organizational Analysis of how High School Students are Discharged as Dropouts." In *Research in Sociology of Education and Socialization*. A.M. Pallas (ed). New York: JAI Press.

Reyhner, J. 1992. "American Indians Out of School: A Review of School-based Causes and Solutions." *Journal of American Indian Education* 31(3): 37–56.

Robertson H. 2003. "Decolonizing Schools." *Phi Delta Kappan*. 84(7): 552.

Rowe, K.J., and P.W. Hill. 1998. "Modelling Educational Effectiveness in Classrooms: The Use of Multi-level Structural Equations to Model Students' Progress." *Educational Research and Evaluation*. (4): 307–347.

Rumberger, R.W. 1987. "High School Dropouts: A Review of Issues and Evidence." *Review of Educational Research*. 57(2): 101–121.

Rumberger, R.W. 1995. "Dropping out of Middle School: A Multilevel Analysis of Students and Schools." *American Education Research Journal*. (32): 585–625.

Rumberger, R.W. 2003. "The Causes and Consequences of Student Mobility." *The Journal of Negro Education*, 72(1): 6–21.

Siggner, A.J. 1986. "The Socio-demographic Conditions of Registered Indians." *Canadian Social Trends*. (Winter): 2–9.

Smith, D. 1999. "Educating Inner-city Aboriginal Students: The Significance of Culturally Appropriate Instruction and Parental Support." *McGill Journal of Education*. 34(2): 155–171.

Stairs, A. 1995. "Learning Processes and Teaching Roles in Native Education: Cultural Base and Cultural Brokerage." In *First Nations Education: The Circle Unfolds*. M. Battiste and J. Barman (eds). Vancouver: UBC Press. 139–153.

Sterling, S. 1995. "Quaslametko and Yetko: Two Grandmother Models for Contemporary Native Education Pedagogy." In *First Nations Education: The Circle Unfolds*. M. Battiste and J. Barman (eds). Vancouver: UBC Press. 73–98.

Swisher, K., M. Hoisch, and D.M. Pavel. 1991. *American Indian/Alaskan Native Dropout Study, 1991*. Washington DC: National Education Association.

Swisher, K. and M. Hoisch. 1992. "Dropping out Among American Indians and Alaska Natives: A Review of Studies." *Journal of American Indian Education*. 31(2): 3–23.

Tsuji, L.J.S. 2000. "Modified School Years: An Important Issue of Local Control of Education." *Canadian Journal of Native Education*. 24(2): 158–168.

Vallerand, R. J. and L. Menard. 1984. "Increasing the School Attendance of Native Students: An Application of Cognitive Evaluation Theory." *The Canadian Journal of Native Studies*. (2): 241–255.

Van der Woerd, K.A. and D. N. Cox. 2003. "Educational Status and its Association with Risk and Protective Factors for First Nations Youth." *Canadian Journal of Native Education*. 27(2): 208.

Wall, C.S., and P.R. Madak. 1991. "Indian Students' Academic Self-concept and their Perceptions of Teacher and Parent Aspirations for them in a Band-controlled School and a Provincial School." *Canadian Journal of Native Education*, 18(1): 43–51.

Ward, C. 1995. "American Indian High School Competition in Rural Southeastern Montana." *Rural Sociology*, 60(3): 416–35.

Ward, C. 1998. "Community Resources and School Performance: The Northern Cheyenne Case." *Sociological Inquiry*. 68(1): 83–113.

Wehlage, G. and R. Rutter. 1987. "Dropping Out: How Much do Schools Contribute to the Problem?" In *School Dropouts: Patterns and Policies*. G. Natriello (ed). New York: Teachers College Press.

White, J.P., P. Maxim and N. Spence 2004. "An Examination of Educational Success." In *Aboriginal Policy Research (Vol 1)*. White, J.P., P. Maxim and D. Beavon (eds). Toronto: Thompson Educational Publishing. 129–148.

White, J.P., and N. Spence. 2006. "A New Approach to Understanding Educational Outcomes: The Role of Social Capital." In *Aboriginal Policy Research: Moving Forward, Making a Difference* (Vol III). White et al. (eds). Toronto: Thompson Educational Publishing. 69–86.

9

Churn Migration and Educational Attainment among Aboriginal Adolescents and Young Adults

Dan Beavon, Susan Wingert, and Jerry P. White

Introduction

In this chapter, we address the question: What are the consequences of mobility among Aboriginal peoples? It has been widely recognized that the Aboriginal population is, on average, more mobile than the non-Aboriginal population (Norris, Cooke, & Clatworthy 2003). While research has documented many of the antecedents to and reasons for frequent moves in this population, little work has examined the social consequences. Here, we theorize that frequent moves between communities break the bonds that enable people to access social capital, which, in turn, undermine community social cohesion. One consequence of this process is hypothesized to be lower levels of educational attainment.

While the process of "churn" migration is believed to affect a wide range of outcomes, we have chosen to examine educational attainment, since it is a foundational component of socio-economic status. There is also widespread support within the Aboriginal community for improving educational outcomes as a way of improving individual and community conditions (RCAP 1996).

Literature Review

Educational Attainment

In general, national data on educational attainment among Aboriginal peoples in Canada suggest that there have been improvements, but, as Hull notes in this volume, relative gaps remain. Aboriginal people tend to be overrepresented in the less than high school category and underrepresented in the high school diploma, college or university certificate or diploma, and university degree categories (Mendelson 2004). According to 1996 data, Aboriginal young adults were 2.6 times less likely to have completed high school compared to non-Aboriginals, and were 50% less likely to have completed post-secondary (Tait 1999). As has been widely noted, Aboriginal women have slightly higher levels of educational attainment. In addition, Aboriginal lone mothers were more likely than mothers in two-parent families to attend school (Tait 1999).

It appears that there are barriers to education that are unique to or more prevalent among Aboriginal peoples. The 2001 Census shows that young adults from every ethnic minority group had higher rates of high school completion compared to Aboriginals (Beavon & Guimond 2006). Potential explanations include negative attitudes toward education as a result of the residential school legacy, fewer perceived returns on education, a lack of economy within or near community, a disconnect between traditional culture and pedagogical approach, geographical isolation from higher education institutions, and discrimination or alienation within the school system (Maxim & White 2006, R.A. Malatest & Associates Ltd. 2004, Richardson & Blanchet-Cohen 2000, Spence & White forthcoming, White, Spence, & Maxim 2006). Rates of school non-completion are highest among the Inuit, followed by Registered Indians, non-Status Indians, and the Métis (Beavon & Guimond, 2006). Tait (1999) noted that the Métis are less likely to live in remote communities or the North, and have had formal education and greater connection to mainstream institutions, historically. Opportunities for higher education and employment are often limited in Inuit and First Nations communities, which mean that people have to leave their communities, social supports, and way of life behind in order to attend post-secondary institutions.

Research has shown that there are significant benefits to higher education for Aboriginal peoples. Hull (2005) found that, among all Aboriginal groups, labour force participation increases and government transfer dependence decreases with education. Gaps in labour force participation among Aboriginal persons compared to non-Aboriginals were very small at the same educational level. There also appears to be threshold effects with the likelihood of unemployment decreasing significantly at the secondary graduate, post-secondary certificate and university degree levels (Hull 2005, Tait 1999). Walters, White, and Maxim (2004) found that, controlling for socio-demographic characteristics, level of schooling, and field of study, Aboriginal post-secondary graduates earn more than non-minorities and visible minorities. The advantage was particularly pronounced at the university degree level.

Mobility Patterns

While there is a persistent myth of a mass exodus from reserves to urban centres, the migration pattern of Aboriginal peoples is more aptly characterized as "churn" into and out of cities and within cities (Norris & Clatworthy 2003). Registered Indians with ties to reserves tend to move back and forth between their First Nations communities and urban centres (Norris & Clatworthy 2003). Between 1991 and 1996, the largest percentage of individuals who left reserves, moved to urban centres (61%) while the majority moving to reserves came from cities (69%) (Norris, Beavon, Guimond, & Cooke 2004). The off-reserve population is even more highly mobile. Among those in large cities, at least half of all moves were within the same community (Norris & Clatworthy 2003). Mobility patterns have been linked to age with young adults having the highest rates (Norris & Clatworthy 2003). Major reasons for migration include family, housing, education, employment, and community factors (Beavon & Norris 1999, Distasio, Sylvester, Jaccubucci, Mulligan, & Sargent 2004, Norris & Clatworthy 2003). While we often think of the on- and off-reserve populations as being completely distinct, they are often connected through mobility, as well as culture and politics (Graham & Peters 2002).

Social Capital and Social Cohesion

Social capital "can be defined as the networks of social relations within the milieu, characterized by specific norms and attitudes that *potentially* enable individuals or groups to access a pool of resources and supports" (White & Maxim 2003, 67). Coleman (1988) argued that social capital is "a variety of different entities, with two elements in common: they all consist of some aspect of social structures, and they facilitate certain actions of actors—whether persons or corporate actors—within the structure" (S98). Social capital is produced through changes in *relations* among individuals that facilitate certain actions (Coleman 1988). Individuals can use the resources and supports available through social networks to achieve their own goals. In addition, there are also effects that improve conditions in the community and may enhance the well-being of residents who are comparatively isolated. Communities with high levels of social capital have dense webs of personal connections, established rules of conduct, and generalized reciprocity all of which build trust (Putnam 2000). The literature has generally suggested that social capital is a source of: 1) social control; 2) family support; and 3) access to resources in networks outside the family (Portes 1998). While most theoretical and empirical work on social capital has emphasized positive dimensions, it also has negative ones, including "exclusion of outsiders, excess claims on group members, restrictions on individual freedoms, and downward levelling norms" (Portes 1998, 15).

Social cohesion can be considered a framing concept since there is no consensus about its precise definition (Beauvais & Jenson 2002). It can be thought of as "the capacity of community members to live in harmony" (Policy Research Initiative Project 2005, 8). The literature discusses four different aspects of social cohesion: 1) common values and civic culture, 2) social order and social control, 3) social solidarity and low levels of inequality, 4) social networks and social capital, and 5) belonging and identity (Beauvais & Jenson 2002). Community ties have been identified as a key determinant of social cohesion particularly when defined as social networks, capital, or solidarity (Beauvais & Jenson 2002).

Social capital and social cohesion are interrelated concepts. For example, Beauvais and Jenson (2002) argued, "higher levels of social cohesion raise the return to social-capital investment" (26). However, the distinction between the two concepts is that "*social capital* comprises individual actions like joining an organization or doing volunteer work. *Social cohesion* is a characteristic of a group

Figure 9.1: Conceptual Model

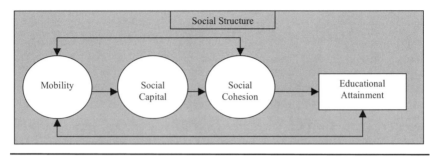

of people, determined by their propensity to invest in social capital" (Beauvais & Jenson 2002, 26).

Conceptual Model

The conceptual model used here draws upon theoretical work by White and Maxim (2003) and Beavon and Norris (1999). White and Maxim's (2003) model proposed that there are reciprocal relationships among human, physical, and social capital within communities. In turn, social capital affects social cohesion, which affects population outcomes. "If levels of migration are high, either measured as net migration or in terms of the rate of 'churn,' the probability of forming associations, clubs, parent-teacher groups, sports clubs, and so on is diminished. Any community civic life would be negatively affected" (White & Maxim 2003, 7). Beavon and Norris (1999) theorized that high levels of mobility, which are influenced by demographic, political, and legal factors along with push and pull dynamics between community of origin and destination, undermined community social cohesion, which contributed to a higher incidence of social problems that further fuelled churn migration. The authors theorized that churn migration patterns were related to a range of economic and social outcomes. The model used here borrows from this latter part of the model by proposing links between social capital, social cohesion, and educational attainment (See **Figure 9.1**). The social structure provides the context in which these patterns occur, which is why we include controls for gender, community ties, family structure, labour force participation, and economic family income. While any degree of mobility has the potential to break bonds of social capital, moves that occur between communities are most likely to disrupt social networks both spatially and temporally (Beavon & Norris 1999). Data limitations prevent us from examining "within community" moves; however, we are able to capture the "between community" moves that are more likely to be detrimental to social capital networks.

There is some research on non-Aboriginal populations that support parts of this model. For example, Prubesh and Downey (1999) used two waves of data on high school students from the national Education Longitudinal Survey to examine the relationship between residential and school moves and academic performance.

They found that school-only, residential-only, and combined school and residential moves were associated with declines in social capital and academic performance. Importantly, most of the difference in effect between movers and non-movers was due to difference in the groups predating the move. The authors concluded that the family types that tend to move more often also experience other forms of social and economic disadvantage.

Aman (2006) examined educational outcomes among different cohorts of Aboriginal students in British Columbia. She found that student mobility was associated with level levels of school completion. Part of the explanation appears to be that where there is more than one school in the centre, mobile Aboriginal students tend to cluster in schools in communities with poorer economic and social conditions. However, she also found that "higher proportions of Aboriginal students *(notwithstanding* these higher proportions may be more likely to occur in schools in where poor socio-economic conditions prevail) are linked to increases in Aboriginal graduation *and* Band graduation at the school level" (93). This finding suggests that bonding on the basis of ethnicity may buffer against the effects of negative socio-economic conditions.

Method

The data for these analyses come from the 2001 Aboriginal Peoples Survey (APS) Public Use Microdata File (PUMF) of adults (aged 15 and over) off-reserve (i.e., excluding individuals living in First Nations communities or reserves).[1] The APS is a post-censal survey that targets individuals who reported Aboriginal ancestry, identity, or Indian Band, Indian Treaty, or Registered Indian status in the Census (APS 2006).

Respondents in the 15 to 19 (N=4,279) and 20 to 24 (N=3,351) age groups were selected. We theorized that these two age groups represented key periods during which frequent moves would have the greatest impact on the likelihood of dropping out, completing high school, and pursuing post-secondary education. We analyzed the groups separately since the 20 to 24 year olds were old enough to have completed high school, while most members of the younger group were not.

We generated a dependent variable that classified respondents according to whether they had graduated from high school—with diploma or General Educational Development (GED) diploma—and whether they were currently attending a secondary or post-secondary program. Those who indicated on their highest level of educational attainment that they had completed some post-secondary, a certificate or diploma program, or a university degree, were coded in the post-secondary group even if they were not currently enrolled. Four categories were created: 1) dropouts (had not completed high school and were not currently attending); 2) non-graduates (had not completed high school, but were currently attending); 3) graduates (had graduated high school, but had not pursued post-secondary); and 4) post-secondary (had graduated high school and pursued post-secondary).

Independent variables included frequency of moves, which was divided into five ordered categories based on two variables in the APS that identified whether respondents had ever moved and how many times they had moved in the past five years, excluding moves within the same city, town, or community. It is important to note that this variable misses movement within municipalities and neighbourhoods. However, we are still able to capture those moves that are most likely to disrupt social capital networks. Given that respondents in the APS PUMF were living off-reserve at the time of the survey, we would expect the data to underestimate the within community mobility characteristic of the off-reserve population, but to capture the churn migration typical of the on-reserve population. The reference category included those who had moved three or more times in the past five years compared to those who had never moved, as well as those who had moved zero, one, or two times in the past five years.

Sex was dummy coded with males as the reference category. We created a variable to capture community ties. Those who reported North American Indian as part of their identity and were members of an Indian Band or First Nation were coded as having strong ties to reserve. Those who reported being Inuit, or non-Inuit living in the Arctic, were coded as having ties to the Arctic. All others were coded as having stronger ties to off-reserve communities since they are not eligible for housing on-reserve and do not live in the Arctic. Dummy variables were created with reserve ties as the reference category.

The family structure variable in our model is based on Statistics Canada's census family status, which includes married or common-law couples with or without children and lone-parents whose children live in the same dwelling. Grandparents living with grandchildren are considered census families if the children's parent(s) do not live in the household. Children who are married, common-law, or have children are not considered to be part of their parents' census family even if they share the same dwelling. Non-census families include people living alone, with other relatives, or non-relatives. We created three categories: 1) child living with parents or grandparents; 2) common-law, married, or lone-parent; and 3) non-census family. Ideally, we would have liked to use variables that provide a broader view of household structure. For example, the challenges facing lone parents living on their own are likely greater than their counterparts who continue living with their family of origin, enabling them to pool resources such as money and social support. Unfortunately, the variables necessary to discern living arrangement were not available in the dataset.

Labour force participation was coded according to whether a respondent was employed, unemployed, or not in the labour force (not working for pay or looking for employment). Income used the economic family income variable, which sums all of the income for family members (related by blood, marriage, common-law, or adoption) in the same household. We felt that this variable more accurately captures the actual level of differential resources available to the family. There were seven categories ranging from less than $10,000 per year to 80,000 plus.

The proposed model conceptualizes that social capital gives rise to social cohesion. There are no variables that adequately capture social capital in the APS PUMF. We used social support as a proxy measure of social capital since support is one resource that may be accessed from networks (Policy Research Initiative Project 2005). The limitation of this approach to measuring social capital is that it primarily taps into bonding social capital as opposed to linking or bridging. It also misses potential negative consequences of social capital, such as involvement in gangs or other groups that engage in illegal or socially deviant behaviours. Respondents were asked to rate how frequently various forms of social support were available to them on a four-point Likert scale ranging from all of the time to almost none of the time. Variables were reverse coded so high scores reflect high levels of social support. We coded variables into three dimensions of social support: 1) social interaction, which combined variables measuring how often respondents have someone with whom to do something enjoyable, relaxing, or to have a good time); 2) emotional support, which combined variables related to having someone to listen, confide in, or count on for advice; and 3) affectionate support, which was based on a variable measuring the availability of love and affection. The subscales were given equal weighting and combined. The scale was adjusted so it ranged from 0 to 27. Cronbach's Alpha was 0.84. We also found limited measures of cohesion in the APS PUMF. Our measure of cohesion was based on a series of questions that asked respondents to respond yes or no whether suicide, family violence, sexual abuse, drug abuse, or alcohol abuse were a problem in their community. Responses were coded so that "no" was given a value of 0 and "yes" was given a 1. Responses were summed and the scale reversed so high scores reflect higher cohesion. Cronbach's Alpha was 0.85.

Data were analyzed using multinomial logistic regression models in Stata. Only cases with complete data on the model variables were included. In the 15–19 age group, there were 3,491 complete cases (18.4% missing); while in the 20–24 age group, there were 2,761 complete cases (17.6% missing). Multiple imputation was performed using Amelia II to address the missing data. The analyses presented here use non-imputed results since the parameters did not differ substantively. All data are weighted using the survey weights provided by Statistics Canada.

Results

Descriptives

Figure 9.2 shows the weighted percent of cases in each mobility category. Those who have never moved make up the largest proportion of respondents in both age groups; however, the older group is more likely to have moved in the past five years compared to the younger group. In particular, the older group is twice as

Figure 9.2: Mobility by Age Group

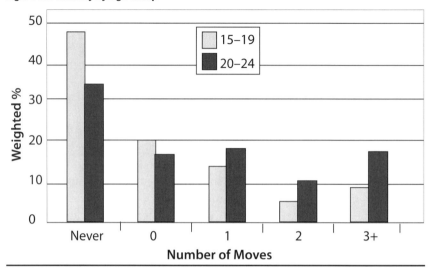

Figure 9.3: Sex by Age Group

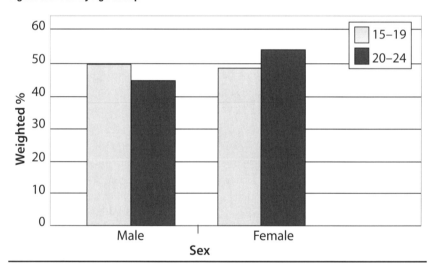

likely to have moved three or more times in the past five years compared to the younger group.

The sex distribution by age is presented in **Figure 9.3**. The distribution is very near 50/50 for the younger group, but females are overrepresented in the older group, perhaps reflecting the tendency of females to move more frequently and from on- to off-reserve (Norris, Beavon, Guimond, & Cooke 2004, Norris & Clatworthy 2003). Research has found that Aboriginal women tend to move in a family context while men tend to move as lone persons for economic reasons (Peters 1994). Women often leave their home communities in search of better

Figure 9.4: Community Ties by Age Group

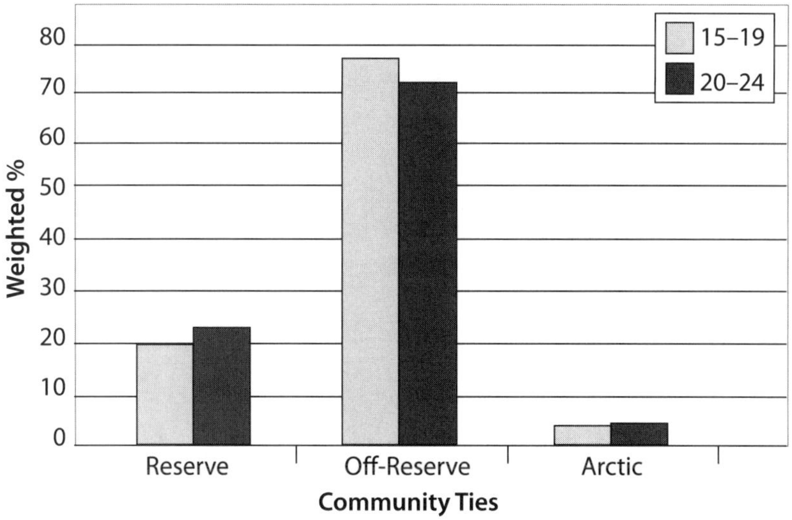

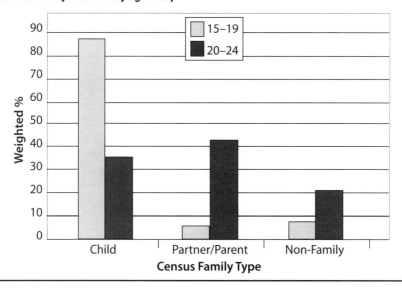

Figure 9.5: Family Structure by Age Group

housing, services, or employment; to escape abusive situations; or following the breakdown of a marital or common-law relationship (Cooke & Belanger 2006, Norris, Beavon, Guimond, & Cooke 2004, Peters 1994).

Figure 9.4 clearly shows that almost three-quarters of respondents in each age group have stronger off-reserve ties, which is not surprising given that the PUMF was limited to adults living off-reserve. The slightly higher proportion of members from the older group with on-reserve ties may reflect greater mobility

Figure 9.6: Labour Force Participation by Age Group

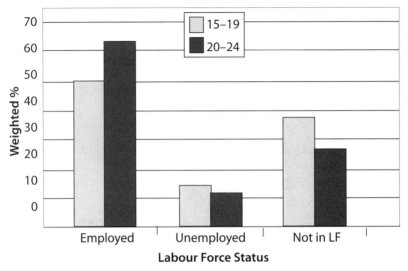

Figure 9.7: Economic Family Income by Age Group

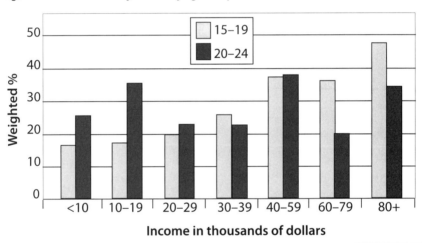

in this age group. We would expect that some young adults from First Nations communities choose to leave during this life stage in order to pursue education or work opportunities off-reserve.

Age differences in family structure are readily apparent in **Figure 9.5**. The vast majority in the younger age group are children living with parents or grandparents compared to just over a third in the older group. Close to half of the older group were living with a partner or were a parent compared to less the 6% of the younger group. Similarly, one-fifth of respondents in the older group had a non-census family arrangement compared to one-thirteenth of the younger group.

Figure 9.8: Social Support by Age Group

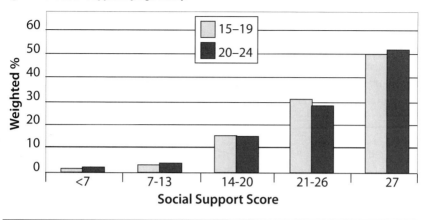

Figure 9.9: Community Cohesion by Age Group

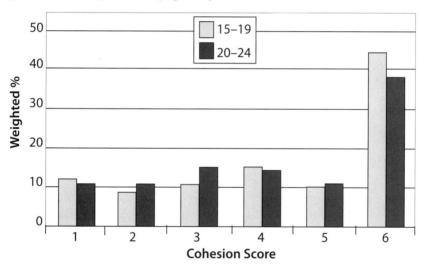

When we look at indicators of socio-economic status, it is evident that being employed is the most common status, with the older group having a higher rate (63.1%) than the younger (49.6%) (**Figure 9.6**). Among the younger and older group, respectively, 13.5% and 11.1% were unemployed. The unemployment rate was 21.4% for the younger group and 15% for the older group, which is substantially higher than the Canadian youth unemployment rate in April 2001 of 12.7% (Statistics Canada 2001). Those in the younger group were more likely to not be in the labour force (36.9%) compared to those in the older group (25.8%).

Results for economic family income (**Figure 9.7**) demonstrate that the younger group tend to have higher levels of income because they are more likely live with parents. The older group is overrepresented in the lowest income categories. It is notable that at least half of respondents reported household incomes of $40,000 or more.

Approximately half of the young adults in the sample reported the highest level of social support (**Figure 9.8**). Less than 1% indicated a score of less than 7. Fewer than 5% fell into the 7 to 13 score range. Approximately 15% and 30% were in the 14 to 20 and 21 to 26 score range respectively. There were no appreciable differences in support levels between the two age groups. The majority of respondents indicated relatively high levels of social support.

We see a similar pattern for community cohesion, with the largest number of respondents indicating very high levels of cohesion (**Figure 9.9**). Nevertheless, approximately 11% of the sample indicated that they lived in communities with all six social problems, which corresponds to a cohesion score of 1. There was no clear pattern by age group, suggesting that the higher mobility in the older group did not have a strong effect on perceptions of social cohesion.

The dependent variable, school attendance, shows a clear age pattern (**Figure 9.10**). The percentage of dropouts (DO) is roughly equal (about 16%) between the two groups. In the younger group, we see—as expected—over half are non-graduates (NG), indicating they have not graduated but are still attending school. This rate drops to 3.7% in the older group, representing a small number of individuals who were held back at some point or left for a period of time and then returned, which other studies have found to be a common pattern among Aboriginal peoples (Hull, 2005). In the younger group, almost 16% had graduated high school (G), compared to a slightly higher number in the older group (21%). When we look at rates of post-secondary (PS) attendance, the difference is dramatic, with only 16% of the younger group attending compared to 59% in the older group. In the younger group, 82% of those in the post-secondary category indicated "some post-secondary" as their highest level of educational attainment and 18% had attained a certificate or diploma (results not shown). As expected, given their young age, none had earned a university degree. Among the older group, 61% indicated "some post-secondary," while 31% had attained a certificate or diploma, and 8% had earned a university degree.

Multivariate Analyses

The results of the multinomial logistic regression models for the 15–19 and 20–24 age groups are presented in **Figures 9.11 to 9.26**. The factor change scale indicates the odds ratio (expß) while the logit coefficient scale represents the raw coefficient (ß). Letters are used to indicate each category of the dependent variable: D for dropout, N for non-graduate, G for graduate, and P for post-secondary. The dropout category is set as the reference. Outcomes to the right of another letter indicate higher odds while those to the left correspond to lower odds. The distance between a pair of outcomes indicates the magnitude of the effect. The lines connecting outcomes indicate that the odds are *not* significantly different between the pair. Significance was set at the 0.1 level. The area of the outcome

Figure 9.10: School Attendance by Age Group

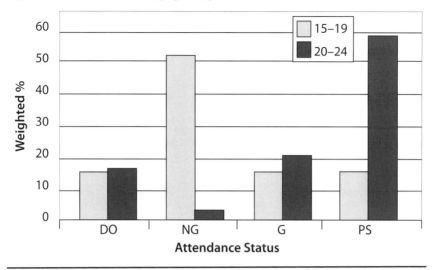

Figure 9.11: Odds of School Attendance by Number of Moves (Ages 15-19)

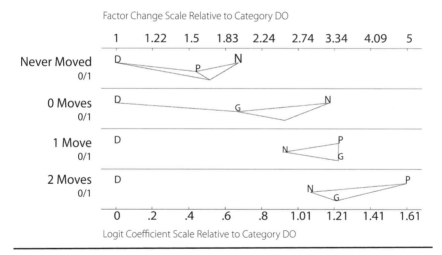

letter is proportional to the size of the change in probability of an outcome given a one unit change in independent variable controlling for all other variables. It can be interpreted as the substantive impact of the variable on the outcome (Long & Freese 2006).

Figure 9.11 shows the odds of school attendance by number of moves for the 15–19 year old group. The reference group for number of moves is the three or more moves category. For the dependent variable, the odds of each outcome are relative to the dropout group, which takes a value of 1 across all categories of the independent variable. STATA calculates significance tests for each pair of

Figure 9.12: Odds of School Attendance by Number of Moves (Ages 20-24)

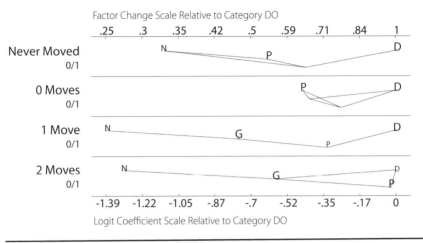

Figure 9.13: Odds of School Attendance by Sex (Ages 15-19)

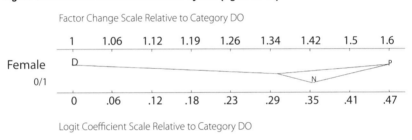

Figure 9.14: Odds of School Attendance by Sex (Ages 20-24)

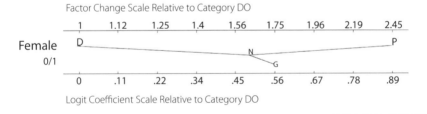

educational outcomes, which are *not* connected by a line if significant. If we look at the never moved category, we see that the dropout and non-graduate groups do not have a connecting line indicating that compared to those who have moved three or more times, those who have never moved have 1.97 higher odds of being a non-graduate than a dropout. There were no significant differences between dropouts and graduates or post-secondary. If we look at the next category, those who indicated 0 moves in the past five years, relative to the reference group, were 225% more likely to be a non-graduate and 154% more likely to be in post-secondary than being a dropout. There was no significant difference between the odds of being a graduate and a dropout between non-movers and frequent movers, as indicated by the line connecting these two outcomes. If we move down to the "one move" category, we see that those who had moved once in the past five years, compared to the reference, were 2.53, 3.42, and 3.43 times more likely to be a non-graduate, graduate, and post-secondary attender, respectively, than being a dropout. The lines between post-secondary and non-graduate, non-graduate and graduate, and graduate and post-secondary indicate no significant differences in the odds of being in these groups between one time movers and frequent movers. Finally, among those who had moved twice in the past five years (the last line in the chart), compared to those who had moved three plus times, the odds were higher for being a non-graduate (193%), graduate (239%), and post-secondary attender (400%) than being a dropout. There were no significant differences in the relative odds between two-time movers and three-time movers in terms of being a non-graduate, graduate, or post-secondary attender.

Unlike the 15 to 19 year olds, less frequent moves were associated with poorer educational outcomes among 20 to 24 year olds (**Figure 9.12**). Those who had never moved had 0.33 lower odds of being a non-graduate and 0.54 lower odds of attending post-secondary, compared to dropping out. Respondents who had not moved in the past five years, compared to the reference, had 0.64 lower odds of attending post-secondary relative to dropping out. Those who had moved once were 75% less likely to be a non-graduate and 53% less likely to be a graduate compared to a dropout. However, moving once was associated with a greater likelihood of attending post-secondary (OR=2.90) compared to not graduating. Even those who had moved twice in the past five years were less likely to be a non-graduate than a dropout (OR=0.27), but more likely to be a post-secondary attender than non-graduate (OR=3.61), than those who had moved three or more times. Rerunning the analysis with never moved as the reference, confirmed that among the older group, moving two or more times significantly increased the likelihood of attending post-secondary compared to dropping out (results not shown).

Compared to their male counterparts, females aged 15 to 19 had 1.42 and 1.60 greater odds of being a non-graduate or post-secondary attender than a dropout (**Figure 9.13**). The pattern was similar for the 20 to 24 age group (**Figure 9.14**). Females, relative to males, had 1.71 greater odds of being a graduate and 2.45 greater odds of attending post-secondary compared to being a dropout. In addition, females were 1.40 times more likely to be in post-secondary compared to being a graduate.

In the younger group, those who had stronger ties off-reserve, relative to those with stronger ties on-reserve, were 63% more likely to be a non-graduate, 95% more likely to be a graduate, and 75% more likely to be a post-secondary attender than a dropout (**Figure 9.15**). On the other hand, respondents with stronger ties to the Arctic, compared to those with reserve ties, were 50% less likely to be a graduate and 52% less likely to attend post-secondary. Among the older group,

Figure 9.15: Odds of School Attendance by Community Ties (Ages 15-19)

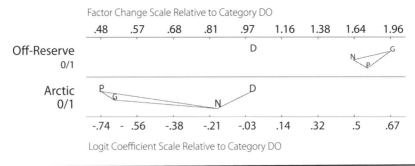

Figure 9.16: Odds of School Attendance by Community Ties (Ages 20-24)

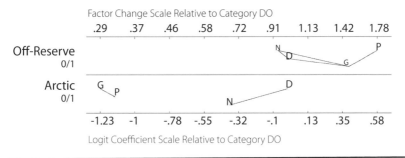

having stronger ties off-reserve, compared to on-reserve, increased the likelihood of attending post-secondary relative to dropping out by 78% and relative to being a non-graduate by 90% (**Figure 9.16**). Among those in the Arctic, the odds of being in the graduate category was 0.29, relative to being in the dropout category and 0.43, relative to being in the non-graduate category for the older group. They also had lower odds of being in post-secondary compared to dropping out (OR=0.32) or not graduating (OR=0.48).

When we look at family structure, we see that among the younger age group, being a partner or parent, rather than a child, decreases the odds of being a non-graduate compared to a dropout by 0.11 (**Figure 9.17**). However, it is also associated with 4.27 higher odds of being in post-secondary and 4.85 higher odds of being a graduate than being a non-graduate. Relative to being a child, being in a non-family is associated with a greater likelihood of attending post-secondary relative to the other categories (302% relative to dropping out, 410% relative to not graduating, and 123% relative to being a graduate). In addition, the odds of being a graduate compared to a non-graduate are 129% higher. In the older group, compared to those who identified as being a child, those who were partners or parents were less likely to be in post-secondary, relative to being a dropout (34%) or a graduate (43%) (**Figure 9.18**). Those in non-families, compared to those still living with parents or grandparents, were more likely to be a graduate (OR=2.06) or post-secondary attender (OR=2.13) compared to being a dropout.

Figure 9.17: Odds of School Attendance by Family Structure (Ages 15-19)

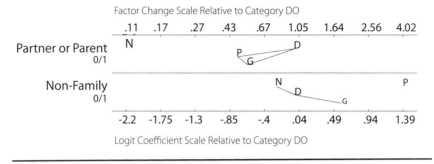

Figure 9.18: Odds of School Attendance by Family Structure (Ages 20-24)

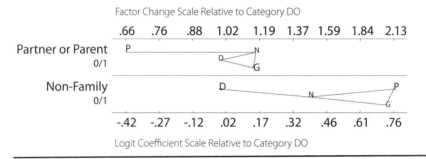

Labour force participation patterns show that among unemployed 15–19 year olds, relative to their employed counterparts, the odds of being a graduate relative to being a non-graduate are 0.61 lower (**Figure 9.19**). Similarly, the odds of being in post-secondary compared to being a non-graduate are 0.55 less. Among those out of the labour force, compared to respondents who were employed, the likelihood of being a non-graduate (289%) or post-secondary attender (59%) were greater than being a dropout. Interestingly, the odds of being a graduate were lower by 0.53 compared to being a dropout. The odds of being a graduate or post-secondary attender relative to being a non-graduate are 86% and 59% lower. The odds of being in post-secondary, relative to being a graduate, are 3.02 times greater. In the 20 to 24 age group, compared to those who are employed, those who are unemployed were less likely to be a graduate (OR=0.46) or have gone on to post-secondary (OR=0.47) compared to dropping out (**Figure 9.20**). Those who were out of the labour force, compared to their employed counterparts, were 95% more likely to be a non-graduate than a dropout, but less likely to be a graduate by 59% and less likely to be attending post-secondary by 44% than be a dropout. They were also 79% less likely to be a graduate compared to a non-graduate and 71% less likely to attend post-secondary compared to being a non-graduate.

Figures 9.21 to 9.26 plot the predicted probabilities of each outcome across the independent variable for each age group. **Figure 9.21** shows that, as expected, given their age, 15 to 19 year olds have the highest overall probability of being a

Figure 9.19: Odds of School Attendance by Labour Force Participation (Ages 15-19)

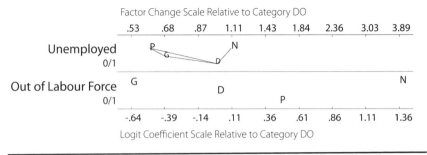

Figure 9.20: Odds of School Attendance by Labour Force Participant (Ages 20-24)

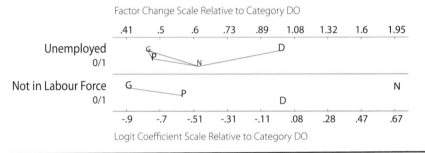

Figure 9.21: Probability of School Attendance by Income (Ages 15-19)

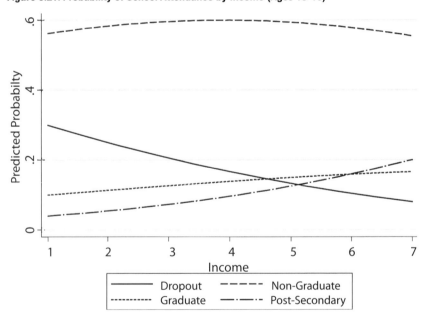

Figure 9.22: Probability of School Attendance by Income (Ages 20–24)

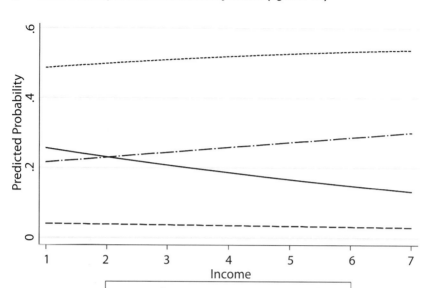

non-graduate and the lowest of being in post-secondary. However, income affects the chances of educational outcomes. The probability of dropping out decreases quite dramatically as income increases, while the odds of graduating or attending post-secondary increase. **Figure 9.22** plots the results for the older group, which reveals a similar pattern. In this case, the odds of being a graduate are highest overall and being a non-graduate is lowest. There is little effect of income on the probability of being in these two categories. On the other hand, the odds of dropping out decline as income increases and the odds of attending post-secondary also rise slightly.

Figure 9.23 indicates that, as social support increases, the predicted probability of dropping out decreases by more than half. The chances of being a non-graduate or graduate increase while post-secondary attendance remains fairly constant across support levels. The same graph for 20 to 24 year olds shows that the probability of dropping out decreases substantially among those with higher levels of social support (**Figure 9.24**). The probability of being a graduate increases slightly while that of being a non-graduate is fairly constant. The chances of a respondent attending post-secondary more than double across social support scores.

The only variable in the model that failed to achieve statistical significance for any of the educational outcomes or age groups was social cohesion. **Figures 9.25** and **9.26** confirm that it had little effect on educational outcome probabilities.

Figure 9.23: Probability of School Attendance by Support (Ages 15–19)

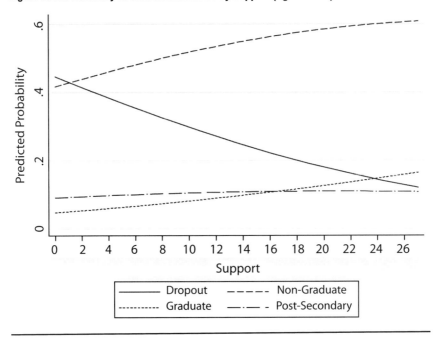

Figure 9.24: Probability of School Attendance by Support (Ages 20–24)

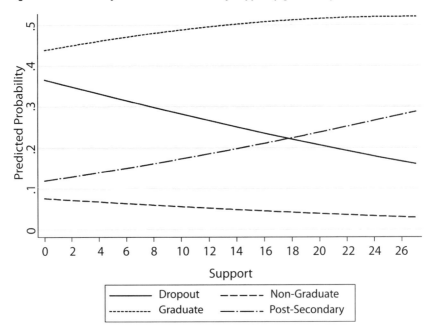

Figure 9.25: Probability of School Attendance by Cohesion (Ages 15–19)

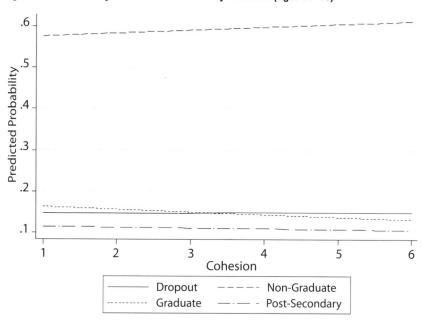

Discussion

Despite data limitations, we feel that the conceptual model proposed in this chapter has the potential to assist researchers in unravelling the complex relationships between mobility, social capital, social cohesion, and social and economic outcomes. Based on these analyses, it appears that movement is a double edge sword with respect to educational attainment. The results suggest that among 15 to 19 year olds, frequent moves increase the likelihood of dropping out of secondary school. However, some movement in the past five years was associated with the highest odds of attending post-secondary. We can conclude that the odds of staying in school, graduating, and continuing on to post-secondary are higher for those who move less frequently. However, those who had moved once or twice in the past five years had higher odds of graduating or attending post-secondary, which suggests that some movement normatively accompanies the completion of high school.

Cross-tabs confirm that, among 15 to 19 year olds, those living with parents have a higher expected frequency of being non-movers (results not shown). Those who are married, common-law, or a single parent are overrepresented among frequent movers. Individuals not in a census family have a higher than expected frequency of moving once, twice, or three or more times. There are also differences by age in the relationship between labour force participation and educational attainment. In this group, those out of the labour force had a greater likelihood of attending school, either high school or post-secondary, while those who were

Figure 9.26: Probability of School Attendance by Cohesion (Ages 20–24)

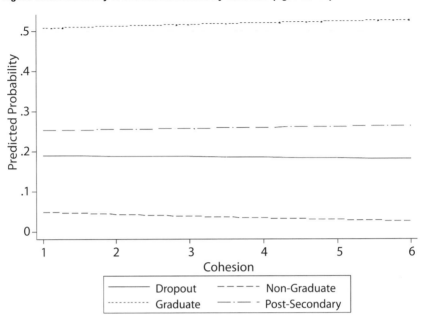

employed were more likely to have graduated. The picture seems to be that among adolescents residential stability, living with parents or guardians, and being out of the labour force is beneficial in terms of staying in school. This pattern is quite consistent with our basic model. However, following the completion of school, it is advantageous to move in order to purse opportunities, either a job or post-secondary training. This period of pursuing opportunities may involve several moves without significant detriment to educational attainment. However, forming families early, either by partnering or parenting, is associated with frequent moves and lower levels of attainment. Hull (2005) also found that lone parenthood was a barrier to higher education among 15 to 24 year olds.

In the older group, the pattern was more complex. Those who moved three or more times in the past five years had the highest odds of being a non-graduate compared to non-movers. If we use the results from the younger cohort to provide context, we can speculate that some of these individuals were also frequent movers when they were younger and may have fallen behind their peers or dropped out and subsequently returned. Longitudinal data is needed to trace moving patterns across childhood and adolescence and its relationship to cumulative advantage or disadvantage. On the other hand, those who had moved two or more times in the past five years also had higher odds of attending post-secondary compared to non-movers. These findings reinforce the conclusion that some movement in order to pursue opportunities is advantageous with respect to educational attainment. Another possibility suggested in the literature is that strong bonding ties may be detrimental when group norms discourage the pursuit of higher education (White, Spence, & Maxim 2005). Movement may serve to break or weaken bonding ties in order to minimize pressures to maintain low educational norms. Studies of the Aboriginal cohort in the Youth in Transition Survey (YITS) confirms a connection between parents' attitudes toward education and educational attainment (Maxim & White 2006). No suitable data was available to test what proportion of young people may have moved for this reason. In other cases, strong bonding capital is an asset. For example, those with strong bonding social capital networks that are linked to resources and bridged with other educational institutions tend to have positive effects on the graduate rate and transition to post-secondary (White, Spence, & Maxim 2005). More direct measures of the types and characteristics of social capital are needed to uncover the dynamics that influence attainment.

In terms of family status, compared to those living with parents, individuals with their own families were much less likely to attend post-secondary while those in non-family arrangements were more likely to have either graduated or pursued post-secondary. Therefore, these results suggest that continuing to live at home following graduation or while pursing post-secondary is less normative. Even in this older cohort, family formation decreases the odds of pursing higher education. What we cannot tell from this data is whether there is a difference between those who became a partner or parent during adolescence versus those who made this transition as an adult. It is more common among Aboriginals, especially Aboriginal women, to form families early (Anderson 2002) and attend post-secondary later on (see Clement in this volume). Therefore, if we were able to look at these individuals later in adulthood, the differences in educational attainment may be less dramatic. The relationship between moving and family status (cross-tabs not shown) reveal that those who have never moved are more likely to be living with parents. Those who are living with partners or children are have a higher than expected frequency of not moving in the past five years, but a lower frequency of never moving, which is to be expected since many will have established their own households. Interestingly, there appears to be greater residential stability among individuals who form families at this stage, compared to the younger cohort. Individuals who were not in a census family were less likely to be non-movers and more likely to have moved at least once. In this group, it is clear that frequent movement is beneficial for those who have graduated and are ready to move on to post-secondary. Family structure is also important with those living in non-family arrangements being in a better position to pursue post-secondary. In this age group, compared to being employed, unemployment is related to lower attainment, especially with respect to graduating and attending post-secondary. Those who were not in the labour force were much more likely to be still in high school and less likely to be graduates or in post-secondary. It seems in this age group, employment is associated with higher odds of educational attainment. In fact, a reverse causation explanation is possible with those who completed high school or trade, college, or university training being more likely to find employment.

The pattern by gender is consistent in both groups, with females having higher levels of attainment compared to males. Other researchers have reported similar findings (for example, see Hull 2005). Similarly, those with ties to off-reserve communities have greater odds of continuing or completing their educations, while those in the Arctic are less likely to do so, compared to those with on-reserve ties. Cross-tabs examining the relationship between community ties and mobility show that there is a very high association between living in the Arctic and having never moved (results not shown). Therefore, the churn migration pattern is less common among Aboriginal peoples from this region. One other interesting finding was that moving at least once was more common among 15 to 19 year olds with strong ties to reserves, but not among their older counterparts. This pattern may reflect movement as part of a family unit.

It is also the case that higher economic family incomes are associated with a notable reduction in the odds of dropping out and an increase in the odds of attending post-secondary, which suggests disadvantages associated with poverty, lack of faith that higher education will have tangible pay-offs, and/or pressures to make money interfere with school completion. Future research may shed light on what distinguishes those who complete secondary from those who dropout within the same socio-economic strata. Even more dramatic was the decline in the odds of dropping out as social support levels increased. In general, social support was positively associated with higher educational attainment, which implies that social capital networks that enable individuals to access positive forms of support are essential. To what extent support may buffer the negative effects of socio-economic disadvantage and mobility are questions for future research.

The lack of significant findings for social cohesion warrants comment. Unfortunately, the only measures available in the APS PUMF that are essentially types of social disorder capture only the negative extreme of the concept's valence. Two key dimensions mentioned in the literature include inequalities and social exclusion, and the strength of social relations, interactions, and ties (Beauvais & Jenson 2002). These variables miss positive dimensions of cohesion, such as participation in community life, sense of belonging, and levels of trust. Since cohesion is a multifaceted concept, measures that tap into different dimensions may provide a deeper understanding of how it operates. Better concept measurement is needed before we declare cohesion to be unrelated to educational attainment.

Directions for Future Research

An important limitation of this research is that it is cross-sectional. The life course perspective (for example see, Elder, Johnson, & Crosnoe 2003) can help us situate individuals within contexts of their own and family life history and historical period. In particular, by taking a long view of personal history, we can examine how movers and non-movers differ prior to moves. We can also examine the effect of mobility history rather than mobility within a limited time period. We may discover there are different consequences depending on whether moves are normatively or non-normatively timed. It may also matter what triggers the move and what other events are occurring within the family or community. For example, the consequences of mobility may be particularly negative when triggered by or accompanied by martial breakdown. The life course would also enable us to link family members' personal histories in order to understand these interrelated dynamics.

Research has suggested important interaction effects with family structure. Research on children has suggested that high mobility is not detrimental to school performance among children who live with both biological parents, while any mobility negatively affected children living in other family structures (Tucker, Marx, & Long 1998). It may be that family transitions reduce human and social capital, which creates conditions in which the loss of community capital is injurious to educational outcomes (Hagan, MacMillan, & Wheaton 1996, Tucker, Marx, & Long 1998). In addition, we know little about the long-term effects of mobility in childhood. Hango (2006) used data from the 1986 Canadian General Social Survey (GSS) to examine the impact of childhood mobility on educational attainment among 25 to 79 year olds. The results suggested that for most individuals, the positive benefits of childhood mobility outweighed the potential negative losses of social ties in the short-term and the heightened stress. Over the long-run, living in more than one community before the age of 15 had a positive effect on educational attainment. However, it is important to note that longer-distance moves were more common among higher socio-economic status families. These findings further stress the potentially important effects of the impetus for the move, family characteristics, and resources available in the new location.

Research has suggested that groups that are prone to exclusion, which include Aboriginal peoples, may have strong bonding social capital, but lack bridging ties with other social groups or local institutions and linking ties with powerful social organizations and institutions (Policy Research Initiative Project, 2005). Our measure of social capital primarily taps into positive bonding dimensions, but does not capture the role of negative aspects of bonding, bridging, or linking ties. Future research can examine how bridging ties and linking social capital may be affected by socio-demographic characteristics and mobility, and in turn influence social and economic outcomes. "Understanding the contextual conditions in migration decision making is also necessary if we are to identify the types of policies that could make migration transitions easier to the individuals involved" (Cooke & Belanger 2006, 159).

Policy Implications

The analyses presented here along with the findings of other scholars suggests that there is a distinction between moves in which people are forced to leave in order to find housing, escape violence, access services or supports, for example, and those in which people choose to leave to pursue opportunities that are perceived to have long-term benefits, such as pursuing higher education and better employment. If this is the case, then policy can reduce forced mobility by providing resources such as suitable and affordable housing or protection, services, and support for those who are leaving abusive situations. It can also facilitate movement among those who are pursing opportunities by providing things such as financial support and programs to remove or reduce barriers. In both cases, the key is to assist individuals in maintaining existing ties and building new ones within new communities. Linking individuals to local institutions may be particularly important for achieving goals related to employment or education. There is also a need to provide services with a family focus since residential changes often are precipitated by changes in family structure or function. Appropriate supports for parents and children may reduce the negative effects of breaking social and community ties.

Putnam (2000) argued "social capital is not a substitute for effective public policy but rather a prerequisite for it and, in part, a consequence of it" (Social Capital and America's Ills, 14). The Policy Research Initiative Project (2005) concluded that social capital perspectives are particularly useful in addressing the needs of populations at risk of exclusion during life transitions, and in promoting community development. Social policy can assist citizens to acquire human and social capital, which enable them to fully participate in their communities and nations (Policy Research Initiative Project 2005).

Endnotes

1 Surveys of the on-reserve Aboriginal population have been limited by incomplete enumeration of reserves and undercoverage on-reserve. These analyses are not subject to these limitations since the data were collected from the off-reserve population.

References

APS. 2001. *Aboriginal Peoples Survey User's Guide to the Public Use Microdata File (adults off-reserve)*. Ottawa: Statistics Canada.

Aman, C. L. 2006. *Exploring the Influence of School and Community Relationships on the Performance of Aboriginal Students in British Columbia Public Schools*. Unpublished Dissertation. Vancouver: University of British Columbia.

Anderson, K. 2002. *Tenuous Connections: Urban Aboriginal Youth Sexual Health and Pregnancy*. Toronto: Ontario Federation of Indian Friendship Centres.

Beauvais, C., and J. Jenson. 2002. *Social Cohesion: Updating the State of Research*. Ottawa: Canadian Policy Research Networks.

Beavon, D., and E. Guimond. 2006. *Demographics and Well-being of Aboriginal Youth in Canada*. Paper presented at Investing in Youth: Evidence from Policy, Practice, and Research, Ottawa.

Beavon, D., and M.J. Norris. 1999. *Dimensions of Geographic Mobility and Social Cohesion: The Case of Aboriginal Peoples*. Paper presented to the Research and Analysis Directorate, Ottawa.

Coleman, J. S. 1988. "Social Capital in the Creation of Human Capital." *The American Journal of Sociology*, 94 (Supplement: Organizations and Institutions: Sociological and Economic Approaches to the Analysis of Social Structure): S95–S120.

Cooke, M., and D. Belanger. 2006. "Migration Theories and First Nations Mobility: Towards a System Perspective." *Canadian Review of Sociology and Anthropology*, 43(2): 141–164.

Distasio, J., G. Sylvester, K. Jaccubucci, S. Mulligan, and K. Sargent. 2004. *First Nations/Métis/Inuit Mobility Study: Final Report*. Winnipeg: Institute of Urban Studies.

Elder, G. H., M.K. Johnson, and R. Crosnoe. 2003. "The Emergence and Development of Life Course Theory." In J. T. Mortimer and M. J. Shanahan (eds.), *Handbook of the Life Course*. New York: Kluwer Academic. 3–19.

Graham, K. A. H., and E. Peters. 2002. *Aboriginal Communities and Urban Sustainability*. Ottawa: Canadian Policy Research Networks.

Hagan, J., R. MacMillan, and B. Wheaton. 1996. "New Kid in Town: Social Capital and the Life Course Effects of Family Migration on Children." *American Sociological Review*. 61:368–385.

Hango, D.W. 2006. "The Long-term Effect of Childhood Residential Mobility on Educational Attainment." *The Sociological Quarterly*. 47:631–664.

Hull, J. 2005. *Post-secondary Education and Labour Market Outcomes*. Ottawa: Indian and Northern Affairs Canada.

Long, J.S. and J. Freese. 2006. *Regression Models for Categorical Dependent Variables using Stata* (2nd ed.). College Station: Stata Press.

Maxim, P. S. and J. P. White. 2006. "School Completion and Workforce Transitions Among Urban Aboriginal Youth." In J. P. White, S. Wingert, D. Beavon and P. S. Maxim (eds.). *Aboriginal Policy Research: Moving Forward, Making a Difference* (Vol. 3). Toronto: Thompson Educational Publishing. 33–52.

Mendelson, M. 2004. *Aboriginal People in Canada's Labour Market: Work and Unemployment, Today, and Tomorrow*. Ottawa: The Caledon Institute of Social Policy.

Norris, M. J., D. Beavon, E. Guimond, and M. Cooke. 2004. *Registered Indian Mobility and Migration: An Analysis of 1996 Census Data*. Ottawa: Strategic Research & Analysis Directorate, Indian and Northern Affairs Canada.

Norris, M. J., and S. Clatworthy. 2003. "Aboriginal Mobility and Migration Within Urban Canada: Outcomes, Factors, and Implications." In D. Newhouse and E. Peters (eds.), *Not Strangers in These Parts: Urban Aboriginal Peoples*. Ottawa: Policy Research Initiative. 51–78.

Norris, M. J., M. Cooke., and S. Clatworthy. 2003. "Aboriginal Mobility and Migration: Patterns and Policy Implications." In J. P. White, P. S. Maxim, and D. Beavon (eds.), *Aboriginal Conditions: Research as a Foundation for Public Policy*. Vancouver: UBC Press. 108–129.

Peters, E. 1994. *Demographics of Aboriginal People in Urban Areas, in Relation to Self-government*. Ottawa: Department of Indian Affairs and Northern Development.

Policy Research Initiative Project. 2005. *Social Capital as a Public Policy Tool: Project Report*. Ottawa: Policy Research Initiative.

Portes, A. 1998. "Social Capital: Its Origins and Applications in Modern Sociology." *Annual Review of Sociology*. (24):1–24.

Pribesh, S., and D. Downey. 1999. "Why are Residential and School Moves Associated with Poor School Performance." *Demography*. 36(4): 521–534.

Putnam, R. D. 2000. *Bowling Alone: The Collapse and Revival of American Community*. New York: Simon and Schuster.

R.A. Malatest & Associates Ltd. 2004. *Aboriginal Peoples and Post-secondary Education: What Educators have Learned*. Montreal: Canada Millennium Scholarship Foundation.

Richardson, C., and N. Blanchet-Cohen. 2000. *Survey of Post-secondary Education Programs in Canada for Aboriginal Peoples*. Victoria: University of Victoria.

Royal Commission on Aboriginal Peoples. 1996. *Royal Commission Report on Aboriginal Peoples*. (Vol. 3—Gathering strength). Ottawa: Canada Communication Group.

Spence, N., and J. P. White. (2007). "Modelling Educational Success of First Nations Students in Canada: Modelling Community Level Perspectives." *Canadian Ethnic Studies*. 39 (1/2): 145.

Statistics Canada. (2001, May 11). Labour Force Survey. *The Daily*, from <**www.statcan.ca/Daily/ English/010511/d010511a.htm**>.

Tait, H. 1999. "Educational Achievement of Young Aboriginal Adults." *Canadian Social Trends*. (Spring): 6–10.

Tucker, C.J., J. Marx, and L. Long. 1998. " 'Moving on:' Residential Mobility and Children's School Lives." *Sociology of Education*. (71): 111–129.

Walters, D., J.P. White, and P.S. Maxim. 2004. "Does Post-secondary Education Benefit Aboriginal Canadians? An Examination of Earnings and Employment Outcomes for Recent Aboriginal Graduates." *Canadian Public Policy*. 30(3): 283–301.

White, J.P. and P.S. Maxim. 2003. "Social Capital, Social Cohesion, and Population Outcomes in Canada's First Nations Communities." In J. White, P. S. Maxim & D. Beavon (eds.). *Aboriginal Conditions: Research as a Foundation for Public Policy*. Vancouver: University of British Columbia Press. 7–33.

White, J.P., N. Spence, and P.S. Maxim. 2005. "Impacts of Social Capital on Educational Attainment in Aboriginal Communities: Lessons from Australia, Canada, and New Zealand." In *Social Capital in Action: Thematic Policy Studies*. Ottawa: Policy Research Initiative. 66–80.

White, J.P., N. Spence, and P.S. Maxim. 2006. "A New Approach to Understanding Aboriginal Educational Outcomes: The Role of Social Capital." In J.P. White, S. Wingert, D. Beavon & P.S. Maxim (eds.). *Aboriginal Policy Research: Moving Forward, Making a Difference* (Vol. 3). Toronto: Thompson Educational Publishing. 69–86.

10

rt Two: Causes, Cost

dian Registry

is based o

Previous

Resear

sion

First Nations Educati
Assessing Determina
Social Context Le

Nicholas Spence and Jerry P. Whi.

Introduction

The essential role of education in numerous social outcomes is well known. The Census data indicate that average educational attainment levels of First Nations are below national averages (Hull 1996; Norris and Siggner 2003). No doubt, the implications for Aboriginal communities are vast. This is captured by recent analyses, such as the Community Well-being (CWB) Index examining the relative differences in well-being between Aboriginal and non-Aboriginal communities (White, Beavon, and Spence 2007). Considering the importance of this ongoing issue, an attempt is made in this paper to explore the characteristics of successful schooling for First Nations communities. This approach begins with the community as the unit of analysis, with the realization that there are multiple levels of influence when discussing educational attainment, including intrapersonal, interpersonal, and contextual (community, province, country) and institutional. Unfortunately, the availability of data to examine educational issues in a comprehensive manner is the single greatest obstacle facing researchers. This analysis does not privilege contextual effects, which focus on the community, but underscores that they are an integral component of the overall picture of Aboriginal educational success. It is the process of exploring the community-level characteristics that explain educational success that is our main preoccupation in this paper.

There are five categories of explanatory variables used in our model: geographic isolation, school type, demographic, economic, and human capital. This study is the first of its kind where the explanatory power of the community is examined. We add to the information on Aboriginal school experience and contribute to a better understanding of the indicators of attainment by looking at three issues related to quality: graduate rate, withdrawal rate, and age-appropriate rate. We consider these indicators to be important as they focus on the school and community.[1]

We are studying those individuals who fall under the jurisdiction of the Department of Indian and Northern Affairs Canada (INAC). Accordingly, we evaluate the education outcomes of all First Nations students who report that they reside on a First Nations reserve, have qualified to register under the *Indian Act*, and appear

Information on such students is reported to INAC, and our
those data and the 1996 Census.

Research

on Aboriginal educational attainment is rare. In fact, the Royal Commis-
on Aboriginal People (RCAP) (1996) noted that there is a critical problem
terms of data availability and a lack of assessments of educational attainment.[2]
Much of the time spent discussing the issue centres on the perceived problems and
the assumed patterns of underachievement. Empirical work is often restricted to
small case studies or regional investigations and, at best, descriptive measures of
trends. While previous studies are sparse, there is some research to evaluate.

Studies of First Nations education indicate that certain patterns exist. Firstly,
off-reserve Indians have a greater educational attainment than those on-reserve
(Government of Canada 1971; McDonald 1991). Hull (1996) notes that this pattern
is particularly noticeable in the case of secondary and university completion rates.
Using data from 1986, Armstrong, Kennedy and Oberle (1990) found that only
25% of Canada's First Nations people completed high school compared with one
half of the non-Indian population. In terms of the transition to university, only
23% of First Nation graduates proceeded to this next stage of education compared
to 33% of the non-Indian population. The total First Nation population with a
university degree was 1.3% compared to 9.6% of the general population. Data
from Hull (1996) using the 1996 Census indicates that 37% of Registered Indians
attained "some post secondary" education (university, trades schools, and other
non university post secondary education);[3] however, this figure was much smaller
than the other Aboriginal population (47%) and the greater Canadian population
(51%).[4] Since 1986 the Registered Indian population with some post-secondary
attainment has increased 14% from 23% to 37% (ibid.). Among the Registered
Indian population 15 years and older not attending school, Hull (ibid.) found that
44% have completed secondary school or continued with some post-secondary
education although this figure is smaller than the percentage for the Aboriginal
identity group (51%) and other Canadians (67%). In terms of university degrees,
only 3% of Registered Indians attained this level of education compared to 4% of
other Aboriginal identity groups and 14% of other Canadians. While the indicators of post-secondary success have improved for Registered Indians, the relative
success of this group compared to the general population has been offset to some
extent because of the latter's increased success.

What about at lower levels of education? Studies suggest significant improvements in educational attainment in recent years. As Tait (1999) notes, the percentage of young Aboriginal adults with less than a high school diploma dropped from
60% to under 45% between 1986 and 1996. While the 1980s had been a time of
great change, as King (1993) notes, education levels of Aboriginal people are
still too low compared to the non-Aboriginal population. For instance, in 1986

Aboriginal people were 2.2 times more likely not to complete high school than non-Aboriginals. By 1996, this figure had increased to 2.6 times (Tait 1999). This implies once again, as with post secondary education, that the relative improvements in lower levels of education of the Aboriginal population tend to be offset to some degree by the increases in attainment found in the general population.

The importance of education is most clearly seen when one examines the returns.[5] Several researchers have found that the return to education for Aboriginals is greater than for other groups (George and Kuhn 1994; Patrinos and Sakellariou 1992; and Sandefur and Scott 1983) although this finding is not consistent (e.g., Lian and Matthews 1998). Jankowski and Moazzami (1995) found that there is an earnings return to education for First Nations persons of about 7.8% for each year of elementary and secondary school completed, and 31% for university training. Other studies, such as Drost (1994), also find positive outcomes for education in terms of labour force participation. Analyses indicate that the largest gains in reducing the risk of unemployment come from improvement of completion rates for elementary and high school (Ryan 1996).

The provinces of British Columbia and Saskatchewan have undertaken research to highlight some of the issues surrounding First Nations education. In British Columbia studies have found that 14% of Aboriginal students do not progress to high school as compared to 4% of non-Aboriginal students. In addition, Aboriginal students score significantly lower on Foundation Skills Assessments (FSA) in the standard testing in grades 4, 7, and 10 (British Columbia Ministry of Education 2000a). The British Columbia Ministry of Education and the Saskatchewan Department of Education have found that some of the most influential proposals for building effective schools and enhancing education attainment for First Nations students are premised on the community setting. Communities that generally engage in activities supporting both home and school are found to be a key to success (British Columbia Ministry of Education 2000b; Epstein 1987, 1988; Levesque 1994).

The striking point about Canadian assessments of First Nation and Aboriginal education is the lack of any real modelling of reasons for the particular patterns of educational attainment—it is this void that we wish to fill. Given the limitations of data in Canada, we looked at what is available and asked what we could model that would be useful. Our models use aggregate data, but the results must be interpreted with caution. Specifically, one must avoid making the ecological fallacy (i.e., making inferences at the individual level based on findings from the aggregate level); in other words, relationships observed at the aggregate level are not necessarily reproduced at the individual level (see Robinson 1950).[6, 7] The Organization for Economic Co-operation and Development (OECD) (2007) has implicitly addressed this issue in its discussion of educational indicators; specifically, a distinction is made between the various levels of educational indicators and related determinants that may be examined, and it is emphasized that the data must be appropriate, given the goals of the research. In this case, using aggregate data to assess macro-level propositions is an acceptable and commonly used method of inquiry (Snijders and Bosker 1999).

Hypotheses

Educational attainment has been found to vary by place of residence. Those outside metropolitan areas have less educational attainment by age and cohort than those in urban centres (Ward 1995). Isolation from economic centres probably makes many parts of the educational system seem somewhat irrelevant to students as a result of the high unemployment and shortage of opportunities available. Is location of the community also predictive of educational attainment in Canada? We believe that this is the case; in other words, we hypothesize an inverse relationship exists between the distance of a community from economic centres and educational success.

We think that school type is directly related to educational success in Canada. The literature has documented the difficulties faced by band schools in hiring and retaining qualified and experienced teaching staff. In short, band school teachers tend to have lower salaries and less job security, opportunities for change and advancement, professional development, and employment benefits than their peers because these institutions are not governed by district or provincial collective agreements (Bell 2004, RCAP 1996). Moreover, the teaching climate is characterized by a shortage of specialists and resources within the school which facilitate the learning process (ibid). A school system that aims to arm students with the human capital, cultural capital, and social capital to succeed in mainstream society may appear as pointless and disparate from reality as First Nations students know it, in the absence of well-qualified teachers who are able to bridge the gap using appropriate pedagogy.

Another issue is the lack of a national system of quality control to evaluate the education received by students (ibid). The absence of mandatory common benchmarks for monitoring purposes could quite possibly contribute to a perpetual system of long-term ineffectiveness in these schools with little accountability, even after taking into account differences in student intake and community contexts.[8] In the case of provincial and federal/private schools, the role of vertical ties, that is, increased interaction between ethnic minorities and the dominant groups may result in the former becoming more familiar with the dominant culture, acquiring accepted cultural capital and establishing networks (social capital), which can be used for educational attainment. Thus, we hypothesize that the provincial and federal/private schools would positively affect educational success while band schools would have a negative effect on educational outcomes.

In American studies of minorities poor achievement and dropping out is found to be related to an inability to translate education into work. Therefore, poor socio-economic development in a particular community could be linked with poor educational attainment or school leaving (Snipp and Sandefur 1988). One aspect not examined in the empirical literature is whether the economic status of communities (e.g., income and employment) affects rates of educational outcomes. Higher income and employment would be expected to be related to the level of educational resources available in the community, positive norms of attainment as the incentive or link between education and jobs would be concrete, and there would be greater focus on educational attainment at a collective level (see White, Spence, and Maxim 2005). Also, a high proportion of students may withdraw from school early in order to take advantage of job opportunities on-reserve (high employment rate on-reserve) if they believe that short-term gains from employment will outweigh the long-term benefits of human capital accumulation associated with remaining in school. This process is, however, mediated by the type of job and degree of competition in the market. If there are no jobs then there is no reason to study; if there are only low-end jobs available there is no reason to study; if there is a mix of low, medium, and high end jobs with competition, then school becomes more salient. Previous research has found that only a small proportion of withdrawers tend to be employed (White, Maxim, and Spence 2004). We expect that higher levels of economic success will have a positive effect on educational success.

A variable associated with economic development is the degree of occupational diversity in a community. The more occupational diversity on a reserve, the more incentive there will be for a band to increase investment in human capital. Hence, this variable is expected to have a positive effect on education outcomes because it measures human capital opportunities that exist. There may be a large percentage of the labour force employed, but all in a few occupations. This limits the demand for a comprehensive educational system and narrowly focuses attainment towards those occupations. Similar to our discussion of income and employment, the effect of occupational diversity on educational demand and outcomes is influenced by competition and the nature of the skills required for the job.

We expect that demographic variables would be determinants of the educational outcomes of First Nations bands. Demographic conditions, such as the age-dependency ratio, marital status, family size, and the sex ratio affect the educational outcomes of on-reserve students through their determination of the community's collective needs and goals. For example, the more children there are in the band, the more educational needs (financing, schools, teachers, etc.) there will be. The extent of education provided to meet these needs depends on the collective goals of the community, that is, how much education and of what quality do they want their children to possess, as well as the resources available to meet their needs and goals. Since bands tend to have young populations, the need for educational services is high; however, this need is countered by a relatively smaller proportion of adults who are able to provide for such services, beyond those provided by the government. We hypothesize that this phenomenon of a high age dependency ratio would have an adverse effect on educational success. Similarly, a high proportion of larger families would be characterized by a greater distribution of finite community social resources to accommodate the needs of children, which would decrease the investment in children and, therefore, lower educational success. This is similar to the popular "resource dilution theory" in the literature on effects of sibling size in families on various social outcomes but at a community level (see Steelman et al. 2002 for a comprehensive discussion). Family type is also predictive, as the proportion of single parent families is positively correlated with the prevalence of community problems and poverty (Bianchi 1999, Bursik and Grasmick 1993, Sampson 1992), which is antagonistic to the educational attainment process. Bands that have a higher proportion of single and/or divorced/separated/widowed people would be expected to have a higher proportion of single parent families, which be would an indication of lowered community cohesion, and less focus on education than bands with a greater proportion of married people. Thus, we expect that the proportion of single or no-longer-married people in a band would be correlated with lower rates of educational success, and the proportion of married, two-parent families would be positively correlated with educational attainment. The sex ratio—adult females to 100 males in a band—will also affect educational outcomes. Lower female-to-male ratios can result from a high rate of spousal abuse on-reserve, resulting in females migrating off-reserve, signalling serious societal problems that interfere with the education outcomes of students.[9]

Parental high school completion rates have been linked to lower dropout rates and reduced age inappropriateness (Ward 1998). Human capital accumulation on reserve is estimated using adult education levels. Conceptually, this variable can be thought of in terms of community norms and values. A high-achieving community provides the yardstick against which members measure themselves. In other words, the ideological context is one which places a premium on educational attainment, and this is probably reflected in the resource allocation of the community. Community human capital will have an effect even after taking into account the isolation, school type, demographic, and economic variables. Higher adult education levels in a band are expected to increase the educational attainment of children in the band even above the effect of income (see White, Spence, and Maxim 2005).

In summary, our main hypotheses are as follows:

1 The distance of a community from metropolitan areas will have a significant effect, with increasing distance of a community from economic centres having a negative effect on educational success.

2 School type will have a significant effect, with attendance at provincial and federal/private schools having a positive effect on educational success.

3 The employment rate, average income, and occupational diversity will have a positive effect on educational success.

4 a) The sex ratio (adult females to males) will have a positive effect on educational success.

b) The age dependency ratio will have a negative effect on educational success.

c) Family type will have a significant effect, with the proportion of single adults and separated, divorced, and widowed adults having a negative effect on educational success.

d) Family size will have a significant effect, with the proportion of one-child families having a positive effect on educational success, and the proportion of families with two or three or more children having a negative effect on educational success.

5 Human capital attainment will have a significant effect, with community attainment at all levels of the educational system having a positive effect on educational success. Further, as community attainment increases at *higher levels* of education, the effect on educational success will be stronger.

Sample

This analysis uses band-level data from the 1996 Census and Department of Indian Affairs and Northern Development Program Data—Education Survey for the school year 1995/1996, including all Registered and non-Registered (negligible) Indian and Inuit students who live on-reserve in Canada.[10] There are 397 communities that are used in the study.[11]

Measures[12]

The Educational Attainment Variables

Three different measures of educational attainment are used in this study: age-appropriate rate, graduate rate, and withdrawal rate. These measures are widely used throughout the literature and are considered standard outcomes of interest for this population (OECD 2007; RCAP 1996).[13] The **age-appropriate rate** is the percentage of age-appropriate grade 12 and 13 students in a band.[14] This gives us an analytically simple measure of the number of students that are behind the norm. In our sample, the average age appropriateness of students in our bands is 46.8%.[15] Our second measure of educational success, the **graduate rate**, is the proportion of grade 12 and 13 students, ages 16 to 22 years, in a band who were included on nominal roles and graduated. The average graduate rate is 19.8%. The third measure of educational success, the **withdrawal rate**, is the percentage of grade 12 and 13 students on the nominal rolls who withdrew from high school in 1995–1996. For the purposes of this measure we exclude students who transfer to other schools, move off reserve, died and/or graduate. This leaves those individuals who, for whatever reason, do not proceed with their education. The average withdrawal rate is 17.8%. Our focus upon grade 12 and 13 students is intentional; it is a critical point in the educational system in two respects, that is, a minimum entry point into the job market and post-secondary training or studies.[16, 17]

Table 10.1: Descriptive Statistics of Variables

Variable N=397	Mean	Std. Dev.
Dependent Measures		
Age-appropriate rate	.468	.249
Withdrawal rate	.178	.210
Graduate rate	.198	.206
Spatial		
0 to 50 km	.312	.464
51 to 350 km	.491	.501
More than 350 km	.197	.398
School Type		
Proportion of band school attendance	.214	.317
Proportion of provincial school attendance	.772	.320
Proportion of federal and private schools attendance	.014	.072
Demographic		
Sex ratio (female to 100 males)	92.7:100	10.965
Age ratio (0–14 to 100–15+)	55.9:100	20.259
Proportion of married adults	.324	.120
Proportion of single adults	.530	.128
Proportion of separated, divorced, and widowed adults	.146	.062
Proportion of families with no children	.188	.169
Proportion of families with one child	.262	.183
Proportion of families with two children	.230	.167
Proportion of families with three or more children	.321	.200
Economic		
Ratio of employed to total population of working age	39.5:100	12.356
Income of population 15 years and over (Canadian $)	7742.00	6981.15
Human Capital		
Proportion of adults with no high school graduation diploma	.557	.176
Proportion of adults with high school graduation diploma	.065	.051
Proportion of adults with trade certificate or other non-university post-secondary education	.242	.128
Proportion of adults with some university (no degree)	.112	.094
Proportion of adults with bachelors degree or higher	.024	.033
Occupational diversity	.795	.126

*Percentages may not equal 100 due to rounding

Isolation Variable

A revised version of the original one developed by INAC, this variable measures the distance from a First Nation community to the closest major centre, as well as accessibility to the community (i.e., road access). It provides a measure of the degree of isolation of a community from the greater society. In our sample, 31.2% of bands are 0–50 km away from a major centre; 49.1% of bands are 51–350 km away from a major centre; and 19.7% of bands are more than 350 km away from a major centre, with some communities having no year-round road access. [18]

School Type

This measure examines the proportion of students from a band attending a specified type of school: band schools, provincial schools, and federal/private schools. In our sample, the average figures are 21.4% , 77.2%, and 1.4% respectively.

Demographic Variables

This analysis uses four demographic measures: the sex ratio, age ratio, marital status, and number of children. The **sex ratio** is the number of females per 100 males in a band. This figure is 92.7 in our sample. The **age ratio,** a form of dependency ratio, is a measure of the number of children (0–14 years) to 100 adults (15 years and over) in a band. Among our sample of First Nations bands, there are 55.9 children to 100 adults. For our measure of **marital status**, the proportion of the adult band population with a particular legal marital status is examined: married, single, and separated/divorced/widowed. In our sample of communities, on average, 32.4% of adults are married; 53.0% of adults are single; and 14.6% of adults are separated, divorced, and/or widowed. The **number of children** is examined as a proportion of families with a specified number of children: none, one, two, and three or more.[19] The averages for our sample are 18.8%, 26.2%, 23.0%, and 32.1% respectively.

Economic Variables

There are two measures of the economic status of a community: the **ratio of employed to the total population of working age** and **average income.** These two indicators provide a point of comparison that gives us a view of the economic activity in and around the First Nation community and the adaptation of the adult population to that economic market. Sometimes analysts calculate the employment to population ratio. This measures the percentage of the total population 15 years and older employed during the week prior to the Census. While this is an interesting measure, some analysts exclude those in school from the population to calculate the ratio as we have done. Thus, one must be cognizant of this issue when comparing studies. This figure is 39.5 to 100 for our sample.

The other indicator of the economic status of First Nations communities is the average income of communities. This is a crude measure, but it is a proxy for wealth. Many studies have linked income and well-being (e.g., Wilkinson 1997).

Table 10.2: Hierarchical Regression of Age-appropriate Rate, Withdrawal Rate, and Graduation Rate on Community-level Predictors

	Age-appropriate rate n=397 β	$\sqrt{}$ Withdrawal Rate n=397 β	$\sqrt{}$ Graduate Rate n=397 β
Step 1: Isolation			
0 to 50 km (reference)			
51 to 350 km	-.042	-.035	.071
More than 350 km	-.074	.008	.008
F change (df, df)	8.613 (2,394)***	.660 (2,394)	.778 (2,394)
R^2 change	.042	.003	.004
Step 2: School Type			
Proportion of band school attendance (Omitted)			
Proportion of provincial school attendance	.116*	.004	.080
Proportion of federal/private schools attendance	-.057	.072	-.053
F change (df, df)	4.445 (2,392)*	5.099 (2,392)**	1.957 (2,392)
R^2 change	.021	.025	.010
Step 3: Demographic			
Female to male ratio	-.032	-.079	-.024
Age ratio	.004	.084	-2.39***
Proportion of married adults (omitted)			
Proportion of single adults	-.203**	.137*	-.219**
Proportion of separated, divorced, and widowed adults	-.016	.071	-.087
Proportion of families with no children (omitted)			
Proportion of families with one child	-.038	-.005	.109
Proportion of families with two children	.082	-.042	.222***
Proportion of families with three or more children	-.038	-.138	.312***
F change (df, df)	3.312 (7,385)**	2.363 (7,385)*	5.916 (7,385)***
R^2 change	.053	.040	.096
Step 4: Economic			
Ratio of employed to total population of working age	-.095	.121*	-.161**
Average income of population 15 years and over	-.020	.058	.017

	Age-appropriate rate n=397 ß	√ Withdrawal Rate n=397 ß	√ Graduate Rate n=397 ß
F change (df, df)	0.232 (2,383)	2.502 (2,383)	3.006 (2,383)++
R² change	.001	.012	.014
Step 5: Human Capital			
Proportion of adults with no high school graduation diploma (Omitted)			
Proportion of adults with high school graduation diploma	-.022	.018	.056
Proportion of adults with trade certificate or other non-university, post-secondary education	.188**	.121	-.005
Proportion of adults with some university (no degree)	-.016	-.103	.148**
Proportion of adults with bachelors degree or higher	.085	-.163**	.064
Occupational diversity	.081	-.048	.040
F change (df, df)	2.857 (5,378)*	4.414 (5,378)**	2.277 (5,378)++
R² change	.032	.051	.026
Full Model			
F change (df, df)	3.693 (18,378)***	3.176 (18,378)***	3.676 (18,378)***
R² Total	.150	.131	.149
R² Total (adjusted)	.109	.090	.108

Note: Standardized (ß) coefficients are from the final regression model, with the exception of the isolation block as it is a categorical variable and uses unstandardized (ß) coefficients.

Coefficients for "reference" and "omitted" categories are not entered into the model to avoid singularity.

*p < .05, ** p < .01, ***p < .001

++p < .055 and in the case of the final regression coefficients, (ß) is also meaningful; therefore, we chose to interpret this coefficient.

This measure of economic strength is restricted to the population 15 years and over.[20] The average income for the bands in our sample is $7742.00. First Nations people living on reserves tend to have a much lower employment rate than the rest of the Canadian population, and a high proportion of their income comes from government transfers (approximately 40% of the total income on average). Other income sources such as investments account for less than 2% of reported income. In our sample, 65% of average band income comes from employment. It should be kept in mind that people living and employed on-reserve are not required to pay income taxes; therefore, incomes are not readily comparable to the general population.

Human Capital Variables

There are two human capital variables in this analysis: the **highest level of schooling among adults** and the **occupational diversity**. The extent of educational success in a community indicates past performance and allows us to assess how educational levels in a community influence current attainment. This would include aggregate effects such as norms and community priorities. We look at the proportion of adults in a band attaining a specified level of schooling. Our findings by educational level of attainment are as follows: no high school graduation diploma (55.7%), high school graduation diploma (6.5%), trade certificate or non-university post-secondary education (24.2%), some university with no degree (11.2%), and a bachelor's degree or higher (2.4%). **Occupational diversity** is an index of the diversity of occupations within a band.[21] It allows us to assess the degree of economic opportunities in the community. Interpreting this variable is as follows: the higher the coefficient, the greater the occupational diversity of the community. For our sample, the average is .795.

Results

A series of sequential multiple regression analyses were conducted to assess the extent to which blocks of independent variables are predictive of educational success, that is, the age-appropriate rate, graduate rate, and withdrawal rate. The blocks of independent variables were entered as follows: Block 1—the isolation variable (distance from a band to a centre using dummy coding); Block 2—school type; Block 3—the demographic variables (sex ratio, age ratio, marital status, and number of children); Block 4—the economic variables (ratio of employed to the total population of working age and average income); and Block 5—the human capital variables (highest level of schooling among adults and occupational diversity).

The results of the evaluation of assumptions led to a square root transformation of the dependent variables, the withdrawal rate and graduate rate to reduce skewness and improve the normality, linearity, and homoscedasticity of residuals.[22] The measures reported for this analysis include the change in R^2 and the final standardized regression coefficient of each independent variable for the full model. Changes in R^2 indicate the amount of incremental variation explained in the dependent variable by a block of independent variables having statistically eliminated the effects of previously entered independent variables. An adjusted R^2 value for the full model is also presented. All information can be found in **Table 10.2**.

With the exception of the model for the age-appropriate rate, the isolation variable is unrelated to educational outcomes. This block explains 4.2% of the variance in the age-appropriate rate when entered first into the model. In the full model, the dummy variables for isolation are not found to affect the main results reported here, and a thorough examination did not find these effects to be mediated by the economic block as hypothesized.

When the school type block is added to the regression model in step 2, statistically significant changes in the age-appropriate rate and withdrawal rate appear. This block accounts for 2.1% of the variance in the age-appropriate rate and 2.5% of the variance in the withdrawal rate. An examination of the final betas shows that the only variable with a significant effect is the proportion of provincial school attendance on the age-appropriate rate.

The block of demographic variables contributes significantly to explaining educational outcomes in all three models, beyond the geography and school type variables. Specifically, demographics accounts for 5.3% of the variance in the age-appropriate rate, 4.0% of the variance in the withdrawal rate, and 9.6% of the variance in the graduate rate. The proportion of single adults has a negative effect on the age-appropriate rate and a positive effect on the withdrawal rate. The final beta scores for the graduate rate shows that the age ratio and the proportion of single adults have a negative effect on the graduate rate while the proportion of families with two and three or more children have the opposite effect.

In step 4, we find that the economic characteristics of the community explain a significant amount of the variance only in the graduate rate (1.4%) beyond that afforded by those variables introduced in the first three steps. The final beta scores show that the ratio of the employed to the total population of working age has a positive effect on the withdrawal rate and a negative effect on the graduate rate.

The final step assesses whether community human capital improves prediction of the dependent variables after taking into account the previous blocks. This block has a statistically significant impact, and explains 3.2% of the variance in the age-appropriate rate, 5.1% of the variance in the withdrawal rate, and 2.6% of the variance in the graduate rate. For the age-appropriate rate, the proportion of adults with a trade certificate or other non-university, post-secondary education has a positive effect on this measure of educational success. The proportion of adults with a bachelor's degree or higher has a negative effect on the withdrawal rate. In the case of the graduate rate, the proportion of adults with some university (no degree) has a positive effect. Collectively, the full model explains 15.0% of the variance in the age-appropriate rate, 13.1% of the variance in the withdrawal rate, and 14.9% of the variance in the graduate rate. The adjusted R^2 values in this analysis are 10.9%, 9.0%, and 10.8% respectively.

Discussion

This study has revealed several key findings. The effect of isolation is only important for the age appropriate rate when entered first into the model. School type effects for the age appropriate rate are seen with the proportion of provincial school attendance. We believe that the unique positive effect of this variable is best understood in terms of the earlier discussion of vertical ties. As ethnic minorities interact with the dominant groups, they may become familiar with the dominant culture, acquire accepted cultural capital and establish networks (social capital) which can be used for educational attainment. In terms of the withdrawal rate, the effect of the school type block's variables disappears in the presence of the demographic, economic, and human capital variables.

The demography block plays a particularly important role in this analysis. The age ratio has a strong negative effect on the graduate rate. This is no surprise as we would expect a dilution effect of resources at the community level; that is, there would collectively be less financial, emotional, and time resources available as the proportion of children to adults increases. The end result is the mitigation of educational attainment of youth. The proportion of single adults exhibits an effect across all measures of educational success which reduces educational success; that is, it decreases the age-appropriate rate and graduate rate, and it increases the withdrawal rate. Recall that as the proportion of single adults increases, this is associated with a higher proportion of children in single parent households (lone parenthood) and higher levels of poverty (Bianchi 1999). We argue that these communities tend to be structurally deficient in social capital (e.g., less cohesive networks), which is necessary for the transmission of other forms of capital, such as financial or human (Coleman 1988, Coleman 1990, and Martin 2004). This context would undermine the educational outcomes of the community.

The fertility variables, the proportion of families with two children, and the proportion of families with three or more children are both important in their effects on the graduate rate. Most notable is the strong *positive* effect of these variables on the graduate rate while controlling for all of the other variables in the entire model. How can this be explained? The context of a community—including prevailing norms and priorities surrounding child rearing—is an important consideration. For example, large families are accepted and encouraged among Mormons. The communities play an important supporting role in raising children (we call this social capital), and the social norms dictate that societal resources be prioritized and allocated towards the needs of youth (Downey and Neubauer 1998). What this all means is that cultural context and institutions of governance at the community level can influence the effects of fertility on educational attainment. So it appears that in communities where the proportion of two children increases, the dynamics (e.g., culture, resource allocation, etc.) are such that positive aggregate effects in education are observed. A greater understanding of the positive effect of this fertility variable on educational outcomes in First Nations communities is needed. This could prove quite fruitful in the ongoing discussions regarding sibling size and resource dilution theory (see Steelman et al. 2002). Parental decisions regarding the allocation of various forms of resources could be found through qualitative research. Moreover, this type of research could enable us to better understand the role of culture in social norms relating to child rearing in the community. Our previous work on social capital in Aboriginal communities indicates this would be a useful exercise (White, Spence and Maxim 2005).

The strong positive effect of the proportion of families with three or more children on the graduate rate is noteworthy. This variable has a statistically significant positive effect on graduate rates, with a beta value of .312 (p<.001). An analysis of this coefficient from the bivariate case (r=.03, p>.05) through to the full multiple regression model is informative, since the change in the coefficient between the former and latter is significant. Indeed, in combination, the other variables in the model suppress variance in the proportion of families with three or more children that is irrelevant to prediction of graduate rates, which results in a dramatic increase in the effects of this independent variable. Hence, this variable's importance cannot be understood in isolation of the other variables in the model.[23] At this point we conclude that further analysis needs to be done to understand the dynamics surrounding the suppression of this variable and the possible consequences.

Although the entrance of the economic block does not contribute much in explaining variance in the dependent variables, given its point of entry, the final beta values for the ratio of the employed to the total population of working age are statistically significant for the withdrawal rate and the graduate rate. This effect is adverse for educational success. Following from our discussion earlier, it appears that higher levels of employment may be promoting an acceptable culture of premature exiting of the educational system in order to take advantage of job opportunities on reserve. These school leavers may feel that the short term gains from employment will outweigh the long term benefits of human capital accumulation associated with remaining in school.

The effect of the community's educational levels across all three models in this analysis is most notable. While holding constant the isolation, school type, demographic, and economic variables, the educational attainment levels of a community have a distinctly important role in the educational success of students. When we examine the betas within the human capital block, the proportion of adults with some university (no degree) is an important variable in increasing the graduate rate, and the proportion of adults with a bachelor's degree or higher plays a key role in reducing the withdrawal rate. Thus, it appears that high levels of community educational attainment may breed a social context which values, supports, and expects high academic achievement (high average norms), which could result in high rates of educational success. This effect would not be entirely surprising; after all, since behaviour is socially determined, societal level norm effects are naturally of great significance.[24]

The proportion of adults with a trade certificate or other non-university post-secondary education is important for increasing the age-appropriate rates; in fact, it has the strongest unique effect on educational success out of all the variables in the human capital block. In addition to the norm effects of higher education mentioned previously, we comment that the trades demand individuals who are highly visual, enjoy hands on work, and respect senior workers with more expertise and training who can pass on their knowledge. The key traits of Aboriginal culture include visualization, learning through the process of doing, and passing on teachings from elders. As an increasing proportion of the community attains this type of education and works in these culturally congruent jobs that offer a respectable average pay, the mass perception of the value of education would be apparent, which may result in high age-appropriate rates.[25] This positive relationship between norms, community capacity, and educational attainment in communities has been found in a recent comparative study of New Zealand, Australia, and Canada (White, Spence, and Maxim 2005).

It is our belief that the issue investigated in this work, identifying predictors of educational success, is a crucial area of concern for all stakeholders. Despite the shortcomings, our findings are useful. Indeed, our analysis shows that using different indicators of attainment and success yielded somewhat similar results. A brief analysis of the final beta values demonstrates that despite the similarities in terms of the importance of blocks of variables, certain variables within those blocks appear to be playing different roles in their effects on each measure of educational success. This indicates that researchers must be aware of the validity issues surrounding varied measures of "educational success," as our understanding of the processes of success are shaped by the outcome measure used.[26] In the process of developing and evaluating policies and programs, a clear understanding of these varied causes and determinants is essential to achieve desired outcomes.

It is clear to us that given the relatively low explanatory power of the three models and the residual unexplained variance, there is a need for further research into the determinants of our measures of educational success. Given that this area is under researched, it is not unexpected that our study is an initial glance that tends to spawn many more questions—such is the nature of research. Without a doubt, we believe that further theorizing and empirical analysis is necessary to gain more insight into the complexities of the factors that contribute to educational outcomes. Methodologically, an aggregate cross sectional snapshot of the average effects of the variables used in our analysis limits our understanding of the phenomena at hand. Longitudinal, multilevel, and qualitative studies would be useful in shedding more light upon the processes of attainment in these diverse communities. In terms of variables, cultural content and the use of traditional language in the educational system are obvious directions to proceed. As mentioned earlier, our focus upon grade 12 and 13 students is intentional; it is a critical point in the educational system in many respects, given that it functions as a minimum entry point into both the job market and post-secondary education institutions. However, further work on the effects of community level characteristics at various points in the educational system is needed. Work by White, Maxim, and Spence (2004) indicates that the transition to high school from elementary school is problematic, as educational success measures decline substantially for First Nations. Do the variables used in this model explain educational success at lower levels of the educational system? Are the effects of these variables constant at all levels of the educational system? Are there variables absent from this analysis that are fundamental for explaining educational success at lower levels of the educational system? Stakeholders, including policy makers, require this type of research to arm them with the knowledge necessary to develop and implement meaningful social policy, programs, and initiatives at strategic points in the educational system.

Social Policy

From a policy perspective, this research does not provide a perfect recipe for the educational success of First Nations. However, a policy lens that recognizes community effects as more than the sum of the individual-level characteristics of members of the community is a step in the right direction. Moreover, our findings indicate that policy, programming, and initiatives aimed at the following areas would potentially yield positive results:

1 Supporting communities with a high proportion of single parents through long-term sustainable initiatives to offset economic disadvantage and associated social problems. Children in disadvantaged families are likely to experience a life course trajectory that differs from their advantaged peers in a negative way. The cumulative effect of disadvantage over the life course carries a great cost to society, across a range of social indicators, including health, education, and income. It is the case that inequality produces further inequality; therefore, intervening at an early stage in the life course to eliminate inequalities is the most efficient way to proceed.

2 Providing resources of various kinds that reinforce the importance of both youth and education as priorities in a community; for example, creating public meeting places, opportunities for exchange and interaction in a community can facilitate the development and reinforcement of these community norms. Working with communities to identify and implement culturally appropriate initiatives is of principal importance.

3 Building social capital in communities to enhance outcomes.[27] This process is particularly important where there is a high rate of community problems (e.g., crime, family disintegration, etc).

4 Promoting community capacity strategies and economic development in a manner that promotes a highly educated populace.

5 Collecting data in future surveys that captures detailed individual-, as well as contextual-level variables. It is difficult to make definitive claims on any phenomenon without good data. Efforts can be focused on collecting high quality data and, where possible, data that is amendable to multilevel analyses. Given the various levels that influence educational success, including intrapersonal, interpersonal, and contextual (community, province, country)/institutional, data that would enable us to distinguish the relative strength of these various levels and their associated variables would be useful. Finally, one of the longstanding debates in the social science literature, "structure versus

agency," can be addressed using multilevel data. This line of research opens a number of research avenues, such as the way intrapersonal characteristics (e.g., motivation) may vary in their effects by social context (e.g., educational norms of community-average educational attainment) or interpersonal relations (e.g., social support) are amplified or mitigated by social context (e.g., income inequality).

More informed policy can only be made after data has been collected that will provide meaningful insights into the processes of the trends documented in this research.

What can we conclude from this study? Instituting social policy that can foster the development of human capital in the Aboriginal population is a key starting point to economic development and the well being of communities. Thus, improving the rates of educational success of Aboriginal students in the educational system is paramount. We know that the structural components of society impact on the decisions individuals make in their day to day lives. Decisions are always made in a given social context. If that social context is not supportive or conducive to staying in school, then we can expect poor educational attainment outcomes. Our regression analysis has shown that the social structure of the community affects educational success. Thus, educational policy can only be examined in the context of other social policy. Through further research, it is our hope that more light can be shed upon the key determinants of human capital in Aboriginal communities. We understand that there are various levels at which it is strategic to intervene, including the individual, community, province, and country levels. This work has shed some insights into the mechanisms related to achievement at the community level. While we are edging closer to articulating the process through which these determinants operate to affect educational outcomes, we have much to learn. Utilizing and combining various modes of research (qualitative/quantitative) will be very useful. Given the paucity of research in understanding the structural issues surrounding educational attainment in Aboriginal communities, we see this as an area ripe for much theorization and deliberation.

Endnotes

1 This study builds on work by White, Maxim, and Spence (2004).

2 A clear example is the issue of native language instruction in schools. Language and culture are thought to play vital roles in the improvement of attainment since the preservation of traditional languages is extremely important for all Aboriginal peoples (King 1993; see also Ledlow 1992 and White and Cook 2001). Kaulback (1984) states that students from some cultures may have a different way of processing information than those children who have been raised in mainstream culture. Despite the call by First Nations for more traditional culture and language in the curriculum, there has been a slow institutional uptake. Moreover, there seems to be little research into how this is accomplished and a lack of good data to do any rigorous testing.

3 The higher percentage in this category reflects the large number of training courses offered to Registered Indians through INAC programming.

4 It is useful to differentiate between Registered, Status, or Treaty Indians (those who are registered under the *Indian Act* of Canada) and other Aboriginals. Registered Indians are persons who are registered under the *Indian Act* of Canada and can prove descent from a band that signed a treaty. The other Aboriginal population includes all of those individuals who report Aboriginal identity but are not Registered Indians. It includes those who identify themselves as Métis, Inuit, or North American Indian (First Nations) and those with multiple Aboriginal or Aboriginal and non-Aboriginal identities.

5 Returns to education can be observed in a number of social outcomes such as income and health as well as community well-being.

6 Educational outcomes are a product of numerous effects at the micro- and macro- levels of analysis as discussed earlier. The best approach to address this methodological issue is to use multilevel models. Multilevel models have been used in modelling educational outcomes to separate out the various levels of influence, for example, school and community effects as well as individual level effects (e.g., Goldstein 1995). Unfortunately, the researchers were unable to secure individual data to match individuals to communities because of confidentiality issues. Nevertheless, this paper is useful as it provides a model of educational outcomes that focuses on community effects as opposed to basic descriptive data.

7 Particularly in the areas of population health, community-level variables have gained prominence in the social sciences in recent years.

8 Band school authorities make several important points for not requiring their schools to take existing provincial assessment programs, such as the biases of the measures, unfair comparisons with provincial schools, and the potential loss of autonomy and control over their community's education (Bell 2004).

9 Property laws and band practices tend to favour the male keeping the reserve residence, which can force women to migrate to cities. Thus, although spousal abuse and sexist formal laws and practices are both linked to the sex ratio, these effects cannot be distinguished using this measure alone.

10 We use data from 1996 because the 2001 Department of Indian Affairs and Northern Development Program Data is not currently available.

11 Approximately 2% of cases had missing data and were deleted from the analysis.

12 Please contact the authors regarding questions related to the derivation of variables.

13 These three variables are analytically and statistically independent. Statistically, we found that the variables do not come close to any known criteria for constituting a scale. The Pearson's correlation coefficient between the three variables are as follows: $r_{\text{(age appropriate rate, graduate rate)}} = 0.101$; $r_{\text{(age appropriate rate, withdrawal rate)}} = -0.259$; $r_{\text{(graduate rate, withdrawal rate)}} = -0.303$;

14 The equation for the age-appropriate measure is provided below:

age-appropriate rate = number of age appropriate/total

total = age-appropriate + not age-appropriate

age-appropriate = (Age – 7) – grade, which will result in a value < 0

not age-appropriate = (Age – 7) – grade, which will result in a value > = 0.

We used a more generous 7 years instead of the usual 6 years as our age-appropriate base level for grade one, to account for the likelihood that students on-reserve would not be age-appropriate compared to the rest of the population as a result of a higher rate of absenteeism.

15 See **Table 10.1** for the mean values for all variables.

16 "Minimum" refers to the minimum accepted level of educational attainment in general Canadian society. Non-completion of high school is considered an absolute liability to economic involvement.

17 Ontario was the only province with grade 13 in the dataset, and one might expect rates to therefore differ; however, an analysis of the data found no significant difference between Ontario and the rest of the country.

18 INAC uses four zones used to describe isolation, but because of low frequency counts in zones three and four we have combined them.

19 Our decision to group families with three or more children into one category is based on a few important reasons: 1) we feel that issues related to family size do not change at three and over; 2) the proportion of families with four, five, six, etc., children, are very small and the analytic value diminishes with the increasing number of categories. Thus, the low end is more important to capture for the analysis.

20 Measurement error is created by the rounding of data in the Census to protect the privacy of individuals in bands with small populations; however, the implications are trivial for this analysis.

21 The data does not distinguish between occupations on- and off-reserve. The coefficient ranges from 0 to 1, as given by the following formula:

$$1 - E\,(P_i^2)$$

P_i = population in occupation i/total population in all occupations

$i = 1...12$ [1]

Note that 'i' is indicative of twelve different occupations: management, administration, clerical, science, health, law, teaching, art, sales, food/travel, construction/trades, manufacturing, machine operation, and primary industries.

22 The graduate rate (Statistics = 1.446, Std. Deviation = 1.625) and withdrawal rate (Statistic = 1.625, Std. Error = .121) were transformed to reduce skewness, resulting in the square root transformation of the graduate rate (Statistic = .020, Std. Error = .121) and withdrawal rate (Statistic .260, Std. Error = .121).

23 Deriving theoretical explanations for suppression results is questionable unless these findings are replicated (Maassen and Baker 2001). Moreover, it is recommended that any attempts to test for the presence of a suppression effect should be based on a priori assumptions about the theoretical relation between the variables and the role of the suppressor variable (MacKinnon, Krull and Lockwood 2000). The idea of suppressor variables and their utility has come under scrutiny by many. Readers are advised to see the discussions on this issue by Wiggins (1973), Cohen and Cohen (1992), Pedhazur (1982), and Maassen and Baker (2001).

24 Structural approaches to examining social issues have underscored the effects of social norms on a number of social outcomes (e.g., Durkheim 1979; Kawachi, Kennedy and Lochner 1997; Rose 1992; White, Spence and Maxim 2005.)

25 The Alberta Aboriginal Apprenticeship Program has been heralded as groundbreaking and extremely successful. The premise of the program is that apprenticeship training is essentially congruent with the core values of Aboriginal culture (Alberta Human Resource Development Council of Canada 2004). Thus, we are not surprised to find a positive effect on educational success.

26 The entire domain of the concept "educational success" is vast. Indicators of educational success are numerous, such as standardized testing, employment rates after graduation, average earnings after graduation, student attitudes/self-evaluations, etc., and we are limited in terms of the number of indicators available to use due to the availability of data. Conceptual debates on the content validity of this concept continue (OECD 2007).

27 A recent study by White, Spence, and Maxim (2005) confirms the payoffs of using the social capital lens in developing Aboriginal educational programming and policy.

References

Alberta Human Resource Development Council of Canada. "The Alberta Aboriginal Apprenticeship Project." Available from <**www.ahrdcc.com/en/view.php?page=AAAP**> [accessed 10 September 2004].

Armstrong, R., R.J. Kennedy, and P.R. Oberle. 1990. *University Education and Economic Well-being: Indian Achievement and Prospects*. Ottawa: Indian and Northern Affairs Canada, Quantitative Analyses and Socio-Demographic Research, Finance and Professional Services.

Bell, D. 2004. *Sharing Our Success: Ten Case Studies in Aboriginal Schooling.* Kelowna: Society for the Advancement of Excellence in Education.

Bianchi, S.M. 1999. "Feminization and Juvenilization of Poverty: Trends, Relative Risks, Causes and Consequences." *Annual Review of Sociology.* 25: 307–333.

British Columbia Ministry of Education, Aboriginal Education Branch. "How Are We Doing: An Overview of Aboriginal Educational Results." Available from <**www.bced.gov.bc.ca/abed/results**>[accessed 10 March 2000].

British Columbia Ministry of Education, Aboriginal Education Branch. "Aboriginal Education Improvement Agreements." Available from <**www.bced.gov.bc.ca/abed/agreements/**> [accessed 10 March 2000].

Bursik, R. and H. Grasmick. 1993. *Neighborhoods and Crime.* New York: Lexington Books.

Cohen, J. and P. Cohen. 1975. *Applied Multiple/Correlation Regression Analysis for the Social Sciences Second Edition.* New York: Wiley.

Coleman, J. 1988. "Social Capital and the Creation of Human Capital." *American Journal of Sociology.* 94: S95–S120.

Coleman, J. 1990. *Foundations of Social Theory.* Cambridge: Harvard University Press.

Department of Indian Affairs and Northern Development. 1995. *Highlights of Aboriginal Conditions 1991, 1986: Demographic, Social, and Economic Conditions.* Online Catalogue number R32-154/1-1986E. Ottawa: Minister of Public Works and Government Services Canada.

Downey, D. and S. Neubauer. 1998. "Is Resource Dilution Inevitable? The Association Between Number of Siblings and Educational Outcomes Across Subgroups." Paper presented at the 93rd Annual Meeting of the American Sociological Association, San Francisco.

Drost, H. 1994 "Schooling, Vocational Training and Unemployment: The Case of Canadian Aboriginals." *Canadian Public Policy.* 20 (1) 52–65.

Durkheim, E. 1979. *Suicide.* Free Press: New York.

Epstein, J.L. 1987. "Toward a Theory of Family-School Connections: Teacher Practices and Parent Involvement Across the School Years." In *The Limits and Potential of Social Intervention.* K. Hurrelman and F.-X. Kaufman (eds). Berlin/New York: DeGruyter/Aldine.

Epstein, J.L. 1988. "How do We Improve Programs for Parent Involvement?" *Educational Horizons.* Winter: 58–59.

George, P. and P. Kuhn. "The Size and Structure of Native–White Wage Differentials." *Canadian Journal of Economics* 27 (1994): 20–42.

Goldstein, H. 1995. *Multilevel Statistical Models.* London: Halsted Press.

House of Commons Standing Committee on Indian Affairs. 1971. *Minutes of Proceedings and Evidence of the Standing Committee on the Annual Reports of the Department of Indian Affairs and Northern Development, 1967–68 and 1968–69.* Ottawa: Government of Canada.

Hull, J. 2000. *Aboriginal Post-Secondary Education and Labor Market Outcomes Canada, 1996.* Ottawa: Indian and Northern Affairs Canada.

Jankowski, W. and B. Moazzami. 1995. "Returns of Education among Northwestern Ontario's Native People." *Canadian Journal of Native Studies.* 15(1): 104–111.

Kaulback, B. 1984. "Styles of Learning Among Native Children: A Review of the Research." *Canadian Journal of Native Education.* 11(3): 27–37.

Kawachi, I., B. Kennedy and K. Lochner. 1997. "Long Live Community: Social Capital as Public Health." *The American Prospect.* 35: 56–59.

King, C. 1993. *The State of Aboriginal Education in Southern Canada.* Ottawa: Royal Commission on Aboriginal Peoples.

Ledlow, S. 1992. "Is Cultural Diversity an Adequate Explanation for Dropping Out?" *Journal of American Indian Education.* 31(3): 21–36.

Levesque, D.M. 1994. *Cultural and Parental Influences on Achievement Among Native American Students in Barstow Unified School District.* Paper presented at the National Meeting of the Comparative and International Educational Society. March, San Diego.

Lian, J. and D.R. Matthews. 1998. "Does the Vertical Mosaic Exist? Ethnicity and Income and Canada." *Canadian Review of Sociology and Anthropology.* 34(4): 461–483.

Maassen, G. and A. Baker. 2001. "Suppressor Variables in Path Models: Definitions and Interpretations." *Sociological Methods and Research.* 30: 241–270.

MacKinnon, D., J. Krull and C. Lockwood. 2000. "Equivalence of the mediation, confounding and suppression Effect." *Prevention Science.* 1(4): 173–181.

Martin, M. 2004. "Producing and Reproducing the Family: Economic and Family Behavior in Two Generations." *Dissertation Abstracts International: The Humanities and Social Sciences.* 64(8): 3088-A.

McDonald, R.J. 1991 "Canada's Off Reserve Aboriginal Population." *Canadian Social Trends.* Winter: 2–7.

Norris, D. and A. Siggner. 2003. *What Census and the Aboriginal Peoples Survey Tell Us About Aboriginal Conditions in Canada.* Presented at the 2003 Aboriginal Strategies Conference, Edmonton Alberta, 2003. Available online at <**http:// 209.123.49.177/~statcan/presentations/_dougnorris_ 01.pdf**>

OECD. 2007. *Education at a Glance 2007.* Paris: OECD.

Patrinos, H. and C.N. Sakellariou. 1992. "North American Indians in the Canadian Labor Market: A Decomposition of Wage Differentials." *Economics of Education Review.* 11(3): 257–266.

Pedhazur, E.J. 1982. *Multiple Regression in Behavioral Research: Explanation and Prediction.* New York: Holt, Rinehart and Winston.

Robinson, W. 1950. "Ecological Correlation and the Behaviour of Individuals." *American Sociological Review.* 15: 351–357.

Rose, G. 1992. *The Strategy of Preventive Medicine.* Oxford: Oxford University Press.

RCAP. 1996. *Guide to the Principles and Recommendations of the Final Report of the Royal Commission on Aboriginal Peoples.* Ottawa: The Royal Commission on Aboriginal Peoples.

Ryan, J. 1996. "Restructuring First Nations' Education: Trust, Respect and Governance." *Journal of Canadian Studies.* 31(2): 115–132.

Sampson, R. 1992. "Family Management and Child Development: Insights From Social Disorganization Theory." In *Advances in Criminological Theory: Volume 3, Facts, Frameworks and Forecasts.* J. McCord (ed). New Brunswick: Transaction. 63–93.

Sandefur, G. and W.J. Scott. 1983. "Minority Group Status and the Wages of White, Black, and Indian Males." *Social Science Research.* 12: 44–68.

Snijders, T. and R. Bosker. 1999. *Multilevel Analysis: An Introduction to Basic and Advanced Multilevel Modeling.* New York: Sage.

Snipp, C.M. and G.D. Sandefur. 1988. "Earnings of American Indians and Alaskan Natives: The Effects of Residence and Migration." *Social Forces.* 66(4): 994–1008.

Steelman, L., B. Powell, R. Werum, and S. Carter. 2002. "Reconsidering the Effects of Sibling Configuration: Recent Advances and Challenges." *Annual Review of Sociology.* 28: 243–269.

Tait, H. 1999. "Educational Achievement of Young Aboriginal Adults." *Canadian Social Trends.* 52 (Spring): 6–10.

Ward, C. 1995. "American Indian High School Completion in Rural Southeastern Montana." *Rural Sociology.* 60(3): 416–434.

Ward, C. 1998. "Community Resources and School Performance: The Northern Cheyenne Case." *Sociological Inquiry.* 68(1): 83–113.

White, J., D. Beavon, and N. Spence (Eds). 2007. *Aboriginal Well-being.* Toronto: Thompson Educational Publishing, 2007.

White, J.P., P. Maxim, and N.D. Spence. 2004 "An Examination of Educational Success." In *Aboriginal Policy Research: Setting the Agenda for Change, Vol. 1.* J.P. White, P.Maxim and D. Beavon (eds). Toronto: Thompson Educational Publishing. 129–148.

White, J.P., N.D. Spence, and P. Maxim. 2005. "Social Capital and Educational Attainment Among Aboriginal Peoples: Canada, Australia and New Zealand." In *Policy Research Initiative Social Capital Project Series, Social Capital in Action: Thematic Studies.* Ottawa: Policy Research Initiative, Government of Canada. 66–81.

White, W. and P. Cook. 2001. "Thunder-birds, Thunder-beings and Thunder-voices: The Application of Traditional Knowledge and Children's rights in Support of Children's Education." *American Review of Canadian Studies.* 31 (Spring-Summer): 331–347.

Wiggins, J. 1973. *Personal and Prediction: Principles of Personality Assessment.* New York: Addison-Wesley.

Wilkinson, R.G. 1997. "Comment: Income, Inequality and Social Cohesion." *American Journal of Public Health.* 87(9): 1504–1506.

11

A New Approach to Understanding Aboriginal Educational Outcomes: The Role of Social Capital[1]

Jerry P. White, Nicholas Spence, and Paul Maxim

Introduction

In recent years, social capital has received much attention and has been the subject of great debate in the social sciences and policy arenas. Whether social capital has the capacity and utility to produce meaningful change in achieving the goals of society, is one focus of that debate.

This paper examines the impacts of social capital on Aboriginal educational attainment in Canada, Australia, and New Zealand. The focus for Canada is First Nations and in other countries it is a similar population. Our aim is to explore how social capital theory has been applied to Aboriginal contexts in each country, and we seek to determine if social capital plays, or can play, any role in improving educational attainment for Aboriginal populations. Does social capital figure in the formation of programs and policies? Should it be a consideration? What are the specific contexts in which social capital can have an effect on educational attainment? We approached these questions by creating as extensive an inventory of policies and programs as possible for each of the countries. Also, we supplemented our inventory with email, phone, and face-to-face interviews with experts, such as Robert Putnam in the US, David Robinson in New Zealand, Canadian Aboriginal students, and government policy officers in all three countries. We thank everyone who took time to work with us.

We developed a synthesis looking for patterns and distilling the role of social capital. Our research looked at conscious applications of the concept, but also where we could discern its implicit part in educational attainment. In writing our results we chose programs and policies that illustrated our synthesis.

Why Aboriginal Education?

The focus on educational attainment and human capital development is strategic. Much research has illustrated the gap in the standard of living between the greater Canadian society and Aboriginal people, and the foundations for understanding these outcomes (White, Maxim, and Beavon 2004). Recurring themes are the lagging levels of educational attainment, and the consequent poor labour market outcomes among Aboriginals compared to the non-Aboriginal Canadian population. The 2001 Census data demonstrates these gaps clearly. Among the population 15 years of age and over, 48% of Aboriginals have less than a high school graduation certificate compared to 30.8% of the non-Aboriginal population. The percentage of Aboriginals with high school and some post-secondary education is 22.4% compared to 25% for the non-Aboriginal population. For trades or college, 23.7% of Aboriginals possess this credential compared to 25.9% of the non-Aboriginal population. At the high level of attainment—university—only 4.4% of Aboriginals have achieved this credential compared to 15.7% of the non-Aboriginal population (Statistics Canada 2003). However the picture is not, totally bleak. For example, 2004 Indian and Northern Affairs Canada (INAC) data shows that there have been some improvements in educational attainment over time, but the gaps are still noteworthy.

Our paper is anchored by the desire to develop more insight into the solutions to these problems using the social capital lens. The trends we have documented are not exclusive to Aboriginal Canadians. Indeed, Aboriginal populations across all three countries have less attainment than the general population, and this issue has not gone unnoticed by their governments. Although our preoccupation with this issue originates within the Canadian context, a logical step is to compare the work done in other countries and develop a general framework of social capital as it relates to Aboriginal educational outcomes. This is what we have done.

Defining Social Capital

Conceptually and theoretically, social capital has various faces and dispositions. Recently, there has been a move to arrive at a single conceptualization and definition of social capital—these efforts have met with much resistance. We do not resolve this issue but match our working understanding with the definition set out by some members of the government, including the Policy Research Initiative. We leave the theoretical debates regarding the "correct" definition of social capital for another forum.

We adopt a structural approach to the concept, which emphasizes social networks as the focal point of investigation. Social capital is defined as the networks of social relations within the milieu, characterized by specific norms and attitudes that serve the purpose of *potentially* enabling individuals' or groups' access to a pool of resources and supports. Social capital is conceptualized in three different forms: bonding social capital (intragroup relations), bridging social capital (horizontal intergroup relations), and linking social capital (vertical intergroup relations in a society stratified by class, status, and power relations) (Woolcock 2001).

Outline

In the introduction we have dealt briefly with the focus of the study, our approach to data, and the definition of core concepts. Part I presents our model for understanding how social capital operates in the Aboriginal context we studied. The four dimensions of social capital we identify were derived inductively from the study of policy, practice, and outcomes in our target countries. We integrate a small number of examples into this section to make the model grounded and easier to understand. In Part II we explore some examples of policies and programs that illustrate our synthesis. Finally, we return to the four dimensions, integrate our examples into the model, and draw some further lessons for policy making.

Part I—The Four-Element Model

We can draw the following general conclusions from our study of social capital and Aboriginal educational outcomes: social capital is not an extremely powerful explanator; it functions as an independent variable that explains some variance in population and individual outcomes. However, understanding what seems to impact on the effectiveness of social capital provides interesting insights into its potential strengths and weaknesses.

We found that there are four elements that interact to influence the policy and program effects of social capital. They are:

1. Levels of Social Capital

Social capital seems to have more influence at set threshold points. For example, in the case of Port Harrison in Canada, the movement of the community to a new location led to the destruction of social capital as it broke generational ties. Parents and elders used to teach the young how to hunt and build ice houses. The relocation to a place where there were no hunting possibilities led to a breakup of the traditional system where young people traveled with the elder skilled hunters, learning many skills, such as language, traditions, etc., during the hunting season. Prior to the move, this community had high levels of educational attainment because in the off-season the community studied at the school. After the relocation, this community spiraled downward as evidenced by many social indicators: suicide increased, school non-attendance became endemic, fertility rates declined, and rates of illness rose (White and Maxim 2003). Thus, the state had destroyed, perhaps inadvertently, the social capital of the community.

As social capital approaches zero, there seems to be a relatively great effect on population outcomes. In communities that are decimated of social capital networks, educational attainment is very low. The rebuilding of social capital in these communities can have a positive effect; however, given the threshold effect, as we build social capital to even moderate levels, the effect may be negligible, or, depending on the existence of the following three other elements, we may see declines in positive outcomes as social capital grows very strong.

2. Norm Effects

Increasing levels of social capital are not necessarily related to increasing educational attainment. This can be understood by examining what we call norm effects.

Simply put, where parents and family have low educational attainment and high levels of bonding social capital, the child's educational attainment is likely to be low. This is why we see a high correlation between mothers' and children's educational attainment (White and Maxim 2002). The post-secondary students we interviewed for this study all came from communities where their family-clan networks had relatively high educational attainment. Ward's (1992) work examining the Cheyenne in the US found that the level of educational attainment in the clan group is critical to the educational success of the children. In another US examination of policy, Ward (1998, 102) notes that the more successful Busby community and its tribal school utilize the highest educational achievers, where "adults with education are the role models and sources of support for students." This is a case where the norms available for the child are critical, and substituting higher norm adults for the bonded network of the family has positive effects.

Where we have low educational norms embedded in a child's family, it is counterproductive to build bonding social capital. The higher the bonding social capital, the more the low norms are reinforced, and the lower the educational attainment is likely to be. In Part II we have several indications of this process. In Queensland, Australia, they had truancy problems and developed a program whereby buses went to the homes of every Aboriginal student to get them in the morning. They discovered that the parents who had little schooling would not wake the children to get on the bus—they preferred to have them sleep.

3. Cultural Openness Contexts (Building Relationships Based on Cultural Context)

Where bonding social capital networks are integrated into wider society (either bridged or linked), there is greater potential for increasing educational attainment. Even remote communities can experience more improvement if culturally open. Open cultures can exist in a few ways. For example, where language use includes dominant languages, people engage in the wider economy, and traditions are not exclusionary. Openness is a relative concept; hence, if that which is "outside" can be made more like the target group's culture it simulates a more open situation, and allows bridging and linking. Highly closed dominant cultures and marginalized or non-integrated ethnic groups can have high levels of social capital and very low educational attainment. Integrated and open cultural contexts that have much lower social capital will have more potential for educational attainment.

This phenomenon can be understood in different ways. For example, if we look at the more successful endeavors in our target countries, we can understand the process as one where the dominant cultural group gathers a clear appreciation of the Aboriginal culture. This appreciation is translated into behaviours that are consistent with the norms within the Aboriginal culture, which facilitates the development of relations and allows linking and bridging to take place. We find this process most clearly manifested in New Zealand. Williams and Robinson (2002) have sought to identify Indigenous applications of social capital.

Interestingly, they argued that "the nature of social capital in New Zealand can only be understood by taking into account elements of social capital important to the Maori," which led to their development of a Maori concept of social capital (ibid, 12). Robinson and Williams (2001) argued that there were nine key factors or emphases in a Maori concept of social capital. Our review of their work indicates that the key differences involve the role of primary network. For example, in their estimation social capital is not produced outside of family. The extended family in Maori thinking is the community. Imposition of networks outside the family or community are deemed to be less functional. Robinson and Williams (2001, 55–60) outline their theory:

> A Maori concept of social capital emphasizes the following elements: Extended family relationships are the basis for all other relationships. The whanau [family] is the nucleus of all things. Maori community values and norms come from traditional values that are rooted in the whanau ... It is essential to have knowledge of, and to know one's place in ... the hierarchy of whanau, hapu and iwi[2] ... Relationships in Maori society develop around informal association rather than formal organisations ... The connectedness that is derived from this association ... The holistic, integrating nature of relationships and networks are of primary importance, while their use or functional activity is secondary ... Family, tribal and community networks may take priority over functional contracts with specified agencies such as health, education or welfare ...
>
> Membership in customary Maori associations is based on an exchange of obligations and acceptance by the group. Conditions for joining are verbal, implicit and obligation-driven—rather than rule-driven, specified and written down ... The concept ... includes obligations based on a common ancestry and the cultural dimension that obliges one to act in certain ways that give rise to the development of social capital. Key concepts of Maori society that relate to social capital include hapai (the requirement to apply the concept of uplifting/enhancement) and tautoko (providing support within the community).

So New Zealand views of social capital imply that relationships must be built through informal associations as opposed to formal institutionalized structures, and the informal relations that lead to the connectedness and networks that are created have specific functions and expectations at the family kin group (whanau), sub tribe (hapu), and tribal (iwi) level. According to Williams and Robinson (2002) these relationships take precedence over formalized contractual relations in things such as education. The traditional culture has two social capital–related processes that New Zealand policy can utilize: hapai (bridge or connect) and tautoko (support or commitment) which we will see in the form of drawing the family into pre-school.

From a practical point of view, the problem is how to utilize the strong bonding capital networks within the community at the family and clan level to enhance population outcomes. The simple approach to this would have included bridging and linking them to wider social capital networks. Robinson (2004) notes that success depends on two factors: creating or drawing on a collective historical memory of relations held by the iwi (tribe) with another community that facilitates the bridging process (i.e., the memory and history of relations with the central government in this case); and the perception of, or lack of, shared understandings. These are assessed and developed through interaction. Interaction takes place in traditional forums such as the hui—a ceremonial gathering that allows people to get to know each other in a recognizable context. It seems from our assessment that this recognition can, therefore, manufacture a collective knowledge/memory of shared understandings which permits linkages.

New Zealand has developed a Maori concept of social capital where it is only produced in the extended family (whanau), and cannot be created for the Maori from the outside through linking or bridging networks. Thus, programs that involve the imposition of networks outside the family or community are deemed to lack functionality. Success rests on bridging networks based on relationships that must be built through engagement in informal associations at the whanau (family), hapu (clan), or iwi (tribe) level. Informal associations that work can eventually be translated to more formal institutionalized structures.

The Maori have specific practices where whanau, hapu, and iwi levels develop understandings of each other. These specialized meeting and exchange structures, such as the hui, are used to create higher level linkages and bridges between social capital networks. You will see, in the program and policy examples below, how this has been utilized.

So in New Zealand, we found that government policy and program development was preceded by an understanding of Maori culture. The implementation of the programs to help with educational attainment issues could only be done by creating the conditions for bridging and linking, which meant opening the cultural context by adopting the Maori ways.

There are many examples around the world where Aboriginal cultures have changed and become more open. Exogamy creates more openness for example. In Australia and Canada, the residential schools were an attempt to force assimilation. We can see that these attempts to create linkages are very destructive.

4. Community Capacity

Strong bonding social capital networks, with high attainment members, that are bridged to school networks and linked to resources seem to have a positive effect on the transitions to high school and post-secondary institutions, graduate rates, and overall educational success. The context within which social capital works seems much more important than the "strength" or "level" of the bonded network. Networks cannot hold all the resources necessary to ensure educational attainment. They must operate in capital-rich environments; that is, they require other forms of capital in order to have a positive influence on educational attainment. This is why we observe that communities with low economic development (high unemployment) have low educational attainment. Those willing or able to integrate with wider capital formations (e.g., physical capital), or who have the capacity to develop such capital based on their infrastructures tend to have high educational attainment.

Our investigation of Australia demonstrated this dimension very clearly. Stone, Gray, and Hughes (2003) argue that using social capital generated by low-capacity communities can reinforce low capacity. They looked at this in the context of job searching, but it has implications for education. Interventions to network low-achievement parents with the schools may encourage a reproduction of the lower achievement according to the Australian approach.

Hunter (2000) notes that unemployment of adults is a key problem in creating and sustaining poor educational results for children. Community capacity is once again seen as playing a fundamental role in educational processes. Hunter's study of social capital concludes that reinforcing social capital in a community with low employment levels reinforces lower norms of achievement, and leads to children uninterested in educational attainment.

A study by the Centre for Aboriginal Economic Policy Research (Hunter 2000), however, does call for Australia to vet all policies (as per Putnam's call) to determine the effects on social capital, and how to ensure that policies increase the involvement and connection of Aboriginal society with wider Australian society. This "connectiveness" may actually increase integration and mitigate the effects of high levels of bonding capital, which works with low education norms to reinforce separateness. There has been considerable research on Portes's four negative attributes of social capital and their application to the Australian Aboriginal context. Hunter (2004) notes that the "exclusion of outsiders" prevents access to services, especially in the area of education; "excessive claims on group members" plays out as "demand sharing" that may undermine educational involvement by youth; "restrictions on group members' freedom" can undermine autonomy where norms dictate non-involvement; and "downward leveling of norms" creates a non-achievement context as we noted in the previous studies.

The Australians are developing a theoretical model that differs from the one used in New Zealand and advocates the need to intervene to build community capacity, including at the level of network construction. They have also placed cultural specificity at the core of approaching the issue of social capital and educational attainment, but it appears somewhat differently (more interventionist) in practice as we will see in the policies we review in Part II.

Conceptual Modelling of the Four Elements

If we examine some combinations of cases, the interrelationships and impacts of the four dimensions may become clearer:

> *Scenario 1*: Aboriginal children with moderate to high social capital, where educational attainment norms in their networks are moderate to high, who live in communities with cultural openness and low unemployment levels, will have high educational attainment.

> *Scenario 2*: Aboriginal students who have high levels of social capital with low educational attainment norms in their network and low economic

development, will have low educational attainment. This scenario is often compounded by being resilient to outside network bridging and linking—a result of being culturally closed.

Scenario 3: Aboriginal children with zero or extremely low social capital will have no educational attainment norms to draw upon and will have low educational attainment. In this case alone, building social capital is a key prerequisite to increasing educational attainment.

Part II—Selected Policy and Program Examples in New Zealand, Australia, and Canada

Part II explores some of the policies and programs aimed at confronting problems of educational attainment among Aboriginals in New Zealand, Australia, and Canada. This is not designed to be an exhaustive review of the activities in each region; instead, it examines some key illustrations of the four-dimension model we presented earlier.

New Zealand

New Zealand has targeted educational attainment for the Maori as the key to reversing the negative population indicators all too common among Indigenous populations worldwide. The New Zealand Ministry report small, yet positive, improvements based on two identified factors that have made the biggest difference in engaging students and raising their achievement: the quality of teaching and the relationship between whanau/home and school (New Zealand Ministry of Education 2003). We will concentrate on the second issue, the relationship between family and school, because this is clearly connected to the use of social capital to increase educational outcomes, and provides the clearest indication of opening relationships based on cultural context.

Since 1988 the New Zealand government has moved to "hand over responsibility for governing educational institutions to the local community and make communities accountable ... [R]eforms have encouraged more innovative ways for communities and education institutions to work together" (Ministry of Maori Development 1997,10). The evaluation of the reforms overall, cited that the successful initiatives occurred when there was a developed community–school co-operation, and when the community families proposed, developed, or participated in and supported the programs (ibid.).

One of the first policies developed and translated into programs was the stepwise creation of pathways for parents to be involved in supporting their children's learning. The Parent Support and Development Program (PSDP), Study Support Centres (SSC), and Parents as Mentors (PAM) initiatives were set up as partnerships between schools, whanau (family), and communities. If social capital is created in the kin group or whanau, and social capital in the form of networks of support are key to improving school achievement, then building network connections between schools and whanau would be the way to proceed. This is exactly what they have done. The building block of their improvement program is increasing Maori involvement, but that cannot be done top down; it must be done bottom up (recall our discussion in Part I).

The Parents as First Teachers (PFT) program is one of the most illustrative. It focused on providing support and guidance to parents with children 0 to 3 years of age. Maori children tend to come less prepared for elementary school, which leads to performance and discipline issues. This led to a widespread discussion between those running the program and the whanau and communities about establishing and running preschools in those communities to increase the preparedness of the children. From our modeling perspective we have to ask: "How did the Ministry get the whanau to be involved?" The Ministry set up stalls at community events, attended *hui* (special meetings with dialogue), etc., and the Ministry networks became "known" to the Maori. Recall that relationships in Maori society develop around informal association rather than formal organizations, and so family, tribal, and community networks may take priority over functional contracts with specified agencies. Thus, building the personal informal links was a precursor to more formalized relations. After being known to Maori families, the New Zealand Ministry explained the benefits of preschool, and helped parents set up their own early childhood programs, or helped children enroll in the founding ones. In 2003, 3,000 Maori families were involved in the PFT program (Farquhar 2003, New Zealand Ministry of Education 2003).

The case of New Zealand illustrates the need to build culturally sensitive pathways that open the bonding social capital networks up to linking and bridging resource-rich networks. Also demonstrated is the role of norms and the relative unimportance of levels of social capital in the basic bonding networks.

Australia

In this section we want to highlight what is distinctive in the Australian approach and point out how their understanding contributes to our model. While the Australians have launched a myriad of programs to improve teacher cultural understanding, train new teachers, develop preschools, and integrate parents, they see building community capacity as integral to making education relevant to Indigenous peoples. Thus, jobs and access to markets are the foundation of success. They also see that the skills of the labour force have to increase in order to take advantage of any development. There is little evidence that the Australians are looking at any particular strategies that involve utilizing or developing social capital in this process. However, some exceptions are notable. The Gumala Mirnuwarni (Coming Together to Learn) Program, West Australia, was established in 1997. The House of Representatives Standing Committee (2004,189) reports that the impetus for this program was the community's desire to see their children more actively participate in school: "It has involved collaboration and partnership between children, parents, schools, State and Commonwealth education authorities, three resource partners and a philanthropic organization, in a program designed to improve educational outcomes for local Indigenous students." A representative of the mining company Rio Tinto outlined one element of the project, a personal commitment contract that reads: " 'I, the child, agree to go along to school and I, the family member, agree to support my child going to school ... ' If the child does not participate in school, then they are not welcome at the after-school program ... that has been set up for them. So there is an expectation that their participation in school will lead to enhanced benefits"[3] (House of Representatives Standing Committee 2004, 189).

The Gumala Mirnuwarni has been successful because of the attempts to link family networks, students, and school networks together utilizing reciprocity mechanisms. The Government noted that they recognize the success of the project, and have proceeded to use it as a foundation for other initiatives. They have developed the notion of compacts around the country in which diverse stakeholders forge beneficial working relations, for example, families with schools and industry (House of Representatives Standing Committee 2004). This has the effect of increasing the apparent benefits of school. The use of networks in the community is less developed and less widespread than in New Zealand; however, an analysis of policy development does show the employment of networks. The Australians are cautious on social capital issues.

The Australian experience indicates the relationships between the goals of being educated and the motivation to be involved in the process of being educated. Where there is development in the community (higher capacity) there is a tangible reward or return for the work of going to school. Where there are no opportunities for work or societal involvement, the rewards are unclear and involvement in the educational process diminishes.

Canada

The last set of examples we will cover are from Canada. This section is broken into two parts as we want to look at examples from National program and policy, delivered under the auspices of INAC, and some provincial examples.[4]

National Policies in Canada

INAC operates two major sets of programs. First, the Elementary/Secondary Education National Program aims to "provide eligible students living on reserve with elementary and secondary education comparable to that required in provincial schools ... where the reserve is located" (INAC 2003a, 3). Funding is transferred to a variety of deliverers that can include the Bands (communities) themselves; the provincial school boards, if they are delivering the services; or federal schools maintained by the government. INAC outlines the expenditures acceptable for funding. Second, the Post-Secondary Education Program's objective is to "improve the employability of First Nations people and Inuit by providing eligible students ... access to education and skill development opportunities at the post-secondary level" (INAC 2003b, 3). Moreover, this program aims to increase participation in post-secondary studies, post-secondary graduation rates, and employment rates (ibid).

Canada launched a review in 2002 to identify and address the factors of a quality First Nations education (INAC 2002). Several initiatives have been started in the past few years, but more time will have to elapse before we can evaluate these initiatives. However, we can see that many of these initiatives parallel those that have been successful in other countries.

Provincial Initiatives

There are many policies and programs across the country affecting Aboriginal people that are aimed at enhancing their educational and labour market outcomes. We look at only a few illustrative examples in British Columbia, where the work that has been done is quite extensive.

The Best Practices Project by the First Nation Schools Association and First Nations Education Steering Committee of British Columbia (1997) is a very successful initiative. For example, the First Nations Role Model Program in School District 52 (Prince Rupert) involves the use of very successful First Nations role models in the classroom. The goal is to promote awareness of First Nations cultures and issues for all students and teachers, while promoting self-esteem and pride in cultural heritage. There is a benefit to the school and students as the mentor links the students to the resources of the outside world, and they substitute for the low educational norm context of the parental networks. Not only can the mentor's resources be potentially drawn upon, but they establish a relationship that is grounded in a culturally familiar context. The provision of a higher-norm model substitutes for the lower attainment levels in the child's bonding capital group (family) while fostering openness. The key is not building bonding social capital, which can reinforce low attainment (scenario 2).

The Summer Science and Technology Camps Initiative, funded by INAC and coordinated by the First Nations Education Steering Committee, targets First Nations youth, engaging them in science and technology issues, and exposing them to the numerous education and career opportunities available. The program includes local elders and other community members through the process of having First Nations communities and organizations develop the initiatives in accordance with their local priorities. Through partnerships with institutions outside of the community, such as BC Hydro, BC Gas, Ministries of Fisheries and Forestry, Science World BC, and the University of British Columbia, the reason for education becomes clear. In a way, this initiative connects the students directly to the job market, and makes education seem to have a purpose. In that respect, it plays the role that higher levels of community capacity and development would play. This is an illustration of what the Australians are arguing, concerning the need for resource-rich environments for social capital to operate. As well, links are forged between the communities (children) and resource-rich institutions. The immediate effects are increased interest in science subjects, and the long-term establishment of relations between the community and the labor force.

Policy and Program Implications

As we developed Parts I and II of this synthesis we drew some tentative linkages between the policy and program initiatives, and the four elements that we feel interact to enhance success generally and optimize social capital–based initiatives particularly. We can draw some more general conclusions in this section, and push a little deeper into how we can approach the critical issue of Aboriginal educational attainment. Policy and program success seems highly sensitive to context.

In New Zealand where the Maori are a large proportion of the population, we find well-developed programs to build educational attainment levels. They are also based most closely on a homegrown, culturally specific notion of social capital. As we noted, New Zealand has determined that social capital is only created in the communities at the family level. Given that the families and sub-clans all have high-bonding social capital levels, and that the higher tribal organizations are built on this social capital base, any bridging or linking that is going to take place must be rooted in the core family networks. They have a restricted yet functional view of using social capital, where the high levels of bonding social capital must be shaped and utilized in the wider institutions to promote the norms of external networks. We saw for example that the programs began at the preschool age with the families running the preschool, which changed attitudes towards schooling. Parents (the whanau) became involved in preparing children for school, which was often done in the school setting, by passing school skills onto them. It is through this process that the school system becomes a part of the family. The school networks, including teachers, principals, etc., became "known" and began to "share a history" with the Maori while developing "knowledge of the customs and norms." This process allowed the whanau to be bridged and linked to the educational institutions, which precipitated the flow of the bridged and linked resources. The policy aimed at creating a context of cultural openness in this case.

Openness can be created in two ways. First, one can transform aspects of the cultural norms of the target populations, although this is the most difficult and runs the risk of being seen as assimilationist. A second approach is to make sure the program is delivered in a way that is not challenging to the Aboriginal culture, using the ways of the people to the greatest possible degree. This has the effect of making the institution, such as a school, more like the people and less "outside." A closed cultural context is one that has two approaches that are culturally distant. Narrowing the gap through the introduction of Aboriginal language, community elder participation, and using the forums that are acceptable (e.g., the hui in New Zealand) helps create a more open context.

Specific policies and programs across the three countries all reinforce the importance of this condition being fulfilled. Many have aspects of their programs tailored, albeit often unconsciously, to reinforce openness. This process is clearly seen in initiatives such as "Teaching the Teachers," which teaches Aboriginal culture as well as programs that integrate community cultural leaders and make use of family and elders.

The Australians have a greater focus on economic development as a necessary condition for improving educational attainment. They are generally more skeptical of the concept, noting that the high levels of bonding social capital combined with poor norms around schooling reinforce non-attainment. Australia seeks a more step-wise process to improving educational attainment, where the key is community development and improved community capacity. Having access to jobs enables citizens to understand the utility of education. Also, this strategy retains those with human capital in communities, which in turn provides better norm models. Recall, Queensland had a problem with school attendance and developed a program to have buses drive to each student's house every morning to take them to school. The result was poor because the parents would not wake the kids if they were sleeping. Attendance, leading to graduation, leading to jobs was the needed understanding. The successful programs have developed partnerships with the business community, creating job opportunities. These partnerships around the country link industry and community interests, giving meaning to educational attainment. They created the integration of the family bonding capital networks with the resources that made education more important. In these cases it was the building of community capacity that was key, and the other elements, while important, needed to be less prominent. Building social capital at the community level (bonding) was of little importance, and may have been detrimental in the absence of economic development given the low educational norms.

Using our framework, and incorporating the Australian experience, we might argue that given our examination of initiatives, in unsuccessful programs, parents were not easily involved because they had little understanding of the importance of schooling due to their low educational attainment. Given the low community capacity in terms of economic development, the purpose for supporting the schools and promoting higher educational attainment for the children was unclear to both the community and the students. The more successful programs were, indeed, linked to job paths.

In Canada, at the federal level, some of the recent initiatives that have been started in the past few years parallel initiatives that have been successful in other countries. These initiatives have not had sufficient time to develop and evaluate at this stage. The provinces have developed programs that address specific local needs. The provincial programs that are most successful target the specific problem associated with our model. For example, in the Science and Technology Camps, the inclusion of local elders and other community members as teachers led to the First Nations communities and organizations developing the initiatives in accordance with their cultures; consequently, family networks were bolstered by having adult participants that came back and encouraged support for education.

In the case of the First Nations Role Model Program, the mentors substituted for the low educational norm context of the parental networks. Other initiatives examined but not discussed here showed similar patterns.

In conclusion, we would argue that understanding social capital is important in promoting educational attainment. However, it has a moderate influence, and rarely acts alone. It influences outcomes for Aboriginal educational attainment in conjunction with other resources (human and economic/physical capital). It is contingent on the context and this can be assessed by using the four elements we have discussed throughout our paper. We have argued the following:

1. It is key to identify the specific context and interrelation of the four identified elements, and address programming toward the specificity of the situation. Just building social capital would rarely be the most effective strategy. Where communities, families, and clans face grave social problems and have low bonding social capital, then it is appropriate to build that resource. It could, however, under certain conditions, be the wrong strategy.

2. Where there are very low educational norms in the child's networks, reinforcing social capital in those networks is the wrong approach. It will reinforce low norms and non-attainment strategies. Substituting higher norm roles is one strategy for overcoming this problem; however, that involves bridging and linking to the child and their networks, which depends on the appropriateness of strategies and the degree of openness of communities to outsiders.

3. The ability to engage children depends on how open their communities are. Schools, ministries of education, federal departments, and teachers will have to depend on the target groups having accepted or incorporated aspects of the dominant culture and goals in order to connect with their programs and resources; or the dominant culture and its institutions can adopt, and adapt to, the Aboriginal minority culture, and create an openness context to connect in that manner. Such adaptation must be context specific. However, even where connections can take place, there is no guarantee of any "buy-in" to goals of educational attainment.

4. Enthusiasm for education is linked to seeing a purpose for the effort. This point is key particularly where past experience has been negative for the parents. For example, residential schooling in Canada and Australia created a legacy of mistrust and anger among Aboriginal peoples. The key to providing purpose is related to the development of community or related capacity.

Future Research

The development of a better understanding of the interrelationship between the four identified elements is the next step. This should involve two separate processes. First, the development of methods to measure the different elements will allow us to produce useful diagnostic tools. The second process is to develop a simple planning tool that gives its user a way to draw conclusions about the relative problems across the four dimensions: levels of social capital, norms effects, cultural openness, and community capacity. The planning tool could be a crude guide to assess existing programs, diagnose problems, and design improvements.

Endnotes

1 This is a revised version of a paper originally published in the Policy Research Initiative's *Social Capital Thematic Studies Book* in 2005.

2 Whanau is family, hapu is sub clan, and iwi is tribe.

3 "The programs involved Education Enrichment Centres where students can study after school, with supervision and support. Homework and individual tutoring was undertaken. The centres were set up with educational resources including computers with internet access ... Students were assigned a school-based mentor ... who also worked on well-being. Extracurricular activities could be arranged to develop confidence and abilities including ... visits to industry ... and cultural awareness camps ..."(Western Australia Department of Education n.d.).

4 In Canada, education falls under provincial jurisdiction in the Constitution. However, note that INAC funds basic elementary and secondary education for the 120,000 students who live on-reserve (INAC 2004). The federal government also provides funding that supports roughly 26,000 First Nation and Inuit students in post-secondary education each year. About 4,000 of these students graduate annually (ibid).

References

Farquhar, S.E. 2003. *Parents as First Teachers: A Study of the New Zealand PAFT Program.* Wellington, NZ: Early Childhood Development.

First Nations Schools Association and First Nations Education Steering Committee. 1997. *First Nations Education: Best Practices Project Volume 1.* Vancouver: First Nations Schools Association and First Nations Education Steering Committee.

House of Representatives Standing Committee on Aboriginal and Torres Strait Islander Affairs. 2004. *Many Ways Forward: Report of the Inquiry Into Capacity Building and Service Delivery in Indigenous Communities.* Canberra, Australia: Parliament of the Commonwealth of Australia.

Hunter, B.H. 2000. "Social Exclusion, Social Capital, and Indigenous Australians: Measuring the Social Costs of Unemployment." Technical Report Discussion Paper No.204, Centre for Aboriginal Economic Policy Research, Australia National University.

Hunter, B.H. 2004. "Taming the Social Capital Hydra? Indigenous Poverty, Social Capital Theory and Measurement." Retrieved October 2, 2004 <**www.anu.edu.au/caepr/Publications/topical/Hunter_social%20capital.pdf**>.

INAC. 2002. *Our Children—Keepers of the Sacred Knowledge: Final report of the Minister's National Working Group on Education.* Ottawa: Indian and Northern Affairs Canada.

INAC. 2003a. *Appendix A: Elementary and Secondary Education–National Program Guidelines.* Ottawa: Indian and Northern Affairs Canada.

INAC. 2003b. *Appendix B: Post Secondary Education–National Program Guidelines.* Ottawa, Canada: Indian and Northern Affairs Canada.

INAC. 2004. Personal Communication. November 11. Indian and Northern Affairs Canada.

Ministry of Maori Development. 1997. *Making Education Work for Maori: Talking Points for Parents and Whanau.* Wellington, New Zealand: Government of New Zealand.

New Zealand Ministry Of Education. 2003. *Nga Haeata Maturauranga: Annual Report on Maori Education.* Wellington, New Zealand: Government of New Zealand.

Robinson, D. and T. Williams. 2001. "Social Capital and Voluntary Activity: Giving and Sharing in Maori/Non-Maori Society." *Social Policy Journal of New Zealand.* (17):51–71.

Robinson, D. 2004. "Forming Norms and Implementing Sanctions–Deliberation and Sustained Dialogue in a Social Capital Framework." Notes prepared for panel presentation at ISTR Conference, Toronto, July 11–14, 2004.

Statistics Canada. 2003. "Selected Educational Characteristics, Aboriginal Identity, Age Groups, Sex, and Area of Residence for Population 15 Years and Over, 2001 Census – 20% Sample Data." Catalogue No. 97F0011XCB01042. Ottawa: Statistics Canada.

Stone, W., M. Gray, and J. Hughes. 2003. *Social Capital at Work: How Family, Friends and Civic Ties Relate to Labour Market Outcomes.* Research Paper 31, Australian Institute of Family Studies, Melbourne.

Ward, C. 1992. "Social and Cultural Influences on the Schooling of Northern Cheyenne Youth." PhD dissertation, University of Chicago.

Ward, C. 1998. "Community Resources and School Performance: The Northern Cheyenne Case." *Sociological Inquiry* 68(1):83–113.

Western Australia Department of Education. *GUMALA MIRNUWARNI–"Coming Together to Learn."* Retrieved September 20, 2004 <**www.dest.gov.au/archive/iae/analysis/learning/1/gumala.htm**>.

White, J.P. and P. Maxim. 2002. "Correlates of Educational Attainment in First Nations Communities." *Aboriginal Policy Research Conference*, Ottawa, Nov. 26–28, 2002.

White, J.P. and P. Maxim. 2003. "Social Capital, Social Cohesion, and Population Outcomes in Canada's First Nations Communities." In *Aboriginal Conditions: Research as a Foundation for Public Policy*. White, J.P., P. Maxim, and D. Beavon. Vancouver: UBC Press. 7–34.

White, J.P., P. Maxim, and D. Beavon (eds). 2004. *Aboriginal Policy Research: Setting the Agenda for Change. Volume I.* Toronto: Thompson Educational Publishing.

White, J.P., P. Maxim, and D. Beavon (eds). 2004. *Aboriginal Policy Research: Setting the Agenda for Change. Volume II.* Toronto: Thompson Educational Publishing.

Williams, T. and D. Robinson. 2002. "Social Capital Based Partnerships, A Maori Perspective – A Comparative Approach." In *Building Social Capital.* D. Robinson (eds). Victoria, New Zealand: Institute of Policy Studies Victoria University.

Woolcock, M. 2001. "The Place of Social Capital in Understanding Social and Economic Outcomes." In *The Contribution of Human and Social Capital to Sustained Economic Growth and Well-Being.* Human Resources Development Canada and Organisation for Economic Co-operation and Development. 65–88.

12

Breaking the Gridlock in Aboriginal Education

Jerry Paquette, Gerald Fallon, and J. Marshall Mangan

Introduction

With a few notable exceptions, there has been little attempt to integrate fully an understanding of Aboriginal issues with wider theoretical orientations, as evident in the tendency in mainstream social scientific and educational journals to concentrate the few articles that do appear on Aboriginal education into special thematic issues. (Wotherspoon and Schissel 1988)

This chapter offers a potential platform for authentic dialogue with and among Aboriginal communities and among policy-makers, scholars, and students interested and involved in Aboriginal education. In the wake of our work aimed at developing a comprehensive framework for understanding Aboriginal and, in particular, First Nations educational policy, we have come to view the central goal of Aboriginal education as nurturing "word warriors" (Turner 2006) and "fringe dwellers," Aboriginal persons who acquire a deep philosophical and institutional understanding of mainstream society *while retaining the fullness of their indigeneity*, persons who can speak Aboriginal truth to mainstream power credibly and effectively. Cultivation of such Aboriginal word-warrior-fringe-dwellers offers the most promising way out of "parity-paradox paralysis," that is, the need to provide education that is "equal" but also distinctively Aboriginal. We also believe that authentic dialogue and true interdependence require non-Aboriginal fringe dwellers, mainstream persons who have a deep philosophical and institutional understanding of mainstream society but who also *succeed in achieving authentic communion with Aboriginal ways of knowing and understanding*.

Our principal task here, however, is not to synthesize those broader literatures but rather to provide theoretically insightful, as well as practically useful, critique of recent and current Aboriginal and especially First Nations educational policy, critique situated clearly and consistently within those broader literatures. In doing so, we seek to "integrate fully an understanding of Aboriginal issues with wider theoretical orientations," admittedly an ambitious (some, of course, would argue impossible) agenda but one that, as Wotherspoon insists, is very long overdue.

Ongoing Gridlock in First Nations Education

First Nations and non–First Nations communities are frequently portrayed as deadlocked in irreconcilable conflict. In this view, each has its own interests to protect and neither is likely to give ground to the other. In this section, we examine critically the ways in which this conflictual stance of First Nations *versus* non–First Nations sustains and exacerbates ideological separation between First Nations peoples and mainstream Canada. Although a pervasive mainstream political narrative champions First Nations causes, it does so even as the Canadian political establishment and its policies in regard to First Nations subvert First Nation aspirations and worsen fragmentation and diseconomy of scale among First Nations communities.

Recent and current federal and Indian and Northern Affairs Canada (INAC) policies focus on devolution of basic managerial oversight (instrumental agency) to the community level and on local (seen as synonymous with "community") control of First Nations education. At best, such policies delegate low-level managerial responsibility and control. Furthermore, although often packaged as solutions to issues of First Nations empowerment, they completely overlook the dynamics of fragmentation. In the end, only a fundamental shift toward constructive engagement, collaboration, and aggregation among First Nations communities, areas, and regions offers the possibility of breaking the current gridlock that has characterized and paralyzed First Nations and non–First Nations relations in education as in other policy domains.

Policy for Compliance, Conformity, and Fragmentation

Until recently, federal policies aimed at improvement of Aboriginal communities' capacity for self-governance have aimed mainly, if not exclusively, at delivery of educational outcomes as close as possible to those specified in mainstream provincial and territorial education. The oxymoronic intent behind such self-governance capacity-building measures, limited as they were, was to help First Nations communities conform to provincial educational purposes, programs, norms, and expectations. These capacity-building initiatives, in short, aimed at little more than enabling First Nations communities to assume *operational* control of their local education "system," a deceptive euphemism for community school(s). Their architects never questioned whether provincial governments should retain responsibility for everything other than funding that really mattered in terms of educational outputs in First Nations schools (curriculum policies, assessment, and graduation standards). Such unquestioned and seemingly unquestionable overarching control by non-Aboriginal educational institutions undermined any significant local and especially *aggregated self-governance of Aboriginal education.* This "devolution" narrative of First Nations governance empowerment, moreover, ignored—and for the most part, continues to ignore—great disparity among First Nations communities in ability to participate in self-governance. Many First Nation communities are severely limited in human, financial, and material resources needed for meaningful self-governance of their schools. This lack of essential "building blocks" for capacity contributes to their marginalization and helps sustain pervasive fragmentation and diseconomy of scale in First Nations education.

Moving Beyond Gridlock: Self-Governance in a Fragmented Environment

Over the last three years we have conducted an extensive analysis of policy documents and reports dealing with capacity building for self-governance. This review and analysis exposed capacities crucial to making Aboriginal communities and education successful and sustainable but that were conspicuously absent from policy discourses (Hurley and Wherrett 1999, INAC 1982, 1997). Perhaps most fundamental among them—and most conspicuously missing from the status quo—is the capability of Aboriginal communities and entities to act, to organize themselves, and to influence others in a world where distinct but overlapping Aboriginal and non-Aboriginal groups compete for resources to build and sustain their capacity to engage in an ongoing open-ended process of self-definition (Schouls, 2003). Policy documents, for instance, are generally silent on the necessity for Aboriginal communities to develop capacities that enable them to relate productively to other policy players in the socio-cultural, political, educational, and economic context in which they exist. Similar silence envelops the challenge of building legitimacy in the eyes of key policy actors in mainstream society. The necessity for Aboriginal communities and aggregate entities to develop capabilities to adapt and self-renew, to master change within themselves or with and among other non-Aboriginal players, and to adopt new ideas also passes largely under a similar cloak of silence.

Accountability verges on impossibility where "self-governance" is implemented in a fragmented policy and administrative space. Numerous reports on Aboriginal policy (Breaker and Kawaguchi 2002, Dion, Hathaway, Helin, and Staats 1997, Hawthorn, Tremblay, and Bownick 1967, Hurley and Wherrett 1999, INAC 2004, RCAP 1996), distinguish between "exogenous" and "endogenous" accountability. The former is accountability that Aboriginal recipient governments have to provincial and federal governments; accountability that is driven by the audit and political accountabilities of these governments. Endogenous accountability is accountability of a system or organization (Aboriginal self-governed entities) to its own constituencies and members. Currently in First Nations education the sole binding accountability is fiscal accountability to INAC and thus exogenous. Authentic, formal, and effective endogenous accountability mechanisms that connect First Nations educational governance organizations to their constituents in regard to either program or financial matters seem to be next to non-existent.

At present neither rule systems nor related accountability mechanisms, where these exist at all, reflect the wide dispersion of authority within and among organizations overseeing Aboriginal education (from community and education authorities to local aggregated organizations and on to INAC itself). Policies formally intended to devolve control of Aboriginal education to the local level have resulted in an era of fragmentation and aggregation "*ad hocery*" among First Nations communities. This local and area "*ad hocery*" has fostered a policy arena which has favoured, if not required, a broad array of local forms and modes of educational governance with few if any enforceable endogenous rule systems and accountability mechanisms. The one very partial exception to this rule is a tenuous program-accountability connection to provinces in the case of First Nations that operate "private" secondary schools.

Across Canada today, First Nations communities are simultaneously fragmenting and integrating. These two seemingly opposed tendencies, moreover, are in fact interactive and feed on each other. In the absence of any overarching rules and structure, effective forms of aggregated governance and accountability mechanisms to regulate and channel the resulting tensions have failed to emerge. Could endogenous and exogenous accountability mechanisms be developed that would constructively harness tensions between fragmentation and integration for First Nations that seek meaningful control over what it means to educate and be educated in an Aboriginal educational *system*? Currently, diseconomies of scale, government policies that encourage fragmentation, and pluralistic developmental aspirations and educational purposes among Aboriginal communities exacerbate rather than harness these tensions. A new form—really a new level or instance of Aboriginal self-governance—in education is urgently needed, one that ensures reasonable order and consistency over time and space in micro–macro interactions (interactions between local authorities and community members, among communities at a regional level, and among regions across Canada). Such a new self-governance form will require reasonable policy and funding coherence and fairness across the multiplicity of diverse Aboriginal communities implicated in the governance of First Nation education. Only functional aggregation of community-level units can lead to endogenous First Nations accountability within a context of responsible self-governance—"Indian control of Indian education" in other words. Only functional integration of community-level units can stem the tide of debilitating First Nations governance fragmentation and provide a basis for effective, efficient, and appropriate governance at the area, regional, and Canada-wide level.[1]

Such a governance structure would require overlapping agreement on broadly shared purposes of education among area and regional Aboriginal communities, notwithstanding great diversity in languages, traditions, and developmental aspirations. No such agreement will emerge without considerable compromise and accommodation on all sides. The path to self-governance of Aboriginal education resting on broad agreement about fundamental purposes is fraught with potential difficulties and roadblocks, especially the problem of competing priorities. Communities within an aggregated self-governance structure might have substantially different developmental aspirations[2] and educational purpose. In that case, they are likely to have conflicting priorities on values and principles as well. In the end, no one can guarantee that such a self-governance model based on compromise and agreement can necessarily accommodate all the voices that may seek to be hear However, *aggregation is a necessary limitation to Aboriginal pluralism;*

compromise is the price of functional aggregation. A central purpose of aggregation is to define fundamental limits to Aboriginal pluralism. Such limitations should be grounded in understanding human experiences broadly shared among Aboriginal communities (judgments made about common ends and purposes of Aboriginal lives and what constitute broadly shared foundations necessary to allow all—or at least most—Aboriginal communities to flourish).

Aggregation of Aboriginal education organizations should, then, seek out and respect shared purposes, values, and beliefs that reflect an overarching concept of human nature framed around capacities essential to a worthwhile life. Although the process of defining it would be a difficult one, we are convinced that an account of essential First Nations capacities could be framed in terms sufficiently general to encompass cultural and historical diversity among First Nation communities. We are also convinced that such an account could provide a uniquely promising basis for First Nations to flourish. Notwithstanding specific circumstances associated with particular socio-cultural settings and contexts, such an account of essential First Nation capacities should guide and shape the creation of aggregated self-governance institutions. Neither Aboriginal socio-cultural life, nor an efficient, effective, and appropriate educational preparation for it, of course, can be reduced to a set of rules or structural accommodations. But we believe that a framework in which tensions and conflicts could be substantially reduced and contained within limits set by policy aimed at functional compromise is possible. Within such a framework, moreover, true First Nations political "community" could at last be achieved. This framework would need to be essentially a First Nations one; it would need to specify at least generally what it means for a First Nation to flourish.[3] Finally, it would need to provide a workable basis to evaluate political, cultural, social, economic, institutional, and governance practices in terms of their contribution to the realization of that ideal.

Such a broadly cooperative political and conceptual self-definition undertaking by First Nations could lead to a workable definition of accountability that has sufficient credibility, political appeal, and clarity to be acceptable both to First Nations and to non–First Nations communities and could thus provide a much-needed workable blueprint for overcoming the current gridlock in First Nations education. No one, of course, can predict how First Nations would ultimately organize themselves and, therefore, no one can know in advance the precise shape and evolutionary trajectory of resulting aggregated forms of self-government. Any such broadly cooperative process will almost certainly be shaped by underlying non-linear and hence difficult-to-predict dynamics.

Educational quality is locked in an ongoing symbiotic relationship with capacity to develop and administer aggregated forms of governance. Neither can *assure* the other, but poor education inevitably begets poor governance and, just as surely, poor governance yields poor education. There is no escape from this relationship. It can translate into either a vicious circle of incapacity, or a symbiosis of developing capacity and continual improvement in performance.

Past and Current Models of Self-Government in First Nations Education: Managing Compliance and Devolution While Fostering Fragmentation and Diseconomies of Scale

The federal government and, to a lesser extent, provincial governments have relied on devolution of operational management to Aboriginal education entities as their key strategy for increasing "local control" of Aboriginal education. In effect, they have "faxed the crisis" of chronic Aboriginal educational deficit—and much of the public blame for it—down the line to more "autonomous" local educational institutions. Ironically, devolution in First Nations education has tightened provincial and territorial control over formal curriculum, imposed at least nominal accountability based on provincially or territorially specified outcomes, and reinforced graduation standards of non-Aboriginal educational institutions. Aboriginality has been central to the policy-definition/implementation divide within the policy process; Aboriginal communities are virtually excluded from involvement in producing educational policy that they are nonetheless mandated to implement at the local level.

Awareness of the interrelatedness and interdependence of Aboriginal and non-Aboriginal communities has arguably increased since the publication of the Royal Commission on Aboriginal Peoples report in 1996. This vision of interrelatedness and interdependence transcends conceptual boundaries of cultural separateness and difference generally used to frame contemporary discourse and jurisprudence on Aboriginal rights and is being pursued within various institutions still undergoing self-definition by Aboriginal communities (Schouls 2003, Turner 2006). Unfortunately no conceptual, much less institutional, framework has emerged that could provide a plausible basis for either Aboriginal self-government or Aboriginal control of Aboriginal education systems. No such framework currently exists to accommodate and channel creatively the tension and conflict among overlapping Aboriginal and non-Aboriginal groups competing for resources to secure their survival and foster their capacity for ongoing open-ended self-definition (Schouls 2003). Trace outlines of such a framework for autonomous self-definition, however, are already being tested by some individuals, communities, and networks.

Although much of the form and content of First Nations education has been and continues to be determined externally, the relationships of Aboriginal communities to education have, to some degree, varied over time in the wake of their evolving conception of what their societies ought to become. This overarching sense of social purpose is shaped by history, geography, current and potential modes of educational governance, forms of political representation within both Aboriginal and non-Aboriginal institutions, and perceptions of appropriate governance arrangements for different educational levels and types (elementary, secondary, post-secondary education, continuing adult education, and non-formal education). Within this complex web of influence, changes to Aboriginal modes of governance (or lack of such changes) have had multiple and complex effects on the purposes, quality, and relevance of Aboriginal education. This complexity calls for more nuanced historical analysis, especially of the assumptions and claims associated with "Indian control of Indian education." In particular, we need to call into question the extent to which various Aboriginal communities, groups, and nations have been able to exercise meaningful choice in education within past and current policy frameworks and, even more fundamentally, the degree to which they *wish* to participate in defining the purposes, nature, quality, and relevance of the education provided to their children. Divergent perspectives on possibilities for reshaping power relationships between Aboriginal and non-Aboriginal communities have produced various self-governance models. In this section we review critically existing and potential modes of First Nations self-governance in education.

Assimilation, Integration, and Devolution of Power: Policy Directions from the 40s to the 90s.

Until the 1990s the main policy directions in First Nations governance and education were assimilation and integration. Only through assimilation and integration, non-Aboriginals were convinced, could First Nations realize their potential as human beings within mainstream Canadian society. While sometimes allowing at least marginal accommodation to First Nations needs, interests, and capacities, First Nations education was designed to foster, indeed to present as the only conceivable possibility for education, a "universal" understanding of the self and acceptance that such an understanding was necessary to neutralize or eliminate divisive cultural differences and thus promote essentially undifferentiated membership in mainstream Canadian society. Such "universal" conceptions, in fact, framed ideas about what it means to be a "normal" human being—for all human beings including Aboriginal persons.

During this period, the overarching purpose for First Nations education was to contribute to minimizing cultural differences between Aboriginal and non-Aboriginal communities in Canada by ensuring that Aboriginal communities conformed increasingly to mainstream Canadian cultural norms. Far from seeking to accommodate cultural differences between Aboriginal and non-Aboriginal communities, policy-makers attempted to order power relationships so that these differences were either eliminated (through assimilation or integration or simply by divesting the federal government of the "Indian problem" in keeping with what Turner aptly labels "white paper liberalism") or at least no longer caused conflict and division.

The main purposes of federal education policy for First Nations, then, remained unchanged from the time of the residential schools: subordination and marginalization of First Nations, First Nations cultures, and First Nations languages. Prior to 1972, policy discourse on First Nations education failed to imagine any involvement of First Nations communities in the education of their young beyond a purely advisory role with regard to policies aimed at improving already existing educational programs or creating new ones patterned after provincial or territorial education programs (Hawthorn, Tremblay, and Bownick 1967). Capacity development in Aboriginal self-governance of education was thereby limited a priori to improving the ability of First Nations *to make suggestions relative to the delivery of educational programs and services* to First Nations students and communities—programs whose shape and content, however, would be determined exogenously. In the 70s and 80s, the National Indian Brotherhood's report entitled *Indian Control of Indian Education* (National Indian Brotherhood, 1972) spawned increasing interest in Aboriginal jurisdiction and control over education. This influential report called for control of education on reserves *by individual First Nations*. It envisaged eventual complete jurisdiction and autonomy over education, and, toward that end, called for First Nations representation on local school boards serving First Nations students. In its eventual response to *Indian Control* the federal government chose not to consider policies that might have enabled Aboriginal communities to assume full control eventually of their own education *systems*. Instead, the Federal government opted to delegate ("devolve") managerial control over education to Aboriginal communities.

Because of such policy directions, First Nations protests that they were systematically denied a degree of educational agency comparable to that found in mainstream society fell on deaf ears in Ottawa. First Nations education continued to be largely defined by non-Aboriginal representational practices. These practices *shaped, controlled, and above all constrained production, transmission, and propagation of Aboriginal knowledge and identities*. In doing so, they made mainstream Canadian societal visions and courses of action appear normal and possible, indeed inevitable, and all others abnormal and impossible for First Nations.

This fundamental orientation toward assimilation, and later integration, of First Nations into non-Aboriginal learning institutions and programs as non-negotiable Aboriginal education policy directions was grounded in a "universalizing" conception of Aboriginality on the part of non-Aboriginals, which effectively denied distinctive Aboriginal needs and capacities by subsuming them within positivist industrial/post-industrial paradigm assumptions about human good and excellence. What First Nations people needed, according to this approach, was to become good mainstream Canadians. The assimilation objective was implemented through re-education and replacement of ancestral First Nations cultures by mainstream values. Aboriginal people after all, policy-makers imbued with liberal ideology reasoned, were *individuals*. For their well-being as individuals they needed to be subordinated to mainstream society as a whole, to become Canadian citizens like all other Canadian citizens. To achieve such mainstream identity, they needed to be trained never to think of or experience their indigeneity beyond the "script" of a socio-economic system in which they occupied, and still occupy today, the lowest position. Aboriginal persons, no less than non-Aboriginal persons, had to come to regard individual "success" as "universal" human excellence achieved through hard work, self-discipline, and conformity to mainstream society and its social, cultural, and especially economic projects. "Aboriginality" needed to be redefined to that end. On the basis of that redefinition of Aboriginality, non-Aboriginal policy-makers pursued policies that would frame First Nation educational, cultural, political, economic, and social life in ways that disadvantaged and marginalized First Nation visions of human good, and silenced their voices in the process. Despite considerable policy-maker rhetoric about the need to build capacity and partnership, those who directed Indian Affairs in Ottawa were prepared to give up little, if any meaningful control, preferring instead to impose changes that *they* deemed best for First Nations peoples.

Policies imposing assimilation, and subsequently integration of First Nations students into non-Aboriginal public schools, were basically prescriptions for "normalizing" First Nations students into educational practices and institutions that would at last contain Aboriginal communities within a "hierarchical encapsulation" of mainly personal identity pluralism (Moon 1993). Hierarchical encapsulation is a way of managing and containing pluralism. Within it, the dominant group (non-Aboriginal society) excludes all others (First Nations) from genuine political participation.

> Sometimes a subject group will play a specialized role in politics, one that they are given precisely because of their status as "outsider," but one that also renders them ineligible to compete for higher or more significant forms of power. Hierarchical encapsulation can also be combined with indirect [partial delegated] rule, in which direct [local managerial] authority over particular groups is exercised by a "declared" elite group within the group who (e.g., Chief and Band Council), whatever...[its] traditional authority might have been, has come to owe...[its] power mainly to...[its] relationships to the ruling stratum. (Moon 1993, 15)

Framed within the assumptions behind these policies of assimilation and integration of First Nations into the mainstream Canadian society, First Nations education assumed specific socio-cultural, political, and economic functions. Its socio-cultural functions were twofold. First, education promoted acceptance by First Nations people of a society in which their beliefs and self-understandings as Aboriginal people were disallowed. It thus encouraged them to accept voluntarily the legitimacy of social, political, and economic inequality as it progressively enculturated them into believing that some groups in society are naturally better suited than others to fill certain socio-economic, cultural, and political roles.

Second, education for First Nations people was to initiate them into the industrial and post-industrial paradigm ideals (Valois and Bertrand 1980) of progress and consumerism and thus foster in them a vision of human creativity as synonymous with economic, technological, and scientific progress.

This assimilationist/integrationist policy promoted educational and institutional practices aimed at maintaining an "oligarchic social structure of society, acceptance that an elite minority makes decisions on behalf of the majority, and thus [serves to] legitimate a hierarchical decision-making structure," (Bertrand and Valois 1980, 173) in effect, an hierarchical encapsulation. Such educational policy goals for Aboriginal students "promote [suitable] intellectual aptitudes, contribute to reproducing the existing social division of work, and promote the legitimacy of the established order and its value" (Bertrand and Valois 1980, 178). Overall, policy-makers viewed education for First Nations students as but one among many tools for maintaining the status quo in society as a whole. Despite partial devolution of managerial authority over education to individual First Nation communities, "Along the way, Indian control of education became synonymous with local control. Admittedly, the policy paper was short on details in terms of what actually constituted Indian control. But local control as an objective was clearly enunciated in the document and INAC cheerfully accepted this interpretation of Indian control because it fit conveniently with its emerging policy on devolution" (McCue 2004, 4).

During the 90s, the RCAP (2006) outlined two basic educational options available to Aboriginal communities with regard to education. One option was to exercise their inherent right to define and organize their own education systems. Doing so, according to the Commission, would involve passing their own laws and regulating all dimensions of education including policies on educational goals and standards, administration of schools, tuition agreements, and purchase of provincial or territorial services. The second option was working to improve existing public education systems by increasing Aboriginal control over Aboriginal education in those systems through mechanisms of community and parental involvement to strengthen identity and resolve problems of quality, adequacy, and appropriateness of education and to implement culturally based curriculum. In both cases, the RCAP viewed capacity development for self-governance over education as learning and knowledge-generating processes aimed at empowering Aboriginal communities to develop and implement needed changes through educational entities or systems defined and controlled by Aboriginal people.

Gathering Strength: Canada's Aboriginal Action Plan (INAC 1997) eventually provided the federal government's response to the RCAP report. In it the federal government renewed its commitment to devolve program responsibility and resources to Aboriginal communities but also committed to assisting Aboriginal organizations in order to strengthen Aboriginal governance and to support education reform on reserves, with the objective of improving the quality and cultural relevance of education for Aboriginal students, improving the effectiveness of teachers and teaching practices, supporting parents and community involvement in the decision-making process in schools, and improving the management and support capacity of Aboriginal education systems across the country.

Gathering Strength marked a substantial shift in policy discourse with its emphasis on supporting First Nations organizations and capacity development. At least on paper, it moved beyond the micro-perspective of the traditional INAC development focus on the internal functioning of individual First Nations. It began to embrace Aboriginal "cultural ownership" by at least acknowledging that Aboriginal communities should be able to express and analyze the conditions of their lives and, in theory at least, to collaborate on collective and sustainable solutions and actions to common problems, to think in strategic terms, and to see the contribution of non-Aboriginals in broader and more interconnected ways. With *Gathering Strength*, capacity development for self-governance arrived at least nominally on the "radar scope" of federal policy aimed at assisting Aboriginal communities in recovering the autonomy necessary to initiate and manage change, to resolve conflict, to establish networks, to manage institutional pluralism, to deepen and enhance coordination and collaboration among communities, to foster communication, and to ensure that knowledge generated in the course of self-governance is shared for the common good of all.

However, notwithstanding a policy discourse that espouses devolution of power and control of Aboriginal education to First Nations, the reality remains that

> the education clauses in these agreements [SGAs] clearly indicate that the federal government still supports their 1950 policy of integration—every one of the SGAs referred to [The Federal Framework for Transferring Programs and Services to Self-Governing Yukon First Nations, 1998 (YFN); Mi'kmaq Education in Nova Scotia, 1997 (ME); The Manitoba Framework Agreement, 1994 (MFA); Nisga'a Treaty Negotiation: Agreement in Principle, 1996 (NTM); The James Bay and Northern Quebec Agreement (JBNQA); The United Anishaabeg Councils Government Agreement-in-Principle, 1998 (UAC)] includes a clause or clauses that in effect say that the education that the affected First Nation(s) provides as a result of the SGA must be comparable to the provincial system, or that students must be able to move from the First Nations education program to a provincial school without penalty. (McCue 2006, 6)[4]

McCue thus argues, rightly in our view, that supposedly new policy directions in First Nations educational governance have entailed little change in practice. Notwithstanding policy rhetoric that vaunts empowerment of Aboriginal communities in shaping their educational "systems," changes necessary to authentic "Aboriginalization" of First Nations education have been systematically ignored by Aboriginal and non-Aboriginal policy-makers and their respective advocates. Like McCue, we doubt that significant change in the governance and content of First Nations education is occurring at all. We also share McCue's concern that history is only repeating itself, that shifts in First Nations education policy, including those supposedly embedded in the SGAs, have not brought about any fundamental change.

The 90s and Beyond: Adaptive Policy Initiatives for Increased Aboriginal control of Education

It seems quite clear that as late as the late '90s, policy on First Nations educational governance remained essentially unchanged. Aboriginal control of education offered a convenient rhetorical packaging to foster the illusion of more autonomous First Nations governance in education and elsewhere as well as in economic development of Aboriginal communities—all vaunted at the time as key elements of decolonization though devolution of power. The federal government, and some provincial governments as well, promoted self-government and control of education in particular as a means of ushering First Nations into a rapidly globalizing market society and thus, allegedly, free them from traditional colonial constraints. However, this view of the central purposes of self-government seems far more neo-colonial than "decolonizing" and effectively denies Aboriginal peoples' capacity to formulate their own conceptions of person and society.

Once more, this model resulted in various kinds of advisory structures at the local community level in some provinces (such as guaranteed representation on local public school boards). This integrated model was followed in turn by a delegated-authority model which enabled Aboriginal communities to administer provincial laws and procedures for the education of Aboriginal children on behalf of the province. Within this model, the province retains ultimate authority over laws, regulations, and policies pursuant to education standards and criteria for academic success (See the Framework Agreement signed by the federal and provincial governments and First Nations in British Columbia, (*Bill C-34: First Nations Jurisdiction over Education Act*, 2006).[5] Therefore, Aboriginal communities have acquired local managerial powers, but not the legislative or executive powers usually associated with self-government.

To date, then, no policy changes that reflect real change in attitudes, norms, values, or perceptions have emerged to frame authentic First Nations self-governance in education. No substantive policy has appeared that offers much hope of fundamentally changing and renewing Aboriginal and non-Aboriginal political and power relationships in the field of education. Current policies only seek to improve the efficiency and effectiveness of existing policy and practice without disturbing them, without disturbing basic organizational features, or without any real change in the way that Aboriginal and non-Aboriginal communities relate within the existing power structure. They simply bring forward in time the existing goal of conformity to provincial and territorial education programs—especially in regard to learning and socialization goals, structures, and roles in providing education to their people. Policy-makers continue to insist that First Nations schools and educational institutions should be organized according to a simple template whose only requirement is conformity—at least in formal terms—to programs set by provincial and territorial education ministries, an approach which obviously raises serious issues of legitimacy.[6]

Ironically the policy thrust toward increased Aboriginal self-governance in education during the late 90s and early 2000s preserved dynamics that sustained, indeed probably worsened, the existing tendency toward fragmentation among Aboriginal communities. Perverse fixation on radically local control has deprived First Nation communities of the capacity to establish relevant, healthy, and sustainable education *systems*. The dynamics of this fragmentation, encouraged at every turn by policy, have continued to contribute to the plurality and dispersion of administrative authority. They have also increased significantly the probability of an eventual authority crisis in Aboriginal education among Aboriginal and non-Aboriginal communities. They have sapped the ability of Aboriginal communities to cope with deepening and increasingly rapid change, so that meaningful self-governance has diminished rather than increased as the complexities and contradictions of fragmentation and diseconomies of scale have become more pervasive and pragmatically consequential given the broader context of education both in Canada and within an increasingly globalized knowledge economy.

Therefore, notwithstanding that the call for local Indian control over Indian education remained at the centre of policy directions in the late 90s and early 2000s, the discourse of local control of Aboriginal education has failed to increased the capacity of leaders in Aboriginal education to know when, where, and how to engage effectively in collective action for self-governance in education. Despite ongoing preoccupation with the lack of relevance in Aboriginal education and with uncertainties associated with the current dynamics of fragmentation, no new policy direction has emerged to nurture effective collective action through functional, self-determining aggregated governance institutions that reflect Aboriginal conceptions of how authority should be organized and exercised in the field of education and for what societal purposes (Cornell, Jorgensen, and Kalt 2002).

Concluding Observations

First Nations education is fraught with complexity and uncertainty. Yet some of its features underscore the potential for functional aggregation in its governance. Educational and related social purposes, interests, and developmental aspirations on the national stage are so numerous, diverse, and disaggregated that a hierarchical national or even regional or province-wide structure with a single mechanism for self-governance seems unlikely in the near future. Nonetheless, although both informal and formal First Nations governance steering mechanisms exist, and although some have more potential scope for influencing what matters in education than do others, none is presently capable of orchestrating or catalyzing effective self-governance in Aboriginal education.

Development of functionally integrated aggregate models of self-governance in First Nations education will require further discussion and negotiation on the scope, mandate, and lines of accountability of First Nations aggregated governing entities. Notwithstanding, all First Nations are to some degree part local and part global. If meaningful self-determination for First Nations in education and elsewhere is ever to arrive, these two dimensions will have to meld in new and functional ways. Such melding would, within the parameters of aggregated self-governing entities, redefine to a significant extent who First Nation peoples are. Pure Aboriginal localists seek vainly to turn back the clock to an obsolete, discredited, and dysfunctional model of self-governing First Nation *communities*; pure aggregationists, on the other hand, might well be seen by critics as individuals who have lost their local footing. Aggregated self-governing educational entities can only sustain and renew themselves by respecting, balancing, and nurturing diverse First Nations local cultures and by giving them *reasonable* autonomy to support their own ways of looking at the world on the one hand—but doing so with due respect for the unforgiving realities of economy of scale on the other.

Progress toward more effective, accountable,[7] and legitimate[8] self-governance in First Nation education can only occur incrementally so long as each individual First Nation community can continue to decide unilaterally whether it will participate in an aggregate organization at all, as well as when, under what circumstances, and to what extent. Our brief overview of self-governance in Aboriginal education provides a salutary warning that prospects for effective, efficient, legitimate, and accountable forms of self-governance are highly problematic, that such progress might take decades, and that the probability of evolution toward harmoniously interdependent political relationships between Aboriginal and non-Aboriginal communities may not be greater than the chance of deterioration toward tension-filled and retrogressive political relationships. Beyond that troubling conclusion lies the inescapable bottom-line question in First Nations education governance reform: how, and in what time frame, might the current radically disaggregated Aboriginal education non-system be transformed into—or replaced by—effective, efficient, and appropriate self-governance?

Structural Failure

In this section of the chapter we focus tightly on governance, jurisdiction, and control, and thus on governance structures and processes. Nonetheless, questions of purpose inevitably frame that discussion if one believes that in governance form should follow function—in preference to "tail wagging the dog" approaches. However desirable it may be to craft form around purpose, even in the best of situations the tail often does wag the dog in educational governance. This unhealthy dynamic, however, has been strikingly evident in First Nations education. Broad agreement exists that First Nations people, even when the matter is examined purely in terms of conformity with mainstream educational standards, are, for the most part, collectively and individually victims of a major educational deficit. That deficit is, to a considerable extent, one of the principal legacies of the residential system and of the penury and myopia within which it was conceived and operated. First Nations students are systematically *behind*—and they are not catching up very fast. In fact, the Auditor General of Canada recently concluded in a now often-cited claim that, at the current rate of progress in closing the gap between the educational achievement of First Nations students and mainstream Canadian students, another 28 years would be required to complete the process (2004, 1). More ominously still, the gap between First Nations students and mainstream students in regard to completion of a university certificate or diploma seems to be growing (Clement, forthcoming).

Figure 12.1: Simplified Representation of First Nations School Governance

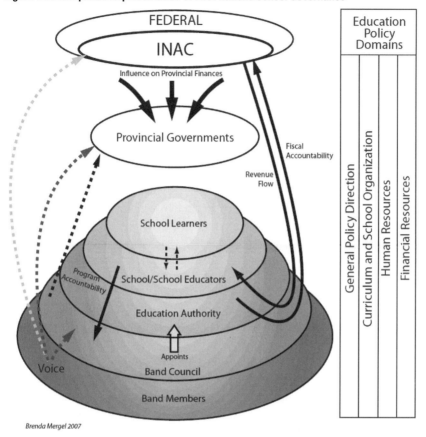

Brenda Mergel 2007

Adapted and extended from Smith, Paquette, & Bordonaro, 1995

First Nations Governance and Control

Figure 12.1 is a simplified[9] schematic representation of First Nations school governance focusing on the flow of "voice," "authority," and "accountability." We use these terms in ways that differ from the meanings many readers associate with them in everyday language, specifically:

- voice is the right, conferred by law, to participate in policy-relevant decision-making processes without having the right to vote or participate in any final decision
- authority is the right, conferred by law, to make decisions about a particular matter in an education system
- accountability is legal responsibility for defined results (program accountability) or use of financial resources (financial accountability); program accountability may be based on either effectiveness criteria (were results produced) or efficiency criteria (were results produced at a

"reasonable" cost), or both[10]

Band members are entitled to vote in federal elections. As with all other citizens, federal education programs, including education programs addressed to First Nations learners, are one area of potential voter interest and choice, *among a great many others*, to First Nation voters. While First Nations education is presumably of greater interest to those living in First Nation communities than to most other voters in federal elections, even for them, it can only count as one among many issues that shape their voting choice. Given the tiny *relative* importance of First Nations education in shaping federal voter behaviour, even, in all likelihood, in shaping the voting behaviour of First Nations voters living on a reserve, the relative electoral "voice" of First Nations citizen-residents in federal funding and policy affecting the education of children in their community school is very small and tenuous (hence the ephemeral "voice" connection to the federal level in **Figure 12.1**).

Notwithstanding, virtually all financial resources for most band-operated schools come from the federal government through INAC. Most of the political mandate for appropriation and allocation of First Nations *education funding comes from the Canadian electorate at large* and that mandate therefore "flows in" to the artificially closed-system representation we offer for simplicity's sake. At the local level, band members do express their preferences with regard to education in band-council elections. In these same elections, however, they also simultaneously make choices with regard to a host of other issues, preferences, and allegiances. In most cases, band members elect band councillors who then appoint members of a band's education authority. The electoral mandate of band-education-authority members have toward their school(s) differs in two fundamental ways from that of members of provincial boards of education:

- in most cases band-education-authority membership results from an electoral process that melds education with a broad spectrum of social, infrastructure, and local political issues that, taken together, shape band-council election results; unlike school-board elections, band-council elections therefore generally *dilute* educational issues in a plethora of other local-governance issues
- generally in band-council elections band members elect "proxies" (band councillors) to decide band-education-authority membership; band elector voice in choosing band-education-authority membership is thus *indirect* in addition to being *diluted* by a host of non-educational issues and considerations (the reduced voice in education at the local level is shown schematically by an intermittent dot pattern in the "voice" line to the band council/band education authority level)

In addition, non-resident band members are eligible to vote in band-council elections. The voting behaviour of non-resident band members who choose to vote in band elections thus "flows into" our artificially closed-system depiction of voice, financial accountability, and resource flow and further dilutes the flow of resident voice to community schools at the band level. In the band-education-authority governance mode, the only significant line of resident voice to band schools is through the diffuse band electoral process. It is, moreover, in every way that matters, almost completely separated from revenue flow from the federal government through the band education authority. Not surprisingly, therefore, band residents have little meaningful control over what occurs in their schools. A major reason for this state of affairs is that the band election process separates political/electoral mandate from band residents to their school(s) from the lines of funding that provide resources and financial accountability that bind school administrators and personnel.

Furthermore, **Figure 12.1** exposes another crucial problem. While the revenue–financial-accountability circuit (however imperfect the financial accountability mechanisms may be) is between the federal government, as represented by INAC, and the local band education authority, the line of program accountability, to the extent it can be said to exist at all, flows *to the province*—which, of course, is completely outside of the main revenue–financial-accountability circuit for First Nations schools. No meaningful program accountability to INAC exists. Further-more, INAC has always insisted that band schools, like federal Indian day schools before them, conform to *provincial* curricula and standards. Such conformity, of course, is almost always more nominal than real, a fact to which the gaping and resilient educational-achievement gap between First Nations students and main-stream Canadian students testifies eloquently (Auditor General of Canada 2004, 1). In striking contrast to the situation of provincial public schools, then, the main, although not surprisingly tenuous and problematic, line of program accountability for First Nations schools diverges from the main revenue and fiscal accountability circuit.

The status quo in First Nations governance reflects a profoundly assimilation-ist stance and does so in a particularly insidious way. In our view, the recent and historic approach of INAC and the federal government to First Nations education can most accurately be characterized as one of "benign neglect"—fund the process with minimal attention to adequacy or purpose, and impose a diffuse and unclear mandate to follow provincial curricula. Otherwise, ostensibly in the interest of furthering "Indian control of Indian education," INAC leaves First Nations to do what they want to do in their community schools. This self-defeating even oxymoronic approach to "Indian control" fails to address the issues of disecon-omy of scale, fragmentation, and an urgent need for functional aggregation of community-level units (not merely purchase of services on an ad hoc perceived-need basis from so-called "second-level service" providers") to make possible purposeful, coherent provision of services such as curriculum development (and implementation), or Aboriginal language and culture programs in particular—and, of course, supervision, administration, or administrative support.

Figure 12.2: Layers of Governance in First-Nations Education

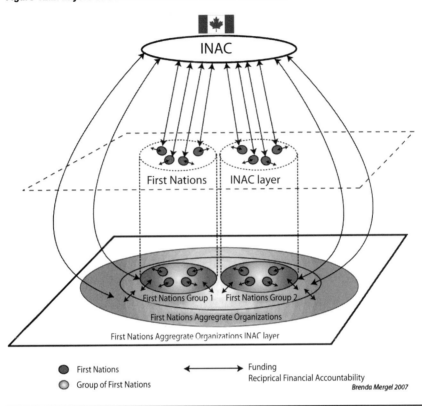

First Nations

INAC layer

First Nations Group 1   First Nations Group 2

First Nations Aggregrate Organizations

First Nations Aggregrate Organizations INAC layer

⬤ First Nations
◯ Group of First Nations

◀———▶ Funding
Reciprical Financial Accountability

Brenda Mergel 2007

Crossed Lines of Governance, Level 1: INAC and First Nations

Lines of governance in First Nations education, it should now be obvious, are severely "crossed." They are crossed, moreover, in two dimensions. In fact, we believe it is both useful and appropriate to think in terms of two "layers" of crossed governance in First Nations education.

The First Nations–INAC layer is the one on which we have focused so far. **Figure 12.2** presents this layer only partially in that it shows only the INAC-to-individual–First Nations dimension of that crossed-governance layer (and thus omits, for example, nominal program accountability of First Nations education authorities to provincial and territorial ministries of education). **Figure 12.2** exposes clearly, however, the conflicting governance relationships across the two layers of First Nations educational governance.

The INAC-direct-to–First Nations layer includes all First Nations with band-operated education programs (elementary, secondary, and post-secondary). The top layer of **Figure 12.2** is best thought of, therefore, as a composite of single band-school-to-INAC governance relationships as depicted in **Figure 12.1**. Bands, however, as we have noted, frequently join together in aggregate organizations such as tribal councils, educational councils, and band associations to pool capacity for certain purposes in education and in other social policy areas. As shown in **Figure 12.2**, moreover, these aggregate organizations themselves often join together in larger aggregations such as the Chiefs' Committee on Education (CCOE), National Indian Education Council (NIEC) initiatives, and/or ultimately the Assembly of First Nations (AFN). First-level aggregate organizations, moreover, sometimes establish links with one another for particular purposes and activities although more typically they are linked through second- and higher-level aggregations. These linkages range from nominal to authentically collaborative.

First Nations aggregate groups also compete with one another for recognition, credibility, and scarce federal dollars. They often receive funding, moreover, as **Figure 12.2** indicates, *both* from INAC and from member bands. This duality of funding sources often simultaneously pulls First Nations aggregate groups in very different directions.

Another telling point can be made regarding the First Nations–INAC structure of governance and lines of accountability illustrated in **Figure 12.2**. In the end, the government of Canada seems to be positioned as the only credible potential guarantor of stability for First Nations The highly salient corollary is that any new forms of First Nation self-governance that might emerge without active support by the Canadian state would be marked by instability and disorder.

Overall, then, INAC's policy of devolving power to the local level has not created any new "political space" within which First Nations might exercise real control over their education system. Instead, informal and non-institutional local and aggregated forms of mainly *devolved low-level managerial power* have emerged to complement, not to replace, the long-established and centralized authority embodied in INAC.

Figure 12.2 can provide a useful basis from which to begin rethinking the current model of governance in Aboriginal education along the lines of a multi-level form, a web-like process of self-governance in education and especially for meeting the challenges of fragmentation. Such a multi-level, web-like model of governance would, however, have to employ rule and norm systems (anchored in binding mechanisms of governance and a common conception of human good). These rule and norm systems would be needed to steer educational issues through both hierarchical and networked interactions across levels of aggregation that would encompass all the diverse First Nations communities that would participate in the process of self-governance of education. It would also need to respect, as far as possible, the evolving individual identities of members of these communities. To overcome the current fragmentation in First Nations education, such a governance model would require authority over education that would be reasonably dispersed and decentralized, while at the same time avoid the incoherence of fragmentation. Functional governance in First Nations education, in short, will depend on authority that flows as much horizontally as vertically but that does so through clearly defined participatory and accountability channels. To work effectively, such a governance model will require political acceptance of broad collaboration through aggregated forms of governance and of the need to undo the current fragmentation in part by renouncing the fallacy of community-level control as synonymous with "Indian control." An immediate corollary is that success with such a governance model will also require capacity on the part of First Nations and non-First Nations communities to establish conditions conducive to convergence around shared values and substantial agreement about developmental aspirations.

Breaking Free of the Gridlock

Ironically, by constructing the concept of "Indian control" as a synonym for radically local control, INAC policy on devolution of control brought forward in time and applied to education a fragmented governance dynamic that led to dysfunctional diseconomies of scale and to paralysis and stagnation of First Nations education "systems." In a further irony, it did so even as it presented, then justified, such fragmented governance dynamics within a discourse of community empowerment and capacity building. Agency, after all, is a process of social engagement that allows members of a community (in the broad sense of a distinct ethno-cultural identity group, not in the narrow sense of a village or small local municipality) to critically shape their own responses to problematic situations or catalytic events (Emirbayer 1998). Current fragmentation of control over First Nations education, and especially the radical disaggregation of First Nations authority over education that it has fostered, raise two crucial questions. First, do functionally aggregated forms of governance offer a relevant way of addressing current fragmentation challenges; and second, if the answer to the first question is affirmative as we believe it is, how could such functionally aggregated governance be achieved in the future?

In the final section, we explore further certain issues surrounding a "governance of fragmentation" (an oxymoronic concept at best). More importantly, we propose a way forward toward forms of governance in First Nations education that would alleviate diseconomies of scale while enhancing relevance of educational programs, effectiveness of educational services, quality, ethics, and the effectiveness and efficiency of governance. This vision of authentic governance is built around multiple levels of *functional* aggregation that would encompass all the relevant diversity of First Nations communities and peoples. Fragmentation dynamics, in our view, constitute the most difficult, complex, and pervasive challenge facing those who seek to exercise meaningful control over First Nations education. Our discussion is framed around two key questions that organize our thoughts on the current gridlock within which First Nations control of First Nations education is embroiled: (1) what are the probabilities that the current radical disaggregation of First Nations control over education can achieve efficient, effective, and ethical governance; and (2) in a context where First Nations communities and institutions are simultaneously fragmenting and sometimes weakly integrating, what forms of First Nations governance can be developed in education and what process can be used to steer fragmentation-integration tensions in constructive directions towards creation of authentically self-determining aggregated forms of First Nations educational governance?

Disaggregation of First Nations Control over Education: Issues of Values and Purpose

Disaggregation of First Nation Control over Education

In any complex, pluralistic society, multiple levels of functional interdependence are embedded in aggregated organizational structures that link various levels of government with both public and private institutions. Among First Nations bodies in charge of governing education, this level of functional interdependence and aggregation is strikingly absent and its absence impedes most attempts to rework, coordinate, and integrate modes and instances of governance of First Nations education. This lack of inter-institutional interface is a major part of the perverse "Indian control of Indian education" (ICIE) legacy. The ICIE mode of thinking about governance of education offers only a balkanizing and debilitating fixation on strictly *local* control, a fixation that promotes endless competition and turf wars over education among and within individual First Nations. Each community wants to *control* every aspect of education in *its* school. The cruelly ironic result is that it controls next to nothing that counts. Instead of asking the key question, how can we collaborate strategically to improve the education of young First Nations persons in our area or cultural-linguistic group, those responsible for school operations and problems focus mainly on protecting the "turf" of *their* community school "*system*," a perfect recipe for preserving and deepening dysfunctional diseconomies of scale.

Diseconomies of scale lead to an inescapable no-pain, no-gain control paradox in First Nations education. Unless, and only to the degree that, individual First Nations are willing, and empowered fiscally and in law and policy to collaborate in deep functional integration of key educational infrastructure services such as curriculum development, administration, supervision, program support, and so forth, *First Nations control of First Nations education will remain an illusion*. If First Nations control is the objective, *deep and comprehensive functional integration* will be necessary.

Schouls summarizes the broader dimensions of the diseconomies-of-scale problem in these terms:

> Many First Nations are small in both population and reserve size, making it difficult and perhaps unrealistic for some of them to administer the services and financial resources necessary for self-government. First Nations may therefore choose to delegate authority to political entities such as tribal councils in functional areas beyond their capacity such as policy development, higher education, and human resource training. However, it is First Nations at the band level that are invested with

statutory political authority, and for this reason they are the focus of my attention (2003, 54).

The evidence is by now overwhelming; it seems to us, however, that simply "delegating" selectively certain support-service functions to an education or tribal council, while clinging to the illusion of a local community-based "education system," has not been and almost certainly never will provide a platform for meaningful First Nations control of First Nations education. It remains true, of course, as Schouls notes, that the *Indian Act* invests First Nations political authority in local bands. This current legislative reality, however, should not be allowed to stand in the way of creating bodies with the scope and scale to integrate functionally and comprehensively educational services to First Nations communities. To some extent, at least initially, all that is needed is broadening, deepening, and reinforcing the mandate of existing organizations.

Entities which provide deep functional integration of services to First Nations communities need to be created and governed with respect for the wishes and evolving sense of identity of member communities although consensus on all issues will not be possible. Equally essential is the need to equip such organizations with appropriate professional knowledge, expertise, and skills—to ensure on an ongoing basis, that is, development and renewal of institutional capacity to deliver the direction and support needed. Above all, this *institutional-capacity* agenda means that the architects of such collaborative institutions must resolutely resist the temptation to use them as venues for "pork-barrel" appointments to key positions of unqualified but locally well-connected people.

Transforming Values and Purpose

The current balkanization of First Nations educational governance has generally resulted in organizational structures unable to resolve challenges facing First Nations education, challenges that are by their nature large in scale and scope. The task of thinking afresh in replacing fragmentation with solidarity involves more than sensitivity and openness to profound transformations in macro-organizational governance structure, however urgently these may be needed. Functionally aggregated governance in First Nations education also requires breaking out of the cultural and conceptual manacles that currently bind it. The present situation calls for a process capable of synthesizing the relevant knowledge from different Aboriginal perspectives about values and developmental purpose that should underpin First Nations education. Such perspectives should lead to a common, and ideally, a broadly shared understanding of values and overarching purpose for First Nations education on the part of major Aboriginal and non-Aboriginal parties/stakeholders. Without such a process, it is very unlikely that any future governance arrangement would serve adequately either Aboriginal youth or stakeholder requirements for an authentically self-determining education system. Such an exercise would involve Aboriginal and non-Aboriginal communities in a way that would lead to reasonable integration of values and purpose as organizing principles for resolution of contemporary problems of large scale and scope in First Nations education, an exercise in fruitful interdependence, in short, just where it is most needed.

Unless solidly anchored in values, principles, and ethics respected in both Aboriginal and contemporary mainstream Canadian cultures, First Nations education, at least in any meaningful sense, is probably doomed. At its profoundest level, reformulation of governance in First Nations education needs to confront the underlying status quo value system and to recognize its deep ties to a long series of unworkable and unhealthy governance arrangements. To some extent, this focus on values, moral principles, and ethics may yield different nuances of meaning for each Aboriginal community. Nonetheless, most Aboriginal community members would probably agree, on reflection, that each of these things constitutes an important and inevitable dimension of any broad-scope Aboriginal self-determination, and its feasibility.

No significant progress in meaningful First Nations self-determination, in education or elsewhere, and especially in regard to the kind of functionally integrative aggregation we are proposing, will be possible without deep trust on the part of the gatekeepers of power and resources in Canadian society. This proposition is at the heart of what Turner calls "Kymlicka's constraint" (2006, 58). Only in a context of mutual trust will First Nations be able to negotiate new arrangements and relationships that will provide them with appropriate "boundaries" for reasonable self-determination. Such trust is ultimately necessary because, as Turner insists, mainstream Canadian gatekeepers of power and resources are and will remain for the foreseeable future mainly non-Aboriginal. Renewing relationships between Aboriginal peoples and the Canadian state must therefore, however ironic it might seem to some, aim for a self-determination mechanism that reorients contemporary Aboriginal ways of doing things so they are *simultaneously* more responsive both to Aboriginal constituents and to ethical values of central importance in the larger Canadian society. To be effective and efficient, functionally aggregated First Nations educational organizations will need to act in ways consistent with ethical values and developmental purpose mutually acceptable to their own constituents and to the gatekeepers of power and resources in mainstream Canadian society, which is no mean challenge. Only in this way will they be able to enrich, reinforce, and sustain functional aggregative dynamics that harness in helpful ways the interaction of Aboriginal and non-Aboriginal communities.

A Higher Vision—Moving to "Education Plus" from the "Parity Paradox" and Complacent Acceptance of "Education Minus"

The Parity Paradox: Basis for Alternative Educational Visions

The exact-equivalence rationale behind the only substantive INAC policy on education—the ability of any student to transfer to provincial or territorial schools *at any time* without penalty (INAC 2003, 4)—is grounded in what one author long ago labelled a "remediation" policy response to poor school performance on the part of minorities (Paquette 1989). The inescapable seminal assumption underpinning such exact-equivalence policy on the part of INAC is that Aboriginal culture and language have no significant part in the image of an educated person in Canada. All that *really* counts, in this view, is what provincial and territorial governments (and *their* constituents and *their* electors) decide counts. Aboriginal culture and language, in this view, is at best an ornament graciously tolerated by "real education." Nothing could be further from Turner's vision of "word warrior" education except perhaps residential-school-style all-out, no-holds-barred suppression of Aboriginal culture and language.

Cardinal long ago insisted that Aboriginal peoples should be regarded as "citizens plus" (Indian Chiefs of Alberta, 1970). In the same vein, we are calling for a vision of Aboriginal education as "education plus," not as "education minus"—as is, with the rarest of exception, currently the case. To nurture a generation of Turner-mode "word warriors," Aboriginal education will require more than equality. The only way to move beyond the parity paradox—the paradox that First Nations schools must provide meaningful grounding in First Nation cultures and language to justify their existence but must also provide reasonable parity in program and achievement if their students are to be able to participate fully in Canadian society and its economy (Jerry Paquette, 1986)—is to do *more* than provincial schools do. No alchemy, moreover, exists that would provide an easy way to meet this heady challenge. As Churchill told the British people during some of the blackest days of World War II, all we have to offer is the "blood, sweat, and tears" of very hard work necessary to develop the leadership, governance, and pedagogical capacity and commitment to reinvent First Nations education as Turnerian "education plus."

Functional Integration

To be realizable within the First Nations context, "education plus" needs to be grounded in self-determining functionally aggregated mechanisms of First Nations governance and provision. Functionally aggregated forms of self-governance can usefully be thought of as governance that transforms, structures, and integrates knowledge and resources from multiple First Nations educational governance entities to produce a new holistic, integrated, and effectively self-determining organizational structure supporting and overseeing Aboriginal education in local communities and beyond. It is a synergistic whole that is potentially much greater than the sum of its parts. Functional aggregation implies purposefully coherent and coordinated action and it comprises cross-sectoral collaboration, cooperation, as well as ongoing modification for improved performance (including initial transformative changes when necessary). The promises of aggregation include integrative thinking and a perspective on educational issues not possible with organizational fragmentation as well as efficient utilization of scarce resources. Such *functional* integration could go far toward remedying the pandemic diseconomy of scale in education among First Nations communities. Cohesion resulting from functional integration could enable First Nations to increase not only the breadth of self-governance in education but also its depth as well.

The potential advantages of aggregated forms of self-determining governance in First Nations education are hardly news. Despite the tight grip that the myth of "local control" as a synonym for "Indian control" has had on the whole devolution saga, individual First Nations have been working together for decades through various associations, tribal councils, and education councils. Functional aggregation, however, requires more than voluntary participation when and to the extent that such participation suits immediate community educational and political priorities or preferences. Voluntary, largely ad hoc affiliation fuels fragmentation. What is needed is *functional integration*, that is, school-board-like aggregations within regional First Nations education jurisdictions.

"Aggregation" and "deep comprehensive functional integration" are not, of course, neutral words. They are heavily value-laden. Aggregation and functional integration suggest "power" and power in First Nations hands suggests purposes— and especially the ability to define and choose among them. Purposes too are anything but neutral. Purposes, and the capacity to choose them, are central to functional aggregation and integration of First Nations educational-governance entities. These entities should set the agenda for First Nations education, or at least for the part of it over which they might reasonably exercise control. *They* should limit or expand and target the range of First Nations control over their education system. *They* should frame ends and means, ponder alternatives, and decide the key educational choices and trade-offs.

Clear and well-articulated developmental purposes are necessary to coherent, sustained pursuit of certain values in ways of being, acting, and communicating. Functional aggregation and integration are background conditions necessary for coherent and purpose-driven First Nations control over First Nations education; necessary but not sufficient conditions for "education plus." Functional aggregation and integration should not be viewed as an automatic stimulus or foolproof recipe for action that leads to efficient, effective, and appropriate self-governance. *By themselves* they are much more in the nature of "second-order change" that shapes, contextualizes, assists, permits, or inhibits particular courses of action than of "first-order change" that transforms, fosters, or shapes major courses of policy action. The distinction is an important one. It differentiates *authentically self-governing* aggregated First Nations educational entities from aggregations that are mere "agents" of policy crafted by others. It should thus prevent the reader from mistaking second-order for first-order changes, from viewing aggregated First Nations educational entities as an unseen hand that would somehow, in and of itself, "cause" First Nations communities and groups to pursue desirable purposes or goals and undertake action appropriate to that pursuit without awareness of why they do so and, most fundamentally, *without taking responsibility for their conduct and choices.*

Ironically, to exercise meaningful jurisdiction over education, First Nations *must* devolve, or "upload"—cede if you prefer—administration, supervision, and programing to aggregate entities. Aggregate entities, in other words, whether they are called "school boards" or something else, *must be the primary vehicle of control and jurisdiction.* Whatever they are called, in the end they will need to act much like school boards—yet avoid the worst pitfalls of bureaucratic dysfunction to which school boards often fall prey.

Funding should recognize "first-level" aggregation (school-board-like entities) as the main locus of power and administrative and program capacity in First Nations education. In particular, the inherently dysfunctional notion that aggregates are mere "service providers" to individual First Nations must come to an end, and with it, funding and funding mechanisms predicated on it. A new balance between community and regional autonomy is needed. Such a balance can only be struck in the context of a new approach to funding, one that takes account of a much larger and more functionally important role for First Nations aggregate organizations, including area school-board-like entities.

McCue (2004) summarizes persuasively the overall impact of scrambled lines of accountability on meaningful First Nations jurisdiction in education:

> So, regardless of the amount of jurisdiction that the SGA provides to the First Nations (at least, in the ones examined), the affected communities must ultimately adhere to the provincial curriculum and provincial standards to educate their children. In effect, what these SGAs are saying is that, yes, a First Nation can have jurisdiction in education, but that jurisdiction must ensure that the status quo regarding the curriculum and education program are maintained in First Nations schools. There is no explicit recognition of First Nations jurisdiction in this regard. Provincial curriculum continues to be the baseline standard for First Nations education. (6)

Aboriginal education needs to be rendered accountable, in the first instance, to its Aboriginal constituents, particularly parents and community members. Ironically, that can only happen with functional aggregation beyond the community level.

Processes for Creating a Meaningful Form of Jurisdiction

We believe that a strategic, iterative, results-based-management (RBM) approach offers the most promising method of linking and harnessing resource inputs to achieve the highly desirable impact of a creative, fruitful interdependence (culturally, socially, intellectually, economically, and so forth) between Aborigi-

Figure 12.3: A Results Chain

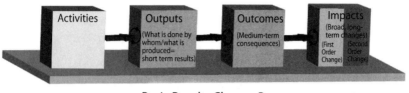

Basic Results Change Process   Brenda Mergel 2008

nal peoples and the rest of mainstream Canadian society. Such interdependence requires renewed relationships that offer appropriate—but by the same token, appropriately permeable—boundaries for Aboriginal self-determination. This type of RBM approach adopts a macro perspective and would deal with issues that underlie most current self-governance problems in First Nations education from an organizational and system perspective. RBM offers a process now broadly accepted in government for linking individual and group capacities to organizational results. This linkage is achieved through sustained focus on the internal working of self-governance to improve internal capacity on the one hand, and on relationships with and influences on and from the external non-Aboriginal environment on the other. Used with insight, commitment, and willingness to apply in-course corrections as needed, it melds institutions, social values, and the political and economic context. RBM utilizes a systemic macro-perspective on developing self-determining forms of aggregated governance by seeing such development as a dynamic process within which interlocking networks of actors (individuals, communities, and formal organizations) work effectively to enhance or change what they do both by their own initiatives and through the support of outsiders. RBM potentially offers a multi-dimensional perspective on the development of self-determining forms of First Nations governance, one where First Nations communities and their learning institutions are viewed as multi-level holistic and functionally interrelated systems. An iterative RBM model allows one to approach self-determination in First Nations education as a process implicating multiple levels and actors (Aboriginal and non-Aboriginal) in power relationships, linkages, and processes that together foster capacity building in technical skills as well as capacity to build networks and relationships, knowledge, and human resource, and finally to manage and sustain change over time.

What we propose offers a promising *process,* rather than a prefabricated solution. We can promise no more than this however strongly we believe that movement toward responsibility, accountability, and transparency within an efficient, effective, and appropriate "education plus" vision of the policy "endgame" is desperately needed in First Nations education. We offer, then, a response to the need to address current challenges in First Nations education *through multi-*

Figure 12.4: Complexity and Risk in Results Chains

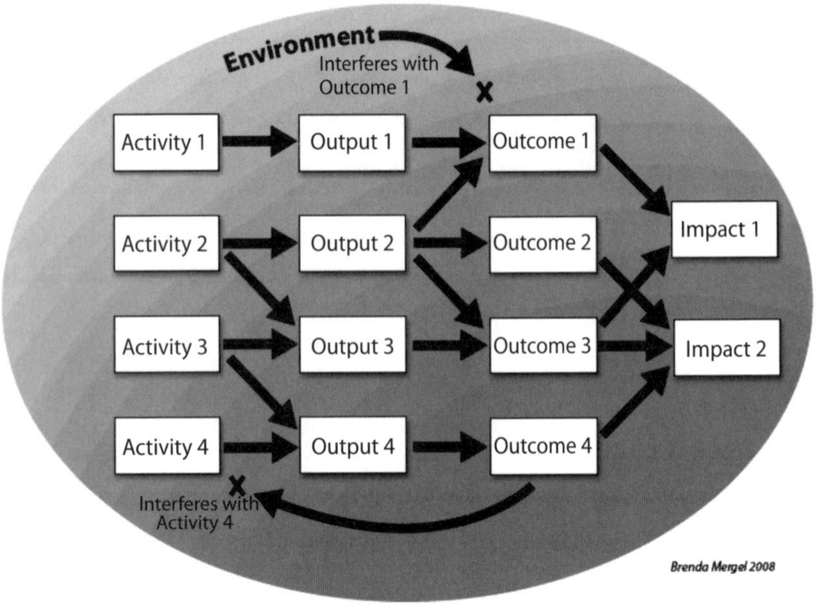

dimensional processes of change, not through a set of discrete or prefabricated policy interventions intended to bring about pre-defined policy outcomes.

The central concept in any RBM model is the "results chain." **Figure 12.3** illustrates such a chain in simplest terms. The key point is that one begins "at the end" of the chain with the ultimate long-term impacts one hopes to achieve. These desired impacts need to be re-evaluated iteratively and may change significantly over the course of any given policy lifespan. As broad, long-term results, impacts provide a working target; in fact, they are the *raison d'être* for everything else in the results chain. One starts at the end and "maps back" to outputs and outcomes that might plausibly contribute to desired "impacts," just as a traveller first decides where she is going and then how she might get there.

"Outputs" are what happens *directly and in the short term* as a result of policy activities associated with a results chain, transitory or short-term results if you will. Outputs consist of "what is done by whom—and to or with whom" and what is produced by activities directly associated with the results chain. "Outcomes" are medium-term consequences of the activities and outputs associated with the results chain. "Impacts," as broad, long-term results, flow directly from the "vision" that motivated and shaped the policy in question in the first place. Impacts are intended to solve or ameliorate perceived problem sets that led policy-makers to pursue a vision of a state of affairs fundamentally better than the status quo. These problem sets reflect a "gap" between what is and what ought to be in the view of the policy-makers, advisers, and bureaucrats who together craft a tentative, "working" (in the sense of "subject to ongoing, iterative adjustment") results chain. Such a process should not, of course, be the exclusive domain of elected and civil-service elites. Rather, it should be embedded within a non-hierarchical participatory development process approach involving all key stakeholder constituencies. This type of process in First Nations education would require significant capacity development to establish, sustain, and empower authentically self-determining and hence participatory aggregated forms of governance. Participatory interventions need to be linked to change outcomes and contribute to building the capacity of First Nations communities and groups to develop their own understanding of what self-determining aggregated forms of governance might look like in practice. *The change process itself, moreover, should never become the main target of change effort.*

To obtain results, activities require resources, first to mount them and then to sustain them. Resources generally come in four forms: human—particularly knowledge and skills—financial, material, and political. Real-world results chains involve numerous activities with multiple outputs, a panoply of outcomes, some, perhaps many, unplanned and unforeseen, and, potentially at least, impacts; impacts which may or may not be those intended in the first place. **Figure 12.4** hints at some of the complexity and uncertainty or "risk" involved in pursuing a results chain. Some activities contribute to more than one output. Activity 3 contributes to both output 3 and output 4. Output 4, however, is leading to an unintended outcome (outcome 4) which is actually interfering with desired impact 2. Outcome 4, moreover, is also changing the way activity 4 is being carried out. Finally, things are occurring in the environment that are actively interfering with outcome 1. This is, of course, a very limited and schematic portrayal of the real complexity involved in trying to apply the results-chain logic to policy implementation. No model can capture the infinite complexity of reality and "the game" really *does* change as one plays it. Such a model, moreover, is not power-neutral. Its dynamic is linked to power issues of various sorts such as competition for limited resources or control which might constrain realization of even a broadly-shared developmental vision for First Nations education. Without doubt the issue of power is linked to focus on desired results. For instance, a focus on short-term project-driven results might undermine a long-term capacity-development priority such as authentic First Nations ownership or sustainable long-term strategies for creation of functionally aggregated self-determining forms of educational governance.

Complexity notwithstanding, such a model raises key questions that should drive policy-making firmly in the direction of an RBM model of accountability: What basic conditions and opportunities do RBM-model reforms require if they are to arrive at real accountability in Aboriginal education?

- To what extent do First Nations students—and their teachers and educational administrators—currently have access to such resources and conditions?

Figure 12.5: Risk in Results—Chain Logic

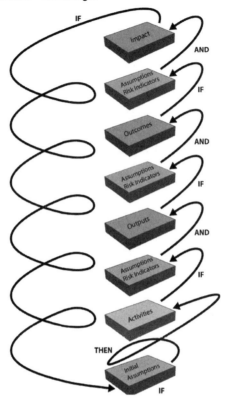

Source: *Results-Based Management in CIDA: An Introductory Guide to the Concepts and Principles.* Canadian International Development Agency, 2006, Figure 6.

Reproduced with the permission of the Minister of Public Works and Government Services, 2009.

- How does the current distribution of these basic educational conditions, opportunities, and resources interface with students' current educational needs to nurturance as "word warriors"—or not?
- Who defines and judges what constitutes aggregated self-governed Aboriginal educational institutions?
- Who should define and judge what constitutes them? Whose analysis will hold sway in defining the issues and problems to be addressed moving toward functionally aggregated self-governed Aboriginal educational institutions?
- To what extent do aggregated self-governed Aboriginal educational institutions' policies ensure that all Aboriginal students have adequate and equitable opportunities to learn what an RBM educational system demands of them?

Figure 12.6: Iterative Use of Performance Information

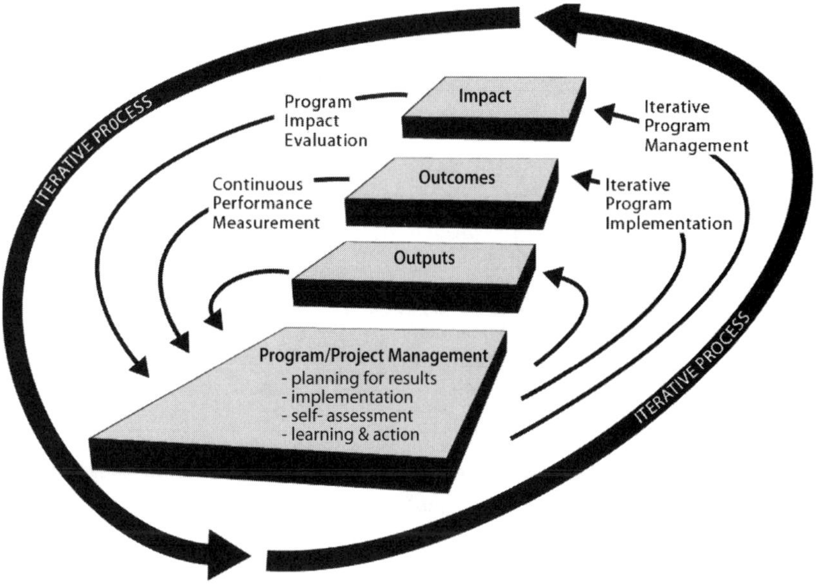

Source: *Results-Based Management in CIDA: An Introductory Guide to the Concepts and Principles.* Canadian International Development Agency, 2006, Figure 9.

Reproduced with the permission of the Minister of Public Works and Government Services, 2009.

What kind of data is available to answer these questions; to whom are data available, and what data are lacking? In short, movement toward authentic "Indian control of Indian education" through an RBM model requires that the model not be denatured into yet another externally delimited ("hierarchically encapsulated") approach to educational accountability that leaves aggregated forms of Aboriginal governance of education unable to prevent, discover, and correct inadequacies in and inequalities among their schools.

Ultimately, the ability of a results chain to achieve planned outcomes and desired impacts depends on three things: usefulness over the short, medium, and long-term of assumptions behind the result-chain model, appropriateness and usefulness of data collected and used for "in-course corrections" during the lifetime of the results-chain policy, and finally unforeseen changes outside and inside policy activities and their multiple results chains. That's a lot of uncertainty entailing a lot of risk. As **Figure 12.5** reveals, moreover, the risk is "cumulative," indeed "compounded." The further one moves along the results chain from starting assumptions toward eventual impacts, the greater the risk of encountering faulty assumptions—or assumptions that once were valid but no longer are. Such cumulative and compounded uncertainty makes it vital to collect, collate, analyze, and use interim data to adjust all aspects of the results chain iteratively over time. **Figure 12.5** captures the general sense of this continuous, multilayered, data-informed "in course correction" dynamic.

Figure 12.7: Awareness and Buy-in—Difficult but Necessary First Steps

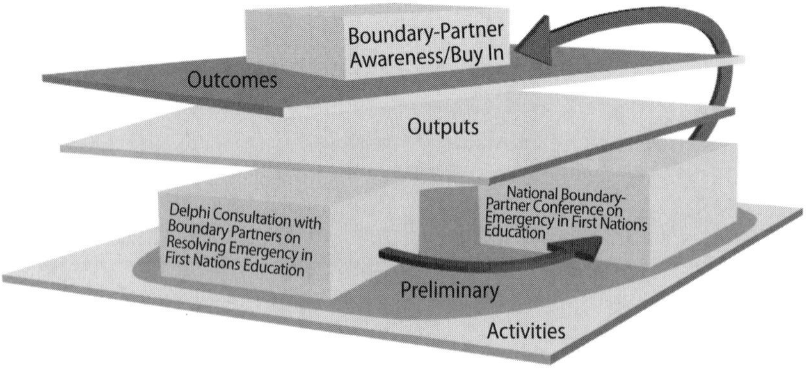

Data relevant to outputs, outcomes, and impacts need to feed back regularly into overall program or policy-management strategic planning. Adjustments should then be made in outputs in order to modify outcomes appropriately and, as necessary, even targeted impacts themselves.

None of this, of course, should be taken as an argument in favour of vagueness and uncertainty in any aspect of the initial planning of the results chain. We simply wish to acknowledge that serious risks exist in any real-world policy results chain and that the only way to exercise some control over them is to take careful account of them iteratively over time (See **Figure 12.6**). The fuzzier one is at the beginning on the desired impacts that justify a results chain and provide direction to it through backward mapping, the greater the chance of confusion, conflict, and failure.

Most "stage theories" of policy implementation or change begin with awareness and initial "buy in" by key stakeholders. **Figure 12.7** translates this difficult but necessary initial step into RBM language and imagery, although it admittedly conceals far more than it reveals. First, it fails to raise the bottom-line political question of what might move First Nations educational leaders who are reasonably satisfied with the current fragmentation of First Nations control of education and resulting local political-economy payoffs from a fragmented status quo to partici-pate in such a process, much less "buy into" the existence of an emergency in First Nations education or a pressing need for serious change—especially change that would fundamentally and permanently alter responsibility and accountability in First Nations education. The only possible response to that question is, after all, "nothing," at least in the current context within which they live and work. It is far easier simply to blame the federal government and inadequate funding for any shortcomings that exist in First Nations education.

Barring an unlikely collective "crisis of conscience" on the part of such leaders, only resolute and courageous action by the federal government to insist on fundamental accountability in the sense obviously intended by the Auditor-General in her highly critical reports on First Nations education is likely to trigger First Nations "buy in" into this type of RBM process. Only federal insistence on accountability in the sense of program value-added for dollars spent in student learning and socialization, would provoke a shared sense of crisis sufficient to trigger this type of fundamental, "out of the box" rethinking of the parameters in the context within which First Nations education currently occurs.

Several policy "wildcards," however, seem to us to be in play at the moment. Taken together, these might make a firm stance on the part of the federal government on the accountability issue more likely than it seems at present. First, the *Zeitgeist* of our time is solidly aligned against waste and in favour of responsibility and accountability. Second, the current prime minister is reputedly closely linked to Tom Flanagan, whose radical "white paper liberal" stance (to use Turner's descriptor) on First Nations issues is widely known (2000). At the moment, it seems entirely plausible that Prime Minister Harper might succeed in obtaining a majority government in the near future in which case all bets are off, in our view, about the sustainability of the status quo in Indian affairs generally but especially in education. Finally, there is always the unexpected. The possibility exists that some unforeseen event that attracts heavy media attention may provoke outrage on the part of either mainstream Canadians or Aboriginal leaders, or even both, about the status quo in Aboriginal education.

Assuming Aboriginal education should arrive at some such "critical juncture" (Koenig, 1986), who are the "boundary partners," "individuals, groups, and orga- nizations with whom the program interacts directly and with whom the program anticipates opportunities for influence" (Patton, 2001) that should be at the table in such consultations and why? Also, how should such consultations occur and why? The national First Nations organizations would have to be central players, but not the only players, in such consultations—and they could not wield veto power over the process itself. Furthermore, such consultations could only be fruitful if it was understood from the beginning by all participants that the status quo was substan- tially untenable *and would no longer be supported by the federal government*. It seems clear to us that at least the Chiefs' Committee on Education (CCOE), the National Indian Education Council (NIEC), the Assembly of First Nations (AFN) and the Assembly of First Nations of Quebec would have to be central players at this consultation table. It is equally clear to us that the Council of Ministers of Education of Canada (CMEC) would need to be at the table as well—and for an excellent albeit not-immediately-evident reason. The CMEC produces the Pan-Canadian Assessment Program (PCAP), successor to its School Achievement Indicators Program (SAIP), a national comparative assessment of learning and reading, math, and science on the part of 13 year olds across Canada. To produce PCAP and SAIP, CMEC has been and continues to be involved in creating national assessments grounded in elementary and primary curricula across Canada and hence in "distilling" the most important components of such curricula, *a major*

Figure 12.8: An RMB starting point for transfer of responsibility and accountability

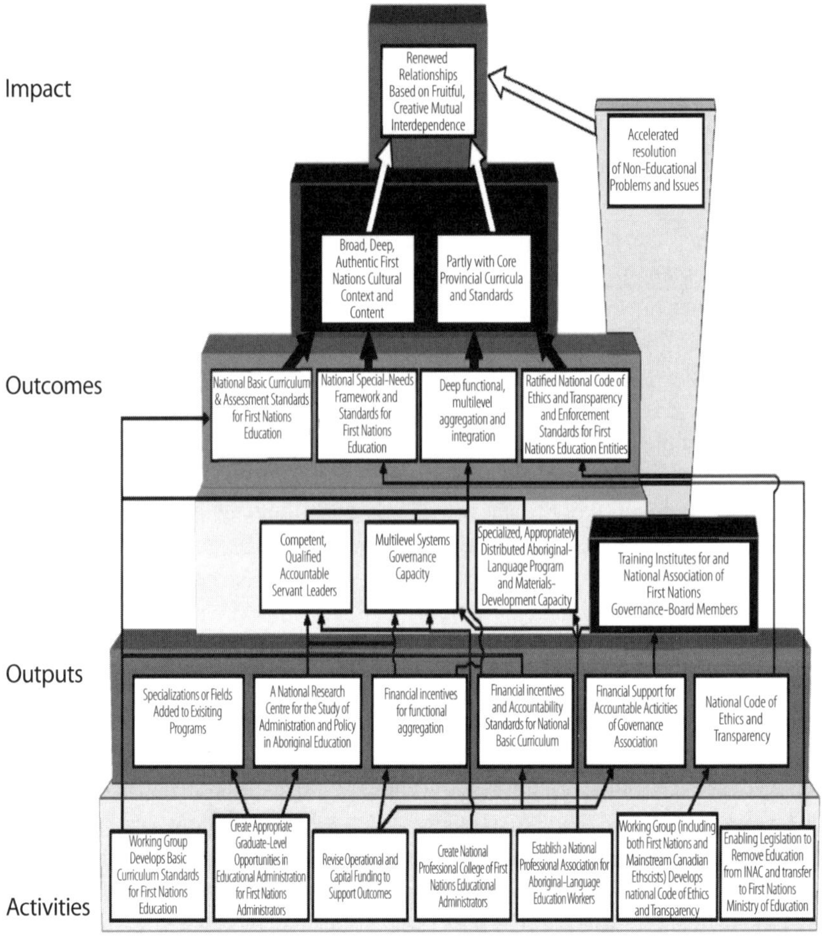

part of what needs to occur in establishing a basic cross-Canada First Nations curriculum framework.

The federal government would also need to be appropriately represented, and that surely means not simply by an education representative from INAC. What is at stake here, after all, is institutionalization of real responsibility and accountability for First Nations education on the part of First Nations entities—once and for all unscrambling crossed lines of accountability. As a crucial step in that direction, all residual education functions of INAC should be targeted for termination in the shortest reasonable time frame. While it is certainly appropriate and necessary that the Minister of Indian Affairs be at the table, the Minister of Finance and Chair of the Treasury Board should also have senior representation at the table since substantial resource issues will arise if the changes we propose go forward.

Such consultations should be reasonably thorough but they should not extend over more than eight months, given the urgency of the need for change. A functional working-committee structure would facilitate the work of the group and firm timelines should be set and adhered to throughout the process with a clear understanding that the process cannot and will not be bogged down by committees that don't do their homework on time. It seems to us that standard "post-presentational" procedures would likely be the most effective (clear description of problems and issues that arise from an initial Delphi exercise followed by delegation to appropriate working committees that would report back to the entire "table" for discussion followed by a two-week period for discussion and notice of motions and then a final meeting for a vote on the motions). The purpose of the preliminary consultation, it should be remembered, would be awareness and "buy in," and hence, necessarily, finding common grounds for that buy-in. Although matters of substance will undoubtedly arise, focus would have to be kept on the endgame—ultimate transfer of real control and responsibility for First Nations education to First Nations entities. Ideally the Prime Minister himself should chair at least the first meeting and should make it clear that the status quo is not an option.

Figure 12.8 offers, in our view, a workable RBM starting point for institutionalization of meaningful responsibility for First Nations education on the part of First Nations entities and for taking major steps away from the current crossed lines of accountability and thus toward a "word warrior" "education plus" that will be a source of pride and satisfaction to all the boundary partners in the process. A real-world RBM would be significantly larger, more comprehensive, and undoubtedly more complex. It would, for example, need to deal explicitly with post-secondary issues. These are present only implicitly in **Figure 12.8**. Still, we believe that **Figure 12.8** provides a reasonably clear idea of what kinds of activities, outputs, and outcomes are needed to move toward a First Nations education plus that joins broad, deep, authentic First Nations cultural context and content on the one hand to parity with core provincial curricula and standards on the other. As we have stressed, any RBM map toward those impacts will need in-course adjustments on a regular basis as it goes forward. Nonetheless, the model portrayed in **Figure 12.8** offers a plausible and potentially useful beginning point, we believe, for a promising alternative to a status quo that pleases no one except those who profit from it.

Not surprisingly, given our treatment of these issues in previous sections of this chapter, the key outcome building blocks in this vision are:

- a national basic curriculum and assessment standards for First Nations education
- a national special-needs framework and standards
- deep functional, multi-level aggregation and integration
- a ratified national code of ethics and transparency with clear and effective

enforcement standards

To realize such outcomes, we think that some minimum "winning conditions" have to be in place, in particular:

- a highly consultative and participatory but also clearly time-delimited process

- openness and transparency—transparent process and decision-making and committed human and financial resources to plan and implement results-oriented actions

- awareness and understanding—all impacted parties/stakeholders are aware of, understand, and accept the issues of self-determining governance of First Nations education, as well as the implied changes and capacity needs

- the presence of the right parties/stakeholders at the table—Who would champion the policy initiatives? Who could provide financial and technical expertise? Who would be impacted? Who would be the direct and indirect beneficiaries? Who with no current voice needs special attention? Who would be supporting and/or opposing such a process?

Furthermore, an adequate pool of competent, qualified, competent, accountable "servant leaders" are needed—leaders with the capacity to operate a complex multi-level education "system" worthy of the name.

To develop a sufficient pool of suitable "servant leaders," appropriate graduate-level programs and concentrations are urgently needed. Resources need major redirection and, almost certainly, significant new money will be needed to realize this vision although we do not believe by any means that all of this money should come from the federal government. Of particular importance are financial incentives to promote and encourage accountable use of a national basic curriculum and related assessment standards. Appropriate support, education, and training for those involved in the governance of First Nations education are urgently needed.

Engaging in such a process will lead to some "hard lessons," by any standards— especially for those who are in favour of and profit from the status quo. However, we believe that such lessons will be welcomed by leaders imbued with a sense of stewardship and of their rightful status as "servants" of Aboriginal learners as by those who seek to renew Aboriginal education as an integral and essential part of renewing First Nations relationships with settler governments and with the non-Aboriginal people of Canada. We firmly believe that an RBM-based process designed through facilitative and participatory approaches can lead to long-term sustainability for functionally aggregated First Nation self-governing learning institutions capable of addressing cross-sectoral educational challenges. Further-more, the RBM-based process seems the only type of process likely to be able to do so. Such a process can provide a much-needed platform for a clear mission and mandate, clear goals, and appropriate ethics and values as well as appropriate functions, systems, and resources.

Concluding Comments

It has become increasingly apparent that the current balkanized approach to First Nations education is an insurmountable impediment to effective, efficient, and ethical self-governance. It fails to develop, sustain, and integrate a critical mass of capacities needed to address educational challenges faced by First Nations communities and, at the same time, it is constrained by values and governance concepts too narrow for the problem of interdependence and trust with mainstream society. The current policy gridlock reality calls for a new governance ethic and different forms of and status for aggregated self-determining governance entities in First Nations education. A move toward functionally aggregated structures of governance in First Nations education will require development of innovative forms of educational organizations that incorporate and are consistent with shared systems of values and developmental purpose for education. Such a transition will require a profound transformation of entire Aboriginal and non-Aboriginal components of society and culture. Both Aboriginal and non-Aboriginal communities will have to change their way of thinking about the governance of First Nations education from a fragmentary to a holistic one and develop a new governance ethic based on coexistence and respectful mutual interdependence within and among First Nations as well as between First Nations and mainstream Canadian society; interdependence framed within evolving Aboriginal identity protected by appropriate boundaries.

We are convinced that First Nations communities will need to undergo pervasive and consequential transformations if they are to regain agency over the education of their children. What we are proposing are transformations that will be so profound that it is hard to predict fully their final nature and implications. However, if and to the degree that these transformations toward functionally aggregated forms of governance in education unfold, resistance to them will inevitably develop. As aggregation and integration of local forms of governance proceed, as has been the case recently in the broader world of public education across Canada, fragmentation tendencies will hopefully dissipate as the processes and fruits of functional aggregation come to be appreciated.

As previously indicated in this chapter, our reasoning about First Nations education is underpinned by conviction that potentially useful critical analysis must go beyond the current understanding of self-governance as strictly local control. Such critical analysis should focus on reversing the resulting balkanization dynamics reflected in absurdly dysfunctional diseconomies of scale, as well as the associated lack of accountability, opaque decision-making process, and absence of over-arching developmental purpose that plague First Nations education in Canada. We find the notion of fragmentation particularly apropos here, as it captures these tensions between forces of disaggregation and aggregation at play in First Nations educational governance. Fragmentation is also a grating word. It is bothersome and uncomfortable. Its annoying connotations, however, may in fact be just what are needed here. Indeed, its abrasiveness forced us to stay in touch through this chapter with its conceptual opposites (respect, cooperation, interdependence, cohesion, and solidarity, for instance) and their hopeful implications for First Nations education.

Finally, our exploration and critique of the phenomenon of First Nations educational governance led us to conclude that it is a rich laboratory for probing, and hopefully reversing, the dynamics of fragmentation and resulting diseconomies of scale among Aboriginal communities. First Nations educational governance should be a site *par excellence* where the main goal should be to integrate the values, practices, and developmental purposes of diverse Aboriginal communities into an aggregated form of self-determining governance. Failing that, however, it could also unfortunately become the site of such powerful impulses toward even greater fragmentation that it would disintegrate into a multitude of locally situated under-performing First Nations educational fiefdoms constantly struggling with one another for a greater share of the resource "crumbs" available to them—resource "crumbs" that could never begin to keep pace with the insatiable demands of a radically fragmented non-system.

Endnotes

1 Good governance depends on transparency, accountability, and equity in ways that are responsive to people's needs.

2 By "developmental aspiration" we mean a vision of the capacities and resources needed by Aboriginal communities to achieve their own understanding of what it is to lead a worthwhile life (conception of human good and ideals of human excellence) as an Aboriginal citizen within the broader Canadian context, or capacities and resources deemed essential to First Nations self-determination.

3 After a great deal of thought and discussion we prefer "flourishing" in this context to the more anodyne—and typically Anglophone—"development" usage. We believe that "flourishing" much more accurately captures what we believe should be the ultimate social and economic policy objective of Aboriginal and First Nations affairs.

4 Some of the Yukon agreements come at it from a slightly different direction—but the coupling to territorial education is nonetheless clear in them.

5 First Nations that opt to participate in educational jurisdiction under this legislation enter into a *Canada–First Nation Education Jurisdiction Agreement*. This agreement will give the participating First Nations in BC control over education in their communities. They will be allowed to design and deliver education programs and services which are culturally relevant for their communities and provincially recognized.

6 These issues of legitimacy may be caused by a lack of fit between the formal institutions of governance and Aboriginal conceptions of how authority should be organized and exercised. The perceived legitimacy among aboriginal peoples of any form of Aboriginal self-governance in education will depend on the fit between those forms of self-governance and Aboriginal political culture (Cornell, Jorgensen, and Kalt 2002).

7 Accountability is basically a matter of responsiveness: are governing institutions and leaders responsive to constituents, funding agencies, and the like, and can they be held accountable for what they do (Cornell, Jorgensen, and Kalt 2002)?

8 Legitimacy is basically a matter of value and beliefs: do members of a community or constituents believe that governing institutions are appropriate for them? Legitimacy of a governing institution arises to a considerable extent from "cultural match," from the degree of fit between the formal organization of government and the community's beliefs about how political things—such as exercising power, making decisions, and representing interests—should be done (Cornell, Jorgensen, and Kalt 2002).

9 School governance, First Nations or otherwise, is never a closed system. To keep our diagram reasonably comprehensible, however, we have not included influences exogenous to the "system" as we have shown it. All manner of issues and contextual realities, national and international, impinge on government policy toward First Nations, including funding levels and allocation for First Nations education. Our purpose here is to focus analytically on voice, authority, and accountability links between citizen-residents (band/community members) and their local schools.

10 This definition, of course, neatly sidesteps the issue of whether the "results" in question are "process" results (e.g., classes provided in certain content areas perhaps taught to certain standards) or "outcome" results such as average test performance, acceptable "gains" in test or multiple-assessment results. The issue is an important one, but for purposes of a simplified model of governance, it's better left to the side.

11 For Levy and Merry (1986), first-order change consists of minor adjustments that do not change the system's core. Second-order changes involve changes in all of the following categories: the organizational paradigm defined as the underlying assumptions that shape perceptions, procedures, and behaviors in an organization; organizational purpose and mission; organizational culture, which includes the beliefs, values, and norms shared within the organization; and functional processes that include organizational structures, decision-making processes, and communication patterns.

References

Auditor General of Canada. 2004. "Chapter 5: Indian and Northern Affairs Canada—Education Program and Post-Secondary Student Program." In *Report of the Auditor General of Canada to the House of Commons*. Ottawa: Office of the Auditor General of Canada. 30.

Bertrand, Y., and P. Valois. 1980. *Les options en éducation*. Québec: Ministère de l'Éducation.

Breaker, R., and B. Kawaguchi. 2002. *Infrastructure and Funding in First Nations Education*. Calgary: Buffalo Signal Associates.

Cairns, A. 2000. *Citizens Plus: Aboriginal Peoples and the Canadian State*. Vancouver: UBC Press.

Canadian International Development Agency. 2006. "Results-Based Management in CIDA: An Introductory Guide to the Concepts and Principles." Retrieved May 16, 2007, from <**www.acdi-cida.gc.ca/CIDAWEB/acdicida.nsf/prnEn/EMA-218132656-PPK**>

Clement, J. (forthcoming). "University attainment of the registered Indian population, 1981–2001: A cohort approach." In D. Beavon and C. Demers (eds). *Horizons: Special Edition on Aboriginal Youth*: Policy Research Initiative. Government of Canada.

Cornell, S., M. Jorgensen, and J.P. Kalt. 2002. *The First Nations Governance Act: Implications of Research Findings from the United States and Canada*: Udall Center for Studies in Public Policy—The University of Arizona.

Dion, M., R. Hathaway, C.D. Helin, and L. Staats. 1997. *Financing Self-Government: The Strategically Positioned First Nations*. Kanaqt, ON: Sixdion; A Six Nations Company.

Flanagan, T. 2000. *First Nations? Second Thoughts*. Montreal: McGill-Queen's University Press.

Hawthorn, H. B., M.A. Tremblay, and A.M. Bownick. 1967. *A Survey of the Contemporary Indians of Canada: A Report on Economic, Political, Educational Needs and Policies: Part 2*. Ottawa: Queen's Printers.

Holmes, M. 1992. "The Revival of School Administration: Alasdair MacIntyre in the Aftermath of the Common School." *Canadian Journal of Education*. 17(4): 422–436.

Hurley, M. C. and J. Wherrett. 1999. *The Report of the Royal Commission on Aboriginal Peoples*. Retrieved September 16, 2005, from <**www.parl.gc.ca/information/library/PRBpubs/prb9924-e.htm**>.

INAC. 1982. *Indian Education Paper: Phase 1*. Ottawa: Indian and Inuit Affairs Program: Education and Social Development Branch.

INAC. 1997. *Gathering Strength: Canada's Aboriginal Action Plan* Retrieved September 20, 2005, from <**epe.lac-bac.gc.ca/100/201/301/gathering/html/1997/chg_e.html**>. Ottawa: Indian and Northern Affairs Canada.

INAC. 2003. *Elementary/Secondary Education: National Program Guidelines*. Ottawa: Indian and Northern Affairs Canada.

INAC. 2004. *Federal Policy Guide: Aboriginal Self-Government*. Retrieved October 9, 2005, from <**www.ainc-inac.qc.ca/pr/pub/sg/plcy_e.html**>. Ottawa: Indian and Northern Affairs Canada.

INAC. 2005. "Chapter 5: Education Action Plan: In Response to the Auditor General's Observations and Recommendations." *November 2004 Report*. Ottawa: Indian and Northern Affairs Canada.

Indian Chiefs of Alberta. 1970. *Citizens Plus*. Edmonton: Indian Association of Alberta.

Koenig, L. W. 1986. "Who Makes Public Policy?" In *An Introduction to Public Policy*. New Jersey: Prentice-Hall Inc. 1–28.

Kymlicka, W. 1989. *Liberalism, Community, and Culture*. Toronto: Clarendon Press, Oxford.

McCue, H. 2004. "An Overview of Federal and Provincial Policy Trends in First Nations Education." In Chiefs-In-Assembly (Ed.), *The New Agenda: A Manifesto for First Nations Education in Ontario*. Toronto: Chiefs of Ontario.

McCue, H. 2006. *Aboriginal Post-Secondary Education: A Think Piece from the Centre for Native Policy and Research*. West Vancouver: Centre for Native Policy and Research.

Miller, J. R. 1996. *Shingauk's Vision*. Toronto: University of Toronto Press.

Minister's National Working Group on Education. 2002. *Our Children: Keepers of the Sacred Knowledge*. Ottawa: Indian Affairs and Northern Development Canada.

Moon, J. D. 1993. *Constructing Community: Moral Pluralism and Tragic Conflicts*. Princeton: Princeton University Press.

Morgan, N. A. 2002. *"If Not Now, Then When?" First Nations Jurisdiction Over Education: A Literature Review Report to the Minister's National Working Group on First Nations Education*. Ottawa: Indian Affairs and Northern Development Canada.

National Indian Brotherhood. 1972/1984. "Indian Control of Indian Education. In J. R. Mallea and J. C. Young (Eds.), *Cultural Diversity and Canadian education*. Ottawa: Carleton University Press.

Paquette, J. 1986. *Aboriginal Self-Government and Education in Canada* (Vol. 10). Kingston ON: Institute of Intergovernmental Relations Queen's University.

Paquette, J. 1989. "Minority Education Policy: Assumptions and Propositions." *Curriculum Inquiry*, 19(4), 405–420.

Paquette, J. 1991. *Social Purpose and Schooling: Alternatives, Agendas, and Issues*. London: Falmer Press.

Patton, M. Q. 2001. "Outcome Mapping: Building Learning and Reflection into Development Programs." Retrieved May 17, 2007, from <**www.idrc.ca/openebooks/959-3/**>. Ottawa: International Development Research Centre.

RCAP. 1996. *Report of the Royal Commission on Aboriginal Peoples* (Vols. 1–5). Ottawa: Canada Communication Group Publishing.

Schouls, T. A. 2003. *Shifting Boundaries: Aboriginal Identity, Pluralist Theory, and the Politics of Self-Government*. Vancouver: UBC Press.

Smith, W. J., J.E. Paquette, and T. Bordonaro. 1995. "Educational Governance in Canada: A Model for Comparative Analysis" (No. Policy Research Paper No. 95-01). Montréal: McGill University, Office of Research on Educational Policy.

Turner, D. 2006. *This is not a Peace Pipe: Towards a Critical Indigenous Philosophy*. Toronto: University of Toronto Press.

Wall, D. 1998. "Aboriginal Self-Governement in Canada." Retrieved September 28, 2005, from <**www.ualberta.ca/~walld/NUNSEPT2.html**>

Wotherspoon, T., and B. Schissel. 1988. *Marginalization, Decolonization and Voice: Prospects for Aboriginal Education in Canada*. Pan-Canadian Education Research Agenda: Council of Ministers of Education, Canada.

13

Aboriginal Youth, Education, and Labour Market Outcomes[1]

Jeremy Hull

Introduction

Recently, there have been many concerns raised in Canada about labour market shortages and the aging of the labour force. Various potential solutions to these problems have been discussed, including reliance on immigration and retaining older workers in the work force. Within this discussion little attention has been paid to another potential resource—the Aboriginal population. Compared to the general Canadian population, the Aboriginal population is young and growing, and it has the potential to partially meet some of the emerging labour market. In some parts of the country, the Aboriginal population makes up a significant share of the potential labour force, especially when demographic trends are projected into the future. In order to fully take advantage of this resource, however, continued improvements will be needed in the education and training of the Aboriginal population. This chapter illustrates another cost associated with lower educational attainment for Aboriginal peoples.

The Aboriginal Population: Younger and Growing

The age structure of the Aboriginal population[2] is very different from that of the general Canadian population, as can be seen in **Figure 13.1**. In this figure the pyramid of the Aboriginal population is super-imposed on the general Canadian population[3] pyramid as of 2001. While the largest age groups among the Canadian population were 35–49 years old, the largest Aboriginal age groups were within the 0–14 age range in 2001. The Canadian population is much older and there are smaller proportions of children in the population, compared to older age groups. By the year 2021 the largest Canadian age cohorts will be over the age of 55. In contrast, the largest Aboriginal age cohorts in 2021 will be 20–34 years old, the ages when people enter the labour force and begin their careers.

The Aboriginal labour force population is projected to grow much more rapidly than the general Canadian population. If these projections hold, the Aboriginal population 15–64 years old will increase rapidly and continuously after 2001, so that by 2026 it will have increased by 48%.[4] During this same 25 year period, the other Canadian population is projected to increase by 18%. In contrast to the Aboriginal population, the other Canadian labour force will reach its peak in about 2016, after which it is not expected to grow. (See **Figure 13.2**.)

Figure 13.1: Population Pyramids: Aboriginal and Canadian Populations in 2001

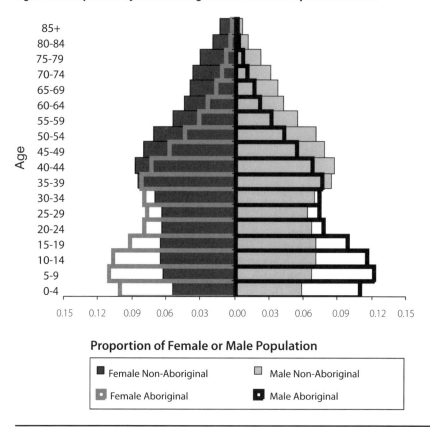

Figure 13.2: Projected Cumulative Growth in the Population 15–64 Years Old by Aboriginal Identity, Canada, 2001–2026

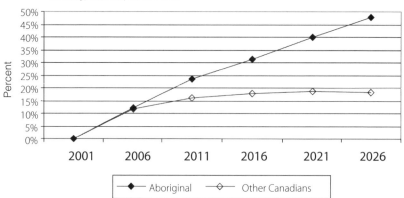

Figure 13.3: Projected Cumulative Growth in the Population 15-29 Years Old by Aboriginal Identity, Canada, 2001–2026

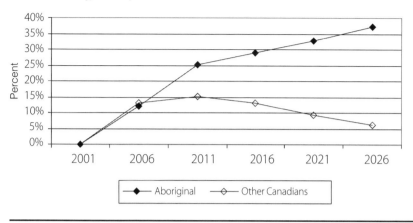

Figure 13.4: Projected Aboriginal Population Turning 15 Years Old per Five-year Time Period, Canada, 2001–2026

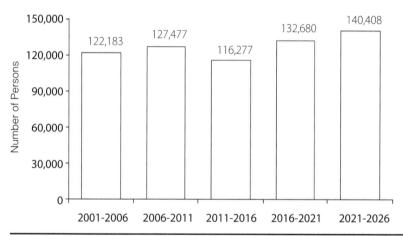

As **Figure 13.1** indicates, the younger Aboriginal population, 15-29 years old, is a relatively large and growing proportion of the population. The population pyramids indicate larger proportions of the Aboriginal population are found in younger age groups. In 2001, 39% of the Aboriginal labour force population[5] was in the 15 to 29 age range, compared to 29% of the other Canadian labour force population. Among the Aboriginal population the younger segment of the labour force, ages 15 to 29, is projected to grow rapidly from 2001 to 2011, and then a little more slowly from 2011 for the next 15 years. By 2026, the younger Aboriginal population is expected to be 37% larger than in 2001. During this same period, the other Canadian population in the 15 to 29 age range is expected to peak in 2011 and then to decline so that it will be only 6% higher in 2026 than it was in 2001. (See **Figure 13.3**.)

Figure 13.5: Projected Aboriginal Share of the Population 15–29 Years Old, Canada and the Prairie Provinces, 2006–2026

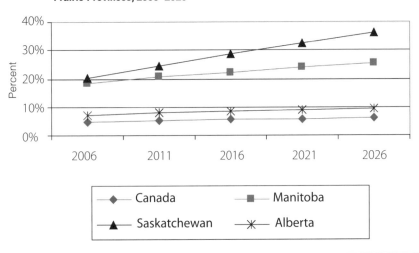

Across Canada it is estimated that about 25,000 Aboriginal youth are turning 15 each year, or more than 125,000 every five years. At this age, most youth are still in school, but they are likely to enter the labour force as they leave school over their next five to ten years. As shown in **Figure 13.4**, the number of Aboriginal youth entering the labour market age population is expected to increase through 2026. Over the course of the twenty-five year period, 2001-2026, more than 600,000 Aboriginal youth will come of age to enter the labour market, with the potential to make a major contribution to the Canadian economy. In each of five provinces—Ontario, Manitoba, Saskatchewan, Alberta, and British Columbia— nearly 100,000 or more Aboriginal youth will turn 15 over the twenty-five year period.

The Aboriginal Population in the Provinces

In 2001, the Aboriginal population was about 4% of the labour force age popu- lation, 15–64 years old, in Canada. As described above, the Aboriginal popula- tion will grow more quickly than the general Canadian population, but it will still only reach about 5% of the total potential labour force by 2026. However, the Aboriginal population is a much larger component of the population of some provinces and regions, especially Saskatchewan, Manitoba and northern Canada. In Saskatchewan, the Aboriginal population already makes up a large share of the total labour force population, and is projected to be 28% of the labour force age group by 2026. In Manitoba, this proportion is expected to reach 22% in 2026, while in Alberta it is expected to reach 8%. In northern Canada, including Yukon, the Northwest Territories and Nunavut, the Aboriginal population makes up a large majority across the whole population.[6]

Figure 13.6: Projected Growth of the Population 15-64 by Identity, 2001-2016, Provinces and Regions with Larger Aboriginal Share of Population Growth

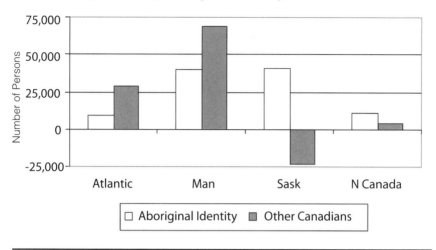

Figure 13.7: Employment Rate of the Population 15–64 By Educational Certification and Identity, Canada 2001

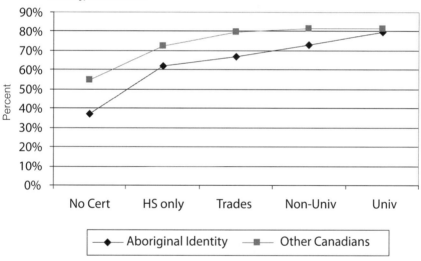

The Aboriginal proportions of the younger age group, 15–29 years old, are even larger. As Illustrated in **Figure 13.5**, 36% of the young labour force population in Saskatchewan is expected to be Aboriginal in 2026. In Manitoba, this proportion is projected to be 28%, while in Alberta, with its larger non-Aboriginal population, it is projected to be 9%. In addition, provincial immigration trends are quite different in these provinces. In Saskatchewan, there would be a projected net loss of labour force age groups if it were not for Aboriginal population growth.

Figure 13.8: Occupational Level of the Aboriginal Population 15-64 Years Old by Educational Certification, Canada 2001

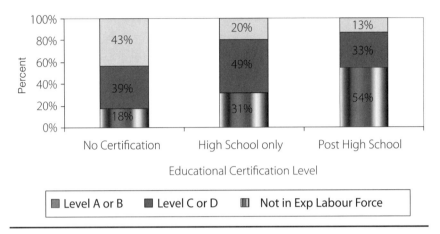

Another way of looking at the importance of the Aboriginal labour force is to consider the Aboriginal component of projected labour force growth. This approach shows that growth of the Aboriginal labour force will make up a substantial part of labour force growth in the Atlantic region, as well as in Saskatchewan, Manitoba and northern Canada between 2001 and 2016. During this period, the Aboriginal component is expected to be about 24% of total labour force population growth in the Atlantic region, about 36% of growth in Manitoba, and about 74% of growth in northern Canada. In Saskatchewan, without Aboriginal population growth there would be a projected decline in the labour force population (see **Figure 13.6**). In other provinces the Aboriginal share of population growth is smaller: 10% in Alberta, 4% in Québec, 3% in British Columbia, and 2% in Ontario. However, a closer look at the regions within these provinces would certainly show that the Aboriginal labour force will be quite important in selected urban and rural areas.

The Role of Education in Labour Market Activity

Past research has shown a strong relationship between education and labour force activity for the Aboriginal population, as well as for the general population (White, et al. 2006). To a large degree, educational attainment reduces the employment gap between the Aboriginal and general Canadian populations. In addition, it has been shown that the key factors are completion of various levels of educational certification, such as a high school graduation certificate or a post-secondary certificate or degree.[7] As illustrated in **Figure 13.7**, the employment rate among the Aboriginal population increases with educational certification, reaching parity with the general population for those with university degrees or certificates, equal to the employment rate of the general Canadian population with this level of education. At lower levels of education, however, there is a gap between the Aboriginal and

Figure 13.9: Percentage of the Population with High School or Higher Certification by Age Group and Identity, Canada 2001

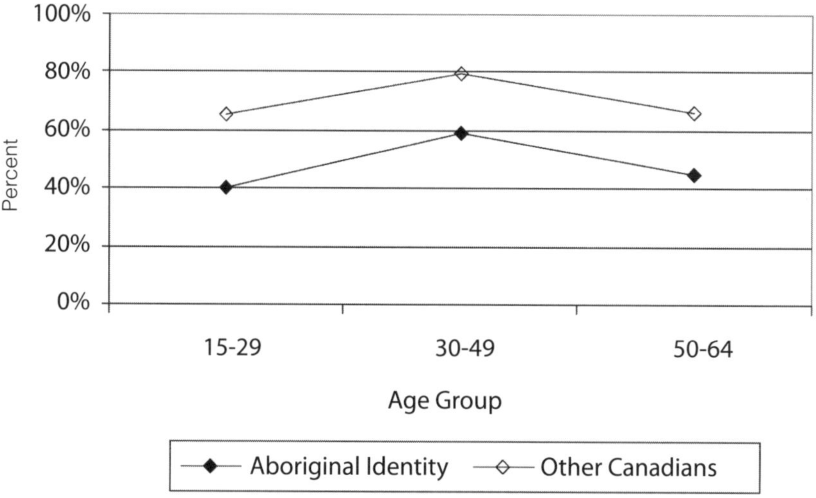

other Canadian employment rates, especially among those without any type of high school or post-secondary certification.

Occupational Skill Levels Are Also Strongly Influenced by Educational Certification

Occupations are often viewed in terms of their required skill levels. These skill levels are closely related to educational qualifications. Levels A and B include management, professional, para-professional, technical, and trades occupations, while levels C and D include semi-skilled and lower skill levels, such as many sales, service, and clerical occupations, processing, assembly, and unskilled labourer occupations. Generally, level A and B occupations require high school completion and either post-secondary training, apprenticeship or other extensive experience and on-the-job training. The relationship between educational certification and occupational skill levels is shown at a broad level in **Figure 13.8**. Among the Aboriginal population without any certification, only 18% have worked in level A or B occupations. Among those with a high school certificate this increases to 31% of the population, while among those with post-secondary certification, the proportion in level A or B occupations increases to 54%. It can also be seen from **Figure 13.8** that a large proportion of those without certification, 43%, were not in the experienced labour force at all, that is they had not been employed during the year prior to the Census.

Figure 13.10: Registered Indian Population with any Secondary or Post-Secondary Certification, Canada, 1991–2001, by Age Group

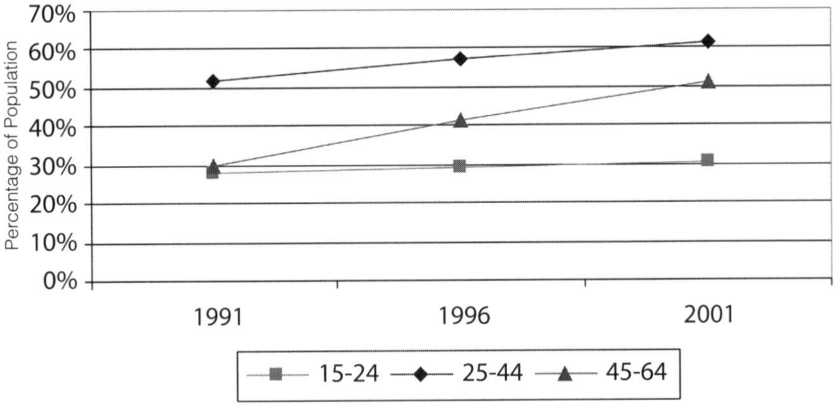

Rates of Educational Certification Among Aboriginal Youth

As can be seen in **Figure 13.9**, the proportion of the young, Aboriginal population with high school or higher levels of certification is low in comparison to the proportion of other Canadians with educational certification. In 2001, only 40% of Aboriginal youth, ages 15–29, had high school or higher certification, compared to 65% of other Canadian youth.[8] Among both the Aboriginal population and other Canadians, these proportions are much higher for those who are 30–49 years old, and the gap between the Aboriginal population and others is somewhat smaller for this age group. Within this age group, 59% of the Aboriginal population and 79% of the other Canadian population have some type of educational certification. This reflects educational patterns in Canada, where many people continue to pursue educational qualifications throughout their lives. This is especially the case among the Aboriginal population, as other research has shown (Hull 2004).

Trends in Educational Attainment

Studies of Aboriginal educational attainment over the past fifteen years have consistently shown increasing educational levels among the Aboriginal population and increasing numbers of Aboriginal students completing high school and attending post-secondary colleges and universities. (See White and Beavon, Chapter 1 and Clement, Chapter 5.) These educational trends are different for different age groups, and are most apparent among the Aboriginal population over the age of 25. As illustrated in **Figure 13.10**, the proportion of the Registered Indian population[9] with any type of secondary or post-secondary certification has been increasing, at different rates, among all age groups. The 25–44 year old population has shown a substantial improvement, while the youngest cohort has

Figure 13.11: Projected Aboriginal Experienced Labour Force 15-64 Years Old in 2016, Comparing Educational Certification Scenarios, Canada

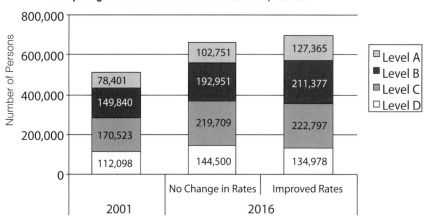

shown a more moderate change. In addition, the trend is that as the older the population group, the higher the proportion who have achieved certification. This shows that the population continues to increase their educational attainment as they age.

Labour Force Participation Increases with Education

When looking at the future Aboriginal labour force it is important to take into account the impact of educational levels. One way to do this is by looking at different scenarios. One scenario would be to assume that Aboriginal educational certification stays at its current level; a second scenario would be to assume Aboriginal educational levels increase as they have done over the past ten years. **Figure 13.11** shows the numbers of Aboriginal people that would be in the labour force in 2016, based on these two scenarios. In 2001 there were about 510,000 Aboriginal people in the experienced labour force.[10] Assuming that the proportions of the Aboriginal population with various levels of education remain the same, it is projected that there will be a little more than 650,000 Aboriginal people in the experienced labour force in 2016. However, if it is assumed that the educational levels of the Aboriginal population will continue to rise as they have over the previous ten years, it is projected that there will be 690,000 Aboriginal people in the labour force in 2016. In other words, there will be approximately 40,000 more Aboriginal people participating in the labour force if Aboriginal educational levels continue to improve than there will be if educational levels do not improve.

The same trend is repeated in the various provinces and regions when we use our two scenarios. The projected numbers of Aboriginal labour force participants in each province or region are shown in **Figure 13.12**. For each province or

Figure 13.12: Projected Labour Force Participants by Educational Scenario, Province or Region, 2001-2016

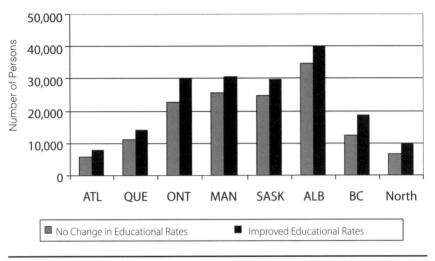

Figure 13.13: Projected Incremental Increase or Decrease in Aboriginal Labour Force Participants Resulting from Improved Educational Certification By Occupational Level, Canada 2001–2016

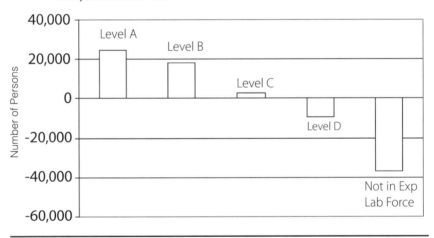

region the different projections for the two educational scenarios are shown. The improved educational scenario is projected to increase the number of Aboriginal labour force participants by more than 7,000 in Ontario by 2016. In the four western provinces, improved educational levels will result in between 5,000 and 6,500 additional Aboriginal labour force participants per province. In northern Canada, the impact is projected to be about 3,000 additional labour force participants, while in Quebec and the Atlantic region, the impact will be about 2,700 and 2,000 respectively.

The Occupational Distribution and Education

Not only will higher educational levels lead to more Aboriginal people in the labour force, it will also lead to increased numbers in higher skill level occupations, and lower numbers in lower skill level occupations. As shown in **Figure 13.13**, the increasing educational levels scenario would result in about 25,000 more Aboriginal people in level A occupations, 18,000 more in level B occupations, and a reduction of about 10,000 in level D occupations. Since the occupations that are most likely to be in demand or to experience labour shortages are in the higher level occupations, the educational trend will help determine the extent to which Aboriginal labour can help meet the need.

Conclusions

We have seen that the Aboriginal labour force is a significant potential resource within Canada. Increased levels of educational certification among the Aboriginal population will pay dividends to the Canadian economy by improving the availability of skilled labour and reducing labour shortages. These improvements will be especially important in certain provinces and regions, particularly in Saskatchewan and Manitoba, northern Canada, Alberta and the Atlantic region. Aboriginal youth, to an even greater degree than other youth, are taking an increasingly long time to complete their education and training, and they continue to both change occupations and upgrade their skills throughout their lives.

Clearly, if we can encourage youth to stay in school and improve the graduation rates, the difficulties that Aboriginal youth experience in entering the labour market will be reduced. As well, various types of post-secondary and adult education need to be made available to the Aboriginal population over the course of their employment and training careers. While post-secondary education institutions and programs have become increasingly flexible in making programs available to mature students, more attention needs to be paid to employer-based training programs that can help integrate Aboriginal youth into the labour force.

We would also argue that a great deal more research needs to be done, particularly industry-specific analyses. This will allow the development of the strategies required to more precisely look at expected skilled labour shortages within local and regional labour markets and target opportunities for recruitment of Aboriginal labour to fill the anticipated demand. Such an analysis would identify specific skills required in the high demand occupations and ways in which the movement of the Aboriginal labour force into high demand occupations can be facilitated, such as through targeted training, recruitment efforts, and removal of job entry barriers.

Endnotes

1 This summary is based largely on the research report, "Aboriginal Youth in the Canadian Labour Market," prepared by Jeremy Hull for Indian and Northern Affairs Canada, Strategic Research & Analysis Directorate, June, 2006. Data for the study are derived from Clatworthy 2007, Statistics Canada 2005 and from the 2001 Census of Canada.

2 Unless otherwise stated, the Aboriginal population referred to in this paper is the population who identified themselves as Aboriginal on the Census of Canada.

3 The Canadian population is the total population, less the Aboriginal population of Canada, and is often referred to as the "other Canadian" population within this article.

4 Preliminary analysis of the 2006 Census of Canada indicates this trend has continued or even slightly sharpened.

5 The term "labour force population" refers to persons potentially available to become particpants in the labour force. This is usually defined as the population between 15 and 64 years of age.

6 Differences in projection methods for the Aboriginal population (Clatworthy) and the Canadian population (Statistics Canada) make it difficult to directly compare these two sets of projection numbers in the North.

7 Other factors, such as age, gender, and geographic location are also important (see Hull 2004).

8 Editor's Note: We use the age range beginning at 15 years as this is recognized as the lower limit for labour market participation. However at this age there are a vast majority of youth that cannot have finished secondary school. This depresses the numbers in the illustration with high school completion.

9 This figure focuses on the population defined as "Registered Indian," that is, those identifying themselves on the Census as registered under the *Indian Act* or a member of a First Nation. This population has been chosen because of the difficulty of comparing the broader Aboriginal population from one census year to another.

10 Editor's Note: By experienced labour force we mean having worked in the previous year.

References

Clatworthy, S. 2007. *Aboriginal Population Projections for Canada, Provinces and Regions, 2001–2026.* Strategic Research & Analysis Directorate. Ottawa: Indian and Northern Affairs Canada.

Hull, J. 2004. *Post-Secondary Education and Labour Market Outcomes Among the Aboriginal Population of Canada, 2001.* Strategic Research & Analysis Directorate. Ottawa: Indian and Northern Affairs Canada.

Statistics Canada. 2005 *Population Projections for Canada, Provinces and Territories, 2005-2031*, Ottawa: Statistics Canada Cat. No. 91-520-XIE.

White, J. and P. Maxim. 2006 "School Completion and Workforce Transition among Urban Aboriginal Youth." In White, et al. *Aboriginal Policy Research: Moving Forward, Making a Difference, Volume IV.* Toronto: Thompson Educational Publishing.

14

Some Estimates of Private and Social Benefits of Improving Educational Attainment Among Registered Indian Youth and Young Adults

Stewart Clatworthy

Introduction

Many studies conducted over the course of the past three decades have documented the large disparity between Aboriginal peoples and other Canadians with respect to educational attainment, labour market outcomes, incomes and income adequacy, health conditions, and a variety of other measures of socio-economic well-being. Most of this research has revealed clear statistical patterns between higher levels of educational attainment and higher levels of socio-economic well-being. Not surprisingly, promoting higher levels of educational attainment among Aboriginal populations has frequently been put forward as a critical step in the process of improving socio-economic conditions among Aboriginal individuals and communities.

A growing body of recent research, conducted among various population groups in several countries, has attempted to determine the extent to which observed statistical associations between education and various socio-economic outcomes reflect "causal" relationships (i.e. that additional education does produce improved socio-economic outcomes). Although more research on this issue is warranted, results to date clearly suggest that higher levels of education produce quite large returns to individuals, in terms of employment, labour market earnings, personal wealth, and other aspects of personal economic well-being (Card 1999, Riddell 2006, Oreopoulos 2006). Collectively, this research has also identified an extensive range of other non-personal or social benefits which are attributable to educational improvements.[1] These broader outcomes include:

- enhanced innovation, knowledge creation, and technological adoption.
- increased productivity and economic growth.
- increased government revenues through taxation.
- improved health and well-being of other family members, including child development (i.e. inter-generational effects).

- improved social cohesion, and enhanced levels of charitable giving, volunteer activity, and other forms of community involvement.
- reduced reliance on social assistance and other social supports and programs.
- reduced levels of criminal activity.

Purpose of the Study

Although statistical patterns between educational attainment and personal outcomes are well-documented, existing research which explores the benefits of educational improvements within the context of Aboriginal peoples in Canada remains quite sparse.[2] This study seeks to provide some preliminary estimates of the potential scale of select benefits (to individuals and to society) that might be realized through future improvements in the levels of education among one segment of Canada's Aboriginal population, Registered Indians. The specific benefits examined include:

- employment outcomes and employment earnings.
- taxation revenues associated with employment incomes.
- savings in government transfer payments to individuals.
- reductions in criminal activity and the costs of crime.

Approach and Data

Estimates of the potential impacts of improvements in education are derived using a series of projections designed to estimate the incremental changes in select outcomes (e.g. employment, employment earnings) that are expected to result from specific changes to the future level of educational attainment achieved by the Registered Indian population 15 or more years of age. The projections are configured using baseline data for the year 2001 and span a twenty-five-year period from 2002 to 2026. Impacts of assumed improvements in educational attainment or of assumed changes in the outcomes associated with specific levels of educational attainment (e.g. changes in the employment rate associated with individuals who finish high school) are estimated using a comparative approach.

A *baseline* projection scenario (referred to as *Growth and Aging*) is configured to examine various outcomes associated with the "hypothetical" context in which future levels of educational attainment achieved by Registered Indians (given their age, gender, location of residence [on- off-reserve], and province or region) remain unchanged from those observed in the baseline year, 2001.[3] This scenario is used to identify changes over time in the distribution of the population by education level, as well as changes in specific outcomes (e.g. the volume of employment) that would be expected to result solely from the growth and aging of the population. Other scenarios are then developed which systematically alter projection assumptions concerning future levels of educational attainment of the population (or assumptions concerning the outcomes associated with individuals who acquire a specific level of education). By comparing the results of these other scenarios with those of the baseline scenario, estimates of the incremental impact on outcomes (e.g. the level of employment) associated with various (assumed) levels of improvement in educational attainment or (assumed) changes in other factors (e.g. improvements in the employment rates) are obtained. Assumptions associated with the various projection scenarios examined in this study are described in some detail in later sections of this report.

The future population estimates, required to support the outcome projections, derive from a recent series of population projections prepared by Clatworthy (2007) for Indian and Northern Affairs Canada (INAC) and Canada Mortgage and Housing Corporation (CMHC). These projections were constructed for the Registered Indian population, as identified by the 2001 Census of Canada, and provide annual estimates of the future population by age, gender, location (on- or off- reserve) and province or region of residence for the period spanning 2002 to 2026.[4]

Patterns of educational attainment of the Registered Indian population and statistical relationships between educational attainment and various outcomes derive from analyses of data from several sources, including the 1996 and 2001 Censuses of Canada, the Canadian Centre for Justice Statistics (CCJS) and Revenue Canada.

Custom tabulations from the 1996 and 2001 Censuses have been used to identify the baseline (2001) distribution of the Registered Indian population by level of educational attainment, as well as changes to this distribution between 1996 and 2001. Estimates of employment rates, average employment incomes, and average transfer payment incomes by level of educational attainment were also derived from analysis of 2001 Census data.

CCJS data from the 1996 snapshot of inmates and 1997 to 2001 data on "admissions to custody" have been used to estimate baseline (2001) incarceration rates of Registered Indians by age, gender, educational attainment, and region.[5] Additional CCJS data concerning federal and provincial custodial costs for 2001 have been used to estimate the average annual cost of maintenance for those held in custody. Estimates of other "non-custodial" costs of crime and justice (e.g. policing, court, and legal costs) prepared for this study rely upon data and analysis reported by Brantingham and Easton (1998).

Estimates of taxation impacts derive from the application of provincial/territorial marginal tax rates for 2001, as identified by Revenue Canada.

Educational Attainment and Employment Among Registered Indians

As noted previously, higher levels of employment and higher employment earnings represent two of the most widely researched and documented benefits ascribed to additional education.[6] As a prelude to examining the potential impacts on employment and employment earnings of improvements in educational attainment, this section of the report provides a brief overview of the level of educational attainment of the Registered Indian population in 2001, as well as indicators of the employment levels and employment earnings associated with those who have achieved specific levels of educational attainment.

Levels of Educational Attainment in 2001

For the purposes of this study, educational attainment data collected by the Census has been configured to distinguish among three groups.[7] These groups include those with:

- Less than High School (including those who have not attained a high school diploma/certificate, or equivalent, and who also have not pursued post-secondary education)
- High School or Post-Secondary Non-University (including those who have graduated high school or pursued post-secondary education but have not attained a university degree)
- University Degree (including those who have attained one or more university degrees at the Bachelor's, Master's or Doctoral level)

Table 14.1 identifies the distribution of the Registered Indian population aged 15 or more years by level of educational attainment, age, and gender. Comparable data for the non-Aboriginal population are also contained in the table. As noted in many earlier studies, the table reveals that sizable gaps in educational attainment existed between Registered Indian and non-Aboriginal individuals, regardless of age and gender. In 2001, less than one-half (about 49%) of the Registered Indian population reported a high school certificate or higher level of education (i.e. some post-secondary education, including university degrees) compared to about 69% of the non-Aboriginal population (a gap of about 20 percentage points). Disparity in terms of educational attainment was greater among males than females and greater among youth (i.e. those 15 to 24 years) than older cohorts.

Table 14.1 also reveals that the proportion reporting high school or higher levels of education was highest among those aged 25 to 39 years, a characteristic common to both the Registered Indian and non-Aboriginal populations. This situation, of course, reflects the fact that many individuals continue to pursue education as young adults. Prior researchers (e.g. Hull, 2005) have observed that rates of school attendance among young adults (i.e. the population aged 25 to 39 years) tend to be considerably higher among Registered Indians than non-Aboriginals, as Registered Indians, who are more likely leave school during their youth, are also more likely to return to school later.

As illustrated in **Table 14.2**, educational attainment among Registered Indians was sharply lower for those living on-, as opposed to off-reserve, among both

Table 14.1: Distribution of Registered Indian and Non-Aboriginal Population Aged 15 or More Years by Level of Educational Attainment, Age, and Gender, Canada, 2001

Age Group	Registered Indian			Non-Aboriginal		
	Less than High School (%)	High School or Post-Secondary Non-University (%)	University Degree (%)	Less than High School (%)	High School or Post-Secondary Non-University (%)	University Degree (%)
Both Genders						
Total	51.4	44.7	3.9	30.8	53.5	15.7
15–24 years	69.4	29.9	0.7	41.7	52.7	5.7
25–39 years	38.0	56.8	5.1	15.7	60.3	24.0
40–64 years	45.8	48.7	5.5	26.5	55.9	17.5
65+ years	82.2	16.4	1.3	57.1	35.6	7.3
Males						
Total	54.3	43.0	2.7	31.0	52.6	16.4
15–24 years	72.4	27.2	0.4	44.5	51.3	4.2
25–39 years	41.2	55.3	3.4	17.6	60.1	22.4
40–64 years	48.1	47.9	4.0	26.5	54.1	19.4
65+ years	81.8	16.5	1.7	53.9	35.4	10.7
Females						
Total	49.0	46.2	4.9	30.7	54.2	15.1
15–24 years	66.5	32.6	0.9	38.7	54.2	7.1
25–39 years	35.3	58.1	6.6	13.9	60.6	25.5
40–64 years	43.9	49.3	6.8	26.6	57.7	15.7
65+ years	82.6	16.4	1.0	59.5	35.8	4.7

Source: Custom tabulations from the 2001 Census of Canada

males and females and all age groups. Individuals reporting high school or higher levels of education formed about 41% of the population on-reserve and about 55% of the population living off-reserve. Registered Indian females reported higher levels of education than males both on- and off-reserve.

Recent Changes in Educational Attainment

Hull's (2005) recent study of educational attainment and labour market outcomes provides a detailed descriptive analysis of changes in levels of educational attainment among Registered Indians between 1996 and 2001.[8] His analysis reveals that although some improvements in the overall educational attainment of Registered Indians appears to have occurred during this time frame, larger education improvements were realized by non-Aboriginals resulting in an increase in the education gap between the two populations.

Table 14.2: Distribution of Registered Indian Population Aged 15 or More Years by Level of Education Attainment, Age, Gender and Location of Residence, Canada, 2001

Age Group	On-reserve			Off-reserve		
	Less than High School (%)	High School or Post-Secondary Non-University (%)	University Degree (%)	Less than High School (%)	High School or Post-Secondary Non-University (%)	University Degree (%)
Both Genders						
Total	58.9	38.8	2.3	44.7	50.0	5.3
15–24 years	75.9	23.9	0.3	62.9	35.9	1.1
25–39 years	46.1	51.3	2.6	31.3	61.5	7.2
40–64 years	51.4	44.5	4.1	41.0	52.2	6.8
65+ years	86.4	12.8	0.8	76.8	21.2	2.0
Males						
Total	61.2	37.4	1.4	47.0	48.8	4.1
15–24 years	78.0	21.9	0.2	66.3	32.9	0.8
25–39 years	49.2	49.3	1.5	33.6	61.1	5.3
40–64 years	53.6	44.0	2.5	42.2	52.1	5.7
65+ years	86.6	12.9	0.5	73.9	22.5	3.7
Females						
Total	56.5	40.2	3.2	43.0	50.8	6.2
15–24 years	73.7	25.9	0.3	59.9	38.7	1.5
25–39 years	43.0	53.2	3.7	29.6	61.8	8.7
40–64 years	49.1	45.1	5.8	40.2	52.2	7.5
65+ years	86.4	12.5	1.1	78.6	20.4	1.0

Source: Custom tabulations from the 2001 Census of Canada

With respect to structuring assumptions for the outcome projection models developed for this study, a particular focus has been placed on changes in educational attainment for the population aged 15 to 39 years. This focus results from the view that the vast majority of future improvements to the education level of the Registered Indian population are likely to result from the achievement of higher levels of attainment by the current and future populations of youth and young adults. This view is supported by recent analyses of school attendance rates across age groups.[9]

Data from the 1996 and 2001 censuses reveal relatively small improvements in educational attainment for the Registered Indian population aged 15 to 39 years. The proportion of this age group that reported high school or higher levels of education increased from about 46.6% to 48.7% during the five-year period (an average annual rate of increase in the proportion of about 0.9%). By way of comparison, the proportion of the non-Aboriginal population reporting high school or higher levels of education was about 74.4% in 2001, roughly 26 percentage points higher than that of the same Registered Indian cohort. Assuming that future improvements in education among the 15 to 39 years cohort continue at the pace observed for the 1996 to 2001 period, the proportion of Registered Indians in this age group that achieved high school or higher levels of education would approach about 61% within twenty-five years.

In addition to the baseline scenario, in which educational attainment levels of the Registered Indian population remain constant (given age, gender, location of residence, and province or region), the projection models developed for this study explore two additional scenarios in which levels of educational attainment gradually improve among cohorts aged 15 to 39 years over the course the projection period. The level of education improvement in the initial scenario (referred to as *Education Gap Reduced by One-Half*) extrapolates the trend observed for this age group during the 1996 to 2001 period, such that the proportion of this segment of the population that has achieved high school or higher levels of education increases (at a constant rate) to about 61% by 2026.[10] If no further improvements in non-Aboriginal education levels occurred during the period, this scenario would reduce the current Aboriginal/non-Aboriginal education gap for this age group by about one-half.[11]

A second, and much more ambitious, scenario assumes that levels of educational attainment among Registered Indians aged 15 to 39 years increase (at a constant rate) over the course of the twenty-five-year period to reach the same levels as those reported by the non-Aboriginal population in 2001. Under this scenario (referred to as *Education Gap Fully Closed*), the proportion of the Registered Indian population (aged 15–39 years) with high school or higher levels of education would rise by about 26 percentage points to 75% by 2026.

Under all of the scenarios, future improvements in education are assumed to occur only among cohorts comprising the population aged 15–39 years. Among individuals forming older age cohorts, levels of educational attainment are assumed to remain unchanged over the course of their remaining lifespan.

Employment Rates by Level of Education in 2001

The projection models estimate future volumes of employment by applying assumed employment rates to estimates of the future population by level of educational attainment, age, gender, location of residence (on- or off-reserve) and province or region. Employment rates for these various segments of the Registered Indian population were calculated from 2001 Census data.[12]

National level estimates of 2001 employment rates by education, age, and gender are provided for the Registered Indian populations living on- and off-reserve in **Table 14.3**. The table also provides comparable rates for the non-Aboriginal population. The table reveals several previously documented patterns. First, rates of employment are considerably higher among Registered Indians who

Table 14.3: Employment Rate of Registered Indian and Non-Aboriginal Population Aged 15 or More Years by Level of Educational Attainment, Age, Gender, and Location of Residence, Canada, 2001

Age Group	Employment Rate (%)					
	Males			Females		
	Less than High School	High School or Post-Secondary Non-University	University Degree	Less than High School	High School or Post-Secondary Non-University	University Degree
Registered Indians On-reserve						
15–24	13.8	39.4	37.5	11.5	38.1	68.8
25–39	38.1	58.8	84.7	32.5	60.7	83.9
40–64	36.7	60.7	80.8	28.3	63.2	82.9
65+	6.9	17.6	28.6	4.0	17.8	28.6
Total	26.2	55.1	80.7	20.9	56.3	82.1
Registered Indians Off-reserve						
15–24	25.4	58.6	60.0	21.0	49.5	72.6
25–39	53.2	71.7	86.6	34.8	60.1	79.0
40–64	43.5	64.6	83.3	29.3	56.7	77.3
65+	6.9	17.1	22.2	3.9	11.6	18.6
Total	37.2	66.6	81.8	25.8	56.3	77.5
Non-Aboriginal (All Locations)						
15–24	42.8	68.9	67.3	37.5	67.7	72.0
25–39	76.8	87.6	88.7	56.4	76.0	81.2
40–64	66.6	81.1	84.5	46.7	69.8	77.3
65+	10.0	14.1	22.2	3.1	6.2	11.6
Total	48.6	74.6	79.5	31.7	64.2	74.1

Source: Custom tabulations from the 2001 Census of Canada

have achieved higher levels of education, regardless of age, gender and location of residence. Among Registered Indian males living on-reserve, for example, those who had attained high school diplomas or completed some post-secondary education (but without university degrees) reported employment rates about 2.1 times higher that those who had not completed high school. Those with university degrees were roughly 3.1 times more likely to be employed than those who had not completed high school. Employment rate differentials by education were of similar magnitude among females on-reserve and among both gender groups off-reserve.

Gender differentials in Registered Indian employment rates were not pronounced on-reserve. In the off-reserve context, however, employment rates of Registered Indian males exceeded those of females among nearly all age and education groups.

Table 14.3 also reveals that sizable employment rate differentials between Registered Indians (both on- and off-reserve) and non-Aboriginals also existed in 2001. Employment rate differentials between Registered Indians and non-Aboriginals, however, were strongly patterned over age and education groups. Quite large gaps in employment rates existed among younger cohorts and among those with lower levels of educational attainment. Disparity in employment rates was substantially lower among those who had achieved high school or higher levels of education. Among those with university degrees, employment rate differences between the Registered Indian and non-Aboriginal populations were very small (and for some groups in the opposite direction).

Although economic theory suggests that overall employment levels could be enhanced by improvements in education, employment levels are also greatly affected by a number of factors (e.g. commodity prices, levels of international demand) which influence the strength of national and regional economies, as well as other factors that affect the quantity of labour required as inputs to production (e.g. technology). As such, forecasting future employment levels and employment rates is extremely difficult. Recent trends in changes in employment rates do not provide a reasonable basis for forecasting future rates.

The employment projections developed for this study have been configured to examine three scenarios concerning the future employment rates of Registered Indians. The initial scenario assumes that the employment rates of Registered Indians remain constant at levels observed for 2001, given level of education, age, gender, location of residence and province/region (***Employment Rates Constant***). A second scenario assumes that future employment rates of Registered Indians improve at a constant rate throughout the projection period to the extent that the observed 2001 employment rate gaps between Registered Indians and non-Aboriginals are reduced by one-half (***Employment Rate Gap Reduced by One-Half***). These improvements are assumed to occur both on- and off-reserve in all provinces or regions, and among all education, age, and gender groups. A third scenario assumes that future employment rates of Registered Indians (given education, age, gender, location and province/region) converge to the levels observed for the non-Aboriginal population in 2001 (***Employment Rate Gap Fully Closed***).

The three employment rate scenarios, when combined with the three scenarios concerning future education levels of the population, result in nine possible projection models. For the purposes of this study, five specific projection models were constructed to present the range of employment outcomes associated with altering the educational attainment and employment rate assumptions.

Assumptions associated with these projection models are identified in **Table 14.4**. Model 1 represents the baseline ***Growth and Aging*** scenario discussed previously. Models 2 and 3 allow one to estimate the incremental impacts on employ-

Table 14.4: Employment Projection Scenarios

Model Assumptions		Educational Attainment		
		Constant	Gap Reduced by One-Half	Gap Fully Closed
Employment Rate	Constant	Model 1 *Growth and Aging*	Model 2	Model 3
	Gap Reduced by One-Half		Model 4	
	Gap Fully Closed			Model 5

ment that would result solely from specific levels of improvement in educational attainment. Models 4 and 5 allow one to estimate the incremental impact on employment that would result from not only specific improvements in levels of educational attainment but also specific improvements in employment rates.

Employment Projection Results

As noted in many prior studies, the Registered Indian population is characterized by having high fertility rates and a "youthful" demographic structure. These attributes of the population imply that substantial levels of population growth can be expected to occur over the course of the projection period. Much of this growth is expected to occur among the population aged 15 or more years, a population commonly used to describe the labour force age group. **Table 14.5**, which provides a summary of the projected changes in the size of the Registered Indian population aged 15 or more years, reveals several important dimensions of the growth and compositional changes which are expected to occur among the labour force age group over the course of the 2002 to 2026 time period. During this period, the size of the Registered Indian labour force age group is expected to increase by about 284,580 individuals, representing an increase of about 68.5% at the national level. Although significant levels of growth are projected to occur both on- and off-reserve, more than two-thirds (about 67.7%) of this growth is forecast to occur on-reserve.

Quite pronounced differences in growth of the Registered Indian labour force age group are also expected among provinces or regions. Growth is expected to occur much more rapidly in the Prairie region, which is expected to account for a majority (about 54.5%) of national growth in the labour force age group during the period.

Table 14.5: Registered Indian Population Aged 15 or More Years by Location of Residence and Province/Region, Canada, 2001 and 2026 (projected)

Province/Region	Population Aged 15 or More Years			
	2001	2026	Change	%
	On-reserve			
Atlantic Region	10,285	19,705	9,420	91.6
Quebec	31,333	56,915	25,582	81.6
Ontario	39,192	70,381	31,189	79.6
Manitoba	34,181	66,321	32,140	94.0
Saskatchewan	28,942	65,760	36,818	127.2
Alberta	27,109	51,497	24,388	90.0
British Columbia	34,927	62,546	27,619	79.1
Northern Canada	8,748	14,362	5,614	64.2
National Total	214,717	407,487	192,770	89.8
Province/Region	Off-reserve			
Atlantic Region	8,846	10,665	1,819	20.6
Quebec	13,303	14,450	1,147	8.6
Ontario	52,365	68,751	16,386	31.3
Manitoba	24,895	43,448	18,553	74.5
Saskatchewan	23,689	43,497	19,808	83.6
Alberta	29,690	53,277	23,587	79.4
British Columbia	43,400	52,431	9,031	20.8
Northern Canada	4,329	5,807	1,478	34.1
National Total	200,517	292,326	91,809	45.8
Province/Region	Total (On- and Off-reserve)			
Atlantic Region	19,131	30,370	11,239	58.7
Quebec	44,636	71,365	26,729	59.9
Ontario	91,557	139,132	47,575	52.0
Manitoba	59,076	109,769	50,693	85.8
Saskatchewan	52,631	109,257	56,626	107.6
Alberta	56,799	104,774	47,975	84.5
British Columbia	78,327	114,977	36,650	46.8
Northern Canada	13,077	20,169	7,092	54.2
National Total	415,234	699,813	284,579	68.5

Source: Custom tabulations from the 2001 Census and Clatworthy (2007).

The age structure of the Registered Indian labour force age group is also projected to undergo significant changes during the period. As revealed in **Table 14.6**, a large majority of the projected growth over the twenty-five-year period is expected to occur among older segments of the labour force age group. The population of youth and young adults (i.e. those 15 to 39 years), which formed about 61% of the labour force age group in 2001, is expected to account for only about 35% of growth during the projection period.

Table 14.6: Projected Growth of the Registered Indian Population Aged 15 or More Years by Age Group, Canada, 2001–2026 (Projected)

Age Group	Growth 2001-26	% of Growth
15–24 years	30,731	10.8
25–39 years	67,960	23.9
40–64 years	118,017	41.5
65 or more years	67,871	23.8
Total 15 or more years	284,579	100.0

Source: Custom tabulations from the 2001 Census and Clatworthy (2007).

Table 14.7: Registered Indian Population Aged 15 or More Years Residing On- and Off-reserve Showing Distribution by Age Group, Canada, 2001–2026 (Projected)

Age Group	Year					
	2001	2006	2011	2016	2021	2026
On-reserve						
Total 15 or more years	214,717	255,937	298,498	334,739	371,073	407,487
% 15–24 years	27.2	29.7	29.4	26.1	23.0	22.0
% 25–39 years	34.0	29.6	28.6	30.6	32.7	31.5
% 40–64 years	31.3	33.0	33.8	34.1	33.7	34.0
% 65 or more years	7.5	7.7	8.3	9.3	10.6	12.6
Off-reserve						
Total 15 or more years	200,517	225,555	249,704	267,959	281,492	292,326
% 15–24 years	24.9	24.5	24.2	21.9	18.7	16.9
% 25–39 years	37.2	32.6	29.7	29.5	30.6	29.9
% 40–64 years	32.5	36.5	38.5	39.1	38.8	38.3
% 65 or more years	5.4	6.4	7.6	9.5	12.0	14.9
Total (On- and Off-reserve)						
Total 15 or more years	415,234	481,492	548,202	602,698	652,565	699,813
% 15–24 years	26.1	27.3	27.0	24.2	21.2	19.9
% 25–39 years	35.5	31.0	29.1	30.1	31.8	30.8
% 40–64 years	31.9	34.6	35.9	36.3	35.9	35.8
% 65 or more years	6.5	7.1	8.0	9.4	11.2	13.5

Source: Custom tabulations from the 2001 Census and Clatworthy (2007).

More detailed information concerning projected changes in the age structure of the labour force age group over the projection period is presented in **Table 14.7**. As indicated in the table, shifts in the age composition toward older age cohorts are expected to occur both on- and off-reserve. These shifts are forecast to be more pronounced off-reserve. One important implication of this shift to older cohorts is that the contribution of education improvements among youth and young adults to educational attainment levels of the labour force age group are likely to diminish over time, as those achieving higher levels of attainment form a declining segment of the labour force age population.

Effects of Growth and Aging

As discussed previously, levels of educational attainment and employment rates are significantly higher among cohorts aged 25 to 64 years, a group commonly viewed as the *prime* labour force age group. One of the consequences of the structure of education and employment over age groups is that the processes of population "growth and aging" can (in the absence of changes in other factors) contribute to shifts in the education composition of the labour force age group, as well as changes in employment volumes (i.e. the number employed). The extent of the effects on educational attainment and employment can be estimated from the results of Model 1, a model in which educational attainment levels and employment rates are assumed to remain constant (given age, gender, location and province or region).

Impacts on Educational Attainment

Projection results for this model reveal that growth and aging would result in relatively small improvements in the level of educational attainment of the Registered Indian labour force age group over the period. The proportion of the population aged 15 or more years reporting high school or higher levels of education would rise from 48.6% in 2001 to about 52.3% by 2026. The share reporting university degrees would increase from about 3.9% in 2001 to about 4.1% by 2026. In other words, maintaining current levels of educational attainment among Registered Indian youth and young adults would have a relatively small impact on the educational profile of the labour force age group in 2026.

Impacts on Employment

Projected employment under the Model 1 scenario is presented in **Figure 14.1**. Growth and aging of the population would result in an increase in the number of Registered Indians employed from about 176,200 in 2001 to about 286,800 by 2026 (an increase of 110,600 individuals or roughly 63%). Employment on-reserve under this scenario is projected to rise from about 77,000 (in 2001) to about 146,500 (in 2026), an increase of roughly 90%.[13] Off-reserve employment during the period would rise by roughly 41% from about 93,600 to about 131,400.

Impacts of Improving Education Outcomes

Results from projection Models 2 and 3 provide the basis for estimating the incremental impacts of hypothetical improvements in educational attainment among youth and young adults on Registered Indian employment. As expected, the levels of educational attainment of the Registered Indian labour force age group would improve significantly under both of these scenarios over the course of the projection period. As revealed in **Table 14.8**, the proportion of the population attaining high school or higher levels of education under the Model 2 scenario would rise from 48.6% in 2001 to 61.7% and the share attaining at least one university degree would rise to about 10.2% (about 6.3 percentage points above the share in 2001).

Figure 14.1: Registered Indian Employment Under Model 1 ("Growth and Aging") Scenario by Location of Residence, Canada, 2001-2026 (Projected)

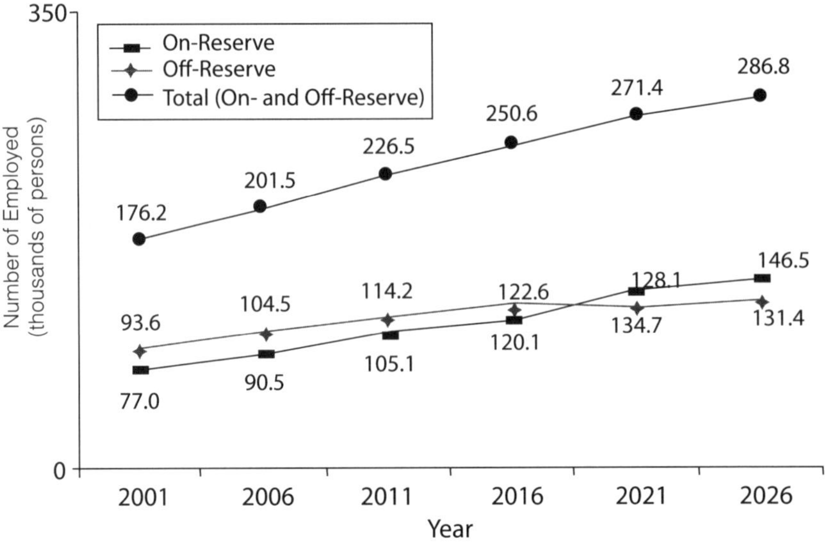

Source: Projections based on analysis of data from the 2001 Census and Clatworthy (2007)

Under the Model 3 scenario, the proportion of the labour force age population attaining high school or higher levels of education would rise to about 68.6%. Those with university degrees would form about 18% of the labour force age group in 2026.

Improvements in educational attainment among the population of youth and young adults would result in significant incremental employment assuming current employment rates remain unchanged. As revealed in **Table 14.9**, a one-half reduction in the current Registered Indian/non-Aboriginal education gap among youth and young adults over the projection period (Model 2) is projected to result in additional employment of 29,300 Registered Indians in year 2026. This represents an incremental impact (resulting entirely from education improvements) of about 16.6% over the employment level in 2001. Eliminating the current Registered Indian/non-Aboriginal education gap among youth and young adults during the period (Model 3) would produce incremental employment (associated with education improvements) of about 49,400 Registered Indians in year 2026, an increase of about 28.0% over the employment level in 2001. About three-quarters of the projected incremental employment resulting from education improvements would occur among on-reserve residents.

As noted previously, future Registered Indian population growth is projected to occur most rapidly in the Prairie region. As revealed in **Table 14.10**, the projected employment impacts associated with improving educational attainment among Registered Indian youth and young adults are also expected to be most pronounced in this region. About 53% of the incremental employment growth associated

Table 14.8: Distribution of the Registered Indian Population Aged 15 or More Years Attaining High School or Higher Levels of Education by Projection Scenario, Canada, 2001 and 2026 (Projected)

Projection Model	Educational Attainment	
	High School or Higher (including University Degree) (%)	University Degree (%)
Baseline (2001)	48.6	3.9
Projection Model	2026	
Model 1—*Growth and Aging*	52.3	4.0
Model 2—*Education Gap Reduced by One-Half*	61.7	10.2
Model 3—*Education Gap Fully Closed*	68.6	18.0

Source: Projections based on analysis of data from the 2001 Census and Clatworthy (2007).

Table 14.9: Incremental Registered Indian Employment Resulting From Assumed Improvements in Educational Attainment Among Youth and Young Adults by Location of Residence, Canada, 2002–2026 (Projected)

Projected Employment Impact 2002-2026	Model 1— *Growth and Aging*	Model 2— *Education Gap Reduced by One Half*	Model 3— *Education Gap Fully Closed*
On-reserve			
Incremental Employment (×1000)	69.5	21.9	36.1
% Increase in Employment (over 2001)	*90.3*	*28.5*	*46.9*
Off-reserve			
Incremental Employment (×1000)	37.9	6.6	12.1
% Increase in Employment (over 2001)	*40.5*	*7.1*	*12.9*
National Total			
Incremental Employment (×1000)	110.6	29.3	49.4
% Increase in Employment (over 2001)	*62.8*	*16.6*	*28.0*

Note: The incremental employment estimates reported for Models 2 and 3 reflect growth that results only from assumed changes in educational attainment among youth and young adults. This growth is in addition to that projected under Model 1 (i.e. ***growth and aging*** scenario).

Source: Projections based on analysis of data from the 2001 Census and Clatworthy (2007).

with improvements in education is projected to occur in the Prairie provinces. The projected impacts of education improvements are especially pronounced in Manitoba and Saskatchewan.

Table 14.10: Incremental Registered Indian Employment Resulting From Assumed Improvements in Educational Attainment Among Youth and Young Adults by Province/Region, Canada, 2002–2026 (Projected)

Projected Employment Impact 2002-2026	Model 1— *Growth and Aging*	Model 2— *Education Gap Reduced by One-Half*	Model 3— *Education Gap Fully Closed*
Atlantic Region			
Incremental Employment (×1000)	3.6	0.6	1.1
% Increase in Employment (over 2001)	*46.7*	*7.8*	*14.5*
Quebec			
Incremental Employment (×1000)	10.5	4.3	7.0
% Increase in Employment (over 2001)	*54.4*	*22.6*	*36.5*
Ontario			
Incremental Employment (×1000)	19.0	4.1	7.1
% Increase in Employment (over 2001)	*41.6*	*9.1*	*15.6*
Manitoba			
Incremental Employment (×1000)	19.5	6.0	10.0
% Increase in Employment (over 2001)	*88.8*	*27.1*	*45.6*
Saskatchewan			
Incremental Employment (×1000)	20.6	5.2	8.6
% Increase in Employment (over 2001)	*118.5*	*29.7*	*49.6*
Alberta			
Incremental Employment (×1000)	20.8	4.5	7.6
% Increase in Employment (over 2001)	*82.6*	*17.9*	*30.2*
British Columbia			
Incremental Employment (×1000)	13.5	3.9	6.8
% Increase in Employment (over 2001)	*40.2*	*11.5*	*20.1*
Northern Canada			
Incremental Employment (×1000)	3.3	0.7	1.1
% Increase in Employment (over 2001)	*57.3*	*12.6*	*20.0*
National Total			
Incremental Employment (×1000)	110.6	29.3	49.4
% Increase in Employment (over 2001)	*62.8*	*16.6*	*28.0*

Note: The incremental employment estimates reported for Models 2 and 3 reflect growth that results only from assumed changes in educational attainment among youth and young adults. This growth is in addition to that projected under Model 1 (i.e. *growth and aging* scenario).

Source: Projections based on analysis of data from the 2001 Census and Clatworthy (2007).

Impacts of Improving Employment Rates

The report's previous discussion of employment rates noted that with the exception of those who had attained university degrees, rates of employment among Registered Indians lag behind those of non-Aboriginals. While improvements in education are expected to result in improvements in Registered Indian employment rates (as those who attain higher levels of education enjoy higher levels of

Table 14.11: Incremental Registered Indian Employment Resulting From Assumed Improvements in Educational Attainment, Among Youth and Young Adults, and Employment Rates Canada, 2002–2026 (Projected)

Projected Employment Impact 2002-2026	Model 1— *Growth and Aging*	Model 4— *Education and Employment Rate Gaps Reduced by One Half*	Model 5— *Education and Employment Rate Gaps Fully Closed*
On Reserve			
Incremental Employment (×1000)	69.5	62.2	109.9
% Increase in Employment (over 2001)	*90.3*	*80.9*	*142.7*
Off Reserve			
Incremental Employment (×1000)	37.9	28.8	53.3
% Increase in Employment (over 2001)	*40.5*	*30.8*	*56.9*
National Total			
Incremental Employment (×1000)	110.6	94.3	169.0
% Increase in Employment (over 2001)	*62.8*	*53.5*	*95.9*

Note: The incremental employment estimates reported for Models 4 and 5 reflect growth that results from both assumed changes in educational attainment among youth and young adults and assumed changes in Registered Indian employment rates. This growth is in addition to that projected under Model 1 (i.e. "growth and aging" scenario). Estimates prepared for on- and off-reserve geographies exclude estimates for Northern Canada. National total estimates include Northern Canada.

Source: Projections based on analysis of data from the 2001 Census and Clatworthy (2007).

employment), considerable incremental increases in Registered Indian employment could also be achieved through reducing the existing employment rate gap between Registered Indians and non-Aboriginals. Projection Models 4 and 5 have been constructed to illustrate the approximate scale of additional employment impacts that could result from improving employment rates.[14] Projection results associated with these models are presented in **Table 14.11**.

Model 4, which assumes that Registered Indian/non-Aboriginal gaps in both educational attainment (among youth and young adults) and employment rates are reduced by one-half over the projection period, estimates an incremental increase in Registered Indian employment at the national level of about 94,300 by 2026 (an incremental gain of roughly 54% over the number employed in 2001). Approximately 69% of the projected employment increase (65,000 individuals) results from the assumed increase in Registered Indian employment rates.[15]

Substantially larger impacts on Registered Indian employment would result from totally eliminating the gaps in employment rates between Registered Indians and non-Aboriginals. Model 5 assumes that Registered Indian employment rates and the levels of education attained by youth and young adults converge over the projection period to match those observed in 2001 for the non-Aboriginal population. The model yields an incremental increase in Registered Indian employment of about 169,000 in 2026. This represents an incremental employment gain of about 96% over 2001 employment estimates. Roughly 71% of the projected increase (119,600 employed individuals) is associated with the model's assumptions concerning improvements in employment rates.[16]

The employment impacts associated with improvements in employment rates (under either Model 4 or 5) would be largest on-reserve. Results from both models suggest that about 62% of the incremental employment gains resulting from assumed improvements in Registered Indian employment rates would accrue to residents on-reserve.

It should be emphasized that the improvements in Registered Indian employment rates on-reserve assumed in Models 4 and 5 would require substantial levels of economic development and job creation over the projection period either on-reserve or in surrounding off-reserve regions accessible to reserve residents. Annual job creation requirements needed to support the assumed levels of improvement in employment rates on-reserve range between 5,270 (Model 4) and 7,180 (Model 5), roughly 1.9 to 2.6 times higher than recent (1996–2001) levels of employment growth on-reserve.[17]

Employment Income Projection Results

The employment projections discussed above have been extended to provide estimates of total employment income. Average employment incomes in 2000 were calculated from the 2001 census for population sub-groups distinguished by level of educational attainment, age, gender, location of residence, and province or region. These estimates were adjusted upward by 3.1% to approximate employment income levels in 2001, the baseline year for the projections.

As revealed in **Table 14.12**, quite large differentials in average employment earnings existed between Registered Indians and non-Aboriginals in 2001, regardless of educational attainment level and gender. Average employment earnings among both Registered Indians and non-Aboriginals were substantially higher among those with higher levels of education. Ratios comparing average employment incomes among education groups (e.g. those with high school or some post-secondary versus those with less than high school) did not differ greatly between Registered Indians and non-Aboriginals. This suggests that in proportionate terms, the employment earnings benefits associated with additional education may be of similar magnitude for both populations.[18]

The average employment earnings estimates calculated for the population reporting employment at the time of the Census, were applied directly to the projected employment estimates to calculate the total employment earnings of the *employed* population. Earnings estimates for the employed population were then adjusted (upwards) to account for the additional employment earnings of the non-employed population. This latter population includes individuals who are temporarily unemployed, as well as others who may work on a seasonal or periodic

Table 14.12: Estimated Average Earnings of Employed Registered Indians and Non-Aboriginals by Level of Educational Attainment and Gender, Canada, 2001

Educational attainment	Average Employment Earnings ($2001)		
	Male	Female	Total
Registered Indian			
Less than High School	17,573	12,019	15,255
High School or Post-Secondary Non-University	24,980	18,230	21,632
University Degree	35,633	26,626	29,744
Non-Aboriginal			
Less than High School	23,970	14,911	20,242
High School or Post-Secondary Non-University	33,785	21,746	27,973
University Degree	48,489	32,851	40,624
Registered Indian/Non-Aboriginal Gap			
Less than High School	6,396	2,892	4,987
High School or Post-Secondary Non-University	8,805	3,516	6,341
University Degree	12,856	6,225	10,880

Note: Estimates of employment earning reported for 2000 have been adjusted to reflect the baseline year 2001.
Source: Custom tabulations from the 2001 Census of Canada.

basis. As configured for this study, the employment projections do not estimate employment associated with this latter population group.[19]

The study presents estimates of total employment earnings for the same five models developed for the employment projections. In the case of Models 1 to 3, future average earnings (given level of educational attainment, age, gender, location of residence and province or region) are assumed to remain constant over the course of the projection period. Model 4 makes a further assumption that the Registered Indian/non-Aboriginal gaps in average employment earnings are reduced by one-half over the course of the projection period. Model 5 explores the scenario where the average employment earnings of Registered Indians fully converge to the levels observed for the non-Aboriginal population in 2000.

All of the projected employment earnings estimates presented in this report are expressed in terms of 2001 constant dollars, unadjusted for future changes associated with real wage growth.[20]

Estimates of the total annual employment earnings of Registered Indians are summarized in **Table 14.13** for each of the five models developed for this study. The table also provides estimates of the incremental amount of employment earnings projected by these models. Incremental earnings have been measured in relation to those expected under the *Growth and Aging* scenario (Model 1).

Total employment earnings attributable to growth and aging of the population are projected to rise from about $5.05 billion annually in 2001 to about $8.34 billion annually in 2026. As revealed in the table, the incremental impacts on employment income associated with improvements in educational attainment among youth and young adults during the period (Models 2 and 3) are projected to be substantial. Assuming that the 2001 education gap between Registered Indian and non-Aboriginal youth and young adults could be reduced by one-half over the period (Model 2), annual total employment earnings of the Registered Indian population in 2026 would increase by an additional $1.35 billion. This represents an incremental increase of about 16.2% over that expected under the growth and aging model (Model 1). Elimination of the education gap among youth and young adults (Model 3) is projected to raise the annual total employment earnings of the Registered Indian population by about $2.3 billion by 2026, an incremental increase of roughly 27.5%.

Models 4 and 5, which also assume reductions in the gaps between Registered Indian and non-Aboriginal employment rates and gaps in average employment earnings, suggest that substantially larger incremental growth in total employment income would result if education improvements were to also be accompanied by improvements in these other dimensions of Registered Indian labour market outcomes. Model 5, for example, which assumes that Registered Indian employment rates and average earnings over the period converge to the 2001 levels observed for the non-Aboriginal population, projects total incremental employment earnings of about $9.25 billion annually in 2026.

Estimates of the cumulative increase in total employment earnings associated with improvements in education (as assumed under Models 2 and 3) are summarized by province or region in **Table 14.14**. Cumulative employment earnings for the 2002 to 2026 period under the growth and aging scenario (Model 1) are projected to total about $172.5 billion.[21] At the national level, cumulative incremental employment income resulting from reducing the education gap among youth and young adults by one-half (Model 2) is projected to total about $15.2 billion over the 2002 to 2026 time period. Fully closing the 2001 education gap among youth and young adults (Model 3) is projected to result in cumulative incremental earnings of about $27.1 billion over the period. Under both scenarios of education improvement, cumulative incremental impacts on employment earnings would be most pronounced in Manitoba and Saskatchewan.

As indicated in **Table 14.15**, the projected impacts of educational improvements on cumulative employment earnings are substantially larger (in both absolute and

Table 14.13: Total Employment Earnings of Registered Indian Population by Projection Model, Canada, 2001-2026 (Projected)

Year	Total Annual Employment Earnings (2001$ Millions)				
	Model 1— Growth and Aging	Model 2— Education Gap Reduced by One-Half	Model 3— Education Gap Fully Closed	Model 4— Education, Employment Rate and Employment Earnings Gaps Reduced by One-Half	Model 5— Education, Employment Rate and Employment Earnings Gaps Fully Closed
2001	5,054.3	5,054.3	5,054.3	5,054.3	5,054.3
2006	5,789.9	5,968.6	6,136.9	6,279.6	7,634.6
2011	6,516.9	6,957.6	7,344.0	7,672.9	9,943.1
2016	7,257.7	7,888.7	8,404.1	9,098.1	12,313.8
2021	7,901.1	8,880.0	9,620.0	10,659.1	15,040.0
2026	8,342.2	9,690.7	10,640.0	12,066.8	17,594.1
Year	Incremental Annual Employment Earnings (2001$ Millions)				
2006	---	178.7	347.0	489.7	1,844.7
2011	---	440.8	827.1	1,156.1	3,426.3
2016	---	631.1	1,146.5	1,840.4	5,056.1
2021	---	979.0	1,719.0	2,758.0	7,139.0
2026	---	1,348.5	2,297.8	3,724.6	9,252.0

Note: As in the case of the employment projection models, Models 2 and 3 assume changes only to the levels of educational attainment of Registered Indian youth and young adults. Employment rates and average earnings are assumed to remain constant (given educational attainment, age, gender, location, and province or region) at levels observed for 2001.

Source: Projections based on analysis of data from the 2001 Census and Clatworthy (2007)

percentage terms) for the population living on-reserve. Roughly two-thirds of incremental earnings are projected to accrue to reserve residents.

Estimates of Income Taxation on Incremental Employment Earnings

To this point, the study has provided some estimates of the approximate impacts on employment and employment earnings that could result from improvements in educational attainment among Registered Indian youth and young adults over the 2002 to 2026 time period. The employment and employment earnings impacts presented previously are primarily private, in that the benefits accrue to individuals. However, a substantial body of research demonstrates that the benefits of educational improvements extend beyond individuals to the broader society. One obvious example, in this regard, relates to the additional income which flows to governments from taxation of higher employment incomes. Although other forms of tax revenue are likely to be positively impacted by the effects of education

Table 14.14: Cumulative Incremental Employment Earnings of Registered Indian Population by Province/Region and Projection Model, Canada, 2002–2026 (Projected)

Province/Region	Model 1—*Growth and Aging* 2002–2026 Cumulative Employment Earnings (2001$ Millions)	2002–2026 Cumulative Incremental Employment Earnings (2001$ Millions)	
		Model 2— *Education Gap Reduced by One-Half*	Model 3— *Education Gap Fully Closed*
Atlantic Region	6,707.0	273.1	526.7
% Increase over Model 1	---	*4.1*	*7.9*
Quebec	16,376.7	1,815.6	3,123.3
% Increase over Model 1	---	*11.1*	*19.1*
Ontario	46,689.7	2,846.9	5,149.6
% Increase over Model 1	---	*6.1*	*11.0*
Manitoba	20,445.9	3,191.3	5,751.8
% Increase over Model 1	---	*15.6*	*28.1*
Saskatchewan	17,832.0	2,417.8	4,277.0
% Increase over Model 1	---	*13.6*	*24.0*
Alberta	25,768.8	1,862.3	3,266.4
% Increase over Model 1	---	*7.2*	*12.7*
British Columbia	31,473.8	2,252.2	4,100.2
% Increase over Model 1	---	*7.2*	*13.0*
Northern Canada	7,168.9	534.0	896.3
% Increase over Model 1	---	*7.4*	*12.5*
National Total	172,462.7	15,193.1	27,091.3
% Increase over Model 1	---	*8.8*	*15.7*

Note: As in the case of the employment projection models, Models 2 and 3 assume changes only to the levels of educational attainment of Registered Indian youth and young adults. Employment rates and average earnings are assumed to remain constant (given educational attainment, age, gender, location, and province or region) at levels observed for 2001.

Source: Projections based on analysis of data from the 2001 Census and Clatworthy (2007).

improvements on employment earnings, this study considers only those impacts associated with incremental income tax revenue.[22]

Estimates of the approximate incremental income taxes on employment earnings resulting from education improvements have been constructed by applying the combined provincial/federal marginal tax rates (for 2001) to the amount of incremental employment earnings projected over the 2002 to 2026 time period. As the average employment income projected by the various models developed for this study ranges from about $19,000 to $26,000 (averaged across all sub-groups), marginal tax rates associated with this income range have been used.[23] These rates are assumed to apply to all incremental employment income projected by the various models and are further assumed to remain constant over the projection period.[24]

Table 14.15: Cumulative Incremental Employment Earnings of Registered Indian Population by Location of Residence and Projection Model, Canada, 2002–2026 (Projected)

Total Employment Earnings	Model 1—*Growth and Aging* 2002-2026 Cumulative Employment Earnings (2001$ Millions)	2002–2026 Cumulative Incremental Employment Earnings (2001$ Millions)	
		Model 2—*Education Gap Reduced by One-Half*	Model 3—*Education Gap Fully Closed*
On-reserve			
Employment Earnings	70,788.7	9,675.2	16,919.0
% Increase over Model 1	---	*13.7*	*23.9*
Off-reserve			
Employment Earnings	94,505.2	4,983.8	9,276.0
% Increase over Model 1	---	*5.3*	*9.8*
National Total			
Employment Earnings	172,462.7	15,193.1	27,091.3
% Increase over Model 1	---	*8.8*	*15.7*

Note: As in the case of the employment projection models, Models 2 and 3 assume changes only to the levels of educational attainment of Registered Indian youth and young adults. Employment rates and average earnings are assumed to remain constant (given educational attainment, age, gender, location, and province or region) at levels observed for 2001. Estimates for on- and off-reserve geographies exclude data for Northern Canada. Estimates for the national total also include data for Northern Canada.

Source: Projections based on analysis of data from the 2001 Census and Clatworthy (2007).

The issue of income taxation on employment earnings is complicated for Registered Indians living on-reserve. While Registered Indians working off-reserve are subject to income taxation in the same fashion as other Canadians, employment income among Registered Indians who both live and work on-reserve is exempt from taxation under Section 87 of the *Indian Act*. There appears to be no formal estimate of the proportion of the employment earnings of Registered Indians living on-reserve that is subject to income taxation. Given this situation, the employment income tax estimates prepared for this study have been based on two scenarios. One scenario assumes that 25% of the employment income earned by reserve residents will be subject to taxation. A second scenario assumes income taxation applies to 75% of the employment incomes of reserve residents.[25]

A summary of the results of the study's analysis of taxation on incremental employment income is presented in **Table 14.16**. Cumulative incremental taxes on employment incomes over the 2002 to 2026 time period associated with population growth and aging (Model 1) are estimated to total roughly $6.4 billion (assuming 25% taxable income on-reserve) to $9.2 billion (assuming 75% taxable income on-reserve). Cumulative taxes on incremental employment income that would result from reducing the Registered Indian/non-Aboriginal education gap

Table 14.16: Cumulative Incremental Increase in Taxes on Employment Income by Projection Model and Location of Residence, Canada, 2002–2026 (Projected)

Location	2002–2026 Cumulative Incremental Increase in Taxes on Employment Income (Millions 2001$)				
	Model 1— Growth and Aging	Model 2— Education Gap Reduced by One-Half	Model 3— Education Gap Fully Closed	Model 4— Education, Employment Rate and Employment Earnings Gaps Reduced by One-Half	Model 5— Education, Employment Rate and Employment Earnings Gaps Fully Closed
On-reserve (25% Taxable)	1,391.1	608.5	1,581.4	1,054.7	4,337.7
% Increase (over Model 1)	---	43.7	113.7	75.8	311.8
On-reserve (75% Taxable)	4,173.2	1,825.6	4,744.2	3,164.2	13,013.0
% Increase (over Model 1)	---	43.7	113.7	75.8	311.8
Off-reserve	4,641.1	1,176.5	3,574.1	2,177.6	8,799.2
% Increase (over Model 1)	---	25.4	77.0	46.9	189.6
Total (On-reserve (25% Taxable))	6,415.3	1,896.7	3,419.7	5,538.9	14,130.4
% Increase (over Model 1)	---	29.6	53.3	86.3	220.3
Total (On-reserve (75% Taxable))	9,197.4	3,113.7	5,529.1	8,701.7	22,805.7
% Increase (over Model 1)	---	33.9	60.1	94.6	248.0

Note: As in the case of the employment projection models, Models 2 and 3 assume changes only to the levels of educational attainment of Registered Indian youth and young adults. Employment rates and average earnings are assumed to remain constant (given educational attainment, age, gender, location, and province or region) at levels observed for 2001. Estimates for on- and off-reserve geographies exclude data for Northern Canada. Estimates for the national total also include data for northern Canada.

Source: Projections based on analysis of data from the 2001 Census and Clatworthy (2007)

by one-half among youth and young adults (Model 2) are projected to range between $1.9 billion (assuming 25% of income taxable on-reserve) and $3.1 billion (assuming 75% of income taxable on-reserve). Estimates of cumulative taxes on incremental employment income under the Model 3 scenario (elimination of education gaps among youth and young adults) range from $3.4 billion (assuming 25% of income taxable on-reserve) to $5.5 billion (assuming 75% of income taxable on-reserve).[26]

Substantially larger amounts of income tax would result if educational improvements were to also be accompanied by reducing (Model 4) or eliminating (Model 5) existing Registered Indian/non-Aboriginal gaps in employment rates and average employment earnings. Cumulative incremental income taxes under these latter scenarios range from about $5.5 billion to $22.8 billion.

Impacts on Government Transfer Payments to Individuals

Several studies concerning the impacts of education on government transfer payments to individuals have observed that those with higher levels of education are less likely to rely on public transfers. This has been found to be the case, even when individuals are eligible for benefits. This latter observation suggests that the proportion of the population receiving transfers should be lower among individuals with higher levels of education.

Data from the 2001 Census for Registered Indians do reveal somewhat lower rates of receipt of transfer payments among higher education groups. Differences among education groups, however, were not pronounced, except when controlled for employment status. Among those who reported no employment income, only marginal differences in the proportion receiving transfer payments existed among education groups. Average transfer payment income also did not vary widely by education level among those without employment income. Among those with employment incomes, rates of receipt of transfer payments and the average size of transfers were generally lower and declined sharply with increasing education. This situation suggests that the effects of education improvements with respect to reducing reliance upon transfers result primarily from improved employment and employment earnings outcomes.[27]

Estimates of the effects of educational improvements on government transfer payments developed for this study include all income from government sources except for incomes from the Canada (and Quebec) Pension Plans and employment insurance. Although incomes from these sources are often viewed as government transfers, these programs (although administered by or on behalf of government) are designed to be fully funded by contributors (employees and employers) and can be viewed as revenue/expenditure neutral.

The procedure used to estimate the effects of education on government transfer income involved two stages. In the first stage, rates of receipt of transfer income, calculated from the 2001 Census for population subgroups distinguished by employment status, educational attainment, age, gender, location of residence, and province or region, were applied to the future population of these sub-groups as projected by the employment projection models. This stage produced estimates of the future population of transfer payment recipients for each subgroup. In a

Table 14.17: Cumulative Government Transfer Income and Reductions in Transfer Income Among Registered Indians by Location of Residence and Projection Model, Canada, 2002–2026 (Projected)

Location	Cumulative Incremental Transfer Income 2002-2026 (Millions 2001$) Model 1—Growth and Aging	Reduction in Cumulative Transfer Income 2002–2026 (Millions 2001$)			
		Model 2—Education Gap Reduced by One-Half	Model 3—Education Gap Fully Closed	Model 4—Education, Employment Rate Gaps Reduced by One-Half	Model 5—Education, Employment Rate Gaps Fully Closed
On-reserve	8,394.8	833.9	1,441.1	2,960.0	4,973.4
% Reduction Over Model 1	---	9.9	17.2	35.3	59.2
Off-reserve	5,646.0	375.1	693.2	1,931.1	3,240.4
% Reduction Over Model 1	---	6.6	12.3	34.2	57.4
National Total	14,183.9	1,244.4	2,191.3	5,019.3	8,430.3
% Reduction Over Model 1	---	8.8	15.4	35.4	59.4

Note: Models 2 and 3 assume changes only to the levels of educational attainment of Registered Indian youth and young adults. Employment rates are assumed to remain constant (given educational attainment, age, gender, location, and province or region) at levels observed for 2001. Estimates for on- and off-reserve geographies exclude data for Northern Canada. Estimates for the national total also include data for Northern Canada.

Source: Projections based on analysis of data from the 2001 Census and Clatworthy (2007)

second stage, estimates of average government transfer income, calculated from the 2001 Census for the same subgroups, were then applied to the projected population of recipients (generated in the first stage) to estimate the total amount of government transfers.[28] The projections assume that rates of receipt of transfers and average transfer incomes remain constant throughout the projection period (given employment status, educational attainment, age, gender, location of residence, and province or region). Transfer payment estimates were developed for each of the five employment projection models discussed previously.

Table 14.17 provides a summary of the cumulative incremental amount of government transfer income to Registered Indians over the 2002 to 2026 period projected to result from population growth and aging (Model 1) as well as estimates of the reduction in cumulative transfer income projected under the Models 2 to 5 scenarios. The estimates are also structured by location of residence.

At the national level, Model 1 projects the cumulative incremental amount of government transfer income for the 2002 to 2026 period to be roughly $14.2 billion, about 59% of which would accrue to residents on-reserve. Assuming that the Registered Indian/non-Aboriginal education gap among youth and young adults in 2001 were to be reduced by one-half over the course of the projection period (Model 2), cumulative government transfers over the period would be reduced by about $1.2 billion (or about 9%). About 67% of this reduction is projected to occur among reserve residents. Convergence of the education levels of Registered Indian youth and young adults to the 2001 levels observed for their non-Aboriginal counterparts (Model 3) would lower cumulative transfer income for the period by roughly $2.2 billion (about 15%). About 66% of this reduction is projected to occur among reserve residents.

As revealed by the projection results for Models 4 and 5, much larger reductions in transfer income would be expected if improvements in the employment rates of Registered Indians were also to occur during the period. Reducing the 2001 employment rate gap between Registered Indians and non-Aboriginals by one-half (Model 4) is projected to result in a reduction in cumulative transfer income of about $5 billion (35%). Elimination of the employment rate gap (Model 5) is projected to lower cumulative government transfer income by about $8.4 billion (or about 59%).

As revealed in **Table 14.18**, the effects of education improvements among Registered Indian youth and young adults in terms of reducing transfer income (Models 2 and 3) are projected to be largest (in percentage terms) in Northern Canada, Manitoba, Quebec, and British Columbia. Impacts on transfer income associated with improvements in Registered Indian employment rates (Models 4 and 5) are projected to be most significant in Northern Canada, Manitoba and Saskatchewan.

Impacts on Crime and the Cost of Crime

Sociologists and criminologists have identified powerful correlations between several socio-economic (e.g. income, poverty, education, literacy, employment), psychological (e.g. mental health) and demographic (e.g. age and gender) factors and involvement in criminal activity. Many of these same factors have also been shown to correlate strongly with recidivism (see Karpowitz and Kenner 2004). Several recent studies have focussed on the role of education as a causal factor in reducing criminal activity. Some of the most important works in this regard include those of Grogger (1998), Lochner (2004), Lochner and Moretti (2004), and Groot and van den Brink (2008). This research finds that higher levels of schooling, especially high school graduation, results in lower rates of incarceration, fewer criminal arrests and a reduction in self-declared reporting of participation in criminal activity.[29] Based on their findings, Lochner and Moretti (2004) conclude that reduction in criminal activity may constitute the largest component of the returns to society attributable to education.[30]

For many years, Canadian data have revealed extremely high rates of criminal activity and involvement with the justice system among Aboriginal peoples. In

Table 14.18: Cumulative Government Transfer Income and Reductions in Transfer Income Among Registered Indians by Province/Region and Projection Model, Canada, 2002–2026 (Projected)

Location	Cumulative Incremental Transfer Income 2002–2026 (Millions 2001$) Model 1— Growth and Aging	Reduction in Cumulative Transfer Income 2002–26 (Millions 2001$)			
		Model 2— Education Gap Reduced by One-Half	Model 3— Education Gap Fully Closed	Model 4— Education and Employment Rate Gaps Reduced by One-Half	Model 5— Education and Employment Rate Gaps Fully Closed
Atlantic Region	473.1	15.5	30.1	125.5	205.0
% Reduction Over Model 1	---	3.3	6.4	26.5	43.3
Quebec	1,679.1	171.6	287.7	532.5	826.8
% Reduction Over Model 1	---	10.2	17.1	31.7	49.2
Ontario	2,750.5	198.1	351.3	812.5	1,321.6
% Reduction Over Model 1	---	7.2	12.8	29.5	48.0
Manitoba	2,329.3	244.1	441.7	957.0	1,645.1
% Reduction Over Model 1	---	10.5	19.0	41.1	70.6
Saskatchewan	2,458.6	191.2	335.9	977.5	1,727.7
% Reduction Over Model 1	---	7.8	13.7	39.8	70.3
Alberta	2,186.4	179.8	312.9	750.4	1,260.6
% Reduction Over Model 1	---	8.2	14.3	34.3	57.7
British Columbia	2,163.8	208.7	374.8	735.7	1,226.9
% Reduction Over Model 1	---	9.6	17.3	34.0	56.7
Northern Canada	143.0	35.4	57.0	128.2	216.6
% Reduction Over Model 1	---	24.8	39.8	89.6	151.4
National Total	14,183.9	1,244.4	2,191.3	5,019.3	8,430.3
% Reduction Over Model 1	---	8.8	15.4	35.4	59.4

Note: Models 2 and 3 assume changes only to the levels of educational attainment of Registered Indian youth and young adults. Employment rates are assumed to remain constant (given educational attainment, age, gender, location, and province or region) at levels observed for 2001.

Source: Projections based on analysis of data from the 2001 Census and Clatworthy (2007).

light of recent research findings, the achievement of higher levels of education among Registered Indians appears to have the potential to contribute to significant reductions in criminal activity and the personal and social costs of crime.

Some preliminary and approximate estimates of the effects of education improvement among Registered Indians on crime and the costs of crime have been developed for this study. The study's focus is restricted to the adult population (i.e. those 18 or more years of age). The estimation procedure involved three stages. In the initial stage, incarceration rates (for 2001) developed for subgroups of the Registered Indian population (distinguished by level of education, age, gender, and province or region) were applied to the populations of these subgroups as projected by Models 1, 2 and 3, resulting in estimates of the projected number of Registered Indian inmates annually over the 2002 to 2026 time period.[31] In a second stage, estimates of the average annual custodial cost per inmate (developed from data published by the CCJS for fiscal year 2000/01) were applied to the projected inmate counts to develop annual estimates of total custodial costs. In a third stage, a ratio measuring the estimated total costs of crime (also including the direct pecuniary costs to victims, policing and security, and court and legal costs) in relation to custodial costs, was then applied to the projected annual custodial costs to produce estimates of annual total costs of crime. The ratio of total costs to custodial costs was developed at the national level using research and data published by Brantingham and Easton (1998).[32] The projections assume that future rates of incarceration (given educational attainment, age, gender, and province or region), average custodial costs, and the ratio of total costs to custodial costs remain constant throughout the projection period.[33]

While data from the 1996 snapshot of inmates do allow one to construct incarceration rates by level of education, age, gender, and region for the Aboriginal and non-Aboriginal populations, these data do not distinguish Aboriginal inmates on the basis of Aboriginal identity or Indian registration status. More recent data (which lacks education information) on individuals admitted into custody, however, is available for Aboriginal identity groups and was used to estimate the Registered Indian proportion of all Aboriginal inmates and incarceration rates. The general procedure used for constructing these estimates is described briefly below.

Annual data concerning the average number of individuals in custody reveals an overall decline from the time of the 1996 snapshot, from about 37,540 to about 31,500 in 2001. At that time, Aboriginal inmates formed about 19.1% of the total inmate population (up from about 16.4% in 1996) and were estimated to number 6,158. By applying the Registered Indian proportion developed from the "admissions to custody" data, the number of Registered Indians in custody in 2001 was estimated to be 4,171. Estimates of 2001 Registered Indian inmate counts by education, age, gender, and region were then developed using the distribution (across these variables) identified for all Aboriginal inmates from the 1996 snapshot data. Registered Indian incarceration rates for 2001 were constructed

Figure 14.2: Estimated Rate of Incarceration Among Registered Indian Males by Age Group and Educational Attainment, Canada, 2001

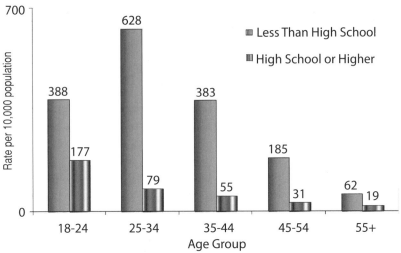

Source: Based on analysis of data from the 1996 *One-Day Snapshot of Inmates in Canada's Adult Correctional Facilities*, CCJS data on inmates and admissions to remand (1996–2001) and the 2001 Census of Canada.

Figure 14.3: Estimated Rate of Incarceration Among Registered Indian Females by Age Group and Educational Attainment, Canada, 2001

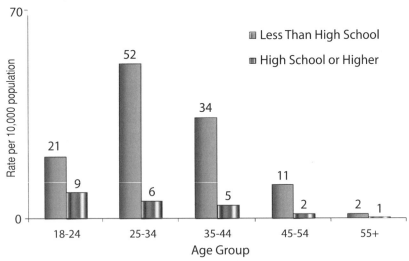

Source: Based on analysis of data from the 1996 *One-Day Snapshot of Inmates in Canada's Adult Correctional Facilities*, CCJS data on inmates and admissions to remand (1996–2001) and the 2001 Census of Canada.

based on these inmate counts and additional population data derived from the adjusted 2001 Census. As a number of assumptions were required in the development of the incarceration rate estimates, they should be viewed as approximations.

The estimated rates of incarceration (per 10,000 population) by age and education group are presented in **Figures 14.2** and **14.3**, for males and females, respectively. Among both gender groups, incarceration rates were highest among young adults (25–34 years) and declined steadily among older age cohorts. The relationship between education and incarceration rates is pronounced for both males and females. Among males, incarceration rates for those who had not completed high school were (depending upon age) between two and eight times higher than those who had completed high school. Differentials of similar scale were also identified for Registered Indian females.

Registered Indian incarceration rates were also found to vary widely by province or region. As illustrated in **Figure 14.4** (for males), incarceration rates were substantially higher among Registered Indians in the Prairie region and Northern Canada. Pronounced differentials in incarceration rates by level of educational attainment, however, were identified for all provinces or regions.

Projected Number of Registered Indian Inmates

Estimates of the number of Registered Indian inmates for the 2002 to 2026 time period are presented in **Figure 14.5** for Models 1, 2 and 3. Assuming incarceration rates remain unchanged (when controlled for educational attainment, age, gender, and province or region), growth and aging of the Registered Indian population (Model 1) is projected to result in an increase in the average annual number of Registered Indian inmates from 4,171 (in 2001) to 7,009 by 2026 (a 68% increase). Reducing the 2001 Registered Indian/non-Aboriginal gap in educational attainment among youth and young adults by one-half (Model 2) is projected to lower the estimated 2026 inmate population by 1,216 individuals (about 17% lower than the number estimated under the population *growth and aging* scenario). Convergence of the levels of educational attainment of Registered Indian youth and young adults over the period to the 2001 levels of their non-Aboriginal counterparts (Model 3) would reduce the projected number of inmates in 2026 by 2,066 individuals (a reduction of roughly 29%).

As revealed in **Table 14.19**, improvements in educational attainment among Registered Indian youth and young adults are projected to result in lower numbers of inmates in all provinces or regions. In absolute terms, these reductions would be largest in the Prairie region. In relation to the projected size of the inmate population under the population growth and aging scenario, reductions associated with education are projected to be most significant in Northern Canada, Quebec, and Alberta.

Figure 14.4: Estimated Rate of Incarceration Among Registered Indian Males by Educational Attainment and Province/Region, Canada, 2001

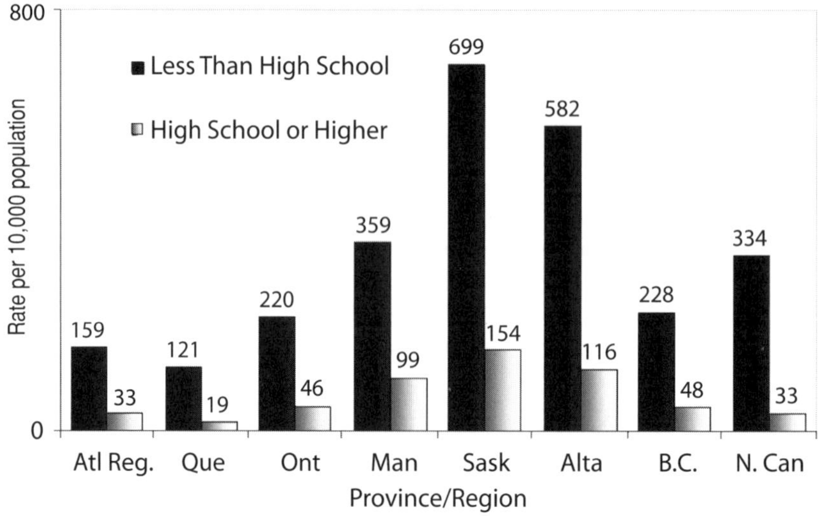

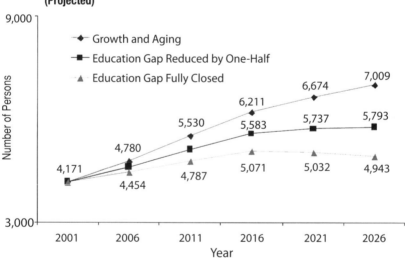

Source: Based on analysis of data from the 1996 *One-Day Snapshot of Inmates in Canada's Adult Correctional Facilities*, CCJS data on inmates and admissions to remand (1996–2001), and the 2001 Census of Canada.

Figure 14.5: Number of Registered Indian Inmates by Projection Model, Canada, 2001–2026 (Projected)

Note: Models 2 and 3 assume changes only to the levels of educational attainment of Registered Indian youth and young adults. Incarceration rates are assumed to remain constant (given educational attainment, age, gender, and province or region) at levels estimated for 2001.

Source: Projections based on analysis of data from the 2001 Census, CCJS data for 1996 and 2001, and Clatworthy (2007).

Table 14.19: Number of Registered Indian Inmates by Projection Model and Province/Region, Canada, 2026 (Projected)

Province/Region	Projected Registered Indian Inmates (2026)		
	Model 1—*Growth and Aging*	Model 2—*Education Gap Reduced by One Half*	Model 3—*Education Gap Fully Closed*
Atlantic Region	104	98	93
% Reduction	---	*5.8*	*10.6*
Quebec	233	175	138
% Reduction	---	*24.9*	*40.8*
Ontario	730	602	517
% Reduction	---	*17.5*	*29.2*
Manitoba	1,220	1,017	869
% Reduction	---	*16.6*	*28.8*
Saskatchewan	2,246	1,923	1,680
% Reduction	---	*14.4*	*25.2*
Alberta	1,686	1,352	1,124
% Reduction	---	*19.8*	*33.3*
British Columbia	613	511	440
% Reduction	---	*16.6*	*28.2*
Northern Canada	178	113	80
% Reduction	---	*36.5*	*55.1*
National Total	7,009	5,793	4,943
% Reduction	---	*17.3*	*29.5*

Note: Models 2 and 3 assume changes only to the levels of educational attainment of Registered Indian youth and young adults. Incarceration rates are assumed to remain constant (given education attainment, age, gender, and province or region) at levels estimated for 2001.

Source: Projections based on analysis of data from the 2001 Census, CCJS data for 1996, and Clatworthy (2007).

Table 14.20: Estimated Cumulative Costs of Registered Indian Criminal Activity by Projection Model and Province/Region, Canada, 2002-2026 (Projected)

Province/Region	Projected Cumulative Incremental Costs of Criminal Activity (2002-2026) Model 1—*Growth and Aging* (Millions 2001$)	Estimated Reduction in Cumulative Incremental Costs (2002–2026) (Millions 2001$)	
		Model 2— *Education Gap Reduced by One Half*	Model 3— *Education Gap Fully Closed*
Atlantic Region	215.5	37.3	71.0
% Reduction	---	*17.3*	*32.9*
Quebec	474.5	322.0	561.5
% Reduction	---	*67.9*	*118.3*
Ontario	1,491.0	844.4	1,486.6
% Reduction	---	*56.6*	*99.7*
Manitoba	3,677.5	1,092.8	1,994.0
% Reduction	---	*29.7*	*54.2*
Saskatchewan	7,794.1	1,769.6	3,212.7
% Reduction	---	*22.7*	*41.2*
Alberta	4,428.8	1,687.1	2,975.9
% Reduction	---	*38.1*	*67.2*
British Columbia	1,050.2	719.4	1,283.5
% Reduction	---	*68.5*	*122.2*
Northern Canada	638.6	539.3	880.8
% Reduction	---	*84.4*	*137.9*
National Total	19,770.3	7,011.7	12,465.9
% Reduction	---	*35.5*	*63.1*

Note: Models 2 and 3 assume changes only to the levels of educational attainment of Registered Indian youth and young adults. Incarceration rates are assumed to remain constant (given education attainment, age, gender, and province or region) at levels estimated for 2001.

Source: Projections based on analysis of data from the 2001 Census, CCJS data for 1996 and 2001, Brantingham and Easton (1998), and Clatworthy (2007).

Projected Total Costs of Criminal Activity[34]

In 2001, the total cost of criminal activity by the Registered Indian population was estimated in this study to total about $2.1 billion. About 55% of these costs were estimated to be incurred by government. A summary of the projected cumulative incremental costs associated with Registered Indian criminal activity for the 2002 to 2026 time period is provided in **Table 14.20** for each of the three projection models.

Assuming stable incarceration rates (given educational attainment, age, gender and province or region) and no increases in inflation-adjusted costs, population growth, and aging over the 2002 to 2026 period (Model 1) is projected to result in cumulative costs associated with Registered Indian criminal activity totalling about $19.8 billion (in 2001 constant dollars). Very substantial reductions in cumulative costs for the period are projected to result from improvements in levels of education among Registered Indian youth and young adults. Closing the 2001 Registered Indian/non-Aboriginal education gap among youth and young adults by one-half (Model 2) is projected to result in a reduction of about $7.0 billion in the cumulative costs of criminal activity for the period. Eliminating the 2001 gap in educational attainment among youth and young adults (Model 3) is projected to lower the cumulative costs of criminal activity by about $12.5 billion. Significant reductions in cumulative costs resulting from education improvements were projected for all provinces or regions. In relative terms, these reductions were largest in Northern Canada, British Columbia, and Quebec. Absolute reductions in cumulative costs associated with education improvements were projected to be largest in the Prairie region.

Summary and Discussion

This study has used a series of projection models to develop estimates of the incremental effects of "hypothetical" improvements in the levels of educational attainment achieved by Registered Indian youth and young adults on several specific outcomes over the 2002 to 2026 time period. The outcomes explored included employment, employment earnings, revenues to government through taxation of employment incomes, government expenditures associated with transfer payments, and the private and social costs associated with criminal activity.

Key findings of the study, which are summarized in **Table 14.21**, suggest that improving educational attainment among Registered Indian youth and young adults has the potential to produce quite large returns to individuals in terms of higher levels of employment and larger employment earnings. In this regard, the projections suggest that improvements which served to close by one-half the education gap that existed in 2001 between Registered Indian youth and young adults and their non-Aboriginal counterparts would increase the volume of Registered Indian employment by about 29,300 individuals (a 26% incremental gain) by 2026. Educational improvements which served to increase the attainment levels of Registered Indian youth and young adults over the period to the same levels as those observed in 2001 for their non-Aboriginal counterparts, would produce incremental employment increases of about 49,400 individuals (or roughly 45%). Additional employment attributable to these education improvements would add between $15.2 and $27.1 billion to the employment earnings of the Registered Indian population over the period (in 2001 constant dollars).

While the estimated returns to individuals associated with achieving higher levels of educational attainment (i.e. higher levels of employment and employment earnings) are clearly substantial, the potential benefits to other individuals and to the broader society are also substantial. The monetary benefits from addi-

Table 14.21: Cumulative Incremental Impacts of Improvements in Educational Attainment Among Registered Indian Youth and Young Adults, Canada, 2002–2026

Incremental Change (2002–2026)	Model 1— *Growth and Aging*	Returns to Education	
		Model 2— *Education Gap Reduced by One Half*	Model 3— *Education Gap Fully Closed*
Private or Personal Returns			
Employment (×1000)	110.6	29.3	49.4
Cumulative Employment Earnings (2001$ Millions)	46,104.8	15,193.1	27,091.3
Social Returns			
Cumulative Increase in Taxes on Employment Income (2001$ Millions)	6,415.3 (*9,197.4*)	1,896.7 (*3,113.7*)	3,419.7 (*5,529.1*)
Cumulative Transfer Income (2001$ Millions)	14,183.9	-1,244.4	-2,191.3
Cumulative Costs of Criminal Activity (2001$ Millions)	19,770.3	-7,011.7	-12,465.9

Note: Estimates of taxes on employment income are presented for the context where 25% of earnings on-reserve are taxable. Estimates for the context where 75% of earnings on-reserve are taxable appear in parentheses.

Source: Projections based on analysis of data from the 2001 Census, CCJS data for 1996 and 2001, Brantingham and Easton (1998), and Clatworthy (2007).

tional taxes on employment earnings, reductions in government income transfers, and reductions in the private and public costs of criminal activity that are expected to result from the scale of improvements in education explored in this study, range between about $10.2 and $20.2 billion for the 2002 to 2026 time period. About 70% of these additional benefits are expected to accrue to governments through increased tax revenue and reduced expenditure requirements.

The study's estimates of the scale of benefits associated with improvements in educational attainment among Registered Indian youth and young adults should be viewed as quite conservative, as only a limited range of potential impacts has been examined. Existing social and economic research, for example, suggests that substantial additional benefits may also result from higher levels of educational attainment, including reductions in health care expenditures (Holzer et al 2007) and reduced needs for a wide range of social support services, such as remedial education and child and family services (Heckman and Masterov 2007). Higher levels of educational attainment would also be expected to contribute to meeting Canada's future labour needs, enhancing labour productivity growth, and increasing national and regional economic output (Centre for the Study of Living Standards 2007).

Although limited in scope, the study's findings clearly suggest that the potential benefits associated with increasing educational attainment among Registered Indian youth and young adults are likely to greatly exceed the costs. From a public policy perspective, there appears to be a very strong rationale for increasing levels of investment in the education of Canada's Registered Indian population. Perhaps the more pressing question (and one that was not addressed in this study) relates to what needs to be undertaken by the various stakeholders, including First Nations peoples and communities, the federal and provincial governments, educational institutions, and the private sector, to achieve higher levels of educational attainment among Registered Indians, and close the gap with other Canadians.

Endnotes

1   Non-personal and social outcomes can be viewed as those which accrue to individuals or groups of individuals other than those who acquire additional education. These outcomes can be either positive or negative. Some recent reviews of research concerning the non-personal and social outcomes of education are provided by Wolfe and Haveman (2001) and Riddell (2006).

2   Hull (2005), using data from the 1996 and 2001 Censuses of Canada, provides an extensive descriptive analysis of the statistical patterns involving educational attainment and personal outcomes related to employment and labour market behaviour for Registered Indians and other Aboriginal peoples in Canada. Many similar analyses have been conducted using data from earlier Censuses and special surveys. Research conducted by George and Kuhn (1994), using micro-level data from the 1991 Census, appears to represent the only rigorous attempt to measure the employment income returns to education among Canada's Aboriginal peoples. A more recent study, prepared by the Centre for the Study of Living Standards (2007), provides some estimates of the potential benefits to individuals (in terms of labour market outcomes) and society (in terms of labour productivity and economic growth) of hypothetical improvements in the educational attainment of Aboriginal peoples in Canada.

3   The baseline scenario also assumes that relationships between educational attainment and outcomes remain unchanged over the course of the projection period. In the case of projections involving employment outcomes, the baseline model assumes that the employment rates of the population also remain constant over time, given age, gender, educational attainment, location of residence, and region.

4   For this study, provincial estimates are used except for the Atlantic provinces (which are aggregated to form an Atlantic region) and for Yukon, Northwest Territories and Nunavut (which are aggregated to form a Northern region). The 2001 Census population estimates used for the projections were adjusted to account for the populations residing on non-enumerated Indian reserves and for the populations missed due to survey undercoverage.

5   The 1996 CCJS snapshot of inmates continues to represent the only comprehensive source of information concerning the characteristics of Aboriginal people held in custody in Canada. CCJS has been working with provincial justice authorities to revise current reporting systems to provide a more extensive range of personal information concerning individuals taken into custody (including Aboriginal status). At this point in time, detailed data concerning personal characteristics are not yet available for several provinces or regions.

6   Three main economic theories presently exist to account for the benefits of education to labour market outcomes. Human capital theory posits that higher education leads to additional skills and productive capabilities which increase the individual's value to employers and hence their earnings. Market signaling theory views education as having no effect on productivity, per se. From this perspective, the importance of education results from its effect on a prospective employer's perceptions of the individual's abilities and potential productivity (i.e. education is viewed by employers as a signal of a potential employee's abilities). Thus higher wages accrue to those who are better educated. Job match theory posits that additional education provides individuals with more information about their own abilities, aptitudes and interests, thus better equipping them to search out, acquire, and remain in jobs which they regard to be appropriate (i.e. better job-worker matches). Appropriate job-worker matches benefit both workers and employers, increase productivity, and translate into higher wages.

7   Census data can support much more detailed breakdowns of the population by educational attainment (for example, see Hull 2005). As the projection models developed for this study also differentiate the population on the basis of age, gender, location of residence, province or region, and one or more outcomes (e.g. employment status), more refined education categories cannot be accommodated due to the population size. As configured for this study, the educational attainment variable distinguishes the population according to specific educational achievements (e.g. attainment of a high school diploma or the attainment of a university degree) which have been shown in prior research to greatly affect labour market and other outcomes.

8   Hull's research also provides comparable data and analysis for other Aboriginal groups (including non-Registered Indians, Métis, and Inuit) and for the non-Aboriginal population.

9   While it is recognized that education is not restricted by age, Hull's (2005) data for Registered

Indians revealed that full–time school attendance rates declined quite sharply among young adults and were very low among individuals 40 or more years of age. Part-time attendance rates tended to peak among those in their mid to late 20's and declined gradually among older cohorts. Among those 40 or more years of age, overall attendance rates were in the range of about 5%.

10 Although the discussion focuses on the population with high school or higher levels of education, the assumed rates of improvement were calculated separately for those with high school or some post-secondary (without a university degree) and those with university degrees. Rates of improvements were also calculated separately for all five-year cohorts comprising the 15 to 39 years age group. The proportion of the population attaining university degrees is assumed to increase more rapidly than the proportion reporting high school graduation only or post-secondary education (without a university degree). This assumption is consistent with Hull's (2005) observations concerning changes in educational attainment levels between 1996 and 2001.

11 It is recognized that further improvements in educational attainment are also likely to occur among the non-Aboriginal population over the period. The study's reference to reducing the "education gap by one-half" should not be interpreted to mean that the future gap in educational attainment between Registered Indians and non-Aboriginals will necessarily be reduced by this or any amount. Equal or greater improvements in education could be achieved by the non-Aboriginal population during this time period.

12 The employment rate measures the proportion of the total population that is employed. Employment rates calculated from Census data reflect the population's employment status during the one-week period prior to enumeration.

13 Future employment growth on-reserve can, of course, be constrained by job growth. The extent of on-reserve employment growth forecast under Model 1 (about 70,000 over the twenty-five-year period) is not inconsistent with recent trends in the volume of employment growth reported by reserve residents. Based on adjusted data from the 1996 and 2001 Censuses, the number of individuals employed on-reserve increased (on average) by roughly 2,710 annually. Assuming annual growth continued at this level over the projection period, an additional 67,845 individuals would be employed on-reserve in 2026.

14 Census data concerning the size of the employed population (at the time of the Census) and the size of population reporting employment incomes in the year preceding the Census reveal the latter population to be considerably larger than the former. The ratio of those reporting employment incomes in 2000 to those employed at the time of the census was 1.46. In addition, those who reported unemployment (i.e. not working but seeking work) accounted for only about one-half of those who reported employment income in 2000, but were not working at the time of Census. This situation implies that many Registered Indians are employed on a seasonal or periodic basis. Given this situation, significant improvements in Registered Indian employment rates could conceivably result from improving access to more stable and permanent jobs.

15 The estimate of 65,000 is obtained by comparing the results of Model 4 with those of Model 2. Both of these models use identical assumptions concerning the extent of improvements in educational attainment. Unlike Model 4, Model 2 assumes no improvements in future employment rates.

16 The projected employment impacts associated with assumed improvements in Registered Indian employment rates display a similar pattern over province/regions as those associated with improvements in educational attainment. A majority (about 61%) of the projected incremental employment resulting from improved employment rates would accrue to Registered Indians in the Prairie region.

17 The employment rate improvements assumed in Models 4 and 5 could, of course, be achieved through net out-migration to off-reserve areas. The additional employment needed by Registered Indians to achieve employment rates comparable to those observed in 2001 for the non-Aboriginal population represents only 3 to 4% of recent levels of national employment growth.

18 Some caution should be exercised in interpreting the differences in average employment incomes observed for Registered Indians and non-Aboriginals. These differentials may result from a number of factors: including differences in wage levels, occupations, age, length of employment, employment status (i.e. full-time vs part-time), and location of residence (on- or off-reserve). Data for workers employed on a full-year, full-time (FYFT) basis provide a better basis for

measuring wage differentials. In 2000, employment income gaps between Registered Indian and non-Aboriginal FYFT workers were larger than the gaps measured for all workers, especially among males.

19 Census data for 2001 revealed that the total Registered Indian population reporting employment income in 2000 was 46% larger than the population employed at the time of the Census. The adjustment for the "non-employed" population was carried out using ratios of the total employment earnings of all those who reported employment income in 2000 to the total employment earnings of those who were employed at the time of the census. At the national level this ratio was 1.208 for the total population. These ratios, constructed for population sub-groups differentiated by level of educational attainment, age, gender, location of residence, and province or region, were applied to the earnings projected for the employed population to construct estimates of the employment earnings for the total population.

20 The Institute for Policy Analysis at the University of Toronto has recently forecast future average real wage rates to rise at about 1.43% annually. Assuming this rate of increase, total employment earnings estimates presented in this study for 2026 could be adjusted upwards by about 43% to account for real wage growth expected during the 2002 to 2026 time period.

21 Cumulative incremental employment earnings are estimated to total about $46.1 billion over the time period.

22 Taxation of additional employment income represents only one dimension of the taxation impacts of education improvements. Higher employment incomes are also likely to result in increases in other forms of government taxation including, excise taxes, provincial sales taxes and federal consumption taxes. Among higher income earners, when combined with income taxes, these other forms of taxation result in marginal tax rates that exceed 50%.

23 Readers should note that the use of marginal tax rates for this income group does introduce some error in the income taxation estimates. In Canada, marginal tax rates vary widely depending upon income and are substantially higher among those with higher incomes. Efforts to account for marginal tax rate differentials would require additional assumptions concerning the distribution of incremental employment incomes by income group. This type of analysis was not attempted for this study.

24 As the employment income estimates projected in this study do not account for future impacts in real wage growth, no adjustments have been made to reflect possible changes over time in marginal tax rate thresholds. Federal tax thresholds are adjusted annually to reflect a portion of observed inflation. Most provinces also adjust thresholds periodically.

25 Analysis of Census data concerning the distribution of employment earnings by place of work for reserve residents may provide a stronger basis for estimating the share of earnings subject to income taxation. Such data were not available to this study.

26 Significant levels of incremental income tax are projected for all provinces or regions. Tax impacts are projected to be most pronounced in Quebec, British Columbia, Ontario, and Manitoba.

27 That rates of receipt of transfer income did not vary dramatically by level of education is not surprising, as some government transfers are quasi-universal (e.g. Alberta energy rebates) or available to large segments of the population. Relatively few transfers are targeted on the basis of education (such as bursaries, scholarships, and other forms of student support). Many transfers are geared to income, such that the amount of the transfer declines and eventually reaches zero only among those with higher incomes.

28 The estimates of average transfer incomes from the Census relate to the year 2000. These estimates were adjusted upward (in this case by 1.5%) to reflect inflation adjustments. Although not all transfers are adjusted annually (or by the same amount) most are adjusted at least periodically to offset the eroding effects of inflation on purchasing power.

29 Several economic theories exist which attempt to account for the effects of improved education on criminal activity. These theories suggest that higher education produces higher wage rates thus increasing the opportunity cost of crime; raises the individual's time preference rate and the extent to which future costs are discounted; and increases the amount of productive time that individuals are engaged in through employment or pursuit of further education.

30 Lochner and Moretti (2004) estimate that the benefits of education to society through reductions in criminal activity are in the range of 20 to 25% of the benefits that accrue to individuals. They

further estimate that a 1% increase in the rate of high school graduation among Americans would reduce the costs of crime in the US by about $1.4 billion annually.

31 As discussed later in this section of the report, the incarceration rates developed for this study have been developed to reflect the average number of inmates in custody at any time during the reference year (in this case 2001).

32 Estimates based on data compiled by Brantingham and Easton yielded a ratio of total costs to custodial costs of about 8.87. Their estimates of the total costs of crime should be viewed as quite conservative, as they are based only on crimes reported to police. Data from periodic surveys, such as the General Social Survey, suggest that a large portion of some types of crimes (e.g. break and enters) are never reported. As such, the true ratio may be considerably higher than that estimated for this study.

33 Although rates of incarceration in Canada reveal declines over the 1996 to 2005 time period, there appears to be little by way of published analyses concerning the factors underlying these declines. Some portion of the decline appears to result from the much greater use of conditional sentencing, especially for first-time offenders and those committing "minor" offences. Population aging is also likely to have been a major factor in this decline, as incarceration rates are strongly patterned over age (being highest among youth and young adults). As such, declines in Canada's youth population over the period would have the effect of reducing the aggregate incarceration rate. More recent data for the 2006/07 period reveal a small increase in the aggregate incarceration rate for Canada.

34 The cost estimates of criminal activity prepared for this study reflect only the costs associated with crimes reported to police. As noted earlier, survey-based data suggests that a large proportion of crimes are not reported to police. As such, the cost estimates prepared for this study should be viewed as quite conservative.

References

Brantingham, P. and S.T. Easton. 1998. "The Costs of Crime: Who Pays and How Much (1998 Update)." *Critical Issues Bulletin*. Vancouver: The Fraser Institute.

Canadian Centre for Justice Statistics. 1998. *A One-Day Snapshot of Inmates in Canada's Adult Correctional Facilities*. Cat. No. 85-002XIE, Vol. 18. No.8. Ottawa: Statistics Canada.

Card, D. 1999. "The Causal Effect of Education on Earnings." *Handbook of Labor Economics* 3A. Amsterdam: Holland. 1801–1863.

Centre for the Study of Living Standards. 2007 "The Potential Contribution of Aboriginal Canadians to Labour Force, Employment, Productivity and Output Growth in Canada: 2001–2017." Prepared for the Education Branch of Indian and Northern Affairs Canada, Ottawa, 2007 (draft).

Clatworthy, S. 2007. "Aboriginal Population Projections for Canada, Provinces and Regions: 2001–2026." Prepared for Indian and Northern Affairs Canada and Canada Mortgage and Housing Corporation, Ottawa, 2007.

George, P. and P. Kuhn. 1994. "The Size and Structure of Native–White Wage Differentials in Canada." *The Canadian Journal of Economics*. 27(1) 20–42.

Grogger, J. 1998 "Market Wages and Youth Crime." *Journal of Labor Economics*. 16: 756–791.

Groot, W. and H. van den Brink. 2008. "The Effects of Education on Crime." *Applied Economics*. Tijdschrift.

Heckman, J. and D. Masterov. 2007. "The Productivity Argument for Investing in Young Children." National Bureau for Economic Research, Working Paper No. 13016.

Holzer, H., D. Schanzenbach, G. Duncan and J. Ludwig. 2007. "The Economic Costs of Poverty in the United States: Subsequent Effects of Children Growing Up Poor." Institute for Research on Poverty at the Center for American Progress, Discussion Paper No. 1327–07.

Hull, J. 2005. "Post-Secondary Education and Labour Market Outcomes: Canada, 2001." Ottawa: Indian and Northern Affairs Canada.

Karpowitz, D. and M. Kenner. 2004, "Education and Crime Prevention: The Case for Reinstating Pell Grant Eligibility for the Incarcerated." Paper prepared for the Bard Prison Initiative, Annandale-on-Hudson, NY: Bard College.

Lochner, L. 2004. "Education, Work, and Crime: A Human Capital Approach." *International Economic Review*. 45: 811–43.

Lochner, L. and E. Moretti. 2004. "The Effect of Education on Crime: Evidence from Prison Inmates, Arrests, and Self-Reports." *American Economic Review*. 94(1): 155–189.

Oreoploulos, Philip. 2006. "The Compelling Effects of Compulsory Schooling: Evidence from Canada." *Canadian Journal of Economics*. 39: 22–52.

Riddell, W.C. 2006. "The Impact of Education on Economic and Social Outcomes: An Overview of Recent Advances in Economics." Paper prepared for the workshop on An Integrated Approach to Human Capital Development, sponsored by Canadian Policy Research Networks, the School of Policy Studies (Queen's University) and Statistics Canada, 2005 (revised 2006).

Statistics Canada. 2002. "Adult Correctional Services: 2000/01." *The Daily*. Ottawa: Statistics Canada.

Wolfe, B. and R. Haveman. 2001. "Accounting for the Social and Non-Market Benefits of Education." in *The Contribution of Human and Social Capital to Sustained Economic Growth and Well-Being*. John Helliwell (ed). Vancouver: University of British Columbia Press. 221–250.

Notes on Contributors

Cheryl Aman

Cheryl Aman completed her degree in the Sociology of Education at The University of British Columbia. Her recent work has focused on Aboriginal K–12 students. Currently, she is involved in research on the impact of school change at both the elementary- and secondary-grade levels for a wide variety of ethnocultural groups, including Aboriginal students. She has lived and taught in schools across British Columbia.

Dan Beavon

Dan Beavon is the Director of the Strategic Research and Analysis Directorate, Indian and Northern Affairs Canada. His team's research is motivated by the guiding question: "How can the quality of life be improved for First Nation peoples and their communities?" Their research has been critical to the formulation and implementation of policy related to program delivery, and his research group is a driving force behind evidence-based decision making within INAC. Dan has published dozens of research articles and many books on Aboriginal issues. He is also affiliated with the University of Western Ontario as an Adjunct Research Professor, Sociology. Dan is the winner of the 2008 Gold Medal Award that is awarded to only one scientist/researcher each year by the Professional Institute of the Public Service of Canada. This award acknowledges his outstanding scientific work that has led to the improvement and enhancement of public well-being.

Stewart Clatworthy

Stewart Clatworthy operates Four Directions Project Consultants, a Winnipeg-based management consulting firm specializing in socioeconomic research, information systems development, and program evaluation. Since 1980, Stewart has completed numerous studies on Aboriginal demography and migration; population, membership and student enrollment projections; and socioeconomic, housing, and employment conditions. Through this research, he has gained a national reputation as a leading scholar of Canadian Aboriginal socioeconomic and demographic circumstances.

John Clement

John Clement joined Indian and Northern Affairs Canada in 2001 and currently holds the position of Senior Research Manager. Earlier in his career, he spent ten years with Research and Statistics at the Department of Justice Canada. He holds a BA in Mathematics from Laurentian University. His areas of expertise are survey methodology and design, Aboriginal people, and the criminal justice system. His current projects at SRAD are: Understanding the Strengths of Indigenous Communities (USIC) with York University; Aboriginal Single Mothers 2001; Aboriginal Occupational Outcomes 2001; Aboriginal Contributions to Canadian

Identity and Culture (Volume 1 and 2) book project with Trent University and the University of Calgary; and Economy, Security, and Community Survey (Aboriginal subsample) with Canadian Heritage. John co-edited a report entitled "Urban Aboriginal Women in B.C. and the Impacts of the Matrimonial Real Property Regime" with Judge Karen Abbott.

Gerald Fallon

Gerald Fallon is an Adjunct Professor with the Department of Educational Administration at the University of Saskatchewan, and also serves as a District Principal for Human Resources in School District 68 in British Columbia. Dr. Fallon has authored and co-authored articles addressing issues of second language methodology and curriculum design, policy and education, educational changes and learning communities, governance and ethics, Aboriginal education, and educational law in a variety of scholarly and professional journals.

Éric Guimond

Éric Guimond is of Mi'kmaw and French descent and is a specialist in Aboriginal demography. He is currently Senior Research Manager in the Strategic Research and Analysis Directorate at Indian and Northern Affairs Canada. His educational background includes demography, community health, physical education, and Aboriginal studies. He also possesses university research and teaching experience with expertise in projection models of population and Aboriginal groups and is an Adjunct Research Professor in the Department of Sociology at the University of Western Ontario. He completed his PhD studies at the University of Montreal on the topic of ethnic mobility of Aboriginal populations in Canada. Currently, Éric is engaged in projects related to First Nations Housing and First Nations Kids Having Kids.

Jeremy Hull

Jeremy Hull is a research consultant based in Winnipeg specializing in Aboriginal education and labour market issues. His clients have included federal and provincial government departments, First Nations and Aboriginal organizations, universities, school boards, and non-profit organizations. Since 2000, he has completed a number of statistical studies for Indian and Northern Affairs Canada Strategic Research and Analysis Directorate on post-secondary education, single parents, women, youth, and labour market issues. He is currently working on studies of Aboriginal housing conditions, Aboriginal post-secondary education and the labour market, and is providing technical assistance to a First Nation in support of self-government negotiations.

J. Marshall Mangan

J. Marshall Mangan is an Associate Professor in the Faculty of Education at the University of Western Ontario. He has studied and written on computer applications in education, the social foundations of education, social justice, and the use of computer techniques in education. A PhD graduate from The Ontario Institute for Studies in Education, he has been at Western since 1995. Through his eight authored or edited books, he has contributed extensively to educational development.

Jerry Paquette

Jerry Paquette is Professor in the Faculty of Education at the University of Western Ontario where he has taught for nearly twenty-two years. He specializes in educational administration and policy studies with a particular focus on education finance, minority education policy (particularly Aboriginal education), and educational policy in general. In addition, Dr. Paquette has been a member of the non-medical research-ethics board at Western for nearly twelve years and has chaired it for four of the last five years.

Chris Penney

Chris Penney is a beneficiary of the Nunatsiavut Land Claim Agreement. He is a Research Manager in the Strategic Research and Analysis Directorate at Indian and Northern Affairs Canada, and has previously worked at the First Nations and Inuit Health Branch of Health Canada. During this time he worked in the areas of Inuit health data and the social and cultural factors that affect Inuit health. He holds a BA in Anthropology from Memorial University of Newfoundland, and an MA in Archaeology from York University, England.

Julie Peters

Julie Peters is a PhD Candidate in the Department of Sociology at the University of Western Ontario. She also works as a Research Associate with the Aboriginal Policy Research Consortium. Her research interests include education, race/ ethnicity, social inequality, and gender. Her current research examines the use of provincial standardized assessment systems in First Nations schools in Ontario.

Nicholas Spence

Nicholas Spence holds a PhD in Sociology from the University of Western Ontario. He has worked for the federal government, and he is currently an Adjunct Professor at the University of Western Ontario, affiliated with the Department of Sociology and the Department of Health Sciences. Nicholas is a member of the Aboriginal Policy Research Consortium (International). His research expertise includes statistics and quantitative research methods, inequality/stratification, health, and education. Nicholas has published several articles on Aboriginal policy and coauthored the book *Permission to Develop: Aboriginal Treaties, Case Law, and Regulations* also published by Thompson Educational Publishing, Inc.

Jerry White

Jerry White was Professor and Senior Adviser to the Vice President (Provost) until July 1, 2008 and now serves as Associate Dean Policy, Planning and Graduate Education for Social Sciences at the University of Western Ontario. He is Director of the Aboriginal Policy Research Consortium (International) and Acting Editor -in-Chief for the International Indigenous Policy Journal. Jerry was the co-chair of the 2002, 2006, and 2009 Aboriginal Policy Research Conferences (with Dan Beavon and Peter Dinsdale) and honorary co-chair of the Russian Aboriginal Policy Research Conference (Moscow 2008). Jerry is a member of the Board of Governors for Western and for Kings University. He has written or co-written thirteen books and numerous articles on Aboriginal policy and health-care management. The most recent are: *Aboriginal Well-being: Canada's Continuing Challenge* (TEP), *Permission to Develop* (TEP), and the 5 volume series *Aboriginal Policy Research* (TEP).

Piotr Wilk

Piotr Wilk is the Community Health Researcher/Educator at the Middlesex-London Health Unit, with a research focus on the health and well-being of parents and their children. Dr. Wilk is currently conducting research on how the socio-economic conditions in which children are born and grow up affect their health and developmental trajectories. Dr. Wilk also focuses his research on the health of Aboriginal children by examining the role of contextual predictors related to family characteristics and community/neighborhood characteristics. He is also involved in teaching advanced graduate courses in social statistics and quantitative research methods. Dr. Wilk has a joint appointment at the School of Nursing and the Department of Sociology at the University of Western Ontario.

Susan Wingert

Susan Wingert is a PhD candidate in the Department of Sociology at the University of Western Ontario. She is also a research associate with the Aboriginal Policy Research Consortium. Her research interests include social inequality, race/ethnicity, culture, and mental health. Her current research examines social determinants of mental health in the off-reserve population.

Marquis Book Printing Inc.

Québec, Canada
2009